M000201426

GEORGE WINGFIELD

Wilbur S. Shepperson Series in History and Humanities

GEORGE WINGFIELD

OWNER AND OPERATOR
OF NEVADA

C. Elizabeth Raymond

University of Nevada Press
Reno & Las Vegas

Wilbur S. Shepperson Series in History and Humanities No. 34
(formerly Nevada Studies in History and Political Science)
Series Editor: Jerome E. Edwards

University of Nevada Press, Reno, Nevada 89557 USA
Copyright © 1992 by C. Elizabeth Raymond
All rights reserved
Manufactured in the United States of America
Designed by Kaelin Chappell

Library of Congress Cataloging-in-Publication Data
Raymond, C. Elizabeth.
George Wingfield : owner and operator of Nevada / by C. Elizabeth Raymond.
p. cm. — (Wilbur S. Shepperson series in history and humanities : no. 34)
Includes bibliographical references and index.
ISBN 0-87417-197-0 (alk. paper)
1. Wingfield, George, 1876–1959. 2. Politicians—Nevada—Biography.
3. Businessmen—Nevada—Biography. 4. Nevada—Politics and government.
I. Title. II. Series.
F841.W56R39 1992
979.3'032'092—dc20 92-17980 [B] CIP

The paper used in this book meets the requirements of American National
Standard for Information Sciences—Permanence of Paper for Printed Library
Materials, ANSI/NISO Z39.48-1992 (R2002).
Binding materials were selected for strength and durability.

University of Nevada Press Paperback Edition, 2013

22 21 20 19 18 17 16 15 14 13
5 4 3 2 1

ISBN-13: 978-0-87417-197-6 (cloth : alk. paper)
ISBN-13: 978-0-87417-929-3 (pbk.: alk. paper)
ISBN-13: 978-0-87417-451-9 (e-book)

In memory of George Wingfield, Jr.,
who graciously made his father's papers available
so that this biography could be written

CONTENTS

PREFACE

I FIRST BECAME AWARE of George Wingfield's dominant position in twentieth-century Nevada when I was hired in the early 1980s to organize his
enormous collection of papers at the Nevada State Historical Society. At that
time there was little scholarly history about this important Nevada figure,
but popular legends abounded. I wondered about this millionaire banker who
was also reputed to be a gangster and a sinister political boss. After reading
Wingfield's mail every day for almost three years, I was sufficiently intrigued
to want to tell the actual story, which was as fascinating in its own right as all
the myths and rumors.

George Wingfield's career was controversial, and his legacy to the state
was mixed. Even thirty years after his death, no one that I interviewed was
lukewarm about the man. Everyone had a strong opinion about him, whether
positive or negative. Yet his centrality to Nevada—and especially to its economy, based on marketing legalized vices as recreational activity for tourists—
is undeniable. For a brief period he was, indeed, the virtual owner and operator of the state of Nevada, both politically and economically. I hope that this
biography will explain the origins and the nature of that tremendous power
and will accurately depict Wingfield's uses of it. At the same time I have
tried to present not only the political and economic consequences, but also
the personal context in which these events occurred. Thus my biography of
George Wingfield reconstructs, to the extent possible, his own view of the
events in which he participated.

It is my hope that this book conveys not only the facts, but also the experienced texture of Wingfield's long and influential life. I trust that its appearance will foster further scholarly discussion of what he did or did not do and
assessments of his continuing importance for the state that he did so much
to shape.

Acknowledgments

This biography has been in preparation for more years than I thought possible when I began the project. Along the way I have incurred numerous
debts. Some of them are personal, to supportive colleagues, friends, and
family members who helped in various important ways to sustain my some-

times flagging energies. To all of them I am privately grateful. Other debts, however, have a direct bearing on the production of this volume and deserve public acknowledgment.

Research for this biography was supported by grants from the Nevada Humanities Committee and the Research Advisory Board of the University of Nevada, Reno, through its Junior Faculty Research Grant program. Some of the most tedious work, including hours of reading microfilm, was undertaken by my research assistant, Anita Watson, who persevered through headaches and blurry eyes. Lynn Hilty and Jim Pagliarini also spent numerous hours in libraries on my behalf. Jerome Edwards, Eric Moody, and William Rowley read the manuscript and contributed greatly to its refinement.

Many individuals along the way were kind enough to offer specific help when they learned of my interest in George Wingfield's life. They include Warren Anderson, Jon Aurich, Jr., Chris Driggs, Phil Earl, Robert Nylen, Tim Purdy, Guy Rocha, and Nancy Welch. I am indebted to each of them for sharing their respective documents, stories, and research. Rollan Melton was instrumental in helping me locate the manuscript of the only biography of George Wingfield that was prepared with the subject's cooperation. David and Jana Ketchum and Jack and Jacquie Ellena graciously gave me entrance to two Wingfield houses. George Wingfield, Jr., and Polly Wingfield Kline provided full access to documents and photographs still in the family's possession, without in any way seeking to influence the manuscript that resulted.

Finally, any researcher grows to respect the skill and energy of library staffs. I particularly thank Karen Gash from the Archives at the University of Nevada, Reno; Susan Searcy and Kathryn Totton of the Special Collections Department of the Getchell Library, University of Nevada, Reno; Lee Mortensen of the Nevada State Historical Society in Reno; Jeff Kintop of the Nevada State Archives; and David Millman of the Nevada State Historical Society in Las Vegas. In addition the Central Nevada Historical Society in Tonopah, Nevada, was enormously helpful, especially William and Allen Metscher. Jerry Hess at the National Archives was also of great assistance.

The Huntington Library in San Marino, California, gave permission to reproduce manuscript material from the Papers of Tasker L. Oddie in its collection. Extracts from letters in the Bernard M. Baruch Papers are published with permission of Princeton University Libraries.

Owner and Operator of
the State of Nevada

IT WAS A STORY made for the movies. Born into a modest Arkansas family in 1876, the unlikely hero grew up on a ranch in southeastern Oregon. The area was raw frontier, "an ancient hidden kingdom" where "change and escape do not come easy."[1] The young man became a cowhand because there was not much else to be, but he yearned for the more exciting world of the professional gambler. With a taste for horse racing and alcohol, he drifted aimlessly for a few years in the isolated sagebrush wilds of northern Nevada. Then, through an incredible combination of ability, luck, and gambling prowess, including the fortuitous acquisition of a phenomenal gold mine, he rose rapidly in the world to become by age thirty a mining multimillionaire and the business partner of a U.S. senator. When his partner died, he turned down an appointment to fill the older man's senate seat, instantly becoming a national celebrity. Shunning the political limelight, he chose instead to stay home in Nevada to tend to his beautiful society bride and his burgeoning fortune.

During the next decade he invested the money. Clearly an extraordinary businessman, he came in time to own most of the principal banks of the state, the major hotels in Reno, an international mining company, extensive real estate, and other businesses almost too numerous to count. His thoroughbred racing stable was nationally famous. Some people complained that he owned his adopted state, as well. As a Republican political power and friend to men in high places, his domination of the state was so complete that he was charged with running *both* of its political parties to suit his own purposes. Contemporary media accounts breezily referred to him as the king of Nevada. Outsiders confused him with the governor. Whether they approved or disapproved, most everyone in the sagebrush state of Nevada acknowledged his power and authority.[2]

To be sure, it was not a life without setbacks. When the depression struck, his banks collapsed and desperate measures to redeem them failed. Suddenly and unexpectedly, his empire crumbled and our hero was forced into personal bankruptcy. Yet even then his legendary luck prevailed. Powerful California bankers came to his rescue to protect his hotel properties, and an old friend providentially offered him a share in another fabulous gold mine. A second, though more modest fortune accrued, and national newsmagazines delightedly covered his second rise to wealth. On his eightieth birthday, he was feted by local dignitaries and national luminaries, including a former president. One year later, he was awarded an honorary doctorate in mining economics. At his death in 1959, he left to his wife and children a comfortable estate of over $3 million and to his state a controversial legacy of a renegade image and a tourist-oriented, gambling-based economy.

Unfortunately, the movie was never made. Despite his remarkable personal history, with its dramatic sequence of success, failure, and renewed success, George Wingfield resolutely eschewed all publicity. Modest almost to a fault, he hesitated to draw attention to his role as the owner and operator of a sagebrush fiefdom. Acutely conscious as well of his unorthodox origins and the controversy that surrounded him, Wingfield consistently refused offers to create biographies or movies based on his amazing career.[3] Although he was personally proud of his leading role in developing the modern economy of Nevada, he was loath to have the story repeated by others. Now, more than thirty years after his death, it still remains to be fully and accurately recounted.

In the intervening years, not surprisingly, a vast legend has grown up about the figure of George Wingfield, obscuring some of the details and lending high color to others. During his lifetime he conspicuously combined economic power and political authority in a manner that was possible only in a sparsely settled desert realm like Nevada, where few people tarried between the periodic mining booms. From his roots as a cowboy-gambler, George Wingfield became the central economic and political figure in early-twentieth-century Nevada, from about 1909 until the final collapse of his empire in 1935. Among several who made similar mining fortunes in Nevada, he was unique in remaining in the state with his money. His first fortune (estimates in the press of as much as $25 or $30 million were probably inflated) was almost all invested in Nevada, a state that had few resources and more square miles (110,000) than people until 1940. Such affluence almost inevitably brought power, and Wingfield quickly mastered the use of both.

The purposes to which he put that tremendous power were controversial at the time and continue to be a matter for debate. The daughter of a political opponent harshly charged that Wingfield worshiped money: "He championed no leader; he cared for no cause; he retained to the end the narrow squint of the small-time gambler he had originally been, and that squint was unblinkingly affixed upon his accumulating stacks of silver dollars." But a San Francisco newspaper reporter depicted George Wingfield in 1929 as a far more beneficent capitalist, "always ready to aid his state when it needs assistance":

> Most of the credit due for the financing of numerous industries belongs to George Wingfield. He contributes money to the raising of cattle and other livestock. He grubstakes innumerable prospectors. He aids banks and other business institutions. . . . those who know his good works hold him the savior of Nevada.[4]

Personally, Wingfield always defended all his actions in terms of the prevailing piety of the age, economic development. He was quite sincere when he maintained, "Service to the state of Nevada has become a religion with me," though his notion of service usually involved at least the potential of profit. To him, politics was a means to an end, a way to insure an advantageous business climate and move Nevada toward constructive diversification. Others, less sympathetic, criticized Wingfield's activities as the crudest sort of personal domination, born of nothing more elevated than a "lust for wealth and authority."[5]

Describing Nevada in 1931, shortly after legalization of gambling and reduction of the residency requirement for divorce to six weeks, the sensationalist *New York Evening Graphic* depicted George Wingfield as a sinister dictator of a sinful state:

> When you speak of American democracy, leave Nevada out, for democracy is unknown there. One man controls the politics of the state, whether Democratic or Republican. One man controls the finances. One man controls the wills of the citizens and tells them what to think, what to vote. One man controls the legislature. One man controls the industries.

No one inside or outside of Nevada could deny the man's importance to the state, but opinions about the nature and purposes of his influence differed radically.[6]

Still, his was undeniably a romantic saga, the kind of emblematic western success story that endlessly fascinated certain writers. As early as 1904, years before George Wingfield came to national prominence with the formation of the fabulously rich Goldfield Consolidated Mines Company in south central Nevada, his activities were already being covered in the San Francisco newspapers. Writer Ralph Paine, who met Wingfield in 1905, found the boyish-looking young man remarkable:

> It occurred to me while I was eating ham and eggs alongside this George Wingfield in the Bullfrog hotel that there was romance left even in money getting. Here was a modern buccaneer, if you please, who had diced with fortune, and won by means of daring and enterprise as bold as ever sent men to fight for gold that lay in the holds of tall galleons. He had "made his stake" as a gambler, but in this corner of the West your honest gambler is as respectable a figure as a Standard Oil King of the Atlantic seaboard. I found that young Wingfield was one of the most respected and popular men of the desert not because he is rich, but because he is square and fearless and generous.[7]

Paine's description set the tone for many subsequent accounts, although the details varied over time. Those who were inclined to appreciate adventure depicted George Wingfield in heroic terms, as an honest gambler who achieved great fortune, but remained true to his humble western roots and used his money to help his state. In these positive accounts, Wingfield was everlastingly "square, fearless, and generous."

In later years, as Wingfield's power grew, his actions began to affect more people. Because he never held any major elected office, however, he was beyond any curbing public pressure in the form of elections or constituent lobbying. His influence thus seemed particularly ominous and irresistible, and resentment of him grew. The wealth and power that had so thrilled Paine in the young Wingfield carried darker implications in the middle-aged man. The tone of the stories changed in the telling. An early-twentieth-century Italian immigrant to Reno, for instance, learned from local gossip a very different version of Wingfield's glorious rise to affluence:

> . . . he was not a mayor, but he was more than a mayor; he was like the governor, you might call it. He had banks and he had prostitutes, and these prostitutes would learn from the miner where the gold mine was. And they would find out, more or less, which place it was, and the next day they'd tell George Wingfield where he should buy stock. . . .[8]

In this version, and others like it, corruption and exploitation replaced honesty and daring as the keys to Wingfield's character, and money rather than service became his watchword. As he accrued power, George Wingfield became not just an admirable symbol of western daring, but a potentially dangerous overlord.

Undoubtedly there was some truth in each version. Depending on one's point of view, George Wingfield assumed the character of Nevada's patron saint or contaminating devil. Personally he remained aloof, dissociating himself from both public praise and condemnation. Reserved and poker-faced, not at all charismatic, he barely moved his lips when he talked. One interviewer described Wingfield's characteristic demeanor in 1941:

> For at first glance, as he sits there a chunky figure wearing glasses, he reminds one of a Buddha who would be exceptionally good at poker. And at second and third glances he reminds one of the same thing . . . and he sits there, Buddha-like, waiting for the other guy to talk first, to place his bet. . . . But his expression does not change.[9]

His public silence, however, didn't stop the stories from circulating. Over time they were embellished by numerous retellings and assumed the status of a popular legend centered on Nevada's most powerful early-twentieth-century resident.

This legend further magnified the already fantastic aspects of Wingfield's career. He was rumored, for example, to have killed a man, to have been a pimp, to have discovered, in the company of three other men, a room full of solid gold. In a society that revered the rags-to-riches formula as somehow quintessentially American, it was perhaps predictable that George Wingfield was reported to have gotten his start by borrowing money from the man who would become his future partner, George Nixon. Nixon was then a banker in the small railroad town of Winnemucca and was variously said to have loaned Wingfield money on a diamond ring, or to have staked him in a poker game, or to have lost money outright to Wingfield in a poker game. Although the details varied in different versions, they were unified by the theme of a vaguely illicit transaction between the two future millionaires. These overtones of unsavory activity would become a prominent element of the Wingfield myth in Nevada.

In Goldfield, where he began his rise to fame and fortune as a mine owner, another element—cool courage—was added to the legend. Wingfield was credited with single-handedly facing down a violent mob of angry union strikers. His would-be biographer, Oscar Morgan, best captures the essence of this story in his dramatic outline of the incident:

> At first meeting they [mine operators] turn to Wingfield for leadership. He becomes target for threats of strikers. Never alters habits. Nerve becomes a byword. Foes hate him, but respect his courage. . . . hundreds of strikers watch him with hostile eyes, but none dares to make first move. Later walks through mob in front of bank which had been

chanting "We want Wingfield." He leaves mine operators' meeting, walks through mob, quietly saying, "I'm Wingfield. Who wants Wingfield?" Tosses them a few $20 goldpieces, tells them to buy a drink, returns to meeting.

This inspiring depiction of raw courage was undercut somewhat by Bernard Baruch's later account that when he met George Wingfield, about the same time, the mine owner was heavily armed and traveling the streets of Goldfield with bodyguards. But it was the emblematic tale of the lone man bravely facing down the mob that prevailed.[10]

As both Goldfield and George Wingfield settled into maturity, Wingfield was extolled by local newspapers as "the Napoleon of Nevada finance," a bold man who never retreated in the face of mining market fluctuations, but always advanced. Friend and foe alike credited him with almost superhuman control over the fate of Goldfield mining stocks. This aura of command only increased after Wingfield's move to Reno and involvement in politics. The man who turned down appointment to the U.S. Senate in 1912 attracted whimsical national coverage as "the cowboy who refused a toga," but his decision to refuse public office did not diminish his influence in Nevada. Everyone agreed he was more important than the governor. A 1934 *Fortune* magazine article on Reno dubbed Wingfield "King George." Later a newspaper publisher described the monarch's kingdom: "Every little thing that went on around the town here, everybody said, 'Well, now, how's that gonna get along with the boys up there in "the cave"?' By that they meant the upstairs of that old Reno National Bank building there [where Wingfield and his attorneys both had offices]." [11]

The fact that his attorneys were prominent Democratic party functionaries was often cited as evidence that Wingfield controlled not just the Republican party, but the Democrats as well. This legendary bipartisan political machine, which allegedly ruled the politics of an entire state in order to protect its central figure, was one more manifestation of George Wingfield's tremendous economic, political, and symbolic power in Nevada. When Wingfield's "octopus-like influence" was broken by his economic collapse in the 1930s, the *Sacramento Bee* crowed about the destruction of the hated Wingfield machine: "At a frightful cost to themselves, the people of Nevada have broken partially the iron shackles with which Boss George Wingfield bound them." [12]

Rumors magnified not only the extent of this control, but also its nefarious character. Wingfield's friendship with one of Reno's prominent underworld figures, for instance, led to his association in the public mind with numerous illicit activities, including prohibition-era speakeasies, brothels, and gambling dens. By 1931, when gambling was legalized in Nevada, Reno had a reputation as a wide-open sin city, and George Wingfield was believed by some to be responsible for all of its vices. As *Fortune* put it in 1934:

> [Reno] has two governments (both, remember, under the large, paternal thumb of George Wingfield): an official bureaucracy, dominated by the law corps and by Thatcher and Woodburn [Wingfield's attorneys] in particular; and a large, feudal, and obscure hierarchy, an underworld brought partially into the open, into which are gathered the town's more primitive (and more popular) entertainments.

In short, there was nothing that went on in Nevada for which, in the popular mind at least, George Wingfield was not responsible. As Max Miller observed, "With Wingfield's downfall the State fell, too, rather a left-handed compliment to the power of a lone individual." [13]

Untangling the extent, the purposes, and the sources of that power is the principal endeavor of this biography of George Wingfield. The legacy of the man who became such a controversial legend during his own lifetime has been obscured since his death by the proliferation of tall tales about him. Undeniably the major figure in early-twentieth-century Nevada, Wingfield for a time was the virtual owner and operator of the state. But his domination was neither so absolute nor so insidious as it was rumored to be, and his real significance for the state still remains to be explored. Behind the movie script is a man whose decision to remain in Nevada had profound consequences for the development of its modern society and economy. The contours of his life and times deserve to be viewed dispassionately.

GEORGE WINGFIELD was born in 1876, into a family with a venerable tradition of restless mobility. His father, Thomas Yates Wingfield, was born into a Methodist family in 1846, in Charlottesville, Virginia. They subsequently moved to western Virginia, to southeastern Iowa, and, by 1853, to the military outpost of Ft. Smith, Arkansas, in the western part of the state adjacent to Indian Territory. By 1858, they had moved once again, this time some fifty miles north along the Arkansas River, to Cincinnati, Arkansas.

They were there during the Civil War, which caused substantial suffering as both regular armies and irregular border raiders fought for control of the bitterly disputed territory. Northwestern Arkansas was an area of significant Union sympathy; and one of George Wingfield's uncles (Thomas's older brother, William) enlisted in the Union army. For that reason, it was also a hotly contested region, from which the Wingfield family fled for two years at the end of the war.

From 1864 to 1866, they were virtual itinerants, stopping in Illinois, northeastern Missouri, and finally in southwestern Missouri, at Springfield. By 1866, however, they had returned home to Arkansas. There, shortly after the war, Thomas Wingfield married Martha Matilda Spradling, George Wingfield's mother. Literate, but not well educated, she, too, was a staunch Methodist. A surviving photograph suggests a woman of firm resolve and considerable character. Throughout her life Martha Wingfield remained a member of the church and a supporter of related causes such as the Women's Christian Temperance Union.[14]

Taking advantage of the embryonic cattle industry that sprang up in post–Civil War Texas, Thomas Wingfield became a cattle buyer. As such he continued the family habit of travel, ranging south into Texas to buy stock, then driving them through Indian Territory and selling them wherever he could. George Wingfield later guardedly described his father as a man who "knew that business, and was typical of his day and region."[15] Thomas and Martha had four children while in Arkansas. Morris was born in 1868, Mary in 1870, and Lillian in 1874. The latter died the next year, and son George was born on August 16, 1876, near Cincinnati, Arkansas. He lived in the state for only four years before the family moved west in their perpetual search for greener pastures. With that relocation, George Wingfield's life took on the western contours that would be its most fundamental characteristic. Molded as a boy by the open informality and male-dominated institutions of western ranching society, his tastes and his experiences in turn influenced his views on various social, political, and economic issues central to the development of modern Nevada.

TWO

Roots

IN 1883, when the Wingfield family settled there permanently, nothing in the tiny town of Lakeview, Oregon, gave promise of future greatness. Established in 1876 at the north end of Goose Lake, Lakeview was the county seat of recently settled Lake County. A small ranching and commercial center, in sagebrush country 150 miles from the nearest railroad, it had roughly 300 people, a land office, and high hopes that remained unrealized.

The peripatetic Wingfields first visited it briefly in 1881. After leaving Arkansas in 1880, Thomas Wingfield took his family west to the Redding, California, area, where they spent one winter while he worked as a cattle buyer. Then, following in the footsteps of his father and an older brother, William, Thomas Wingfield moved on, to the same Oregon valley where William had initially bought property in 1874. By 1881, William had already sold his land in Lake County and moved on, in the familiar family quest for a better situation that eventually took him to the Verde Valley in Arizona. At first his younger brother, Thomas, seemed to be following the same path. After an 1881 sojourn in Lakeview, Thomas left for the Willamette Valley, farther west in Oregon. Eventually, though, he returned east with his family to settle permanently in Lake County in 1883. It was there, on several ranches that his father owned or operated, that George Wingfield grew up.

It was a working childhood, typical of the time and place. George Wingfield's Methodist mother disapproved of alcohol and smoking. His sister and older brother excelled academically. After graduating from the Lakeview Academy in 1889, the former won a scholarship and went on to graduate from the University of Oregon. Son George, however, followed another path. He grew up around cattle and the buckaroos who tended them, acquiring in

9

the process the full range of virtues and vices associated with the frontier cattle industry. The family initially lived in Lakeview, and their final child, Sam, was born there in 1885. Eventually they acquired a ranch about two miles south of Lakeview, with a summer range in the mountain meadows east of town. There all of the children learned to ride, although none of them could swim.[1]

They also helped with the ranch chores. From an early age, George accompanied his father and older brother on long trips to round up stock and drive them to shipping points. Since Lakeview was without a railroad, the logistics of cattle sales were complicated. During most of this period, the nearest railhead for shipping stock from southeastern Oregon was more than 200 miles to the southeast, in Winnemucca, Nevada.[2] Making those trips, plus the seasonal roundups in spring and fall to move the cattle to and from summer ranges, gave ample opportunity to skip school. George Wingfield had a grammar school education, but little more. In later life, while his penmanship was excellent and his grammar generally good, he was described by those who knew him as verbally unpolished, a "rough talker." A 1905 newspaper article described him as conversing "well, although with no great fluency." Although he was obviously an intelligent person, whose "acumen is not to be denied," George Wingfield was never intellectually inclined.[3]

Instead he grew to be an archetypal man of action, preferring deeds to words and tangible accomplishment to idle speculation. It was a natural result of a childhood such as his, growing up in a materialistic frontier backwater, where a man's achievement was measured by the cattle he owned and the friends he kept. Despite his mother's Methodist principles, it was the male world of the open range and horse barn that George Wingfield inhabited. The coarse company of his youth gave him a taste for rough pursuits. In the restrained words of his most reliable biographer, George Wingfield "saw a lot of roistering living."[4] He learned to gamble and to drink, developing along the way a renowned poker face and a reputation as an "incorrigible boy." In Lakeview, George gambled heavily in company with a Chinese laundryman, and childhood friends reported that he fancied himself good enough to be a professional gambler.[5]

He also became an excellent shot and a skilled horseman. He recalled hunting birds at a young age, an activity he continued to relish throughout his life. Wingfield's early years riding the range also gave him an eye for good horses that he never lost. Once he had made his fortune, he invested in automobiles for transportation and never again cared to ride when it could be avoided. But he nursed a passion for breeding and racing horses, first thoroughbreds at the Nevada Stock Farm, and later quarter-horses at the

Spanish Springs Ranch. These later predilections were revealed early in life. As a teenager, he left home briefly to try his luck as a jockey at a racetrack in Reno. This trip probably occurred in 1891, at the age of fifteen, since he later told of seeing the victim of Reno's last lynching, Louis Ortiz, hanging from the Virginia Street Bridge. At any rate, his early foray into professional riding was a brief one, and he returned to Lakeview.[6]

He was there for the terrible winter of 1889–1890, which devastated the Great Basin livestock industry as heavy snows and cold temperatures killed thousands of free-ranging cattle. As an old man Wingfield recalled to a newspaper interviewer that, at age thirteen, he was one of a group of young men designated to drive cattle to their winter range in the desert country northeast of Abert Lake. The very first night of the drive, November 11, 1889, two feet of snow fell in a single night. Four-horse teams pulling bobsleds loaded with hay were used to break a trail, but the going was still impossible. Eventually, George Wingfield turned back to Lakeview with his father's cattle, which had to be fed through the winter on the ranches there. While the decision was expensive, it undoubtedly saved stock that otherwise would have been lost during the harsh storms that followed.

So much snow accumulated that winter that it was still impossible to reach the desert even for a delayed spring roundup on May 1, 1890, because bridges were washed out by flood-swollen creeks. It took 150 men from surrounding ranches to handle the roundup, which lasted until July 1, complicated by the high water, the widely scattered stock, and the large number of dead animals. Years later, at age seventy-six, George Wingfield still remembered the catastrophe with awe. Two-thirds of the cattle and sheep had died, and even those that were fed through the winter were severely weakened by shortages of feed.[7] That terrible white winter ushered in a bleak period for Lake County. The national depression of 1893 only made local disaster worse. Livestock prices plummeted, and the county population fell as people departed for greener pastures elsewhere. Among the refugees were some of the Wingfields. Although his older brother, Morris, and sister, Mary Wingfield Campbell, both remained in the area, young George struck out on his own permanently in 1896. Shortly afterward, in 1898, his parents abandoned the struggle, sold their land, and moved with the youngest son, Sam, to Burns, Oregon.

Their second son cut his family ties decisively at age nineteen. At the time, in the spring of 1896, George Wingfield was working cattle in the Paisley area, forty miles north of Lakeview. He rode into the county seat just in time to participate in the grand opening of the saloon located in the showy Hotel Lakeview, then under construction. Undoubtedly he saw the occasion as an opportunity to hone his highly developed gambling skills. Whether or not he was successful, he left Lakeview as a rider for the Grand Junction, Colorado, cattle company of Rockwell and Stevens. His job was to help take a herd of 2,900 head, recently purchased from local rancher George Turner, to the railhead at Winnemucca, for shipment to Colorado. At 5'9" and 165 pounds, Wingfield was neither large nor particularly powerful, but he was an experienced buckaroo, as well as a poker player. He was also restless, a young man with ambitions that lured him beyond the isolated confines of Lake County ranch life. Although he occasionally returned to Lakeview later in life to visit relatives, his departure that spring of 1896 marked the beginning of a new era.[8]

Among other things, it inaugurated his lifelong identification with the state of Nevada. The 215-mile overland trip to Winnemucca took three months. Once the drive was over and the cattle were loaded onto railroad cars, Wingfield was offered a job on the Rockwell and Stevens ranch in Colorado; but he was tired of trail life and elected to stay where he was. At the time Winnemucca was a city of roughly 1,100 inhabitants, tied by the railroad to the larger world that was still remote from sequestered Lakeview. In Winnemucca people came and went for business and pleasure. It was possible to travel rapidly and easily to larger cities like Reno. Wanting the opportunities for easier money that could come only in prospering towns like this, Wingfield took a calculated risk. With a gambler's finely developed sense of odds, he traded security in Colorado for a chancy life in Winnemucca, where there were no guarantees of employment, but tantalizing possibilities to explore.

At first, the decision seemed an ill-fated one. Young Wingfield took lodgings at a boardinghouse run in connection with the Arcade Restaurant by Mrs. G. W. Nelson and settled down to find work or a poker game, whichever seemed most likely to pay the bills. Unfortunately, neither one proved a dependable source of income. For the next few years, Wingfield was in and out of Winnemucca, sometimes working at ranches in the area, sometimes drifting back to the southeastern Oregon country, where he was well known to ranch supervisors as "the Peely Kid," because his light skin never tanned and was perpetually peeling from exposure to the sun.[9] To keep body and soul together, he did whatever he could find to do. He ran mowing machines and pitched hay, played poker with the railroad men (who regularly had cash), and reportedly even worked on a railroad section gang out of Wadsworth, Nevada.[10]

Wingfield later claimed that poker was his most lucrative activity at the time, but Mrs. Nelson, who befriended him, recalled having given Wingfield numerous meals "on credit" during those years.[11] Eventually, however, a combination of frugal living and gambler's luck enabled George Wingfield to transform himself from casual roustabout to established man of property. As with many critical transitions in his early life, poker was the instrument of the change. In this regard at least, Wingfield had learned well the lessons of his youth. His skill as a poker player was legendary and later in life he was almost universally described as "poker-faced." The years of practice around Lakeview and Winnemucca evidently refined his native ability at the game; at least there was no allegation that he resorted to cheating in order to win. An old friend and fellow poker player described Wingfield's facility at the game:

> . . . never has anybody said or hinted that he ever dealt from any place except the top of the deck. He was simply a grand poker-player who won more often than he lost because he knew more about that intricate game which sometimes seems so simple than did those with whom he played. Also his cool, steel-blue eyes very accurately observed the varied, tell-tale mannerisms of his opponents.[12]

George Wingfield always moved comfortably in the world of gamblers and was careful not to alienate the men he saw as a potential source of income. Even in Winnemucca, the pool of gamblers was finite, and any suspicion that he was winning by sleight of hand would have ended Wingfield's gambling career abruptly and permanently. He therefore learned to win *and* lose graciously, often treating those whose money he had taken to cigars and drinks. For the most part, the men who gambled with him respected his ability and remained his friends. In time, he built up a considerable nest egg from his gambling winnings and used the proceeds to make another change in his life.[13]

In 1899, three years after his arrival in Winnemucca, George Wingfield staked his fortune, reportedly some $40,000, on the nearby mining boomtown of Golconda, Nevada. Sixteen miles east of Winnemucca on the railroad, Golconda was the site of a brief copper boom in the last years of the nineteenth century. The major production district was located at the Adelaide mine, twelve miles beyond the town itself. When the Glasgow and Western Exploration Company organized the Adelaide Star Mines Ltd. and built a 90-ton smelter and concentration plant in 1898, it presaged great things for Golconda. In September of that year, a Winnemucca newspaper unabashedly boasted about its neighbor:

> Each week is showing steady improvement at Golconda. Not much is being said, but wonders are being accomplished. A splendid future is assured. Four years ago the voting population of Golconda was twenty.

Two years ago it was ninety. This year it will be 120. Two years hence it will probably be 500.[14]

During a period when Nevada's mining fortunes generally seemed to be flagging, the excitement at Golconda attracted considerable attention. By 1899, the town had its own semiweekly newspaper, devoted to assiduous boosting of "the most promising copper district in the undeveloped West." In February of that year, it featured an advertisement for a new undertaking by a recent newcomer. Billing himself as "proprietor" of the California Saloon, George Wingfield proudly claimed, "If you want a good drink or a good cigar you must go to the California." He drew attention to his stock of choice wines and liquors and to a "first class restaurant" run in connection with the saloon, where meals were served at all hours.[15]

The saloon business was a natural one for a man of Wingfield's interests and abilities. In western mining towns, especially booming ones like Golconda, they were profitable as long as the ore held out. Serving as a center of sociability for workingmen without homes or families, saloons were congenial places likely to attract a clientele that would include gamblers. They were primarily male enclaves, where men who appreciated fast horses or skill with a gun might meet and assess each other's talents without the scrutiny of disapproving women. As one modern scholar puts it, "The tavern keeper was a businessman, but he was also the caretaker of a cultural style that emphasized camaraderie and reciprocity among peers. . . . entertainment was the order of the day." All in all, it was a logical investment for a former cowhand just past his majority, who had some money to burn.[16]

In 1899, with the purchase of two lots and houses in Golconda, George Wingfield appeared on the property tax lists for the first time. It was the modest and unremarkable beginning of a long and fabulous rise to financial domination of a state. Initially, in 1899, he may only have leased the California Saloon, since neither of his houses was described as a saloon. By 1900, however, he was the owner of the Banquet Saloon, located in a prime spot close to the Adelaide mine. In any event, the move to Golconda clearly signaled an elevation in his status. Beginning abruptly in 1899, George Wingfield began to appear in the local papers, his comings and goings from Golconda or Winnemucca a matter for coverage in the local columns.[17]

For two years after his arrival, in 1899 and 1900, he lived the life of a young sport, dabbling in unproductive mining claims around Golconda, traveling frequently to Winnemucca and surrounding areas, and racing horses in Reno and elsewhere. His racing stable was the subject of special attention in the newspapers. When he took two horses to the state fair races in Reno in 1899,

A dapper young George Wingfield posed for a photographer shortly after his arrival in Nevada. (Courtesy of Nevada Historical Society)

the *Golconda News* noted that they would be ridden by "a crack rider from the East" and speculated that "they will make the nags in the wetern [*sic*] part get down and dig." At least one of the colts, Incindiator, proved competitive and took third prize.[18]

Golconda had its own Jockey Club, of which Wingfield was a leading light. The club organized frequent quarter-mile races, and betting pools were prominently featured. During these years, Wingfield owned several horses in partnership with Dick Vanetta, from whom he later purchased the Banquet Saloon. The travels of the horses, and their fate in various races, were diligently chronicled by both local papers. When the two men hired a trainer from the East, in April 1900, it was rumored that they would be sent east to race "to some of the best tracks in the country." Within a few weeks, however, Wingfield had sold his half interest in the horses to his former partner for $770.[19]

The sale coincided with his departure from Golconda, and also with the subsiding of the brief boom there. The mill shut down in the spring of 1900, and Golconda's population began to decline from its peak of approximately 500 people. On June 30, the *Golconda News*, which was itself soon to relocate to Winnemucca, reported that George Wingfield had closed the Banquet Saloon, selling its stock and fixtures and leaving a box of good cigars with the newspaper staff as a token of his esteem. Although he owned his Golconda houses until 1910, Wingfield's period of active involvement in the town was ended and his fortune was considerably depleted. In his own retrospective account of the Golconda years, he summarized the experience breezily: "Prior to the time that he made his large fortune, he made two or three smaller ones that any average man would call enough but these he lost trying to add to them. . . ."[20]

Yet the Golconda years paid a different, nonmonetary dividend to the young gambler. In Winnemucca, and especially in Golconda, he made important friendships that were to prove pivotal in later years. It was in Golconda, for instance, that he met the young mining engineer Herbert Hoover, with whom he used to ride on the narrow-gauge ore train that ran between Golconda and the Adelaide mine.[21] Despite the disparity in education and occupation between the two men, they became good friends. He also met and befriended John G. Taylor, who was by the 1930s the largest cattle and sheep rancher in the state and both a director of and a significant borrower from Wingfield's banks.[22] Friendships such as these, formed in the days before he became wealthy and thus untainted by any suggestion of self-interest, Wingfield particularly cherished. Later in life, George Wingfield was renowned for his dogged loyalty to such companions from the early days, never forget-

George Wingfield, proprietor of the California Saloon,
is on the left, probably with his partner Dick Vanetta.
(Courtesy of Nevada Historical Society)

ting anyone who had been honest or generous with him before his rise to prominence.

Most important of all these associations, however, was his friendship with Winnemucca banker, later U.S. senator, George S. Nixon. Born in California in 1860, Nixon was Wingfield's senior by sixteen years and became a formative factor in the younger man's life. Like Wingfield, Nixon had little formal education, but had learned telegraphy and came to Nevada to work as a station agent for the Southern Pacific and Carson and Colorado railroads. In 1884, he resigned to take a position in a Reno bank, and two years later he organized the First National Bank of Winnemucca, which was financed in part by Reno investors who had confidence in his demonstrated abilities.[23]

The bank was a success and Nixon became active politically, first in Nevada's splinter Silver party and later as a Republican. He was elected to the Nevada Assembly in 1891, attempted the U.S. Senate in 1897, and became president of the bank in 1901. He also served as the state agent for the powerful Southern Pacific Company, which exercised a notorious influence over Nevada politics in the nineteenth and early twentieth centuries. In 1905, further enriched by substantial investments in Nevada's twentieth-century mining boom towns of Tonopah and Goldfield, he was elected to the U.S. Senate by the Nevada legislature. Nixon was a lackluster senator in the venerable Nevada tradition, but he was personable and well liked, with "a twinkling eye, a ready smile." A contemporary described him in terms suggesting the quintessential small-town banker: "a genial man with the faculty of seeing the humorous side of things, . . . the life of any company he honors; energetic, ambitious and optimistic, he succeeds in imparting optimism to others. . . ." These qualities, combined with his wealth and prominence, were sufficient to secure him a second senate term in 1911. In 1912, he died in office, of blood poisoning following a routine operation.[24]

From 1902 on, the two Georges, Nixon and Wingfield, were to become virtually synonymous in the public mind, as they invested and grew phenomenally rich together in the southern Nevada mining boom. Long after Nixon's death, Wingfield remembered him fondly, if laconically, as one of five men he particularly esteemed: " 'All of them were men you could tie to.' "[25] In 1899, however, there was no hint of future greatness for the young Wingfield, and Nixon was content with his modest successes as a banker and political broker.

The beginnings of their famous partnership are now so shrouded in myth as to be almost impossible to recover. One popular version, circulated as early as 1905, has a 19-year-old Wingfield borrowing $25 from banker Nixon on the security of a diamond ring. According to this story, Nixon at first hesitated

Racehorses were a passion throughout Wingfield's life. Here the proud
young man is shown with one of the early specimens.
(Courtesy of Polly W. Kline)

to make the loan to an unknown youth who was "something of a shambler." However, "there was something in the appearance of his unknown visitor that attracted him," so he pursued the matter. After the banker inquired about the value of the ring, Wingfield supposedly convinced him by an exhibition of his characteristic determination: "Quick as a wink [Wingfield] settled the discussion; 'There's the rock. Lend or not. It's up to you.'" Evidently awed by the youth's assurance, Nixon determined to lend him the money, having discerned that he was "the kind of square Western gambler that even a Nevada banker could rely upon." This loan, promptly repaid, was the beginning of a long and mutually profitable association between the two men. Reputedly, Nixon later loaned Wingfield the money that enabled him to move to Tonopah, Nevada, and begin his rise to fortune. Another variant of the story has banker Nixon admiring gambler Wingfield's skill at poker and offering to stake him for $300.[26]

Wingfield himself denied these stories: "It has always been rumored that Senator Nixon 'grubstaked' Wingfield but this is contrary to the real facts of the case." Certainly it is true that Wingfield traveled frequently between Golconda and Winnemucca during the former's boom years. At this time Nixon was operating the Winnemucca newspaper, the *Silver State*, and was extremely active politically. In such a small town, it seems unlikely that the two could have avoided knowing each other in the normal course of business affairs. The details of their meeting may be irretrievable, but their friendship for each other clearly stemmed from contacts made during these closing years of the nineteenth century.[27]

Wingfield's most reliable biographer, Reno newspaperman Oscar Morgan, recounted the most plausible version of the beginning of the business association between the two men, dating from the end of the Golconda venture. According to Morgan, Wingfield needed money to recover from his losses in Golconda. He borrowed $1,000 from Nixon's bank, on a personal note endorsed by a Winnemucca businessman. When the endorser requested early payment of the note, Wingfield consulted Nixon. The latter obliged by 'allowing Wingfield to borrow the money on his own security, thus arranging for repayment of the endorser without inconvenience to Wingfield. Proceeds of the loan probably *were* devoted at least partially to gambling, Wingfield's customary income-producing activity. However, the transaction was on a business basis, secured by an ordinary note, and not in the nature of a grubstake. For the next ten months, from June 1900 until April 1901, George Wingfield was in and out of Winnemucca, Golconda, and Reno, trying to replace the money he had lost in the evaporating Golconda boom.[28]

In 1900, then, Nixon and Wingfield were not yet partners, nor were they even social equals. During his residence in Winnemucca and Golconda, Wingfield was never mentioned in the social columns that frequently featured George Nixon. Although Wingfield's travels to horse races and his appearances in town were duly noted by the newspapers, he was *not* on the guest lists for elegant social occasions such as the Firemen's Masquerade. He had achieved a certain notoriety in the community and the friendship of important men, but nothing approaching the kind of social respectability that Nixon enjoyed as a prominent banker.[29]

The reasons for this disparity in status are not difficult to determine. George Wingfield, even in his flush days in Golconda, remained a sport and a saloon owner. Early photographs taken in Winnemucca show an aspiring young dandy, flashily dressed and prominently displaying a debonair cane. However forthright and dependable he may have been, he moved most comfortably in a male world where the principal activities were drinking and gambling. Even in the outback of late-nineteenth-century Nevada, his occupation as a gambler precluded admittance to the sphere of social gentility controlled by middle-class women.

He may also have been omitted from the invitation lists of polite society because of the unsavory company he kept. The underworld of gamblers, saloons, and horse races that George Wingfield inhabited also included a class of decidedly unrespectable women, at least by prevailing standards of middle-class propriety. In later years, after he had made his fortune, Wingfield was sued by one of them. In 1906, in Tonopah, a woman calling herself May Wingfield brought a scandalous suit for common-law divorce against George Wingfield. May Wingfield, also known as May Baric, haunted George Wingfield for a number of years, although the divorce suit was not successful. At various times she claimed to have been living with Wingfield since roughly 1900 and to have met him in Alaska.[30]

Although her claim about Alaska cannot be verified, evidence abounds that they did live together in Tonopah, and perhaps even earlier, in Golconda. There are also tantalizing suggestions that George Wingfield at least started for the Alaska goldfields. A 1906 biography in the *Goldfield News* noted, "During the Alaska excitement [which began with the discovery of gold in 1898] he started for the northern region, but got no further than the Coast," before returning to Winnemucca.[31] Whether or not George Wingfield actually went to Alaska, and whether or not he met May Baric there, it is clear that his choice of companions as a young man would not have endeared him to the reputable matrons of Winnemucca.

George Wingfield had undoubtedly improved his financial status during his residence in Humboldt County, and he had assiduously practiced his gambling skills, but prosperity eluded him. In 1901, at the age of twenty-four, he was still restlessly seeking some greater success beyond mineral claims and houses in a moribund mining town. As the Wingfields had been doing for many years, he moved on in his search. This time his travels took him elsewhere in Nevada, to the new silver boom town of Tonopah, located in the center of the desert state.

THREE

"Young Men Who Are Willing to Rough It"

I N THE SPRING OF 1901, when George Wingfield arrived there, Tonopah was still a mining camp on its way to becoming a boom town. There were 250 residents, but no frame buildings as yet, and water was still being hauled in barrels. Its extensive silver deposits had been discovered by Jim Butler in 1900, but news of their richness was slow to reach public attention. Even in Winnemucca, located only some 250 miles to the north, the strike wasn't discussed in the newspapers until 1901, when a brief article summarized Tonopah as "a fine place for young men who are willing to rough it to try and accumulate a fortune."[1]

That description fit the 24-year-old Wingfield perfectly. Still seeking to recoup his fortunes after Golconda faded, he had not yet found a situation that suited him. Drifting in and out of Winnemucca, where the papers still described him as being "of Golconda," he was probably gambling. He later recalled leaving Winnemucca on April 7 and arriving in Tonopah on May 7, 1901. The one-month interval is accounted for by his biographer, Oscar Morgan, who places Wingfield in Reno early in 1901. According to Morgan, who interviewed Wingfield while preparing his manuscript, the latter was in Reno because it offered new victims: "Many of his card-playing pals had grown tired of losing with monotonous regularity when they sat in with him for a little game of 'draw' or 'stud.'" Reno, a town of 4,500, promised fresh opportunities. Although he had heard about the Tonopah strike, he apparently wasn't bound there when he left Winnemucca.[2]

He ended up in Tonopah almost inadvertently. In Reno he had been playing cards with jeweler Frank Golden, who was notorious for losing at poker. Golden invited Wingfield to accompany him to Hawthorne, Nevada, a small railroad town 130 miles southeast. Having nothing better to do, and undoubtedly reckoning the chance for meeting new railroad crews in Hawthorne, Wingfield agreed. The two men set out for Hawthorne, where the Tonopah excitement was palpable. Hawthorne was virtually deserted, as men sought transportation southeast to the rich new camp. Wingfield had experience with mining booms, and he knew there was money to be made. He bought train tickets for Sodaville, where he transferred to a "so-called stage" for the final 60-mile leg of the trip, which took 13 hours and necessitated camping overnight at Crow Springs. He arrived in Tonopah on May 7, 1901.[3]

The new town didn't yet have a post office or a newspaper, although both were in the planning stages. Frenzied building was going on, and everything was in short supply, including water and cash. Lumber was especially difficult to obtain. Would-be customers competed for the scarce commodity by walking out several miles into the desert to meet the incoming freight wagons and bidding against each other for rights to the load. Evidently George Wingfield himself was a successful bidder. In later years, he recalled proudly that his was the first house in Tonopah to be built of new lumber, a mansion that measured twelve feet by sixteen feet, furnished with a rug, a dresser, a bed, and three chairs. Many people were less fortunate, however, and lived in tents or in shacks built from oil drums or bottles. Such dwellings couldn't be effectively heated, so saloons and boardinghouses became the customary gathering places for Tonopah's population. It was an ideal environment for an aspiring professional gambler.[4]

Mining was flourishing in 1901. Jim Butler had inaugurated a verbal leasing system at Tonopah, under which he and his partners received twenty-five percent of all net profits. The first leases had been granted in December 1900. By the time of Wingfield's arrival, there were 120 of them, and they were worked through December 31, 1901. Once the leases proved profitable, outside capital was attracted to Tonopah. Mining there became more systematic with the entrance of the Tonopah Mining Company in 1901. Incorporated by a group of Philadelphia capitalists, this company began development of its properties in 1902, after the leases expired. Its manager was one of Jim Butler's partners in the discovery of Tonopah, lawyer Tasker L. Oddie. Later Nevada's governor and a U.S. senator from the state, Oddie was also to become a significant friend of George Wingfield.

In 1901, however, that friendship lay in the future and George Wingfield was feeling his way around the new camp. Wingfield came to Tonopah casually, much as he had gone earlier to Winnemucca and Golconda. He hadn't started out for the silver camp, and he had no motive for staying there except the constant restless familial search for some ill-defined opportunity. This

This tinted postcard bears the title "Early Days in Tonopah."
It depicts the interior of a typical saloon in the new silver mining camp,
including a table of gamblers at right. (Courtesy of Polly W. Kline)

time, however, luck was with him. His sojourn in Tonopah, from 1901 until 1905, was to inaugurate a new epoch in the life of the itinerant gambler.

His start there didn't seem particularly auspicious. According to Oscar Morgan, George Wingfield arrived in Tonopah still owing money on the note to Nixon. Yet things *were* different. A 1906 newspaper account, evidently echoing Wingfield's own rhetoric, put the matter succinctly: "The truth is, he landed in Tonopah with some money and some good friends, and there saw opportunities. He made money from the beginning."[5]

As before, gambling was the instrument of his success. By sheer happenstance, Wingfield made his initial stage trip into Tonopah in company with Tom Kendall, who, along with partner Jack Carey, soon established the new camp's premier drinking establishment, the Tonopah Club. As Tasker Oddie explained somewhat defensively, while describing the new town in a letter to his mother, "Saloons are the first things in a new mining camp. They cannot be kept out. The miners *will* have some place to go in the evenings, and when they have to pay high prices for drinks, (two for 25 cents) they don't drink as much as they do when they buy it by the bottle." When Kendall and Carey added gambling to their saloon business, George Wingfield was occasionally among the dealers, playing poker or faro informally, "when opportunity and the bank roll made it possible." The Tonopah Club was the most important social center in the mostly male camp, and Wingfield was a popular player with both its patrons and management: "When he won he was a spender. When he lost he was still good-natured, and the winners at his game were likely to imitate his generosity. Cigars and drinks were ordered freely from the bar."[6]

At first the arrangement was strictly informal, and Wingfield was simply one of several dealers offering to take all comers. Among the others was John P. Hennessy, a stud poker player who later became Wingfield's partner in a number of investments in both Tonopah and Goldfield. These games were not licensed and limits were imposed only at the dealer's option. Consequently, the bank could be broken by a lucky player, and the dealers frequently lost their entire stake. Sensing real opportunities to make money, Wingfield sought to put the games on a more businesslike basis. He appealed to Kendall, Carey, and Hennessy to participate in a syndicate that would assemble its resources to run a licensed faro game, with prescribed limits and a bank large enough to withstand any player's winning streak. The plan was realized after one extraordinarily profitable night, when George Wingfield won a large sum gambling in an unlimited game with Sammy Tyke and the unfortunate Frank Golden, who had established a branch of his jewelry store in Tonopah. Wingfield used his winnings to invest with Jack

George Wingfield, at right, must have appeared much like this when he presided over poker games at the Tonopah Club. (Courtesy of Polly W. Kline)

Carey in a licensed gambling concession at the Tonopah Club. Carey and Kendall continued to own the saloon, but Wingfield and Carey became the gambling concessionaires. Eventually, perhaps a few years later, Hennessy became Wingfield's partner in the gambling business as well.[7]

In the ensuing months, as Tonopah's leasers grew wealthy from the ore they were extracting from the ground, the gambling concession at the Tonopah Club proved to be as good as the proverbial gold. In a town with a substantial male population and no social outlets other than saloons, gambling and drinking were the major leisure activities. A few years afterward, when George Wingfield had become a nationally famous millionaire, a magazine article made the story of his rise even more colorful, crediting him with a degree of business acumen that was singular for a gambler. According to Barton Curie in 1908, Wingfield had won the Tonopah Club in a card game, but then managed it conservatively: "He fixed the limit for the chances to be taken by the 'house,' and hired an expert accountant to establish the constant net gain from the various tables. Then he doubled the number of tables." Although this degree of orderly supervision seems unlikely in an embryonic mining camp, the profits were clearly phenomenal. Biographer Morgan reported that Wingfield and Hennessy were worth $2 million in 1904, and others credited the two men with annual profits of $200,000 each in that year. Even Wingfield's detractors conceded that he was a skilled gambler, "famed for a half-cunning expression of countenance which deceived his opponents into believing he was bluffing when he wasn't."[8]

From the beginning, then, Wingfield prospered in Tonopah. He was assessed for a house in 1901, the year of his arrival. By 1902, he owned property valued at over $1,500, including additional real estate and a diamond significant enough to be listed separately by the assessor. In June of that year, he expanded his operations by filing his first Tonopah mining claim, the Reptile. This property, along with other claims that he purchased in partnership with Hennessy and J. F. McCambridge, eventually became part of the Boston-Tonopah Mining Company, of which Wingfield was president. This pattern of joint investment was a common one for George Wingfield. Although Tom Kendall was always assessed individually for the Tonopah Club, Wingfield and Kendall were partners in other Tonopah real estate by 1903, and Wingfield and Hennessy were jointly assessed for a mortgage and a horse and buggy in 1904. Tonopah, then, was a much different tale than Golconda. Here Wingfield played the game and won, his success no doubt aided by the veritable orgy of gambling that occurred during the first week of January 1902, when leasers whose terms had expired on December 31 celebrated by wagering the proceeds from their long months of labor.[9]

This boisterous celebration in turn triggered or at least intensified a health crisis, as Tonopah experienced a "plague" of pneumonia. At least thirty residents, all male and undoubtedly weakened both by hard work and by poor conditions, died during late December and early January. The epidemic was diagnosed late in January and was probably amplified by the poor sanitation in the camp, where water was scarce and garbage and tin cans were strewn about with little regard for orderly disposal. George Wingfield himself was initially reported to be among the victims, but the *Tonopah Bonanza* cheerfully contradicted the rumor. Far from being dead, he was "good for many years yet." Before the epidemic ended, however, many residents had fled. Tonopah's population was down to a low of 50 before rebounding in March to 3,000. As conditions improved, and the camp matured into a prosperous town with piped-in water and talk of a railroad, George Wingfield was also emerging from obscurity. In a political debut that was ironic for a man who was to be so prominently identified with the Republican party, Wingfield was elected in September 1902 as a delegate to the Nye County Democratic convention.[10]

In Tonopah he also expanded his network of friends. In various guises, the people with whom he was associated in Tonopah were to prove influential throughout his life. It was there, for instance, that he first met Noble Getchell, later a prominent Republican state senator and business associate. In 1902, Getchell was in the Tonopah Club when Wingfield was being harassed by an irate patron. Getchell and a friend were suddenly startled by a bullet whizzing over their heads and turned to find the patron on the floor and Wingfield looking startled. The gun, which Wingfield had purportedly taken out only to use as a bludgeon, had accidentally fired, missing the patron but piercing five suits of clothing in a closet beside the bar. Wingfield apologized to Getchell and his friend, offering to buy them drinks as the intended victim retreated through the swinging doors. Getchell accepted the apology, and the drink, and began an acquaintance that later grew into close friendship. He repaid the favor in spectacular fashion in the 1930s, after Wingfield's financial collapse.[11]

Similarly, Wingfield in these years first met Key Pittman, prominent Democratic U.S. senator who came to Tonopah in 1902 to practice mining law, and Pat McCarran, another attorney and future Democratic U.S. senator who served for a time as Nye County district attorney. Along with Tasker Oddie, these men were roughly of the same age, went through similar experiences in Tonopah, and remained intertwined in each other's lives in their subsequent political careers in the state. Wingfield's relationship with May Baric also apparently continued in Tonopah. She later alleged that their arrangement was formalized as a common-law marriage there in December 1902, although the newspapers reported that Wingfield attended a Mizpah Club banquet for "wifeless members" the following November.[12]

By far the most important of Wingfield's Tonopah associates, however, was George S. Nixon, who never actually moved there but nevertheless became prominently associated with the camp. The partnership between these two men, which began in October 1902, was to be a remarkable financial and personal success. It made both men millionaires, guaranteed Nixon's political future, and transformed George Wingfield from a shrewd local gambler into a nationally renowned businessman. The circumstances of its beginning, as with many of the events of Wingfield's early life, are obscured by legend. Oscar Morgan tells a detailed version which has the two men negotiating their arrangements almost casually, in the office of the Tonopah Club, and celebrating their arrangement with champagne. Nixon's first visit to the camp was apparently made in September 1902, when the *Tonopah Bonanza* reported that he "will know more about Tonopah hereafter, having been here." His own paper, the *Silver State*, described him giving "glowing accounts of the outlook for the mines there" and being interested in some promising mining claims. Thereafter he made monthly trips to the new camp. Wingfield himself reported that he had been asked by Nixon before leaving Winnemucca "that if he saw anything that looked good around Tonopah to let him know." Their business association began when he acted on that suggestion, in October 1902.[13]

The new partnership of Nixon and Wingfield was an informal one. It existed from 1902 until its dissolution in 1909 without any legal documents and, in Wingfield's words, "depended merely upon the personal honor and integrity of the two men." At first it was not so much a partnership as an agency. Wingfield, after all, was still a gambler, only twenty-six years old and relatively untried in business matters. Nixon, on the other hand, at forty-two, was at the zenith of his career, a prominent banker and politician with substantial capital to invest. The younger man, who was on the ground in Tonopah, took care of business affairs there for Nixon. The latter reciprocated by occasionally making business arrangements for Wingfield in Golconda. The two men invested together in certain ventures, and Nixon was particularly likely to rely on Wingfield for advice in mining matters, but both continued to have private investments, including mining stocks. By November 1902, for instance, Nixon and Wingfield, along with Wingfield's fellow dealer from the Tonopah Club, Jack Hennessy, were buying and selling stock in two promising new mining companies, the Boston-Tonopah and Montana-Tonopah. Nixon also organized the Nye County Bank (later Nye and Ormsby County

Bank) in the fall of 1902, but Wingfield was simply a stock purchaser and not a principal in that venture. Each man advanced money for the other as necessary, and at intervals they reckoned their accounts and balanced them by forwarding checks for the amount outstanding.[14]

The partnership's activities were varied, but followed a pattern familiar to George Wingfield from his years in Golconda. He retained his gambling concession at the Tonopah Club (in which Nixon was not interested) until at least 1904, but also invested in Tonopah real estate, including the Gem Saloon, and loaned money at a healthy two percent monthly interest rate. True to his gambler's instincts, he was particularly intrigued by the financial potential of mining. From the beginning, he gambled on Tonopah's prospects by investing in cheap mining stocks and buying likely looking claims. If the former increased in price, he sold them. Wingfield was a member of Tonopah's Stock Exchange by January 1903, and Tonopah stocks were listed in San Francisco by April of that year. If the latter had potential, he organized companies and sold their stock directly. In the spring of 1903, for example, he made a six-week tour through northern California and his old neighborhood in Lakeview, Oregon, peddling mining stocks to his former associates. His success in both kinds of ventures was legendary: "It seemed that everything he touched prospered for him, and it was not long before those quiet operations of his gave rise to the expression, 'Wingfield Luck.'"[15]

Luck was certainly part of the operation. In distinct contrast to Golconda, Tonopah actually had rich silver deposits which justified the initial excitement. The success of the Tonopah Mining Company swiftly attracted attention from outside investors seeking similar bonanzas. In such a setting, there was money to be made by any man with mines to sell. Having ready access to cash in an economy that was chronically short of it, George Wingfield was in a unique position to act as a middleman. He grubstaked the prospectors who sought out the mines, advancing them money for supplies and expenses in exchange for an interest in any mineral claims that might be discovered. He was known to be a willing investor, and thus, for relatively small amounts of money, was also able to acquire a partial interest in unproven claims that no one else was willing to wager on. The records of mining locations in Nye County testify to the extent of his participation in such arrangements. Beginning in April 1902, dozens of claims each year listed George Wingfield as a ⅙ or ¼ owner, frequently in partnership with Kendall and Hennessy from the Tonopah Club. With so many possibilities, as the gambler Wingfield knew well, the odds on at least a few succeeding were likely to be in his favor. And in the initial boom days at Tonopah, there was a seemingly infinite market for potential mines.

Yet it was not simply luck, or even a speculative temperament combined with ready cash, that made Wingfield a success in what he customarily referred to as "the mining game." Talent and devotion to business were also factors. In the course of investing he began to develop some feel for the technicalities of mining. Never himself a miner, he was nevertheless more than a passive investor in mines. An early account of his business practices, written before the days of his greatest successes, credited some of his achievement to the fact that he personally investigated the properties in which he was interested: "Wingfield is absolutely indefatigable, and as he is alert to every new opportunity, his tirelessness is brought into frequent play. . . . It is nothing unusual for him to make a horseback trip of fifty or sixty miles, take samples of a new claim, and ride back to Tonopah with little or no rest. As a result he is invariably one of the first on the ground in a new country." All his life, George Wingfield was a careful observer. Initially, this trait simply helped him appraise the men he gambled with. Eventually it also taught him the ways of the wider worlds of mining, banking, and politics. That process of education undoubtedly began in Golconda, but it was in Tonopah that the cowboy and gambler started to pick up a modicum of mining expertise from men who were bona fide miners.[16]

George Nixon clearly relied on Wingfield as a scout. The latter's particular combination of basic knowledge, dedication, and personal connections made him an excellent source of advice about investments in Tonopah. Although the Tonopah newspapers eagerly reported that Nixon was planning to move to the new town after his initial visit, there was no need for him to do so with Wingfield there to serve as his eyes and ears. The first significant venture of the two men was the Boston-Tonopah Mining Company, organized in 1902 from claims that Wingfield had been purchasing for several months, located adjacent to the Tonopah Mining Company property. Wingfield and partner Hennessy had been working the claims at least since May, when two shifts were reported to be employed on their property. After the company was organized, work at the mine continued under the professional supervision of J. F. McCambridge, who was also a stockholder. Based on what they expected would be encouraging production figures, the other partners attempted to promote their mine and thereby make a market for their stock.[17]

In this process Nixon, who had experience in organizing and promoting business ventures, was an invaluable source of guidance. He counseled his partners about when and how to sell the stock, always advising caution in order to build confidence among potential investors. The partners exploited local markets. Nixon sold the stock to his friends and associates in northern Nevada, while Wingfield covered northern California and Oregon during his 1903 trip. Ever the conservative banker, Nixon was a voice of restraint in the management of the company. When McCambridge proposed entering into an underwriting agreement, whereby a third party would take an option on the mine and attempt to sell more stock, Nixon advised against it. Even though it promised to pay off the company's debts and bring in more money for efficient operation, he felt it was dangerous. Undoubtedly mindful of future political ambitions, he wrote:

> I cannot afford to have my name mixed up with any fake or extravagant proposition. I imagine he [the underwriter] intends to issue a prospectus promising everything with a view of catching the person with a few dollars to invest, who in case the proposition ends in failure, will feel that he or she has not sufficient money in to make a hard kick. . . . I have several good friends as stockholders in the Company and I cannot allow the Company to get in bad odor through the sale of stock. I much prefer to wait as I am sure that later on we will be able to continue our work on proper lines.[18]

Just in case the point had been missed, Nixon summoned Wingfield to Winnemucca to confer on the offer. Five days after Nixon's first letter, the two men both signed a second note to partner McCambridge, reemphasizing the initial objection:

> Nothing can be added to the letter written you a few days ago by Mr. Nixon further than to state that we must control the advertising of any plan which sellers of the Boston give to the public. You know that we cannot afford to mix up with any jobbery, even if we were inclined to do so, which we are not, and we feel that Brown figures on some kind of a fake scheme to sell stock.

Such a conservative approach surely suited the banker better than the stock promoter. It undoubtedly didn't come naturally to two gamblers like Wingfield and Hennessy, either. But it was Nixon's will that prevailed, and the gambler Wingfield listened and learned. Years later, accused at various times of manipulating stock markets for his own benefit, he echoed Nixon's rhetoric from earlier years. Wingfield always self-righteously insisted, in response to criticism, that it was his business to make mines, not markets for mining stocks.[19]

If the partnership of Nixon and Wingfield was dominated by the business ethos of the former, it was also clearly governed by the mining instincts of the latter. The two men invested together in several other companies, including the Montana-Tonopah, which was the first in Tonopah to pay dividends on its stock. On matters having to do with these companies, Nixon deferred to Wingfield, quoting from the latter when asked by others for advice on Tonopah stocks. The degree of detail in one of these letters from 1902 testifies to Wingfield's active involvement in overseeing the partners' mining interests:

> Everything is improving in every way. Sollender's company, the Cala-Tonopah struck good ore, it runs about $60 and looks like Fraction ore. The Montana cut another ledge different looking ore altogether from the first and better too. . . . Montana-Tonopah is a buy at 80 cents and you will see the day before long when it will reach $3 a share or even more for they have a mine.

By 1904, when it was clear that Nixon would be increasingly involved in politics, he was ready to trust all of the mining decisions to Wingfield. In July of that year, he executed a power of attorney, "so that you can act at all times for me in the mining business." [20]

Nixon's faith in his younger partner was not misplaced. Wingfield's famous luck was not the only source of their success. Wingfield's mining acumen was renowned among his contemporaries: "Young as this man is, he has given such constant study to every phase of the mining situation that he is now a thorough, competent miner in every way, and does not have to depend upon the opinion of others." In later life, Wingfield surrounded himself with experts to provide him with other opinions, but the mining business remained close to his heart even though he also invested in a range of other ventures. Perhaps his early proclivity for gambling gave him a special affinity for the risky business of making money in mining. Clearly, for George Wingfield, as for the western entrepreneurs described by historian Rodman Paul, "Mining was more than a business; it was a state of mind, a way of life." [21]

Over time, although both men continued to make independent investments, the partnership of Nixon and Wingfield matured into a sizable network of joint investments and a personal relationship of mutual respect and trust. Letters from Nixon in 1902 were addressed to "Friend George," but by 1904 they were being directed to "My dear George." Clearly the most significant of the many relationships that began during the Tonopah years, it gave Wingfield not only wealth, but also direction. Nixon, although much different in temperament, was a man who had things to teach the former "incorrigible boy" from Lakeview, Oregon. As his senior not only in years, but also in experience of the business world, Nixon was in a position to serve as a mentor to Wingfield. Just as he learned mining from watching it being done, so George Wingfield learned finance, and later politics, by observing

George Nixon. And it was Nixon who ultimately counseled the younger man to decisively cut his ties to the roughshod past and give up gambling:

> I really believe old man, as you have told me several times that you wanted to get out of the card business, that the time is now ripe for you to do it. In this stock business you can do better than any of those lobsters, and I believe if you should cut out the cards, you Ramsey and myself can open a brokerage office in Tonopah and San Francisco and make all kinds of money. . . . Think it over and when I come out, we will talk it over.[22]

Apparently Wingfield acted on Nixon's suggestion sometime in 1904 or 1905. Although he retained throughout his life a nervous habit of shuffling together stacks of silver dollars with one hand, he never again relied on his gambling skill as a source of income. The increasing prosperity of Nixon and Wingfield had yielded him a reported worth of $2.5 million, and a monthly income of $25,000 to $30,000. By 1905, the partners owned extensive properties throughout the southern Nevada mining districts, including two banks, hundreds of mining claims, interests in numerous mining companies, an exceptionally productive mining lease, and real estate in several different towns, both existing and proposed. They also had shifted the focus of their operations from Tonopah to a second boom town, Goldfield, twenty-six miles to the south.[23]

Although George Wingfield had prospered in Tonopah, and was closely identified with that camp, real fame and fortune came only with the move south to Goldfield, a gold mining area whose notoriety soon far outshone its northern neighbor. Both the partnership and Wingfield personally relocated there in 1905, but their involvement with the new camp began much earlier. Along with Jack Hennessy and Tonopah newspaper editor W. W. Booth, Wingfield was both locating and purchasing claims in Esmeralda County, the site of Goldfield, by 1902. The mineralized district later known as Goldfield was first discovered in December 1902 by two prospectors, Harry Stimler and William A. Marsh, who initially named it Grandpa. Wingfield later claimed that he had grubstaked Stimler and Marsh, "when they made their original location called Grandpa—now—Goldfield—and which was the first money ever put into the Goldfield district." A more contemporary newspaper account, however, clarifies the story. Stimler and Marsh were originally outfitted by Tom Kendall and Jim Butler, the man who discovered Tonopah. When these two declined to throw good money after bad, Stimler sought other backing. He approached numerous Tonopah figures and eventually assembled a syndicate of investors that included gambler Harry Ramsey, William J. Douglass, and Nixon and Wingfield. This latter group, along with Kendall and Butler, thus shared an interest in the group of claims initially staked by Stimler and Marsh on Columbia Mountain.[24]

Within a year of the discovery, both Stimler and Marsh had sold their interests in the Columbia Mountain group (sometimes called the Sandstorm group after the most productive of the claims) to George Wingfield. Rumors about the high sale price, which later proved false, were enough to start a minor rush into Goldfield. Additional publicity resulted from the visit that year of a government geologist from Tonopah, J. E. Spurr, who reported the new region in mining journals. In a community of inveterate speculators, this was enough to justify laying out a town, which was done by a syndicate in July 1903. They tried to interest Nixon and Wingfield in joining their ranks, but the offer was refused. Within a few months, the partners were to pay $10,000 for just one prime Goldfield lot, on which they later built an office building.

But in July 1903 the hectic future of Goldfield was still remote. Ore from the Sandstorm group proved spotty, and the real excitement didn't begin until 1904, after news began to spread about some extraordinarily rich ore that had been shipped in December 1903 from the Combination claim. This mine was located about three miles south of the less productive Sandstorm properties that Nixon and Wingfield owned, and the partners had just missed buying it in 1903. Ultimately it paid its original purchasers more than $1 million in dividends and was finally sold to Nixon and Wingfield, in 1906, for $4 million. Like the leases in Tonopah in 1901, its success was the signal for outside money to begin pouring into the new camp of Goldfield.[25]

In these same years, Nixon and Wingfield were becoming increasingly involved at Goldfield. The newspapers reported visits by both, Wingfield returning in October 1903 with a sackful of fine specimens, and Nixon carefully publicizing his "enthusiasm" about the new district in June of the same year. Both men invested separately, often in partnership with others; but their various interests in the new camp were eventually combined. Thus, for example, Wingfield purchased the Stimler and Marsh interests separately, when Nixon didn't think enough of the twenty-three undeveloped claims to exercise their original option. Later he declared his partner in on the purchase and transferred part of his interest to Nixon. Similarly, in 1904, Nixon began independently purchasing the outstanding interests in the claims that made up the fabulously wealthy Mohawk mine. By 1906, this property had become the most prominent in Goldfield and attracted national attention; but Wingfield was initially interested in it only as a stockholder.[26]

As had been the case in Tonopah, the first profits in Goldfield went to leasers, companies that paid royalties to the owners of mining claims in exchange for the right to work part of the property. These arrangements benefited property owners by placing the burden of development expenses on the leasing companies. If the ground proved profitable, the companies were then in a better position to secure financing and work it on their own account, or to sell the property at a profit. Meanwhile, the leasing companies bet on the productivity of the particular ground they undertook to mine. The partnership of Nixon and Wingfield became interested in several of these leases in Goldfield, including the famous Sweeney and Reilly leases on the Florence ground. In 1904, the profits of the former lease were $600,000, split among Sweeney, Nixon, Wingfield, and Jack Hennessy. The next year, the two principal partners made $350,000 from the same property. Eventually, Nixon, Wingfield, and Hennessy actually controlled a minority interest in the Florence ground, which they deeded in 1905 to the Florence-Goldfield Mining Company. Although not everything that Nixon and Wingfield touched turned to gold, and few purchases were as profitable as the Mohawk or the Florence, they invested early and widely enough to have a notable presence in the new camp. In the words of a contemporary newspaper account, "Each new investment brought more working capital, and they have kept on buying ever since."[27]

By 1904, then, George Wingfield was on the verge of major changes in his life. He was becoming increasingly identified with the fortunes of the burgeoning new camp to the south, and his growing wealth and prominence were already sufficient to merit coverage in the San Francisco newspapers. In September, the *San Francisco Call* noted breezily that Wingfield, then in the city, had received word that he was $100,000 richer from ore uncovered in the "new camp of Goldfield." During this time, too, Tonopah was stagnating. As mining activity there was increasingly dominated by the Tonopah Mining Company, Goldfield must have seemed all the more tempting as a new field of operations. Although Wingfield had not relocated from Tonopah, he was evidently exploring the possibilities of the new camp. In what was by now a familiar pattern, he purchased a saloon and a house in the speculative new town of Columbia, adjoining Goldfield to the northeast. Also in 1904, the partnership of Nixon and Wingfield began to formalize its operations in Goldfield. Beginning in May of that year, dozens of the Goldfield claims that the two men owned were deeded to formally organized mining companies. They also formalized their control, through formation of the Goldfield May Queen Mining Company, of several mill sites that would prove crucial once mining operations expanded in the new district.[28]

With the arrival of telephone and telegraph facilities in Goldfield in January 1904, it was clear that a permanent population center was developing. Over the next decade, in a riotously accelerated cycle of birth and death, another gaudy new metropolis would take shape on the southern Nevada desert. This time, Wingfield was clearly primed, by virtue of past experience in Golconda and Tonopah, recently acquired wealth, and new associations, to play a major role in its development. It is no wonder, then, that he should seriously weigh Nixon's advice in July of that year to give up gambling. Goldfield would be the third time that the still young George Wingfield had gambled on a mining boom. And with Wingfield's by now legendary luck, the third time would prove to be the charm.

FOUR

Nevada's Napoleon

WHEN HE MOVED to the Goldfield suburb of Columbia in November 1905, George Wingfield was in an awkward state of social transition from the venturesome sportsman's world of gamblers and saloon keepers to the more respectable domain of conservative bankers and college-educated attorneys. As George Nixon's associate and an increasingly wealthy mining investor, he was accorded a certain degree of respect in the local press; but he was pointedly *not* included in the private gatherings of the social elite.[1] The years in Goldfield, and particularly the formation of the Goldfield Consolidated Mines Company in 1906, would permanently change all that. In the brief moment of Goldfield's spectacular efflorescence, when it was for a time the largest city in the state and an object of national curiosity, Wingfield became its wealthiest and most prominent citizen and thereby gained his own particular kind of immortality. In Goldfield the course of his life changed forever.

A children's book published in 1909 depicted him on the eve of this final rise. Portrayed in *A Little Princess of Tonopah* as Ned Osborne, the "Golden Eagle Man," Wingfield's social status as a somewhat marginal outsider is clear. Meeting him on horseback in the desert, the proper twelve-year-old heroine of the book is thrilled to discover that he speaks in slang and routinely carries a revolver. Although he is not an outlaw, and already has a fortune of more than three million dollars, he has for her the allure of the forbidden. While he knows some of the same people she does, including her friend Mrs. Hugh Bronson, a character based on the wife of prominent Tonopah attorney Hugh Brown, he doesn't socialize with them: "'I don't go much on the camp's society ways—and besides, outside of business, I've got a name in this place about as bad as a train robber.'" When she asks why, he explains his reputation:

"That's easy—I try to amuse myself some when I'm not workin'—and I've tried different ways—mostly without getting much out of them— but always seeing things to a finish. And I don't think it's worth while takin' the trouble coverin' up things like some fellows do—especially that college set of fellows the town's full of. . . . So just as every one knows they're sure of a square deal when they do business with me— and they know I go it pretty strong when I'm out for a good time— and—" He did not go on, for somehow the things that made up his "good time" seemed things that one ought to be ashamed of before a little girl like Jean.

Predictably, the Golden Eagle Man proves to be Jean's champion in *A Little Princess of Tonopah*. Socially suspect, but ultimately generous and honorable, he plays a male role analogous to the legendary western whore-with-a-heart-of-gold. But in addition to being a western hero, Ned Osborne is also a surprisingly candid rendition of the 29-year-old George Wingfield on the eve of his fame in Goldfield, a man of ambivalent personal qualities but evident importance.[2]

The real George Wingfield was not much different. Through most of 1904, Wingfield oversaw the mining interests of the two partners, including not only organization of their claims into incorporated companies, but also active trading in the new Goldfield stocks. By now skilled at "building a market," Wingfield was credited by friend and foe alike with considerable skill at this arcane financial game. By his friends, he was hailed as "the Napoleon of Nevada finance," a bold figure who never retreated but advanced even under discouraging conditions. By his foes, most prominently the notorious mining con artist George Graham Rice, he was less admiringly described: "Uncouth, cold of manner, and taciturn of disposition, he was the last man whom an observer would readily imagine to be the possessor of abilities of a superior order." Yet even Rice—who probably begrudgingly admired Wingfield's skill in this realm—acknowledged that "Wingfield was said to be behind the market. He was looked upon as the boss of the mining partnership, and Mr. Nixon as a circumstance."[3]

Nixon's attentions were obviously directed elsewhere in 1904, as he prepared to run for the U. S. senate seat being vacated by William Stewart. The success of his campaign hinged on election of a Republican state legislature, since at that time the legislators elected the senator. By now apparently dissuaded from his initially Democratic politics, George Wingfield assisted his partner's bid for office by supporting Republican candidates. Biographer Oscar Morgan reports his success in a later southern Nevada race, in 1912, which pitted Goldfield saloon owner W. S. "Ole" Elliott, a Democrat, against Republican Emory J. Arnold. According to Morgan:

> It was a spirited fight, because "Ole" was well known and popular. Wingfield worked with his usual quietness, while "Ole" toured the district, buying drinks for everybody. When the votes were counted Wingfield's man had won, and "Ole" was greatly disappointed.
>
> "Why, I bought enough drinks to float a battleship," he declared, "but the trouble is the ———— don't vote the way they drink." [4]

Ole Elliott was not the only man to complain about the vagaries of Nevada politics, and George Wingfield himself had cause in future years to murmur about the fickleness of Nevada voters. His role in Nixon's 1904 campaign, however, introduced him to an entirely new game. From that time forward, Wingfield took a special delight in politics, characteristically—as in 1904—operating from behind the scenes, and with the singular vantage point that money could provide in a small state where elections were won by narrow margins. Although he never ran for partisan political office, Wingfield was to be heralded in a few years as the state's major political power broker and the sinister leader of a tightly organized bipartisan political machine. His acknowledged skill in political organization, like his business acumen, he learned during these years by careful observation of George Nixon.[5]

In 1904, however, in politics Nixon was the boss and Wingfield merely a circumstance. When Nixon was elected the next January by the new legislature, Wingfield was in the capital, Carson City, but was unable to offer much assistance. Early in the month, he contracted what was first thought to be acute bronchitis, but was later diagnosed as smallpox. May Baric, from whom he had apparently been estranged for a period of some months, went to his bedside to nurse him; and he spent the next three months recovering, first in Carson City and then in Tonopah. Nixon, meanwhile, swept on to triumph, sworn into office in Washington in March 1905. His senate seat brought new prestige to the partnership, and gave Nixon access to national figures, not only in politics, but in business as well. Although his senatorial career was lackluster, he made excellent use of his financial ties, frequenting the Waldorf-Astoria Hotel in New York. These contacts were to be especially important to Nixon and Wingfield in 1906 and 1907, when they sought to finance their major mining merger.[6]

Meanwhile the partners continued to invest heavily in the burgeoning mining boom of southern Nevada. As promising new discoveries triggered excitement in evanescent towns like Bullfrog, Rawhide, Gold Center, and Silver Bow, Nixon and Wingfield moved in to purchase likely looking claims, to lay out towns, and sometimes, as at Rhyolite in 1906, to build banks. Despite the growing network of investments, Wingfield continued to reside in and be identified with Tonopah. In April 1905, he was elected a member of the citizens' committee on sanitation, and in July of that year he became one of the directors of Tonopah's Board of Trade. Nixon, on the other hand, was betting big on Goldfield. He was building a large three-story stone office building on a prime downtown corner there. When it opened for occupancy on Labor Day, 1905, its tenants included some of the new town's most prominent attorneys and stockbrokers, but notably *not* George Wingfield.[7]

The Nixon Block *did*, however, house another new business venture of the two partners, the banking firm of John S. Cook and Company. In May 1905, Nixon sold his interests in the Nye and Ormsby County Bank of Tonopah to a group headed by former jeweler and Wingfield poker companion Frank Golden. John S. Cook was Nixon's former cashier in that bank, who had resigned in a policy disagreement with some local directors. When he opened his own bank in Goldfield, Nixon purchased a half interest in it on behalf of Nixon and Wingfield. At the same time, Nixon organized a new bank for Tonopah, the Tonopah Banking Corporation, in which Wingfield, following the previous pattern, was a stockholder but *not* a director. Reflecting the breadth of Nixon's new connections, other stockholders in the Tonopah institution included prominent San Francisco banker William H. Crocker, Chicago investor and Combination mine owner J. D. Hubbard, and Southern Pacific Railroad attorney William Herrin.[8]

As a practical matter, Wingfield began to take over more responsibility for the management of their joint affairs as the duties of office increasingly preoccupied Nixon. The two men made a joint tour of their southern Nevada interests, for instance, in April 1905 and again in July and November, but circumstances inevitably forced Nixon to rely on his junior partner more than he might have preferred to do. Observing him at this period, a young mining engineer noted that Wingfield acted and appeared older than his years and was growing into the responsibilities of his position: "A very intelligent man, his administrative ability, while not extraordinary, was excellent for a man of his background, and he was quick to learn. . . ."[9]

Possibly it was recognition of this growing ability or perhaps only reflected glory from the senator that accounted for George Wingfield's gradual rise in local stature. Whatever the cause, by 1905 his activities began to be covered more seriously by the newspapers, and the mere fact of his association with some new mining discovery was deemed sufficiently portentous to be news-

Automobiles were a new feature of Nevada's twentieth-century mining booms. Wingfield, shown here seated second from the left, owned two in Goldfield. He used them to make quick trips to prospects and to escort parties of potential investors in relative comfort. (Courtesy of Polly W. Kline)

worthy. In August, a brush with death when his car broke down in the desert and Wingfield had to walk forty miles in intense heat with very little water was humorously recounted by the *Tonopah Sun*. Wingfield was stranded along with Charles J. Kappler, a Washington attorney and former private secretary to U.S. Senator William M. Stewart of Nevada. The two men were returning from inspecting a Nixon and Wingfield investment at the new camp of Silver Bow, and the newspaper recounted the ordeal as a mock heroic walking race: "Mr. Wingfield held the pole for the first ten miles and kicked alkali dust all over Mr. Kappler, but with a marvelous burst of speed and a short cut around the brow of a hill the attorney forged ahead of the capitalist." What is significant about the story is its tone of amused appreciation, and its reference to Wingfield as "Mr." Previously, although Wingfield's activities had been reported in the newspapers, he had been referred to in the style accorded to the common man, simply as George Wingfield. The courtesy title of "Mr." was one reserved for men of dignity and importance in the community. By 1905, however tenuous his claim to respectability, Wingfield was acquiring that dignity.[10]

In November, his presence was noted as part of a reception committee that traveled 100 miles south from Tonopah to Beatty, Nevada, to officiate at the opening of a new hotel. As a Tonopah paper noted, "The event was . . . in the nature of a christening of the Bull Frog district," and "society from Tonopah . . . assembled at the Montgomery hotel." In Tonopah in 1903, George Wingfield could scarcely have been included as part of any such "society" party. Being so included in Beatty in 1905, he was clearly a man on his way up in the world. Whether the change was due to Nixon's newfound prominence or to Wingfield's own growing wealth, it was a subtle but distinct shift in his status in the community. As it happens, it was the herald of even greater things to come, when George Wingfield's name would become notorious far beyond the borders of the isolated desert state where he made his home.[11]

Prominence and the accompanying publicity were not especially gratifying to Wingfield. Always reticent, and undoubtedly sensitive about his past, George Wingfield routinely avoided the limelight. Described by contemporaries as "quiet and unassuming," he was naturally reserved: "It is difficult for anyone, even his most intimate friends, to get Wingfield to discuss his affairs, he is so quiet and self-contained." Some of this reserve undoubtedly served his business purposes. Once his activities with Nixon began to attract attention, it was the latter who gave interviews and made most of the firm's public announcements. This role fitted Nixon, a gregarious politician who understood the uses of newspapers. Secrecy suited Wingfield better, enabling him to do business discreetly when he wanted to:

He talked little. He was the most difficult man in the camp to get information from. He never tried to have misstatements corrected. He never
volunteered news to the eager mining reporters who were reveling in
huge headlines almost daily. He made his moves so quietly that not until
quite a while after they had been made did others know about them.[12]

Nevertheless, as Goldfield grew and the riches of its mines began to make
waves in San Francisco, George Wingfield's moves inevitably began to be
publicly discussed. Not only those who traded in mining stocks but also those
who sought tips on the location of new mining districts followed his moves
and marveled at his conspicuously growing fortune, symbolized by the acquisition of a personal automobile in 1905. Thus it was a matter of public interest
in Tonopah when George Wingfield decided to move his headquarters south
to the new camp. Significantly, however, he did *not* move to Goldfield, but to
neighboring Columbia, three-quarters of a mile to the northeast. Columbia
was closer to his Columbia Mountain mining properties and for a brief period
he was evidently trying to promote it in competition with Goldfield as the
major population center for the new district. Wingfield's first Goldfield-area
real estate was purchased there in 1904; and in September 1905, the *Tonopah
Sun* reported that he had decided to move his office there, "where he stays
most of the time to look after his mining interests." In direct competition with
Nixon, although on a more modest scale, he was reported to be "putting up a
fine office block at Columbia of hollow cement blocks and has other buildings
in contemplation." The article went on to mention a projected stockbrokers'
office next door to Wingfield's office building, as well as the latter's intention
to open a Goldfield office in the Nixon Block. This was not done until January 1906, when Wingfield acquired an office in the basement of the latter
building. Columbia had a population of 1,000 people in 1905, and was one
of several potential rivals to Goldfield, including Diamondfield, Jumbotown,
and North Goldfield. It proved as unsuccessful as all the others, however,
and Wingfield soon gave up on it. By 1906, he was no longer identified in the
newspapers as being "from Tonopah" or "of Columbia." [13]

In that year, when he turned thirty, George Wingfield's fortunes became
inextricably intertwined with those of the fabulous new town. Founded in
1903, Goldfield really began to grow in 1904, with the arrival of a large contingent of miners from Colorado and the establishment of saloons, churches,
and branches of Tonopah commercial houses. In contrast to the relatively
orderly history of the silver camp, however, Goldfield was a madhouse, a
speculator's paradise of such "mad excitement" that popular writer Rex
Beach declared himself unable to maintain sufficient mental equilibrium to

write while he was there. It reminded former Colorado governor (later U.S. senator) Charles S. Thomas, who also arrived in 1906, of the nineteenth-century rush to Leadville:

> There was the same excitement, the same lure, and the same sort of men and women. Money was abundant, anything looking like a mining claim could be sold or stocked. Criminals and adventurers there were in abundance. The desert had been staked to the horizon, and men were digging holes all over the surface without regard to formation or even to possibilities of success. Saloons, gambling houses and places of questionable amusement abounded and day was turned into night.[14]

Goldfield had all the disabilities of a desert boom town, including poor climate, scarce and expensive water, and a rudimentary social life. One relocated New York attorney described it to an Ohio correspondent:

> . . . climatic conditions . . . are without qualification, bad. The temperature ranges from freezing to boiling on ten minutes' notice. Water is very scarce, there are absolutely no trees or vegetation and a disagreeable, alkali dust is almost constantly blowing. . . . living is high and food rough. . . . It is a mining camp yet and everything goes.

A sheltered young English farm boy thought he was "on the margin of civilization" when he arrived in 1906, "where the harsh and sordid realities of life were not always decently obscured." A more appreciative witness reported that the dance hall girls from the red-light district wore low-neck dresses with skirts above the knee. As in Tonopah before it, lumber and most other building supplies were scarce and expensive until the railroad arrived in Goldfield in September 1905. For several years, demand exceeded supply and many residents lived in tents or tarpaper shacks, although Wingfield had a comfortable home on Crook Street. Yet the population grew steadily, from perhaps 150 in 1904, to 7,000 in 1905, and an estimated 18,000 in 1907.[15]

The tantalizing promise of wealth was in the air, and people flocked to Goldfield to secure their share. For some, the mines themselves were the way to wealth, as miners sought steady jobs at high pay, and investors sought leases on the proven ground of the Combination or Florence claims. News of the fabulous ore discovered in the Reilly and Sweeny leases, among others, was widely circulated by news releases to papers throughout the country. For others, the allure was potential profit on the stock exchange. Established in 1905, Goldfield's Mining Stock Exchange was the scene of a veritable orgy of speculation, with evening sessions to accommodate those who worked during the day. George Graham Rice, who was surely a participant himself, described it in colorful terms: "Outside of the exchange the stridulous [*sic*], whooping, screeching, detonating voices of the brokers that kept carrying the market up at each session could be heard half a block away." His dramatic description of the chaos was echoed by a young clerk writing home to his mother in an office across the street from the stock exchange: "This is evening now and across the street the stock exchange is booming. They are calling the bids and the chairman's voice sounds higher than anyone's. That is the way here . . . everybody is more or less crazy." Such speculative activity was heavier in Goldfield than it had been in Tonopah, where a few companies dominated mining almost from the beginning. The gold camp saw no such early consolidation, however, and ordinary citizens as well as capitalists were eager participants.[16]

Some of them, undoubtedly, were seduced by the storybook tale of George Wingfield and the Goldfield Mohawk Mining Company, familiarly known as Mohawk. That mine, in which Nixon had purchased an interest in 1904, was the site of a phenomenally rich discovery in April 1906, on a segment known as the Hayes-Monnette lease. The discovery—which came after months of discouraging returns and then yielded almost $6 million in the nine months that remained on the lease—caused a flurry of activity among other leasers, as well as the parent company, which quickly began mining on its own account after learning of ore that assayed between $400 and $600 per ton in value. In this effort, George Wingfield, as general manager of the Mohawk Company, was prominently involved. The Hayes-Monnette discovery also, not unexpectedly, caused the stock prices of the parent company to skyrocket in value. Stock that sold for 27 cents per share in January reached $20.00 per share by November. On behalf of Nixon and Wingfield, George Wingfield secured a controlling interest in that stock in April and May 1906. Reputedly his initial purchases cost him only 10 cents per share. Its subsequent rise in price brought him not only fortune, but fame as well. By June, he was being heralded as "the mining king of Goldfield."[17]

His biographer, Oscar Morgan, saw Wingfield's move into the Mohawk as part of a comprehensive strategy to move south from his initial holdings on Columbia Mountain, which had demonstrated only spotty and unreliable values. Purchase of the Mohawk, which he bought "for practically 'a song,'" gave him property close to the already proven ore of the Combination mine. Whatever the motive, Nixon and Wingfield profited not only from the tangible rise in the value of their property, but also from the publicity that it brought to Goldfield mines generally. In August, Wingfield was elected a member of the San Francisco Stock Exchange, where his trading activity had already attracted considerable attention. National interest was piqued in

October, when Al Myers, one of the initial Mohawk locators, sold a block of 100,000 shares to Nixon and Wingfield for the previously contracted price of $4 per share. The partners in turn resold the stock, which by then was worth $6.12 per share, at their original $4 cost to an eastern syndicate headed by Philadelphia whiskey magnate J. H. Carstairs. Among the prominent investors in this deal were steel executive Henry C. Frick and New York banker J. Horace Harding. Publicity associated with the transaction focused attention on Goldfield, and not incidentally made influential eastern friends for Nixon and Wingfield.[18]

The astonishing autumn rise in Mohawk prices was noted in both local and national papers. Stocks and their upward tendencies were part of the story in September 1906, when Goldfield hosted a national lightweight championship fight between black champion Joe Gans and white challenger William Nelson. Special trains brought thousands of fans to Goldfield for the Labor Day event, sponsored by promoter Tex Rickard and underwritten by the Goldfield Athletic Association. Wingfield was the stakeholder for the then unprecedented $30,000 purse. The event helped publicize Goldfield stocks almost as much as it promoted the town itself. Later, when a single carload of Mohawk ore shipped in January of 1907 netted almost $575,000, a veritable Goldfield fever swept the country. Photographs of the check from the smelter were widely reproduced. It was, everyone agreed, the making of Goldfield. It was also the making of George Wingfield and those close to him. Wingfield gave tips on Mohawk to numerous people, including his washerwoman and the bootblack at Goldfield's prestigious Montezuma Club, each of whom made a tidy sum on private transactions in the stock.[19]

Afterward, Wingfield professed to have had confidence in the Mohawk all along:

> "Certainly I had a big thrill when they hit it big on Mohawk, but it would probably have been bigger if I had not all the time believed so thoroughly in that property. I would have been more disappointed," he added with a swift chuckle, "if Mohawk had turned out bad than I was surprised when it turned out to be the camp's biggest mine."

His actions at the time, however, suggest the magnitude of the gamble he had undertaken, and the extent of his relief when it turned out well. On November 2, 1906, the *Tonopah Sun* ran a cartoon showing "The Dance of the Mohawks." It featured Wingfield with a feather headdress, with Nixon and an elephant presumably representing the Republican party in the background, all dancing with glee over their good fortune. The next day, November 3, Wingfield hosted a late-night dinner for seventy-five brokers, bankers, and financial men at Goldfield's most elegant restaurant, the Palm Grill. Guests included familiar figures from Tonopah, such as discoverer Jim Butler, Tom Kendall, Jack Hennessy, and Tasker Oddie. But there were also leading figures from the new camp, including fight promoter Tex Rickard, saloon owner Ole Elliott, and mine owners Tom Lockhart, Al Myers, and Charles Taylor. Wingfield reportedly wanted to invite even more, but the Palm Grill was stretched to capacity by the occasion.[20]

The banquet, complete with flowers, music, and champagne, was ostensibly given to celebrate the price of the Mohawk stock passing $15 per share, but it became a kind of collective love fest for the guests and their hosts. Wingfield later reminisced fondly about the evening as the most outstanding dinner he ever attended. Newspaper accounts at the time reported a prevailing sentiment that the dinner "should have been a testimonial from the city to Wingfield and Nixon, rather than from the latter to the people," because the coming of Wingfield, especially, represented a new era in the town's fortunes: "it was universally admitted that the boys had been up against a pretty stiff game until the arrival of Wingfield brought a change of luck and transformed the camp from a doubtful existence on the desert to a permanent city that now ranks as the greatest city in Nevada." Here, then, in Goldfield, Wingfield's gambles finally paid off. His skillful financial manipulations not only made money, they also made him a local hero. In only a few more days, with the formation of an even bigger mining company that consolidated the Mohawk with several other properties, they were to transform him into a national figure, the leading mining man and one of the richest men in the state. But as the speeches of Saturday night droned on into Sunday morning, that announcement still lay in the future, and George Wingfield was still just one of the boys who had played the game and won.[21]

Among those paying particular attention to Wingfield's phenomenal rise was May Baric, the woman who had apparently been his companion for several years. In March 1906, styling herself May Wingfield, she filed a sensational suit in Tonopah. Claiming to have entered a common-law marriage agreement with George Wingfield in December 1902, she now sought a divorce. She was also asking for monthly alimony of $3,000, attorney's fees of $50,000, and title to half his property. To guard against disposal of any of that property, she also filed a notice of *lis pendens* in both Nye and Esmeralda counties, which tied up all of Wingfield's holdings until the matter could be resolved. May was represented in her suit by four Tonopah attorneys, including later Nevada Supreme Court justice and U.S. senator Patrick McCarran. They cited grounds for divorce that included not only verbal insult, but also beatings severe enough to necessitate calling a doctor, death threats, and the particularly scurrilous charge that Wingfield knowingly inflicted her with syphilis in February 1905, while he had it in his throat. This last incident occurred while Wingfield was in Carson City, supposedly ill with smallpox. Afterward, according to May, he sent her at his expense for six months of treatment at a hot spring.[22]

The breaking point apparently came in February 1906, when Wingfield supposedly asked her to come from Tonopah to his room in the Nixon Block in Goldfield. There he apologized for his past behavior and promised to set her up in a house in Tonopah. She spent the night; but in the morning he changed his mind and put her out again, with only $400 to put her children in school and railroad fare to her mother's home in California. She apparently returned instead to Tonopah to consult with her attorneys, despite the fact that, as the complaint alleged, George Wingfield "told her that she had no recourse, against him, for the reason that he was a man of high political standing" and that "there were no lawyers who would take her case." As it happened, whether because of Wingfield's powerful political influence or her own weak evidence, the divorce suit *was* unsuccessful. When the case was decided in August 1906, every allegation was denied, and Baric was ordered to pay Wingfield's legal fees.[23]

Yet May's suit cannot simply be dismissed as sensationalism or a gold-digger's harassment of a wealthy man. Her presence in Tonopah and status as Wingfield's common-law wife were generally acknowledged, and several factors suggest at least some truth to her claims. One is the complete absence of any mention of her suit in the newspapers of either Tonopah or Goldfield. At this time even the routine daily travels of George Wingfield were sufficiently newsworthy to be reported in the papers. When he returned in April 1906 from San Francisco, where he had survived the great earthquake that destroyed the city, his account of being awakened in the Palace Hotel and being unable to help the "helpless women, nearly mad with fear and anxiety," made the front page of the *Tonopah Sun*. The prevalence in these same papers of articles on celebrity scandals testified to an apparently insatiable public appetite for the gossipy, intimate details revealed in divorce trials. In such circumstances the case must surely have attracted attention. Yet there is no coverage of May Baric or her charges against George Wingfield, which tends to bear out his boast of being invincible. No newspaper editor in 1906 could have risked alienating a man already being heralded as Nevada's Napoleon.[24]

It is also clear that Wingfield negotiated some kind of settlement with her. A comprehensive series of legal documents from May Baric to George Wingfield, all dated March 21, 1906, included a deed, a bill of sale, and a release. Collectively, in exchange for varying but modest amounts of money "and other valuable consideration," they released Wingfield from all claims by Baric, conveyed to him her interest to any real estate, and sold him any right she might possess to any other personal or mixed property such as stocks and bonds. The valuable consideration undoubtedly included a cash settlement, but may also have involved real estate in California. At least when she reappeared in Wingfield's life in December 1906, at the St. Francis Hotel in San Francisco, she was living in San Jose.[25]

Whatever the nature of their relationship, and regardless of any formal agreement, May Baric clearly felt that she had a legitimate claim on the affections and the fortune of George Wingfield. In December, when she attempted to enter his San Francisco hotel room, she still claimed to be his wife and also threatened to pump him full of lead. When she came back again a few days later, she was described as apparently drunk and on the verge of a nervous collapse. On that occasion, however, George Wingfield revealed to the newspaper what may have been the price that May Baric paid for her March financial settlement from him:

> Wingfield makes strenuous denial of any claim upon him by the woman who says she is his common law wife. . . . Wingfield also claims to have *an affidavit in which the woman admits that she is not his wife* and that she is liable to perjury if she should press the charge.[26]

Affidavits and court rulings notwithstanding, May Baric was to plague George Wingfield for several years, returning at the time of his marriage in 1908. Her claims may temporarily have hampered his reception in refined social circles, but his incredible wealth eventually eclipsed any lingering scandal. The San Francisco papers in 1907 smugly reported that "Goldfield mining men" were skeptical of May's hysterical charges against Wingfield. While they were willing to believe that he was "entangled with her" in Tonopah, they were certain that her only object in making trouble was to obtain money.[27]

Wingfield's wealth was considerably augmented in the fall of 1906, as the partnership of Nixon and Wingfield moved to protect the Mohawk ground and expand their operations by buying neighboring mining properties. The very richness of the Mohawk made it vulnerable. Under the terms of the 1872 federal mining law, another company might be able to claim all the Mohawk ore simply by proving that the Mohawk vein had its apex on the outsider's ground. When a lease on the neighboring Combination property began to encroach on Mohawk ground in the summer of 1906, claiming just that, Nixon and Wingfield responded quickly. They filed suit against the Sheets and Ish lease to stop the infringement and retained a noted mining attorney, former Colorado governor and later U.S. senator Charles S. Thomas. On Thomas's advice, they also hired the noted mining engineer John Wellington Finch, former Colorado state geologist and later director of the U.S. Bureau of Mines. After his investigation, Finch concluded that the geological conditions in Goldfield were so muddled that his clients couldn't expect a favorable outcome from their suit. Instead he advised them to purchase several strategic properties around the Mohawk and Combination, including the Florence, Red Top, Jumbo, and January, arguing that they "all belonged to one vein system and should be under one management" and that "unless some merger or consolidation were effected there would be litigation." Clearly Finch's theory was that if Nixon and Wingfield owned most of the nearby properties, they could better hope to win their suit against the Combination and protect the Mohawk.[28]

Thus was born the scheme that culminated November 13, 1906, with the incorporation in Wyoming of the Goldfield Consolidated Mines Company (GCMC), ultimately made up of six different mining properties in the heart of Goldfield's most productive district. On Finch's advice, Wingfield went to work and purchased a controlling interest in the Goldfield Mining Company, which owned the January mine. The partners' next targets were the Jumbo and Red Top mines to the east. Both were producing properties, and Jumbo had been the first company in the district to pay a dividend. A controlling interest in both mines was owned by early Goldfield prospector Charles D. Taylor. Nixon and Wingfield rousted Taylor from his bed at 11 P.M. on October 10 to discuss a possible deal on his stock.

Although there was already a potential purchaser, Taylor offered to give Nixon and Wingfield the same terms, $2 per share for his stock or $1.2 million total, once the first option expired on October 23. When the potential purchaser did not complete his transaction by that date, the partners sent Finch in to examine the two properties. Because Finch's association with Nixon and Wingfield was well known, his presence caused a rise in the stock prices of both Red Top and Jumbo, from $1.50 to $4.00 per share. Despite the fact that they had no written agreement with Taylor, he honored his initial verbal promise about the price when the partners decided to complete the purchase, thereby giving them an instant, if theoretical, profit of nearly 100 percent on the transaction. On November 1, 1906, Nixon delivered a check to Taylor for $1,190,000 ($10,000 had been paid earlier to secure the option while Finch examined the property), and Nixon and Wingfield once again made newspaper headlines.[29]

Nixon framed that canceled check, the largest he had ever written, and kept it as a souvenir on the wall of his office in Reno. The cash for the transaction came from the Crocker National Bank in San Francisco, where Nixon had earlier formed a valuable connection with William H. Crocker, the city's most important banker. Like Nixon, Crocker was another of the men particularly esteemed by George Wingfield, and he was to be a crucial financial support during the crisis of the 1930s. Something of his character is evident in the description given by Bernard Baruch, in the latter's autobiography:

> Crocker had one of the most engaging personalities I have known. Erect in his carriage and meticulous in appearance, he never seemed to have a hair out of place, even in his short, pointed beard. . . . He was the kind of banker who did not desert his clients when things went bad. No matter how distressing were the circumstances, he never lost his good humor or courage.

For Nixon and Wingfield, that confidence was of critical importance in the next few months, as they orchestrated the most significant deal in Nevada's mining history.[30]

Within two weeks of their purchase, Nixon and Wingfield had organized a holding company for their five central properties: Mohawk, Goldfield Mining, Red Top, Jumbo, and Laguna, which was a minor holding to the east of Red Top. The new company, the Goldfield Consolidated Mines Company, was capitalized for $50,000,000, representing 5 million shares at a par value of $10. In keeping with the tremendous scale of the merger, this was a much larger than normal capitalization. Run-of-the-mill Goldfield mining companies were organized on a basis of $1,000,000, with 1 million shares issued at a par value of $1. Although GCMC's capitalization was criticized as too high, it was defended at the time as being vindicated by the estimated ore reserves on the property. Wingfield himself thought that "the values are there [in the ground]" to warrant the capitalization. He also opined that the high price charged for the stock was a good thing, "because the poor people who cannot afford to deal in mining stock cannot buy them and would not be hurt if the stock should fall." In any event, the full capital stock of the company was never issued, which partially solved the problem. By 1908, GCMC's directors had pledged not to issue any stock beyond the roughly $36 million then outstanding.[31]

Stockholders in the companies that were absorbed into GCMC had the option of keeping their original shares or exchanging them on a specified basis for shares in the consolidated company. Eventually, in 1909, the individual companies were fully absorbed into the merger company. For their troubles in effecting the consolidation, Nixon and Wingfield were allotted 250,000 shares (theoretically worth $2.5 million) of GCMC stock. In addition, of course, they controlled shares received in exchange for their stock in the constituent companies that went into the merger. Ultimately, it was enough to give them roughly two-thirds of the outstanding stock, a comfortable margin, in a $50 million mining company.[32]

For the most part, reaction to the merger was enthusiastic. Some such scheme for consolidating the mines in Goldfield had been rumored for months. Already in April, local brokers were reporting that New York financier Charles Schwab was reputed to be purchasing the Red Top and Jumbo mines in order to operate them as a unit. The administrative benefits of consolidation were obvious. The danger of litigation was avoided, or at least minimized. Centralized management would lower operating costs and provide for intelligent and efficient development of the properties. Furthermore, the participation of national figures like Crocker, Frick, and Carstairs lent financial respectability to the entire undertaking. The high per-share price of the stock only added to this air of exceptional solidity. Unlike some of the more speculative mining companies, GCMC stock was accepted by banks as collateral for loans. In addition, dramatic headlines in local newspapers touted the newfound vigor that consolidation would bring to southern Nevada: "Mine Merger Means More Money and Men for Goldfield." The rhetoric of the *Tonopah Miner* on the eve of the consolidation was representative of the prevailing sentiment:

> In the hands of Wingfield and Nixon the work of making both mines heavy producers and steady dividend payers will be inaugurated and before another year has rolled around there will be at least 1000 additional miners receiving regular wages from the Jumbo and Red Top. The bucket brigade is what makes any camp good and every business interest in the entire district will be benefited.

Not only the organizers and investors, but all Goldfield expected to profit. Nixon and Wingfield appointed John W. Finch as general manager of the new merger, and he reassured reporters that his company would begin mining actively on its own account as soon as the leases expired on December 31, 1906. Mindful of the slump that had occurred in Tonopah when a big company took over from leasers, he promised: "we will prevent any possibility of a financial slump in the stock market, and any depression in business as well, from a reduction in the miners employed. . . ." In the first heady days after the organization, the future looked bright to everyone involved.[33]

In a few days, incredibly, the news grew even more fantastic. Under headlines that proclaimed the mine "worth full fifty million dollars," the *Goldfield News* announced on November 24 that Nixon and Wingfield had secured an option on "the great Combination Mines Company," which would be added to the merger. By this coup the partners worked a miracle that attorney Thomas and mining engineer Finch had assumed to be impossible. Not only did they secure a very profitable mining property, with its own mill, but they also permanently insured the rich Mohawk against potential encroachment. It was enough to quiet some of the criticism about capitalization and to make GCMC, in the opinion of *Mining and Scientific Press* editor T. A. Rickard, the "greatest gold mine in the world" in 1907.[34]

Nixon and Wingfield had been seeking all along to buy Combination stock in order to guard against an adverse decision in the Mohawk's suit against the Combination. Unfortunately, the majority control of the Combination rested with a group of Chicago investors who were unwilling to sell such a profitable mine, particularly to the men who were suing them. The merger partners were unexpectedly aided when a New York promoter and former *Century Magazine* editor named Charles H. Botsford approached Nixon for a block of GCMC stock and casually inquired if he would be interested in buying the Combination. When Nixon replied that he would certainly rather purchase than litigate, Botsford went to work. With financial backing from local mining investor James R. Davis, who came up with the $75,000 down payment, he managed to secure an option to purchase the Combination property for the stupendous price of $4 million. Although the terms of their option required that they organize the Combination as an independent company, presumably to guard against its incorporation into GCMC, Botsford and Davis nonetheless offered it to Nixon and Wingfield. The various parties met in the St. Francis Hotel in San Francisco, where George Wingfield had been summoned on November 10 because of the illness of his father, Thomas. The latter, age sixty, died of "chronic stomach trouble," on November 12, 1906, the eve of the formal incorporation of GCMC. Wingfield remained in San Francisco to attend to his mother and other family members, and the conference with Botsford was held there on November 16 and 17. Botsford and Davis sold their option contract on the Combination to Nixon and Wingfield in exchange for 100,000 shares of GCMC stock, worth $1 million at par value.[35]

Nixon then began to work on financing the deal. Securing options on the remaining Combination stock for a total cost of roughly $500,000, he then went to Chicago and renegotiated the Botsford option. He concluded that deal on December 15. It called for payment of approximately $2,588,000 in cash and 175,000 shares of GCMC stock. The first $1 million payment for the Combination was due by January 20, with the remainder divided into two equal payments due in March and May. The second and third payments could be made either in stock or cash, at the option of the sellers. Having borrowed $1.2 million from Crocker just two months earlier, Nixon and Wingfield now had approximately one month to raise at least $1.5 million more. This was made more difficult because the chilling effects of the massive April 18 San Francisco earthquake were spreading throughout western financial circles, and money was hard to come by. Here, however, they were once again materially assisted by William Crocker, who introduced Nixon to eastern financier Bernard M. Baruch. By this stroke, not only did the partners secure financing for the final segment of their consolidation, but they also solidified their ties to prominent eastern capitalists. And for George Wingfield, Baruch was to prove another invaluable friend, perhaps the single most important relationship, after Nixon, of his life.

At the time of his meeting with Nixon and Wingfield, in 1907, Baruch was a successful private investor respected both for his ability and for his sincerity. Known as "a daring and wealthy Wall street operator," he came from a southern Jewish family and was extremely charismatic. Baruch later became a prominent advisor of Democratic politicians, including Franklin D. Roosevelt, chair of Woodrow Wilson's War Industries Board, and the U.S. delegate to the U.N. Atomic Energy Commission in 1946. After he met George Wingfield in Goldfield in the fall of 1907, the two men became fast friends. With characteristic reserve, Wingfield later described Baruch as "able," with "a high sense of honor." Baruch, however, described George Wingfield glowingly after the latter's death: "For over a half century never a shadow was cast over our friendship nor did I know anyone so moved by the best wish with which man is endowed." Despite their different backgrounds, the two men had a great deal in common. Like Wingfield, Baruch was a gambler at heart: "He liked the racetrack or any situation that tested his nerve, knowledge, and audacity. Financial risks did not frighten him." On Wingfield's advice, several times over the years, with varying results, Baruch was to take such financial risks. His first Nevada venture, however, was proposed to him by Nixon.[36]

Nixon and Wingfield had initially consulted William H. Crocker, who couldn't accommodate them personally, but went with Nixon to New York to introduce him to Baruch. Mining attorney Charles Thomas was also present at the meeting, on December 28, 1906, and reported his and Nixon's astonishment that Baruch seemed to know as much about their mining properties as they did. This was fortuitous, since Nixon needed a quick commitment of the money, and a thorough investigation would have wasted months that the partners didn't have to spare. Baruch recalled that Crocker, "a great optimist," introduced Senator Nixon by saying that he needed $2,578,000 and was good for it. When "Nixon made a noise like a dividend," Baruch countered with a strategy of his own. He agreed to loan the company $1 million, in exchange for an option to purchase 1 million shares of GCMC stock at $7.75 per share. He also proposed a plan to insure that the sellers would accept the subsequent payments in GCMC stock. Baruch gave Nixon a certified check for $1 million, enough to make his first installment payment on January 20. He advised Nixon to install himself in the men's bar at the Waldorf-Astoria Hotel, a celebrated gathering place for the financial community. If anyone asked him about GCMC, Nixon was to reply vaguely that it was all out of his hands and display the certified check. Rumors about Baruch's backing immediately circulated.[37]

When Nixon went to meet the Combination owners in Chicago in January, Baruch advised him just to hand over the check and say nothing about the future payments. When the Combination owners started selling the shares of GCMC stock they had acquired as part of the deal, Baruch bought them, thus supporting the price of the stock. After the Combination owners saw such previously unsuspected demand for the stock, they agreed to accept their remaining installments, with the exception of only $31,312, in stock rather than cash, based on a value of $7.50 per share. As attorney Charles Thomas observed at the time, the decision to accept payment in stock "speaks well for their confidence in Nixon & Wingfield as well as for the deal." When the purchase was finally completed in January 1907, it left Nixon and Wingfield in an exceptionally strong position, with only the initial $1 million cash outlay, in addition to the other expenses of the minor stock options, to be repaid from proceeds of the new mine. Jubilantly, Nixon returned to New York and offered Baruch an additional 100,000 shares of GCMC stock as a bonus for his efforts, which the latter accepted "because I thought I had earned them." By this shrewd maneuver, GCMC managed to acquire an extraordinarily rich mine and still have a $300,000 cash reserve to begin development work.[38]

Goldfield, in turn, settled back in anticipation of a new era of more businesslike operation "with a view to the payment of dividends and the conservation of stockholders' interests." Although some commentators worried that this giant merger might be "the first step toward making Goldfield a one man town, crowding out the chances of the men of little capital," others heralded the improvements that Nixon and Wingfield would bring: "Both men have the reputation of paying the highest wages that were ever paid in the western country, and not a voice has been raised against their treatment of their employees." After the financing battle was over, GCMC dismissed all pending suits and announced plans to build its own giant reduction works, in order to reduce its transportation and processing costs. Under Finch's capable direction, a plan for systematic development of the six properties was devised and active mining began on company account. The board of directors, including Nixon as president and Wingfield as vice-president, agreed to liquidate the company's outstanding debts before paying any dividends to stockholders, of whom they were the majority. Nonetheless, despite labor disturbances, they managed to pay their first dividend, of 10 cents per share, in October 1907. There were regular quarterly dividends of 30 or 50 cents until 1913, and sporadic dividends thereafter. By 1917, GCMC was ranked as the 148th largest industrial corporation in the United States. Before it finally shut down its Goldfield mills in January 1919, the company paid out a total of over $29 million in dividends to its stockholders, of which at least $8 million was reported to have been paid to George Wingfield personally.[39]

The triumph of this huge consolidated company was not without controversy. It was plagued during its first few years with serious strikes and with charges of stock market manipulation, which will be considered in the following chapter. Yet it was without question a major accomplishment that brought stability and a degree of permanence to the mining camp of Goldfield and wealth to a network of stockholders. Unlike most Goldfield mines, most conspicuously the wildcat promotions of Wingfield critic George Graham Rice, GCMC actually paid dividends to its stockholders and thus established Goldfield properties as a legitimate business investment. Its success, which was actually due to a number of factors, including rich ground and capable management, was popularly attributed to the presence of George Wingfield: "For where others feared to incur risk, Mr. Wingfield took over numerous prospects, staked his fortunes on them and converted them into great mines." As news of the consolidation's profits reached the national press, former gambler and saloon keeper George Wingfield found himself hailed as "a man of imagination and ambition," who had "made the name of Goldfield, among the well informed, synonymous with business achievement as distinguished from the foam of speculation." In the coming years, much would be expected of this young phenomenon, both in Goldfield and in the state at large.[40]

FIVE

"Compromise Be Damned"

IT WAS A potentially heady position for a man barely thirty, whose reported worth after completion of the consolidation was somewhere between $25 and $30 million, and whose name "was on the tongue of mining men all over the world." Yet money and fame did not go to Wingfield's head in the conventional ways. As a contemporary San Francisco reporter observed with some surprise, the richest man in Nevada "is easy of approach, easy and pleasant in manner and is still 'George' to the boys who knew him of old." This simplicity was consistent throughout his life. George Nixon took his millions from GCMC and built a huge mansion in Reno, where he also memorialized himself by organizing the Nixon National Bank. Wingfield remained in Goldfield, in a relatively modest home at 405 Crook Street, though he did buy a second car, a black Pierce Arrow. Surprisingly for a former gambler, he was not given to conspicuous personal display of his wealth. Although he wore a ring with a star sapphire and two diamonds, and a gold watch and chain, there were no silver doorknobs in his house like those that graced mineowners' homes during the nineteenth-century glory days of the Comstock Lode in northern Nevada.[1]

George Wingfield always lived comfortably. He liked everything around him to be "first class." He wore well-tailored suits, drank fine wines, and ate meat three times a day. He had good guns and good hunting dogs. He never shaved himself but always went to a barber. Yet his personal consumption was never extravagant. Whether it was a vestige of his hardscrabble Methodist upbringing or a certain self-consciousness about his somewhat crooked path to glory, George Wingfield never lived up to the size of his fortune. He modeled his behavior on the twentieth-century man of business, not the nineteenth-century capitalist. Even at the height of his wealth and influence in Reno, he walked to work each day.[2]

Just like Ned Osborne in *A Little Princess of Tonopah*, Wingfield was unsuited by temperament or training for the constrictions of formal society. He delighted in comfortable occasions such as the Mohawk dinner, liberally lubricated by alcohol, when he could socialize with his male friends and associates; but he didn't participate in the elaborate prescribed ritual of formal parties. Unlike those unfortunates described by *Mining and Scientific Press* editor T. A. Rickard, whose sudden wealth ruined their digestion, lost them their friends, and thrust them into "an environment for which, usually, [they were] quite unfitted," George Wingfield managed to grow gracefully into his new role. He permanently abandoned gambling because he knew it would prevent him from associating with the more refined people he was now meeting through Nixon and GCMC. He carved out a new social style that suited him, avoiding situations he was unequal to, but fully mastering the generosity that his money now made possible. The man once noted for "treating" his buddies even when he lost at poker now entertained his more genteel associates in elegant restaurants.[3]

GCMC was thus important to Wingfield on several levels. Not only did it bring him riches and national attention, but it also initiated him into a wider world of politics, finance, and power. Men like Crocker and Baruch would never, in the normal course of events, have met the Tonopah gambler. When they did, courtesy of his connection to Nixon, he benefited, absorbing their knowledge, style, and manners, and learning how to be a proficient capitalist. Buoyed by their spectacular success in Goldfield, Nixon and Wingfield continued to expand their mining operations into new camps including Fairview, 200 miles north of Goldfield, and Greenwater, 150 miles to the south. While most of these properties never became paying mines, some, such as the Fairview claims, ultimately added to the partners' coffers. Whatever the outcome of these investments, Wingfield, especially, was lauded for making them. When he bought the first claims at Fairview, the *Goldfield Review* approvingly noted Wingfield's loyalty to the state where he had made his money: "his movements are interesting to all mining men of our state; especially so for the reason that he chooses to invest his capital in home industries, rather than to take up his residence in the east, as so many other men made rich by Nevada's mines have done." The newspaper was pleased because Wingfield's presence in Fairview would attract other men of means, a pattern that continued as his operations spread out into new Nevada booms at Rawhide, Manhattan, Rhyolite, and Ramsey, as well as Masonic and Coalinga, California. The fame of GCMC and the prominence of Nixon's eastern investment partners helped legitimate the twentieth-century Nevada gold boom, creating an instant legend that enticed thousands in search of similar bonanzas. Nevada prospectors fanned out into the surrounding desert in search of promising ground while Goldfield promoters combed the rest of the country for new investors. Dozens of new camps sprang up, each claiming to be the next Goldfield.[4]

Despite brief successes in some of them, there were to be no new Goldfields. For one reason or another, even the most promising camps at Manhattan, Rawhide, and Rhyolite failed to materialize into permanent mining towns. Although the original organizers in some cases made fortunes through the sale of their properties, most investors did not. Experienced players of "the mining game" knew the risks they were taking. Prominent mining editor T. A. Rickard described the usual sequence in 1898:

> Mines are short-lived. . . . Nine mines out of ten are sold for more than their worth; more money is made by selling than by buying them. . . . A man usually buys a mine not because it is worth the price he gives for it, but because he is justified in the expectation of finding some one who will pay more for it. The syndicate sells to the public, the public sell among themselves. The second man hopes to meet a third with more money and less sense. So the game proceeds. When the sequence has been exhausted, some one gets badly bitten. Then come the lamentations.

Inexperienced investors, especially, were likely to be victimized by wildcats, fraudulent companies organized specifically to sell stock in worthless claims to unsuspecting outsiders. Victims then made accusations of fraud or malfeasance, which were lodged against the just and the unjust alike. As a result, in the very years of GCMC's greatest profit, through 1911, Nixon and Wingfield were frequently forced to defend the legitimacy of their operations against charges of stock manipulation.[5]

And they were men, as one contemporary editorial admitted, who had made enemies in the course of doing business:

> Nixon and Wingfield are men of strong and dominant personality, accustomed to doing things and bringing about results, often without resource to diplomatic methods. As a result they have made many bitter enemies in the West, enemies who hit from the shoulder in much the same fashion as Nixon and Wingfield, and who are always on the qui vive for any mistakes in policy or efforts of judgment made by the Goldfield Consolidated managers, and never hesitate to give expression in voice and action to what they may ascertain. In consequence the Goldfield Consolidated, unlike many other corporations, is attacked quite as much as it is defended. . . .

One of their severest critics was George Graham Rice, a flamboyant promoter who organized more than his share of nonproducing mining companies and had served time for forgery. Operating as the L. M. Sullivan Trust Company, and later as Nat C. Goodwin & Company, Rice ran what was popularly known as a "bucket shop." He sold stocks in companies that he had organized, usually in small blocks and frequently by mail, to individual investors who generally lacked the expertise to evaluate what they were buying. He advertised widely and promoted his companies as located close to producing mines. The Goldfield Stock Exchange refused to list the stock of companies he was associated with, probably due at least in part to Wingfield's influence. Their suspicions were vindicated in 1907, when his L. M. Sullivan Trust Company failed and also caused the collapse of Goldfield's State Bank and Trust Company, which had loaned money on Rice stocks. Rice simply relocated to Reno and reentered the stock promotion business under a new name later the same year. But the incident sharpened his animosity toward Nixon and Wingfield.[6]

Initially his criticisms may have been defensive, intended to distract from his own debatable practices. Rice evidently developed a personal animus, however, which was enthusiastically returned by Wingfield in particular. Wingfield's biographer reports priggishly that Rice attacked Wingfield and Nixon "because they were carrying on reputable mining operations and refused to have anything to do with him," but that is obviously not the whole story. When Wingfield met the associate editor of Rice's *Nevada Mining News*, Merrill Teague, in a Reno brokerage in November 1907, he reacted violently and hit the editor in the face before any words could be exchanged. When Teague tried to flee, Wingfield followed him outside and continued to beat him "until Teague cried for mercy."[7]

In reporting this incident, the local newspaper tried to excuse Wingfield's behavior by explaining his frustration:

> For several months Teague and George Graham Rice have carried on a tirade of abuse against Nixon and Wingfield, and have done everything in their power to "knock" Goldfield over their heads. Wingfield has often said that if they ever made an attack on him personally he would whip them within an inch of their lives.

Evidently carrying through on his threat, he was reportedly cheered by the crowd who witnessed the attack. At first he asked the *Reno Evening Gazette* newspaper editor who was with him not to print a story about it. When the editor, Oscar Morgan, received a similar request from Rice, however, Wingfield relented and instructed him: "Give [Rice] the works." Rice retaliated by issuing an extra edition of the *Nevada Mining News*, but the Tonopah papers, at least, reported that "the sympathy at Reno is all with Wingfield."[8]

This might actually have been the case. Rice's hatred for Wingfield was certainly undisguised. A few years later, in his autobiography, he would give it free play, insinuatingly describing Wingfield, by then nationally known, as being "of stinted, meager frame," with "the extreme pallor that denoted ill health, years of hardship, or vicious habits." Verbally adept as Wingfield was not, Rice described his nemesis as the kind of man "who uses the backstairs, never trusts anybody . . . and does not allow trifling scruples to stand in the way of final encompassment." Thus provoked, and incapable of responding in Rice's terms, Wingfield channeled his anger into physical violence. Fighting was, after all, the cowboy-gambler's customary manner of settling quarrels, the same impulsive behavior that he had displayed in the Tonopah Club on the day that Noble Getchell met him and that May Baric had complained of in her suit. Moreover, in November 1907, George Wingfield was under considerable stress. The attack on Teague occurred when he was on his way to Wyoming for a GCMC directors' meeting, in the midst of tense labor negotiations in Goldfield, and not long after the death by drowning of his older brother, Morris, in southeastern Oregon. Friends in Goldfield may well have been sympathetic. George Wingfield's new status as a multimillionaire, however, made such violent outbursts newsworthy.[9]

Wingfield was not Rice's only target. As a broker, Rice was "bearish" on GCMC, which meant he was betting that the price of the stock would go down. Thus he had a strong financial incentive to criticize GCMC and its management. He did so at every opportunity, and evidently effectively. Rice's publications were the source of many of the negative rumors about the company, including the perpetual canard that Nixon and Wingfield had lost control to outside interests. In a skittish financial market that was already nervous about the Panic of 1907 and the labor troubles in Goldfield, the partners were forced to spend precious time and energy rebutting Rice's charges, embodied in headlines that inferred disaster, such as "New Yorkers Control Consolidated." Wearily, Nixon and Wingfield responded to repeated reporters' inquiries that, indeed, they still controlled GCMC, that they were engaged in mine development, not stock flotation: "It is our conviction that, as development of the Goldfield properties progresses, we will take much more money out of the ground than we could make at the present time in holding upon the market."[10]

As the *Goldfield News* observed editorially, Rice and his associates were engaged in a "propaganda of lies": "Rice is 'sore' on Goldfield and all Gold-field stocks, especially the Wingfield stocks, is short of them, and never cease their their [*sic*] hammering. . . ." This analysis was confirmed by Goldfield attorneys and mine promoters Albert Watson and Edwin Van Dyck, who described Rice's tactics to a New York correspondent:

> Probably you are not unfortunate enough to know G. G. Rice person-
> ally but, were such the case, you would unhesitatingly throw his pub-
> lication, the *Nevada Mining News*, in the waste basket without reading
> it. Rice cannot do business in Goldfield and therefore goes to Reno
> where, under the cover of another man's name, he issues the publica-
> tion which, besides being his own advertising medium, is used to knock
> everybody and everything in Goldfield. He is a sorehead and a man of
> devious ways and you would do well to take your views of this camp
> from more respectable sources.

Under the circumstances, Wingfield's anger against Rice's lieutenant Teague was understandable, if decidedly inappropriate.[11]

Ironically, Wingfield and Nixon had to defend themselves against charges that they were artificially inflating the market at the very time they were also accused of too *little* support of GCMC prices. From the beginning, the announced policies of the GCMC directors were conservative. They deter-mined to pay the company's debts before distributing profits to stockholders in the form of dividends, and in 1907 they announced ambitious plans for a mill that would mean incurring even more expenses before there were profits. Although they were irritated by efforts of Rice and others to "bear" their stock, they were also adamant about not allowing a bull market to drive the price of their stock to unjustifiable levels. Echoing Wingfield's words at the time of the consolidation, Bernard Baruch publicly announced in 1908, and again in 1909, his belief in the wisdom of this company policy:

> It is well known that the insiders were persistently urged on different
> occasions to advance this stock considerably above $9 per share. This
> jump could be accomplished with very little resistance on the open
> market. . . . [Baruch] has always felt, however, that, while an advance
> was no doubt justifiable, still, if something had not turned out exactly
> as it should be, the stock would have quickly returned to its first level,
> with the result that there would have been any amount of grumbling
> from those who had purchased the shares on the way upward.

Instead they tried to keep fluctuation in stock prices to a minimum, ideally but not invariably somewhere between $7.50 and $8.50 per share. In this way, "anyone has been able to get in or out of this stock very close to the figures at which he got into the shares" and in the meantime enjoy the regular 30-

cent quarterly dividends. This policy was decidedly unpopular among those brokers who wanted to see the price reach predicted highs of $12 or even $15 per share.[12]

More modest changes in price kept the market active, but under control. When prices sank too low, Wingfield bought GCMC stock, explaining that it was a good bargain. Early in 1908, on the other hand, when a group of Nevada politicians tried to profit from rising GCMC prices after learning in advance that the legislature would pass a state police bill favorable to the company, Nixon and Wingfield's Goldfield bank threw a block of its stock on the market to force the price down and thwart the lawmakers' scheme. Although profit clearly was a consideration, market maintenance and stability were the principal goals of this type of activity. George Wingfield's function as a market maker was widely acknowledged, but—unlike Rice—he was never accused of wildcatting, of having attempted to defraud in his market operations. When he traveled east in 1909 for Taft's inauguration, for instance, he also stopped off in New York. There he "succeeded in educating the eastern people" about the value of Goldfield stocks, which stimulated new market interest not only in GCMC, but also in many less well known properties, including Wingfield's Sandstorm, Booth, Blue Bull, Portland, and Conqueror, among others. He then proceeded to San Francisco, where he negotiated a sliding commission scale that was expected to encourage trading in the lower-priced stocks by making it possible to profit from minor shifts in price. A man with the practiced instincts of a successful gambler, George Wingfield now bet instead on the likely results of mines and stocks. In the process he did everything possible to maximize his possibility of profit, but he felt, self-righteously, that he was "educating," never willfully misleading anyone in the Rice manner. Wingfield's self-portrait as a maker of mines and only secondarily a player of markets was absolutely sincere. To question it was to challenge his newly developing sense of himself as an honorable businessman.[13]

In 1907 and 1908, however, much more than honor was at stake for George Wingfield. During those years, he was also immersed in an escalating confrontation with Goldfield's labor unions, particularly the radical Industrial Workers of the World (IWW). The Goldfield Miners' Union, a local of the Western Federation of Miners, was organized in 1904, in large part by Colorado miners who had been displaced in the aftermath of the bitter 1903–1904 Cripple Creek strike. They brought with them a legacy of resentment of the mineowners, who had broken the union and instituted a card system which prevented union members from holding jobs, and of nonunion miners who had refused to cooperate with union efforts. In Goldfield those old animosities came to the fore as the contending parties encountered each other once again. The new complicating factor was the presence of the IWW, which was organized in 1905 as an avowedly anarchist organization, opposed to trade unions as well as to capitalists. Its preamble forthrightly declared: "The working class and the employing class have nothing in common. . . . Between these two classes a struggle must go on until all the toilers come together on the political as well as the industrial field. . . ." In the early years of Goldfield, IWW organizer Vincent St. John and others sought by force of oratory and coordination of labor actions to implement their utopian vision of a single dominant industrial union that would at last give workers some power in their unequal struggle with capital.[14]

In September 1905, the miners' union in Goldfield officially affiliated with the new IWW. To men like Charles Thomas and John Wellington Finch, who had both come from Colorado and witnessed the violence there, the IWW was a sinister new force. Thomas described it in terms that left no doubt as to his sympathies: "Every worker of every sort must belong to it. All prices were fixed by it, and those complaining or even criticizing were beaten up or deported." The first trouble broke out in May 1906, in town. After Western Union messenger boys went on strike for higher wages, the IWW issued a demand that all office employees join the union by June 1. A visit from Nevada governor John Sparks and attorney general James Sweeney was necessary to compromise on the issue. Then, in August 1906, the IWW boycotted the *Goldfield Sun* newspaper after declaring publisher Lindley C. Branson unfair to organized labor in a dispute over his Tonopah paper, also called the *Sun*. The Tonopah trouble was soon settled, but the boycott continued in Goldfield. Newsboys refused to sell the paper, and merchants who patronized it were threatened with a boycott. People going in and out of the *Sun*'s office were photographed in order to harass them. Angered by the attempted intimidation, George Wingfield swung into action against the IWW.[15]

First the mineowners locked out union members who supported the boycott. Then Wingfield went to Tonopah to see Branson, fearing he might back down. Wingfield urged the publisher to stand firm against the IWW boycott. According to Branson's account, Wingfield also promised, apparently on behalf of the mine operators of Tonopah and Goldfield, that Branson would not suffer any financial loss if he agreed to defy the union. Thus reassured, Branson took up the fight, publishing articles and editorial cartoons critical of the IWW at a time when, he claimed, there was no "editor of any newspaper in Nevada, on the Pacific coast or in the country who would dare even mention the I.W.W. and the Goldfield miners' union unfavorably." In Goldfield, Wingfield did his part. On September 9, he defied a group of street corner "loafers" who had gathered around a member of the carpenters' union selling the proscribed *Goldfield Sun* near the Nixon Block. The carpenters' union had refused to align with the IWW and thus defied the boycott. When the crowd began taunting the carpenter as a "scab," Wingfield and his companion, a colorful local mining promoter and gunman named "Diamondfield" Jack Davis, joined the fray. Announcing provocatively that "I bought the *Sun* and I am no scab," Wingfield soon found himself surrounded. He and Davis drew their guns, shots were fired, and a few other men rushed out to join them against the menacing crowd. Apparently chastened by the gunfire, however, "which for a time looked serious," the latter retreated, and the defenders dispersed after spending half an hour on the steps of the Nixon Block awaiting "a renewal of hostilities." Despite the distinct strategic advantage that armed men, no matter how few in number, had over a group of unarmed men, newspaper accounts of the incident stressed Wingfield's boldness and courage. This encounter, and the union's coercive tactics, helped alienate many in the community from the IWW.[16]

Neither Wingfield's showdown nor community disapproval, however, was sufficient to save the *Goldfield Sun*. Just five days after the gunshot incident, Branson announced his intention to sell the Goldfield paper, which became the *Tribune* under its new owners, in order to stop his monetary losses and save his Tonopah paper. He later claimed to have lost $7,000 on the transaction, which he made at Wingfield's urging because the latter "had a deal on hand that [he] could not make unless the paper was sold and the boycott stopped." This was evidently the formation of GCMC, which hinged at that point on the willingness of outside bankers to lend money to Nixon and Wingfield. Significant labor disputes in Goldfield might have created doubts that would have jeopardized the partners' intended purchase of the Red Top and Jumbo mines. Although Wingfield denied being a party to any arrangement about the Goldfield paper, Branson felt betrayed by his failure to make good on his promise of financial reimbursement. But sale of the paper had the desired effect. Once the new owners had replaced all the old *Sun* employees, the IWW canceled the boycott, and industrial peace was temporarily restored.

It was not to be permanent, however. The Miners' Union became embroiled in a direct dispute with Goldfield mineowners in December 1906, after George Wingfield dramatically declared war on the practice of highgrading. Many Goldfield mines, including both the Mohawk and the Combination, boasted extraordinarily rich ore, sometimes called jewelry rock or high grade. This ore, in which gold values were so high that even small pieces were valuable, was a target for thefts of various kinds. In October, a series of robberies from two particularly rich Mohawk leases took sacked ores. On a much smaller scale, individual miners stole high grade ore by hiding it in their clothing, in lunch pails, and even in body cavities. Three of them were caught in the act in the Mohawk in December 1906. Potential profits from this pilfering were so great that miners actually bribed supervisors in order to get jobs on favored leases, while leasers without high grade ore had trouble hiring miners even at premium wages.[17]

Collectively, the losses to the owners were staggering. Yet the practice was not universally condemned. The miners contended that their artificially low wages entitled them to seize a share in the owners' profits. Illicit profits from stolen highgrade also fueled Goldfield's speculative boom. Saloons and gambling halls like the Northern, operated by Ole Elliott and Tex Rickard, where miners working for $4 per day were observed to wager hundreds of dollars nightly, "thrived on the money obtained by miners from stolen ore." And there were those who felt that the effects ultimately benefited even the owners. One legitimate assayer never involved in the fencing of stolen ore believed "some of the companies and many of the brokerage houses winked at the high-grading, in the belief that the consequent booming prosperity and wild life of Goldfield were such good advertising with such beneficial results to mine promotion and stock quotations as to be cheap at that price." Furthermore, individual leasers were willing to tolerate the miners' thefts as long as there were no strikes that would jeopardize their own rush to remove as much ore as possible before expiration of their leases.[18]

The new merger company, however, had no such imperative. GCMC had no time pressure, no particular interest in further mine promotion, and absolutely no inclination to overlook employee theft in the interest of cordial labor relations. Nixon and Wingfield needed every dollar to pay off the costs of mine acquisition, mine improvement, and general expansion of operations. Experienced talent like Thomas and Finch wasn't cheap. Part of their credibility as legitimate mining capitalists also depended on the early payment of dividends. The result was a dramatic crusade to stem the losses, launched as part of GCMC's general effort to rationalize and order its affairs as befitted a $50 million corporation.

As part of the campaign, GCMC filed suit against its leasers to stop them from mining only the high grade portions of their ground and ignoring standard mining practices. It put extra company watchmen underground to guard against collusion between miners and supervisors. It also sought legislation in 1907 that would regulate assay offices and ore buyers and force them to keep public records. Perhaps most flamboyantly, it physically seized ore that belonged to its constituent companies. It was this errand that took George

Wingfield, on December 11, 1906, on a wild race to Reno, where he repossessed 44 sacks of gold ore valued at $20,000. Observing the ore being loaded on freight cars at Goldfield, Wingfield surmised that it was part of the booty from the October thefts. Wiring ahead to Reno to arrange for legal papers, he took the same train that held the ore, which had been consigned by a Goldfield assayer to Vallejo, California. Wingfield left the train in Sparks, the division point just outside Reno, raced by automobile into Reno, signed the waiting documents, and then arranged for bonds to protect the sheriff who actually took possession of the ore and oversaw its transfer to the new Nixon National Bank. Although he knew it might be difficult to prove that the ore came from the Mohawk, Wingfield gave notice that his replevin suit against Wells Fargo & Co. was merely the opening salvo in an ongoing effort to crack down on a generally accepted practice of stealing ore. No longer would Goldfield be a community where "the miners openly boast of what ore they get on their shift and how much per pound they get for it."[19]

Perhaps coincidentally, within a week of Wingfield's announcement, on December 18, the Goldfield Miners' Union initiated its own confrontation with the mineowners. A union meeting on that day passed a resolution sponsored by IWW organizer Vincent St. John that threatened a strike unless miners were given an immediate twenty percent wage increase, from $4 to $5 per day. A second, more radical resolution demanding that miners working on leases receive a share in the profits was tabled. The next day, GCMC and most other mines shut down operations, throwing between 1,200 and 1,500 men out of work. In the words of one observer, "It came like lightning out of a clear sky." The mineowners made no further response until December 28, when they appointed an arbitration committee of five men, including GCMC general superintendent Finch. Nixon and Wingfield were both out of the city, the latter in San Francisco in connection with the replevin suit against Wells Fargo. The mineowners agreed to negotiate with a similar committee of five miners, but, in an obvious attempt to eliminate "agitators," specified that it be made up of men who had been in Goldfield for at least six months prior to December 20.[20]

After several arbitration sessions, the mineowners' proposition was submitted to the union on December 31. It provided for maintaining the old wage scale, but for the owners voluntarily to increase wages by 50 cents per day until the owners and union could jointly establish a general store that would reduce the high cost of living by selling goods at only ten percent above cost. The mineowners also sought agreement to a 10-day notice by either side when strikes or shutdowns were contemplated, and permanent establishment of the 5-person arbitration committee to whom disputes could be referred. They promised to lobby the legislature for "relief from the present oppressive exactions of the railroad service," which also added to the high cost of living in Goldfield. Significantly, they also submitted a second, separate proposition that would permit operators to provide change rooms for their employees. This latter issue was designed to cut down on highgrading by forcing the miners to change from their work clothes on company property under the supervision of a watchman. It was extremely controversial, especially with the IWW, and was reportedly the major reason that the miners rejected the offer. Disgusted onlookers, who wanted both sides to get back to business, wished forlornly for a rational compromise, with "the straight $5.00 scale conceded by the operators and the change-room conceded by the union," but it was not to be.[21]

The stalemate continued until the return of George Wingfield on January 5. The mineowners remained adamant, evidently hoping their intransigence might split the union ranks and separate conservative WFM members from the IWW leadership. Aware that their most entrenched opposition came from St. John and the IWW, the mineowners tried to maintain the fiction that it was dealing only with the WFM. Some miners reportedly resented the fanatical IWW leadership as well, but for the moment the IWW was firmly in control of union activities in Goldfield. The extent of its power was graphically demonstrated by the terms of the settlement they accepted on January 9. The mineowners agreed to pay $4.50 per day for unskilled surface labor and $5 for underground work. The proposed cooperative store remained in the agreement. The change rooms did not. From the union perspective, it had won. From Wingfield's perspective, he too had won, by settling an aggravating strike that was interfering with Nixon's delicate negotiations for money to complete the deal for the Combination. His war against highgrading would continue on other fronts, and the relatively moderate wage concessions were a tolerable price to pay for resuming production.[22]

Unfortunately, though, the resumption was short lived. The IWW continued to grow in strength and militancy, boasting by March 1 that it controlled Goldfield. In keeping with its goal of forming a single massive industrial union, the IWW enrolled town workers of all descriptions, reportedly including prostitutes, and attempted to enforce an 8-hour day for them. Resentment of their domination grew accordingly, especially since "there was never any . . . evidence of an idea that the employer had a right to be consulted." Matters came to a head again over an internal dispute between the IWW and the carpenters. The miners' union attempted to force the carpenters, who already had their own AFL-affiliated union, to join with them instead (and thus implicitly with the IWW). To enforce their demands the

IWW called the carpenters' helpers off the job and ordered grocers, water men, and restaurants not to sell to carpenters. In what was clearly an internal dispute about jurisdiction, on March 8 the miners also served notice on manager Finch of GCMC that they would strike unless all workers around the mines (including carpenters) became members of the miners' union. When Finch refused to intervene in the dispute, the miners' representative called his men off from the Mohawk. When they repented and returned to work the next day, they found themselves locked out.[23]

During this dispute, on March 10, a restaurant owner named John Silva, who had defied IWW orders and continued to serve the carpenters, was shot and killed by union business agents Morrie Preston and Joseph Smith while he was arguing with them about a picket of his restaurant. In a town that was already extremely tense, this incident was cataclysmic. Rumors of armed revolution swept through Goldfield: "with the Colorado struggles fresh in their minds it seemed certain that the next step would be the blowing up of the mines and buildings. There seems to be no doubt that the camp was clutched by a spasm of fear." In the midst of that fear, Preston and Smith were arrested, and an attempt to lynch them was narrowly averted. In the following few days, eight other IWW leaders, including Vincent St. John, were arrested and charged with conspiracy. Although these charges were eventually dropped, Smith and Preston were convicted on May 9 of second-degree murder and voluntary manslaughter, respectively, in a trial that depended heavily on tainted testimony. By then, however, the matter had escalated far beyond the dispute between the carpenters and miners, and beyond the guilt or innocence of the two union officials. By then it had become a matter of extreme provocation to the mineowners, and they organized to do something about it.[24]

As Finch put it in a letter to his old associates in Cripple Creek, "Matters here have taken such a form in the struggle with the labor situation that we have been obliged to organize, as against the IWW which control all the other crafts as well as the miners in the district, a Business Men's and Mine Owner's Association." This group was formed March 14 at Goldfield's elegant Montezuma Club, a private association which served as the headquarters for the town's most eminent male citizens. Diagonally across the street from the miners' union hall, the Montezuma Club and its counterpart each became armed camps. Mineowner Jack Davis, GCMC detective Clarence Sage, and others amassed guns to defend the mines against an expected attack. A group of 200 carpenters and tradesmen met to denounce the IWW and form a committee of safety to guard the water pipeline and the Nixon Block among other places. There were rumors that several prominent men, including George Wingfield, had received notices to leave town, as well as threats on their lives. The menace was made more plausible by a shot fired at banker John S. Cook, a noted Wingfield associate, one night as he left the bank. As the two sides faced off, it was difficult to separate rumor from fact, and each was willing to believe the worst of the other. As U.S. District Court Judge Farrington put it in an opinion issued one year later, "It is not necessary that a man should be knocked down to be intimidated." In Goldfield, in March and April 1907, it was safe to conclude that both sides felt victimized, and that each was genuinely intimidated by the unpredictability or the power of the other.[25]

The Mine Operators Association (MOA) maintained that it was not opposed to miners' unions, but only to the IWW. John W. Finch was a member of the MOA executive committee, and undoubtedly drew on his previous Colorado experience in his dealings with the Goldfield union. In any event, the mineowners' position was clear. They demanded the withdrawal of the IWW. On Friday, March 15, they formally ordered the closing of all mines and businesses, with restaurants, grocers, and butchers allowed to open the next day as long as they employed no IWW members. Disavowing any intention to alter the existing pay scale, the MOA promised to keep the mines closed until the matter was settled to their satisfaction. By Monday, most stores had reopened without IWW employees, although saloons, especially, which depended on the miners' business, were reluctant. Support for the IWW gradually flagged among workers other than the miners. In the Goldfield Miners' Union, however, the IWW maintained a stronghold. Despite several attempts by some miners to withdraw from the IWW, the radicals claimed that the WFM and IWW were amalgamated at a national level, so the Goldfield local couldn't unilaterally sever the ties.[26]

In desperation, GCMC contemplated its own unilateral action. Facing continuing disruption as the possibility of profit receded even further into the distance, the company's attorneys, Thomas, Bryant & Malburn, responded with a novel proposal. If it was impossible to deal directly with the IWW-dominated Goldfield Miners' Union, why not legally dissolve it? Contemplating a request for a federal court injunction, GCMC formulated its complaint against the local union, the WFM, the IWW, and twenty-four local officials. The company detailed a history of conspiracy designed to keep it from operating and asked to have the local "abated as a nuisance and perpetually enjoined from any further meeting or action of any kind or nature whatsoever." Such a legal action was actually taken by GCMC nine months later, in December 1907, after John Finch had resigned and Wingfield's patience with labor unions was completely exhausted; but it was initially drafted during the edgy days of March.[27]

Ultimately, it did not have to be deployed then. Instead the matter began to be resolved after negotiations between two new representatives, Senator Nixon, who had arrived from Washington, and C. E. Mahoney, who was acting president of the WFM. They agreed to put the matter of separating the WFM from the IWW to another vote, which was held April 6 but repudiated on April 9. After the MOA presented its settlement terms on April 9, it moved to cut off all supplies from any business employing IWW members. The combination of negotiation and coercion eventually produced a settlement agreement on April 21, which was ratified by the miners on April 22, bringing to an end a 41-day strike. The new agreement was to have a two-year duration and to involve no change in wage scales. It provided that the Goldfield Miners' Union would have jurisdiction over all nonsupervisory employees in and around the mines, although the matter of the carpenters was carefully obscured. A two-thirds vote was necessary for *either* the union or the MOA to declare a strike or a lockout, and no town controversy—which might involve the IWW—was to be allowed to interfere with operation of the mines.

In headlines prematurely proclaiming, "Labor Trouble in Goldfield District Passes into History," the Goldfield newspapers hailed a new era of permanent peace. The relief was palpable. But peace was expensive. The MOA spent over $45,000 during March and April on detectives to infiltrate the union, guards to protect its members, and supplies to defend itself if necessary. Although the cause was, of course, a righteous one in their eyes, that considerable sum of money was raised from men whose source of income was cut off while the mines were shut down. Although GCMC manager Finch was congratulated by a Boston stockholder on his successful management of the negotiations, it meant that the merger company further postponed its own profit. Leasers who had shut down during the lockout were compensated for their losses by having the terms of their leases extended by a like number of days, as well as an allowance for the additional time necessary to bring the mines back into full operation. All in all, it was an expensive victory, but the achievement of labor stability for the future justified the expenditure. By way of celebration, George Wingfield departed in May on a lengthy tour of his mining interests in northern California that also involved some hunting and fishing and a stay of several weeks in Los Angeles and Catalina. He was gone until late July and reported on his return that he had two operations on his throat while he was in Los Angeles.[28]

Within a few weeks of his July 22 return, the stability that had been so acclaimed in April proved to be disappointingly ephemeral. On August 18, GCMC took the next step in its campaign against highgraders and instituted change rooms in the Mohawk. These required the miners to remove their work clothes on one side of a partition, then walk across the room to a locker on the other side to put on their street clothes. The entire operation took place under the scrutiny of a timekeeper and a company watchman. Although GCMC had installed such change rooms earlier on its other properties, the Mohawk was notorious for its high grade ore, and the change there triggered a walkout on August 20. Miners claimed that "requiring the men to parade the length of the room in their underclothes was un-American, degrading, and not to be tolerated." The company countered that it was all an excuse to protect their right to steal ore.[29]

Nixon tried without success to effect a compromise, offering to alter the design of the change room to suit the miners as long as it still served the same purposes. The settlement was ultimately achieved by GCMC attorney W. H. Bryant, who stressed the owners' desire for a *permanent* resolution and arranged for union committees to meet with Nixon and Wingfield in Reno. Work was resumed on September 8 after the company agreed to put the clothing lockers side by side rather than across the room and conceded to the miners' union jurisdiction over any carpenters employed by the mining company. In the interim, however, a special GCMC directors' meeting scheduled to declare the company's first dividend on August 31 had to be postponed.[30]

In this relatively minor confrontation, GCMC's frustration only grew. A reliable, permanent labor agreement was essential to efficient operation of the giant mining company. Stopping operations and starting over again in a mine was expensive. During the idle intervals, water accumulated in the lower levels of the mines and stopes caved in. Time that was lost in resuming operations meant postponing dividends even longer and subjected the miners to dangerous working conditions. Avoiding this unpredictability was thus coming to be the partners' ruling passion. During the change room controversy, Nixon and Wingfield tried to buy stability. They offered union officials a 3-year contract at $5 per day for everyone connected with the mines, but the officials refused to sign the agreement.

As George Wingfield later remembered it, that refusal, which may have been precipitated by other objectionable features of the proposal, was the final straw: "It was then that we saw that it was impossible to get along with them at all, so we fought the thing out." A later federal investigation of the Goldfield labor troubles, which was not particularly sympathetic to the mineowners, agreed with Wingfield on this point: "although the operators had yielded to nearly all the demands of the union, it seemed impossible to secure any settled industrial conditions." The August strike, although resolved relatively easily, clearly reinforced the owners' resentment of the union and their determination to obtain labor peace at any price. Even Goldfield newspapers not associated with Nixon and Wingfield were predicting as much: "If another general strike is brought on by the action of the miners, the mine owners will shut down and will never reopen until Goldfield is an 'open camp,' and the Western Federation is shorn of its power." [31]

Before too much longer, they had their chance. This time the trouble was precipitated by events outside Goldfield, as an economic depression rippled outward from the national financial centers. Late in October 1907, it reached southern Nevada and two of Goldfield's three banks failed, on October 23 and 24. Free and easy banking practices that had been profitable during the boom months of rising prices suddenly spelled danger as the investment market shrank and mining stocks were frantically being sold for cash. Stocks that had been put up as collateral for bank loans proved worthless when those banks went to liquidate them. As George Wingfield put it several years later, "During the boom days you could go to a bank here and borrow a thousand dollars on a paper napkin with I.O.U. written on it." The State Bank and Trust Company, owned by Thomas B. Rickey, was accused of illegally using depositors' money to buy George Graham Rice's Sullivan Trust Company, which had collapsed earlier in the year. Although Rickey, a political rival of Nixon, was acquitted of the charges, his bank never reopened. Neither did Nixon and Wingfield's old bank, the Nye and Ormsby County. [32]

Even the Nixon and Wingfield bank, John S. Cook & Co., was not immune to pressure. There was a run on the bank on October 15, reportedly part of a union conspiracy to close it. It was forestalled by Nixon and Wingfield's pledge to back its deposits with their personal fortunes, and by conspicuous display of large stacks of gold. The specie was part of GCMC funds on deposit at the Tonopah Banking Corporation, but its presence in Goldfield had the desired effect. Anxious depositors were paid in coin, and longtime commercial customers of the bank like the Northern Saloon returned much of it to the bank again in their deposits. By this means the immediate crisis was forestalled. Meanwhile, however, GCMC was laying off large numbers of miners and the economy of Goldfield was in shambles. [33]

The situation was complicated for the mines by the actions of the smelters through which they marketed their ores. Overstocked with ore by October 1907, and suffering like all businesses from the economic slowdown, the "smelter trust" announced a new policy of deferring payment to their sellers until they in turn were paid by the U.S. Mint for the shipments. This effectively imposed a 45- to 90-day waiting period before the ore sellers would be paid. The smelters also raised the treatment costs for Goldfield ores above the rates charged to other mining districts and paid less than the $20.67 per ounce price set by the federal government for gold. What one mining expert described as "legalized robbery" by the smelters put the local companies in the untenable position of having to buy labor and supplies to extract and ship the ore and then wait as long as three months for their payment. At the mercy of the smelters, GCMC stopped shipping the bulk of its ore and resolved to speed up construction of its own mill facilities, which would reduce its reliance on the smelters for processing. In the meantime, it had to rely on the limited facilities of two small mills it already owned (including the one on the Combination property) and simply wait longer for its returns. This meant that many miners from GCMC and other companies were laid off, making matters worse in a region already hard pressed by the general slowdown.[34]

The bank failures in late October spurred Governor John Sparks to declare a state bank holiday and thus created further pressure for John S. Cook & Co. Once again Nixon and Wingfield responded with infusions of cash. They ordered a special express train from San Francisco to bring up $500,000 from Crocker-Woolworth Bank, where GCMC had substantial funds on deposit. In a carefully calculated newspaper interview, Wingfield let it be known that the partners expected their banks in Goldfield, Rhyolite (a branch of John S. Cook & Co.), and Tonopah to be able to meet all obligations. But he also announced that a total of $1 million in personal funds was available if they did not. Apparently the personal funds *were* needed to shore up the banks. San Francisco newspapers reported that Nixon was selling GCMC at a rock-bottom price of $4 per share to get cash to help the banks, and Wingfield later ruefully reported that the panic cost him "a million in cash," although he was proud that no one else had suffered losses in his banks. A 1910 editorial gave the two men credit for raising loans totaling $3 million under difficult circumstances: "the fact that [the banks] maintained their solvency during the crucial period was due solely to the confidence and credit of Senator Nixon and his partner."[35]

Banker Crocker's loyalty may also have had something to do with it, as Nixon had deposited more than $1.5 million of GCMC funds in Crocker's San Francisco bank to help strengthen it during the panic. In any event, although Governor Sparks extended the original 3-day banking holiday until November 4, John S. Cook & Co. reopened on October 29 with $1 million in coin stacked ostentatiously on its counters. The display was enough to allay depositors' fears and there was "no semblance of a run." Thoughtfully, George Wingfield also made arrangements during the bank holiday so that

Goldfield recipients of GCMC's first dividend checks could cash them at the Casey Hotel or the Northern Saloon, both businesses owned by friends of his.[36]

The pleasures of the partners' economic triumph were soon soured by other troubles, however. By November, with smelter shipments at a standstill and money unavailable, many operators could no longer pay their workers in the customary gold coin. GCMC, a victim of the same circumstances, announced that it would meet its November 14–15 payroll half in coin and half in checks. In view of the fact that Nixon and Wingfield had just conspicuously assembled $1 million in coin to decorate their bank counters, and the GCMC directors on the very same day had declared the company's second dividend of 10 cents per share, the miners' displeasure was understandable. They demanded that the owners guarantee payment of any checks that were issued for wages and agree to use any proceeds from the smelters first of all for cash wages. On November 18, the MOA responded with its proposal. All Goldfield companies would pay their employees in bank checks until the financial crisis was ended and local banks (which customarily received the smelter returns on behalf of the companies to whom they advanced operating funds) could again obtain currency. Until that time, the company checks would be exchanged at local banks for cashiers' checks in denominations from $5 to $20. The cashiers' checks would be accepted at face value by local merchants and would circulate for exchange just like a bank draft in any outside city where the local banks had correspondents. It was a good faith offer. The arrangement extended to the miners the resources of a banking system that mineowners and other wealthy men were accustomed to using; but it was utterly alien to the miners, whose recent experiences with bank closures produced justifiable skepticism about any form of money other than gold.[37]

The result was predictable, and probably not unwelcome to the mineowners. On November 26, 1907, the union voted to strike the next day rather than accept payment in "scrip." It was just the opening that the MOA was seeking. That group responded on November 30 with a resolution that the mines would all remain closed until the financial crisis passed, the smelters began paying a return high enough to cover production costs, and—most significantly—labor conditions were settled to their satisfaction. Thus the battle lines were drawn for the final battle in Goldfield's labor wars. Close to 2,000 men were on strike, and the MOA lost no time in lengthy attempts at arbitration.

On December 2, the MOA declared all previous union agreements abrogated because the strike had been called illegally (the strike had been approved by two-thirds of those present at the meeting, but the mineowners argued that it should be two-thirds of the entire union membership). The very same day, a committee including George Wingfield went to Carson City to consult Governor Sparks. Under the guise of discussing the smelter crisis, they urged him instead to call for federal troops to be sent to Goldfield. Sparks immediately obliged and wired President Theodore Roosevelt, seeking federal troops to prevent "serious labor trouble in the district of Goldfield and adjoining camps, which may result in violence and great destruction of both life and property." [38]

The troops arrived from San Francisco on December 7, despite the fact that local residents could detect no trouble. With an efficiency that bespeaks prior planning, the MOA announced on December 9 its intention to reopen the mines in three days. They reduced wages to the Tonopah scale of $4 per day and imposed a card system, which was illegal under then prevailing laws. The card system required every miner to certify before being hired that he was not a member of the Goldfield Miners' Union, the WFM, or any union connected with them. The owners explained that lower wages were necessary in order to allow them to continue profitable operations in low grade ore they were beginning to encounter and were justified by the reductions they intended to force in Goldfield's inflated cost of living. Later they lamely claimed that they had actually approved the lower wages *before* the troops arrived in Goldfield, although they hadn't announced the change at the time. As they had done in January, they promised to reduce the cost of living by running a company store and boardinghouse if necessary. Although Goldfield WFM members for the most part stood firm and refused to return to work under these conditions, the mining companies began recruiting elsewhere. GCMC's new general manager, John H. Mackenzie, who had replaced Finch when the latter resigned in November, asked an employment agency to find him 150 to 200 miners from the Joplin, Missouri, vicinity and promised to pay their transportation to Goldfield. By January 1908, the mines were functioning again with nonunion labor, some of it personally recruited in Utah by George Wingfield.[39]

Almost immediately, Theodore Roosevelt smelled a rat, and a special 3-man commission was dispatched to Goldfield to report on whether the federal troops were actually needed. On December 20, they informed the president that, while no disorder had existed prior to the arrival of the troops, and the only real violence had occurred in March with Silva's murder, the mineowners' actions in reducing wages and breaking the union now made the possibility of violence real. Disgusted, Roosevelt instructed Sparks that peacekeeping was part of the state's police duty and that he would withdraw the troops by the end of the month unless the governor agreed to call a special session of the legislature and secure passage of a state police bill that would give Nevada its own troops. Sparks reluctantly acquiesced and a special session was convened on January 14. After debate over the legality of the card system, the Republican legislators asked the Goldfield MOA to rescind it in exchange for passage of the police bill. When the MOA agreed to abrogate it, the state police bill was passed and signed into law on January 29. The federal troops began to be withdrawn in January and were completely replaced by state police by March 7, 1908.

In the meantime, fearing that Roosevelt would carry through on his initial threat to withdraw the federal troops by December 30, GCMC revived its March suit and filed it on December 27 in federal district court in Carson City. As George Wingfield succinctly summarized the matter, "We have started in to win and we will win." GCMC sought the same relief as in March: an injunction against union intimidation of its workers by picketing or meetings and dissolution of the WFM. Events later made the suit moot, but the ruling by Judge Farrington on March 6 granted the company the relief it sought, including a declaration that the Nevada law prohibiting the card system was invalid. Farrington's ruling did not formally dissolve the WFM, but it might as well have done so. By the time it was issued, the union was effectively dead in Goldfield, and the final vote to accept nonunion watchmen and end the strike in April 1908 was a pathetic formality. In the end George Wingfield had his way. All radical union influence was purged from Goldfield and GCMC could rely on a stable labor force. From then on, the troubles the company confronted in Goldfield were the more intractable ones of improving the efficiency of mining operations and increasing profits for long-suffering stockholders. Finally, and belatedly, Nixon and Wingfield looked forward to enjoying some of the fruits of their labors in assembling the giant mining property.[40]

The long campaign against the IWW had left its scars, however. Perpetually wary of the dangers of radical "infiltration," George Wingfield for years employed detectives at his mining properties to report on any union activities. Clarence Sage, who was appointed as one of the deputies of the new Nevada State Police, and who was arrested later in life for rape and manslaughter, was only the most notorious of these operatives and in fact severed his connections with GCMC in 1911. Other men followed him, however, often furnished by the Thiel Detective Agency of Los Angeles. Anonymously they supplied the information that ended up as a group of names on a "shit-ass list" forwarded to one of Wingfield's mining superintendents by his personal secretary in 1910 or led to the cryptic notation on the pay records of one discharged miner: "cause Socialist." A Goldfield miner discharged from the Mohawk in 1910 because of his WFM membership objected publicly in the newspaper, although he suspected his union affiliation might be just an excuse to cover the real reason, that he hadn't purchased supplies at the company store. In any event, George Wingfield's animosity toward labor was well known. When he was contacted in 1911 for his version of the Goldfield labor dispute, he concluded proudly, "The result is that the Western Federation of Miners and the I.W.W. are now eliminated from the camp of Goldfield and *always will be as long as I am identified with it.*"[41]

This was not simply perversity or malevolence on Wingfield's part. From his perspective, the IWW influence was a genuinely harmful one, leading inevitably to destruction and violence and the kind of fundamental perfidy he witnessed in Goldfield in 1906 and 1907. In 1915, the appearance of a labor sticker caused him to fear a resurgence of labor agitation, and he immediately called the matter to the attention of the governor's office, advising that "action should be taken by the State to avoid another set back like that caused by the same persons, several years ago." In 1920, in the midst of the post–World War I Red Scare, he was lobbying Nevada's Senator Key Pittman for a bill "defining what is meant by I.W.Wism, Bolshevism, Syndicalism, etc., and putting sufficient power in the hands of the proper authorities to apprehend those criminals and have the punishment meted out to them that they deserve." Like later Cold Warriors, George Wingfield was frightened by a worldwide Marxist conspiracy. Condemning what he called "parlor-Bolshevism," he explained it as the idle amusement of people with money who "are all scared to death for fear this Russian business will come to this country and if it does then they can plead their help to the Cause to keep themselves from being executed by the so-called Proletariat." The contemporary observer is reminded again of Farrington's opinion in ruling for GCMC against the WFM: "It is not necessary that a man should be knocked down to be intimidated." Even George Wingfield, one of the most powerful men in the state of Nevada, could be intimidated by the implied threat to his peaceful enjoyment of the fruits of capitalism. Any initial inclination to compromise for the sake of stability had vanished by 1907, as an exasperated Wingfield prepared to wage war against radicalism in all its guises. By 1908, he had won in Goldfield; but he remained throughout his life fearful of a renewal of hostilities and assiduous in protecting his victory.[42]

Late in January 1908, once the suit against the WFM had been filed and the outcome of the special legislative session was clear, Wingfield left town for an extended business trip to Chicago, Philadelphia, Boston, New York, and Washington, D.C. During this trip he undoubtedly reported on the circumstances of his triumph over the miners' union to the major investors in

GCMC and assessed the company's prospects. He also conferred with Senator Nixon. When he returned to Goldfield at the end of March, he was free at last to concentrate his efforts on expansion and organization of the partners' empire. By now that empire extended throughout Nevada and into California. Wingfield had invested in a resort property, Walley's Hot Springs, in the Carson Valley outside Carson City. He and Nixon owned ranches and banks, including the Nixon National Bank in Reno, for which they had purchased a downtown lot in October 1906. In 1907, they built a separate building in Goldfield to house the offices of GCMC. In September 1908, Wingfield announced plans to seek a franchise to operate trolleys between Goldfield, Columbia, and Diamondfield. Tonopah's magnificent 5-story Mizpah Hotel, in which they were investors, opened belatedly in November 1908, after its construction was delayed by the 1907 panic. One month later, in December 1908, the partners' Bonanza Hotel Company took over the even more elegant brick Goldfield Hotel, which had been opened earlier that same year.[43]

All of this expansion was fueled by the rising fortunes of GCMC. That company's $1 million debt to financier Bernard Baruch was settled in September 1907, when Baruch agreed to forego the option he held to purchase 1 million shares of GCMC stock for $7.75 per share. Instead he received $160,000 in cash and a total of 220,000 shares of stock, valued at $7 per share. Thus freed from debt, and with $2 million in its treasury, the company could proceed with its dividend payments and take full advantage of the economy that joint operations effected on the consolidated properties. By May 1908, the regular pattern of dividends was established, and a rich new strike that manager Mackenzie believed "was the most important find made since the camp became established" was uncovered on the Mohawk.[44]

Stock prices continued to soar as the profitable company hinted that it might have evidence for a successful apex suit against the Florence mine. Nixon and Wingfield held a minority interest in this property, which had been recommended by Finch for inclusion in GCMC, but despite an offer of $4.5 million, they had been unable to convince majority owners Tom Lockhart and A. D. Parker to sell. By May 1908, George Wingfield had been dropped from the board of directors of the Florence Goldfield Mining Company, and, although rumors that GCMC would sue the Florence were officially denied, the newspapers concluded that "actions speak louder than words" in the matter. In fact, no suit was filed and the Florence never did come into the partners' possession; but litigation pending between GCMC and the Jumbo Extension, another Lockhart company, was settled in July by effectively giving GCMC control of all future proceeds from that property. By December 1908, as the company's new 100-stamp mill started into operation, local newspaper headlines trumpeted "Sixteen Per Cent Annual Profit on a $36,000,000 Capital Is Now Guaranteed." In view of the continuing good news from Goldfield, with dividends to match, few could quarrel with the *Tonopah Sun*'s conclusion, in April 1909, that GCMC was the "Richest Gold Mine in the World."[45]

And George Wingfield was a major owner and the company's guiding force, a former buckaroo whose name now appeared in the newspapers identified as a "young millionaire." At the top of his game in Goldfield, having acquired polish from his new associations, he was now prepared by maturity and experience to move into a wider world. In July 1908, he took a crucial step in doing so, signifying the completion of his social metamorphosis from gambler to investor by marrying the daughter of San Francisco banker Robert B. Murdoch. His engagement to the beautiful Maude Azile Murdoch was announced July 29, with the wedding scheduled for Saturday, August 1. The groom was just a few days from his thirty-second birthday. The bride was several months short of her eighteenth.[46]

A contemporary of the couple reported later that Maude Murdoch married George Wingfield for his money and that he married her for social respectability; but that was years after the couple's eventual divorce, in 1929. In the meantime, the newlyweds faced complications that might have overwhelmed any marriage. As soon as the engagement was announced, May Baric reappeared in Wingfield's life, threatening revenge and demanding the return of "her" diamonds, which she claimed had been given to Maude. According to her version of events, on the very day of his engagement to Maude Murdoch, Wingfield had paid $2,000 in bills for Baric and begged her to go to New York. He promised to send her $1,000 there; but she demanded $25,000 and later told a newspaper reporter, "He ought to give me at least $50,000 considering I helped him get his start in Alaska and helped him to make money when we first went to Nevada." When Wingfield refused, Baric called the Murdoch home and announced to the bride's mother that her daughter was engaged to a married man. Although Mrs. Murdoch reportedly told Baric that the engagement was broken, in reality the wedding was hurriedly moved up from Saturday to that very evening, Thursday, July 29. After a brief evening ceremony at the San Francisco residence of a Presbyterian minister, the couple hastily took the train south to Los Angeles, supposedly to embark on a honeymoon tour of Europe and the world. In the midst of this excitement, Wingfield found time to remember his friends in Goldfield, wiring "for the boys to go the route" and ordering dozens of bottles to be put on ice at the Montezuma Club, Goldfield Hotel, and Hotel Casey, "for friends of the bridegroom."[47]

*Construction of the 100-stamp Goldfield Consolidated Mill
marked the beginning of a new era in the desert mining town.
The mill's size and elaborate technology were a measure of
the large profits expected from the consolidated mines.
It began operations in December 1908.
(Courtesy of Nevada Historical Society)*

In the meantime, May Baric continued to give newspaper interviews, in which she was denominated "Mrs. Wingfield Number 1." Enraged at having been jilted, and somewhat erratic by nature, she stormed "George is either a fool or a cur. I don't think much of a man that lives with one wife up to within an hour of marrying another." Her 17-year-old daughter, Olivette, was more restrained, explaining that Wingfield had come to their San Jose home the day before his wedding and promised that he would continue to provide for her: "He laid his hand on my mother's shoulder and said, 'If you had acted differently you might now be in the place of the woman I am about to marry.'" Olivette regretted her mother's attitude and claimed that Wingfield had always been good to both her and her mother. But May Baric was not to be dissuaded. By August 4, she was in Goldfield, threatening to sue Wingfield for bigamy and telling her story of how "it made him crazy when I told him that he would have to settle with me before he could marry any one else and he drew a pistol and tried to beat me over the head with it." The $6,000 house he had given her in San Jose was obviously not nearly enough to settle the score in her mind.[48]

Meanwhile, on the same day, August 4, the San Francisco newspapers reported the apparent suicide of an 18-year-old student who was despondent over news of Maude Murdoch's marriage. Vernal Revalk had resolved to go to the Philippines when he initially learned of the engagement; but news of the wedding caught him unprepared. To drown his sorrows, he began drinking heavily. Two days and nights of drinking absinthe finally led to his death on July 31, after writing farewell messages to his friends. Under the pressure of such dramatic and well-publicized exhibitions as these, it was hardly surprising that the Wingfield honeymoon was shorter than originally announced. By August 23, with Baric presumably placated in the interim, the newlyweds were back in Goldfield, in Wingfield's private apartment on the top floor of the Consolidated Building. There they were treated to no fewer than three separate charivaris, each of which could be stilled only by the liberal distribution of silver dollars. The first group actually dragged George Wingfield halfway down the stairs before he caved in and gave them money. By the third, "the sheriff's office was urged for the love of Heaven to stop the racket." All in all, it was a rude introduction to life in Goldfield for Wingfield's elegant young urban bride.[49]

She apparently responded predictably, and negatively, to the misplaced exuberance of the mining town. Despite reports that the couple would buy or build an elegant new house in Goldfield, by October 1908 they were living in a rented home in Reno, a smaller but more sedate railroad town and commercial center located 260 miles to the northwest and significantly closer

This portrait of Nevada's Napoleon was taken about the time of his marriage in 1908. (Courtesy of Nevada Historical Society)

to San Francisco. Although Wingfield's move there was surely instigated by marriage, it also illustrated the old reliable Wingfield luck, which took him out of Goldfield just at the moment when, in retrospect, it began its long downward slide into dormancy. At the time, however, evidence suggests that he was reluctant to sever his connections to Goldfield. For the next four to five years, he returned there frequently, remained actively involved in its affairs, and saw himself—correctly—as absolutely essential to its continued existence.[50]

In 1909, he phrased that connection to Goldfield in terms of raw power, metaphorically flexing his muscles for his GCMC office manager: "As for what Mr. Baruch said to you about Goldfield, being a place of electricity and opportunity, just remember one thing Chester, when I pull up my roots, the grass will grow in the streets." In 1912, in a more humble and public statement, he verbalized the same sentiment more gracefully. Rebutting the rumor that he was out to wreck Goldfield, he pointed out to a Reno journalist that Goldfield's fate was also his own: "I want to make Goldfield a permanent camp, and will labor continually to that end. I want all of Nevada's camps and districts to succeed, whether I am personally and financially interested in them or not." In different tones, both declarations demonstrate the extent of Wingfield's personal identification with this place where he had, both literally and figuratively, made his fortune. When he left it to go to Reno, in another of the series of fateful relocations that had first brought him out of southeastern Oregon, George Wingfield entered a new realm and began to play a new game. Reno was to be his headquarters and the capital of his economic and political empire for the next fifty-one years, until his death in 1959.[51]

SIX

"I Have Took Over Everything"

I N RENO, the 32-year-old George Wingfield experienced the final phase of his metamorphosis to power, as he slowly began to comprehend and exercise the prerogatives that accrued almost inevitably to a man of great wealth who remained devoted to a chronically poor state. Over the years, many terms would be used to depict the scope of that power, and Wingfield was described variously as "king," "governor," or "overlord" of Nevada. Each term was a feeble rhetorical attempt to summarize the pervasive influence he exercised in his adopted state, but none seemed quite right to describe his particular combination of broad political and economic authority. Gradually, as he moved out of the shadow of his partner and widened the scope of his activity and interests, George Wingfield became publicly identified not just with the economic fortunes of Goldfield or the political structure of Reno, but with the destiny of the entire state.

By 1908, many of the significant patterns that would characterize Wingfield's conduct of his business affairs were already well established. Perhaps most important was his reliance on gifted lieutenants for the management of his operations. Business historian Alfred Chandler, Jr., has described a "managerial revolution in American business," in the late nineteenth and early twentieth centuries, which made possible the rise of the large modern business enterprises by virtue of efficient, coordinated administrative hierarchies. Without the benefit of any formal training in management, this is essentially the model that Wingfield followed for his many businesses, with ranks of "middle managers" who focused on running individual companies and a few trusted associates to consult with him on planning for the whole organization. As one biographer succinctly put it, "He doesn't claim to know it all himself." [1]

Intelligent enough to recognize the worth of expert advice and rich enough to pay well for it, Wingfield generally chose these men wisely. Although he made some mistakes over the years, distinguished men like Thomas, Finch, and Mackenzie in Goldfield were but the first in a long list of skilled engineers, attorneys, bankers, accountants, lobbyists, and executive assistants with whom Wingfield was associated over the years. He was generous in his acknowledgment of "those expert and capable persons with whom I have been fortunate enough to surround myself." His reliance on their expertise continued to be remarked throughout his life. In 1929, for example, a journalist portrayed a familiar corporate Wingfield model of operations, conducted by an executive who "surrounded himself with able, energetic associates who know the mining game." Native ability and a certain amount of luck clearly had something to do with George Wingfield's ascent; but it was also true, as the *Goldfield Tribune* put it in an editorial at the time of his marriage, that Wingfield was a man "who knew how to improve the chances that Fate threw in his way." [2]

In that regard one of Wingfield's most important selections during the Reno years was his office manager, Clarence F. Burton. Burton joined Wingfield's staff shortly after the move to Reno, replacing J. M. Fenwick, a GCMC employee who had accompanied Wingfield as his private secretary. Born in Washington, D.C., in 1885, Clarence Burton graduated from law school at Georgetown University and was also a certified public accountant. For an entire decade, until his departure in 1920 for a banking position in Boston, Burton was a valuable Wingfield aide, translating the latter's initiatives into concrete form. He supplied supervision, financial analysis, and counsel not only for the Wingfield office in Reno, but also for the far-flung network of mining superintendents, property managers, engineers, and other employees that came to be referred to as the "Wingfield organization." He was secretary of over forty corporations, a director of several, and an investor in some. Employees of Burton's caliber, well trained, efficient, and systematic, made it physically and organizationally possible for the Wingfield empire to grow beyond the scope of a single man's oversight.[3]

Equally important on Wingfield's staff was his supervising engineer, Estey A. Julian. First employed by Wingfield in 1911, as manager of the Nevada Hills Mine, at Fairview, Julian was another of the mining experts who flocked into Goldfield from the Cripple Creek mines of Colorado. Born in Missouri, he was a proficient engineer. He rose quickly in the ranks of Wingfield employees to become, in 1917, the head of GCMC's new Exploration Department in San Francisco. A trusted confidant and congenial employee, Estey Julian became George Wingfield's principal technical advisor, consulting not only on mining matters, but also on details of bank and hotel construction or technical installations of any sort. In 1919, he was appointed general manager and vice-president of GCMC, positions he held until his death at age seventy-three, in 1955. Over the years Julian's expertise recast George Wingfield from a venturesome mining speculator, willing to take chances on any likely looking prospect, into a conservative mining investor, carefully weighing the indications on any property before deciding to invest in its development.[4]

In addition to his reliance on talented men like Burton and Julian, another Wingfield trait was his pattern of investment, which was diverse, but generally centered in Nevada. George Wingfield was a passionate adopted son of Nevada and believed, quite simply, "in spending his money where he made it." With few exceptions, he adhered to this principle throughout his life. As early as 1905, long before GCMC, he was described as "having more ready money always at his disposal than any other man in Nevada . . . but he never lets it get outside of the State." By 1913, this was no longer quite true. Wingfield owned oil wells in southern California, had invested in a taxicab company in San Francisco, and held shares in a pioneer rice-growing effort in Butte County. But he was still preeminently identified with his home state, where, as a San Francisco reporter described it, "no substantial investments are made . . . in mining or other enterprises that the investor does not first seek the benefit of his counsel." Indeed, it was this fact—that others outside the state looked to him for advice on Nevada investments—that he cited to Governor Tasker L. Oddie when he turned down Oddie's appointment to the U.S. Senate in 1912. Characteristically, Wingfield felt that his role as a conduit for bringing money into the state was more important than any political leadership he might provide, that he could "serve the state better in a private than in an official capacity."[5]

George Wingfield's choice of verb in that statement, his notion that he *served* the state by supervising his own investments, seems disingenuous but was nonetheless quite sincere. The most significant aspect of Wingfield's transition from gambler to investor was the enlarged scope of responsibility that he assumed. At the beginning, in Golconda and Tonopah, he was simply making money for himself in the best American capitalist fashion. His partnerships with Nixon, Hennessy, and others, however, gradually began to broaden his perspective, implicating him in other people's money. By the time GCMC was formed, Wingfield had become a de facto trustee for major investments by important men who were strangers to him. Decisions that he made in Goldfield affected not only his own bank account, but also the fate of an entire town and the direction of markets in New York and San Francisco. No longer merely speculation, a means of personal enrichment, mining had become his business, an activity that involved him in a network of obligations to others. Somewhat unevenly, George Wingfield grew into the dignity, responsibility, and privileges of that role.

When he moved to Reno, his vision broadened further, to encompass the entire state and new activities. Acutely aware of Nevada's dependent status, which effectively made it an economic colony of financial capitals to the east and west, Wingfield set out to aid his adopted state through conscientiously diversified investment. He took seriously his new role as the state's major capitalist and promoted activities that promised more permanent prosperity than mining. Wingfield invested in a broad range of companies in the 1910s, but always with an underlying premise not only of profitability, but also of constructive development for the state of Nevada.

It was the classic banker's philosophy, one that he had learned from watching Nixon. As one biographical sketch summarized it in 1915, "He has done many things for Nevada, simply because he thought it would help make it grow and prosper—where the profit to himself was very little or nothing." A disgusted former employee confirmed that opinion in the same year. Engineer Frederick J. Siebert was proposing to organize a development company to look for new mining properties and boasted of his qualifications: "I made plenty of money for Wingfield at that game and could do very much better for others than I did for him as he would not do any business outside the state and furthermore turned down many good money making things for very foolish reasons." As the acknowledged richest man in Nevada, George Wingfield assumed responsibility for the economic advancement of his adopted state and took seriously his self-imposed obligation to invest within its borders.[6]

Others in the state viewed his expansion in a less flattering light and deplored the insidious pattern they perceived. One of Democratic senator Key Pittman's political lieutenants wrote anxiously to him in 1913, seeking money to support a Democratic newspaper and warning of "Wingfield's blighting hand." In his eyes, George Wingfield was clearly no benevolent capitalist, but a grasping octopus:

> He has ambitions to control the State for his own aggrandizement and has already started his work. He has the Gazette, has bought a ranch and started a creamery at Fallon, furnishing cows to the ranchers on time, has the Buckhorn mill nearly ready and is branching out in other ways. This is no Frankenstein of my mind, but is the cold truth.

Whether Wingfield's economic activities were viewed as development or domination, however, they unquestionably shaped the growth of Nevada over a quarter of a century.[7]

Within limits, Wingfield was generous with the proceeds of his labors.

Although never a public philanthropist on the magnificent, self-aggrandizing scale of an Andrew Carnegie, his acts of charity were numerous. The man who once treated his gambling cronies to cigars and his business associates to champagne was personally generous throughout his life: "All religious denominations are alike to him in the matter of contributions, and his name is to be found on every charitable list." His sympathy for hard-luck stories was legendary, and he advanced money as "loans" to many people from whom he realistically never expected repayment. An employee's wife remembered that his visits to southern Nevada from Reno would always attract eager prospectors, aware both of Wingfield's perennial interest in new mining properties and of his reputation as a soft touch. After the sudden death by drowning of his older brother, Morris, in 1907, he cared for his sister-in-law and two nieces, sending both of the latter through college and providing a modest allowance. A lifelong member of the Elk's Club, which he joined in Goldfield in 1907, he was especially generous to that group. As reserved about his philanthropy as about other aspects of his life, George Wingfield eschewed publicity for these activities, although he pursued them systematically throughout his life.[8]

In 1909, Wingfield could well afford to be charitable. In February of that year, GCMC demonstrated its recovery from previous years' labor difficulties by distributing its greatest single dividend ever, over $1.8 million. Later that spring, another huge find of rich ore was uncovered in the Combination mine, promising even greater profits to come. Yet the year was significant for other reasons, as well, as Wingfield continued the process of disengagement from his past that had begun with the move from Goldfield to Reno. In February, May Baric took her threatened revenge against him by filing a breach of promise suit in U.S. district court in California. Seeking $500,000 in damages, she anticipated a fascinating trial:

> I can prove all that I will claim in this suit, for the whole state of Nevada knows it. He broke me down physically and left me without a cent after living with me as his wife for seven and a half years. He introduced me to hundreds of people as his wife, including Senator George Nixon of Nevada.
>
> Wingfield used to beat me terribly, and I can prove that. He has my diamonds and Mrs. Wingfield No. 2 is wearing them. . . . Then there is the real "dirty" part, which will come out at the trial.[9]

Obviously furious at having been abandoned, and unwilling to disappear quietly, Baric was a woman with nothing to lose and much to gain from causing trouble. Wingfield must have been exasperated at her failure to stay bought and honor their previous agreement. His attorneys went to work, however, and the trial was delayed until he once again reached a settlement with her. In January 1911, in San Francisco, May Baric signed an agreement admitting that she had been "by certain attorneys persuaded" to undertake her suit. She acknowledged that she had previously received satisfaction for all of the alleged charges and had freed Wingfield from any further claims. For the sum of $20 "and other good considerations," therefore, she dismissed her suit, promised not to assert her wrongful claims again, and released Wingfield from any further demands of any character. In his spectacular rise to power and prominence, George Wingfield had simply outgrown the volatile May Baric, who belonged to the flamboyant gambler's world he had left behind. Male sporting companions from those days might safely be retained. They were regarded by the press simply as colorful tokens of the young millionaire's humble origins and broadmindedness. May Baric, though, was a different matter. For the sake of his new reputation, as well as his new wife, all ties with Baric had to be definitively cut.[10]

Unfortunately for Wingfield, Baric was notably unwilling to acquiesce in her own replacement. The notoriety that her protests brought Wingfield hounded him for years to come. The daughter of one employee, from a socially prominent Carson City family, recalled that, although her father remained with Wingfield for some time, "he would not introduce my mother or any of his family to Mr. Wingfield." She added superciliously that "Wingfield's partner, Mr. Nixon, was definitely not like him." Still later, when Wingfield was running for reelection to the post of university regent in 1938, his defeat was attributed at least in part to the female voters' disapproval of him. For the moment, however, the 1911 agreement with Baric promised some relief from harassment, allowing the troubled relationship from his past to fade into uneasy memory.[11]

A change that was more significant in demarcating the Reno years from Wingfield's past life occurred in March 1909, when the partnership of Nixon and Wingfield was dissolved. As the *Goldfield News* summarized it, "Nixon Gets the Money! Wingfield Holds Stock." Their parting, like the years of their association, was amicable. In an interview afterward, Wingfield denied reports of a rift between them: "I can also state that during all the time we were partners we never had a disagreement, and had no misunderstanding when we dissolved. . . . I can say that Senator Nixon is the best man I ever had any business dealing with." A few months later, he put it more succinctly, "I'd go to hell for George Nixon." The dissolution was initiated by Nixon, who had decided to devote himself to banking and sell his 308,000 shares of GCMC stock. Nixon gave Wingfield the right of first refusal on the stock, and Wingfield took 158,000 of the shares for himself at the rate of $8 per share, or a total of $1.2 million. The remaining 150,000 were sold to six individual purchasers. To pay for his GCMC stock, Wingfield turned over to Nixon his share of all their joint banking and real estate holdings, including the Tonopah Banking Corporation, the Nixon National Bank, the Mizpah Hotel, and other properties. He kept only the Goldfield bank, John S. Cook & Co., buying out the Cook brothers to become its sole owner. He also retained all the partners' joint interests in other mining properties.[12]

Negotiations took place over a period of weeks. Wingfield and his wife left in mid-February for a projected one-month trip that would include the Taft inauguration in Washington, D.C., and a GCMC directors' meeting. By late February, they were in New York, where they stayed at Nixon's favorite haunt, the Waldorf-Astoria Hotel. Rumors about the sale were rampant at the time. The *Goldfield News* inaccurately reported that Nixon's shares had been purchased by a syndicate headed by steel magnate Henry Clay Frick and that Wingfield had lost control of GCMC. Many speculated about Nixon's reasons for selling. Some suggested that Nixon needed "to strengthen himself for his coming fight for reelection to the Senate," which would take place in 1910, because "he knew that the Consolidated company's attitude toward labor was too unsavory a load to pack during a campaign." Wingfield denied this version, offering instead a story "simple and quickly told. Nixon wanted to dispose of all his mining interests and concentrate his time and attention upon his banking."[13]

The *Tonopah Sun* probably came closest to the truth of the matter when it summarized, "The partnership simply ceased because Mr. Wingfield is essentially a mining man, while Senator Nixon is essentially a banker and real estate man." For several years, it had suited their mutual purposes to commingle their fortunes and respective areas of expertise. Now, however, each man had different purposes, and separation made sense. Wingfield candidly revealed his assessment of who had made the better deal when he wrote to his accountant, "I have took over everything."[14]

Public sentiment in Nevada generally seemed to favor his view of the matter. Newspaper headlines optimistically promised, "Wingfield to Make Things Hum," "Wingfield Will Inject Fresh Energy into Goldfield Now." As one historian of the southern Nevada mining boom, Byrd Sawyer, points out, Wingfield could be counted on to continue his policy of expansion at a time when most of the other mine operators "had gone to California to enjoy the fruits of their labors." Also, as a Tonopah mine operator pointed out at the time, it would also mean good things for the stock market: "I think in a way that it means a great deal for the state. Nixon was very conservative and wished to attend to the banking end, while Wingfield has more of the gambling spirit and will do much to stimulate the stock game." Even archnemesis George Graham Rice, a most unlikely source, apparently approved of the change, announcing that "the Consolidated company benefited much in public esteem by the retirement of Senator Geo. S. Nixon from its management and directorate."[15]

In any event, the dissolution of Nixon and Wingfield was an important watershed in George Wingfield's life, fully as significant in its way as his society marriage. For the first time since 1902, it put him in complete control of his own business affairs, now vastly more complex by virtue of the $25 million in reported profits made by Nixon and Wingfield over the years. In seven whirlwind years, the former gambler from Golconda had matured into an entirely new man. The *Salt Lake City Telegram* noted the change admiringly in 1912:

> Unlike many men who have made sudden fortunes, he seemingly by instinct knew how to handle his money when the golden stream began to pour into his coffers, and year by year he has grown and broadened until he is recognized in financial circles everywhere as one of the shrewdest and cleverest young financiers of the country. . . . His money and his honors have not changed him in the least in his attitude toward those he knew in his early struggles in the desert. . . . His good fellowship has never changed a whit and his gratitude, though expressed unostentatiously, has been no less effectively.[16]

From George Nixon, and the men to whom Nixon introduced him, he had learned much of business and politics, of the responsibilities and the pleasures of money. From now on, no longer the junior partner of a U.S. senator, he would apply that knowledge on his own. No doubt he was justifiably confident of his abilities to do so, but there is an engaging touch of humility in George Wingfield's response to a reporter for the *Tonopah Sun*, who asked him after the dissolution of Nixon and Wingfield in 1909, "What are you going to do, George?": "I'm going to do the best I can."[17]

His best was not half bad. Moving confidently into the arena he knew best, George Wingfield rapidly branched out in mining. He began reorganizing his "outside" Goldfield properties, those not included in GCMC, and reopened several, including the Sandstorm-Kendall Consolidated Mines Company in January 1911 and the Blue Bull and Booth in 1912. In addition, GCMC continued to systematize its operation, creating in 1909 a wholly owned subsidiary, the Goldfield Consolidated Milling and Transportation Company (GCMT), to operate its new 100-stamp mill, the older 20-stamp Combination mill, the Alkali Springs water plant at Lida, Nevada, the system of pipelines and the reservoir that supplied water to the mills, and the two miles of railroad that connected the new mill with the mines to the north.[18]

This last move created political controversy when Esmeralda County bullion tax proceeds plummeted as a result. GCMT, being a separate company, could charge GCMC for processing its ore, and those costs would be deducted from GCMC's net proceeds, against which the bullion tax was assessed. All profits from GCMT went to GCMC stockholders, however, so that the scheme in fact allowed the company to lessen its tax liability without adversely affecting the stockholders. Although the *Goldfield News* and Esmeralda County officials professed outrage at the perfidy of the county's largest taxpayer, there was little to be done. As Esmeralda County's district attorney philosophically concluded, no laws had been broken: "no power on earth, under existing laws, could prevent the Goldfield Consolidated Mines Company from forming this separate milling corporation, or, having formed it, from paying that corporation a reasonable charge for milling its ores." Depending on one's perspective, this was outrageous exploitation or sound business practice. Wingfield obviously subscribed to the latter view.[19]

Unfazed by local criticism of the administrative reorganization, they continued their largely unsuccessful attempts to solve the vexing problem of highgrading. They employed undercover detectives, including Clarence Sage, to pursue and collect evidence against those suspected of stealing ore, but failed to obtain many convictions from Esmeralda County juries. The highgrading did not blemish the growing national fame of GCMC, however. In March 1910, the *Wall Street Journal* reported favorably on the company, and in June, with great fanfare, it became the only gold mine to be traded on the New York Stock Exchange.[20]

The continued success of his crown jewel gave Wingfield both the capital and the confidence to expand his mining operations into the rest of the state. He plowed his dividends back into Nevada mining. In 1909, for example, he purchased options on two major properties: the Buckhorn mine outside of Palisade, in Eureka County; and the Nevada Hills Mining Company, near Fairview, in Churchill County. In the former company, his partners included steel magnate Henry Clay Frick, Bernard Baruch, and New York stockbroker J. Horace Harding. The latter property was consolidated in 1910 with an adjacent mine that Wingfield already owned, the Fairview Eagle. Once again Frick and Harding assisted with the financing. Although both mines ultimately proved disappointing, Wingfield's reputation as a mining wizard (combined with the positive reports from his engineers) was sufficient to secure the eastern capital needed to erect mills at both sites. By July 1910, after Wingfield's consolidation of the companies and infusion of cash, Nevada Hills was being optimistically described as "the next comer," the "heir apparent" to GCMC on the New York Curb Market.[21]

In addition to his mines, George Wingfield also spent money for other Nevada assets, including ranches and real estate. He acquired two large livestock outfits, the Lander County Livestock Company, which had its headquarters at the Grass Valley Ranch near Austin, and the Pyramid Land and Stock Company, which owned 18,000 acres of land in Nevada and California. He remained devoted to southern Nevada and bought a majority interest in the luxurious 4-story Goldfield Hotel in December 1910. In the years after the split with Nixon, Wingfield also started several entirely new concerns. These included the Churchill Creamery Company, in Churchill County, Nevada; Sutter Butte Canal Company, in Butte County, California; and the Meadowbrook Ranch, north of Reno near Janesville, California.[22]

Wingfield's involvement in Churchill County, site of the first government-sponsored reclamation district at Fallon, began in 1909, with the purchase of a local ranch. Agriculture offered few of the spectacular profits of mining, but it was a relatively stable industry, and one for which Wingfield's ranch background gave him sympathy. In Churchill County he became part of a nascent Nevada agricultural district when he announced plans to run a model dairy farm and establish a "completely-equipped creamery and icing plant." This undertaking was incorporated the next year as the Churchill Creamery, although dairying operations didn't begin until 1913. In that year the Churchill Creamery purchased the Fallon Creamery and began importing blooded Holstein and Jersey dairy cows for sale to local farmers. The cows could be purchased on credit by applying one-half the proceeds of all cream delivered to the creamery.[23]

By 1914, when Wingfield built a new creamery building in Fallon, some 800 cows were under contract to the dairy and Wingfield controlled butter production in Churchill County. His younger brother, Sam, was living on one of the Fallon ranches belonging to the creamery, overseeing farm operations while his brother paid his living expenses. Practicing model farming techniques at his local ranches, Wingfield intended to "demonstrate to all the success that comes through proper methods and the right selection of breeding stock." In recognition of his efforts, George Wingfield was appointed in 1914 to the State Agricultural Society. Unfortunately, the success he anticipated proved elusive. The Churchill Creamery was eventually sold in 1921, after disappointing profits. By 1922, Wingfield was offering his Churchill County ranches for sale or exchange for some property "that is up-to-date, and upon an income basis." For a brief period in the 1910s, however, George Wingfield shared the prevailing faith of the U.S. Reclamation Service and the Lahontan Valley farmers that "this valley will blossom as few sections of the world can do."[24]

And he was willing to invest part of his fortune to bring that faith to fruition. In 1916, for instance, as part of an ongoing search for viable Nevada crops, he invested along with a group from Michigan in the bankrupt Nevada Sugar Company. This company had been founded in 1911, in hopes that Churchill County might become a beet sugar center. Uninstructed local farmers knew little about growing beets, however, and irrigation difficulties decimated the crops. The factory remained idle from 1913 until 1916, when Wingfield and the new investors leased the property to the Utah-Idaho Sugar Company. This time, wartime prices for hay were so high that few farmers cared to sign contracts to produce sugar beets, and it closed again in 1918. Although this agricultural venture, too, proved disappointing, Wingfield undertook it with high hopes, intending once again to demonstrate to a skeptical outside world that Nevada's soil and climate were not deficient.[25]

At about the same time, in 1911, George Wingfield also invested in California agriculture, when he helped organize the Sutter Butte Canal Company in Butte County, near Oroville. This corporation owned no land, but held a valuable water right to the Feather River. Its business was providing irrigation water to farmers by way of 57 miles of main canals and 131 miles of laterals. Wingfield purchased some of the new company's bonds along with GCMC investor J. D. Hubbard and several others, including former GCMC superintendent J. H. MacKenzie. It was to be, along with GCMC, one of his longest-lived investments. Here, in contrast to Nevada, agricultural potential was virtually unlimited. The Sutter Butte Canal Company helped sponsor the initial California rice-growing experiments, with seed imported from Louisiana, which ultimately established the prosperous new industry on a commercial basis beginning in 1913. It also supported orchards in the area. At first George Wingfield was simply an investor and the company was locally run. In 1921, however, he assumed active management and placed the company under the supervision of Estey Julian. Although there were some difficult years during the financially troubled 1930s, the company survived and expanded, and Wingfield continued to own his stock until the company itself was dissolved in 1957, just two years before his death.[26]

Another Wingfield agricultural venture clearly fell into the pleasure category. In 1910, he purchased a 320-acre ranch near the Honey Lake Valley outside Susanville, California, which he named Meadowbrook Ranch. He was familiar with the area from earlier hunting trips there, held under the auspices of the Pacific Coast Bear Club, of which he was a member as early as 1907. A dedicated hunter, George Wingfield prided himself on his skill with a gun. He was a good shot throughout his life. Bear-hunting trips to Lassen County introduced him to the picturesque, forested foothill country seventy-five miles northwest of Reno. He purchased the ranch there as a summer resort for his wife, who made plans for a large, 2-story residence with accompanying guest house, greenhouse, fish ponds, and outbuildings.[27]

Meadowbrook was George Wingfield's first major indulgence since making his fortune, and his excitement was obvious in a letter to Congressman George Bartlett, asking for numerous farm bulletins:

> I am starting to be a farmer so be sure and hustle all of these for me . . . don't you miss one of these numbers or by H. [*sic*] I will not give you one of these geese when they are raised. I am buying a ranch on the west side of Honey Lake and filling it up for a summer home. everthing [*sic*] is going well with me, and if they keep going a little more I will be even on what the panic took away from me.

Sparing no expense, he made the ranch into a showplace. The house was completed that same fall and Wingfield imported numerous exotic animals, including peacocks, buffalo, and a herd of elk that formerly belonged to Governor John Sparks. In 1912, following the same pattern of stock improvement he had announced in Churchill County, he imported an English stallion for Meadowbrook, to be made available to local breeders at such terms "as will give everyone a chance to raise the standard of horse flesh." He steadily purchased more land as it became available, and eventually built two fish ponds which he stocked with trout. By 1913, he owned 1,640 acres of land and a pleasure boat on Honey Lake, which he used both to entertain guests and for duck hunting. Over the years, a number of eminent visitors experienced Wingfield's hospitality at Meadowbrook Ranch, including Nixon, Baruch, Oddie, and Crocker.[28]

The far-flung empire that Wingfield assembled by activities such as these was too vast and complicated for personal attention, and he relied on accurate and detailed field reports from his engineers and managers for the information he needed to make business decisions. As he expanded his operations, therefore, he was in perpetual need of new employees. Individual managers were hired to run the Churchill Creamery and Meadowbrook Ranch, as well as the various mining companies. Wingfield required absolute loyalty and undivided attention from these men. Supervision of all the various scattered operations was then centered in Reno, where Clarence Burton and his successors served as a clearinghouse for information coming in from the field and disseminated instructions from Wingfield. The Reno office also kept the

Wingfield's country retreat at Meadowbrook Ranch,
in northeastern California, was his pride and joy during the 1910s.
His wife and children often spent summers there.
The property is presently operated as a summer camp.
(Courtesy of Polly W. Kline)

Hunting, particularly for ducks and other birds,
was a sport that George Wingfield enjoyed throughout his life.
Here he is seated on the right. (Courtesy of Polly W. Kline)

financial records of the various companies, which were reported for income tax purposes beginning in 1913.[29]

Maintaining familiarity with his businesses and properties was a matter of intricately coordinated effort. Despite his immense fortune, George Wingfield did not retire to a life of leisure. Instead he maintained a strenuous schedule, traveling frequently through the state to visit the banks for quarterly directors' meetings and inspecting his various mining and ranching properties. His scattered employees all required some direction from the central office, and Wingfield liked to keep an eye on his investments. Occasionally illness intervened, as in the summer of 1910, when he spent two months in San Francisco for treatment of what began as ptomaine poisoning and then developed into an abscess on the liver. At such times his absence from his customary activities (apparently amplified in this case by the rancor of George Graham Rice) led to reports in the national press that he was dying. So closely was Wingfield identified with his business interests, particularly the mining companies, that his health and active participation became a matter of keen interest in the financial markets. He had become, in every respect, a public figure, a man whose pronouncements on Nevada and on mining were actively solicited by the press and taken seriously by men who mattered nationally.[30]

In such an atmosphere, it was no wonder that George Wingfield developed a thorough appreciation of his own power and importance in Nevada. Having invested widely and significantly in the state, as no previous mining baron had done, he expected to receive a certain consideration in return. Wingfield candidly described the way he saw things to a Reno newspaper reporter in August 1910, as he announced his intention to oppose certain candidates who were seeking political office "before their feet have become calloused by the burning sands":

> This is a defensive measure, as I am actually and indirectly one of the largest taxpayers in the state. Nevada must be for Nevadans. This is the beginning of a new era, when the men who make their money in the state want to spend it here. . . . If Nevada voters permit the men of capital to leave the state, being really driven therefrom by the vampires, buzzards, and jackals of newspaperdom and politics, the state alone will be to blame.[31]

In 1911, he reiterated the same sentiment, this time privately, in a handwritten letter to his old friend from Tonopah, Tasker Oddie. In February 1911, when he wrote, Oddie was the newly inaugurated progressive Republican governor of Nevada and Wingfield was in San Francisco, recovering from surgery on January 25 to remove his appendix. His tone was less dramatic than in the earlier newspaper interview, but the reasoning was exactly the same:

> No doubt you will be surprised to hear from me, but I always need something to do. Am pretty good again but my locomotion is not good yet.
>
> I notice they [Nevada State Legislature] are trying to pass some drastic labor bills, which of course are annoying. The people of Nevada have always howled because people who make money don't stay there to spend it. Am afraid such legislation will help drive others out who have attempted to stay and help build up the resources of the state. . . . the man who puts his money in the ground should be incouraged [*sic*] instead of discouraged.[32]

As a man of parts, one willing to risk his capital on building up Nevada, George Wingfield felt himself entitled to recompense. He sought to protect his businesses against any legislation that he considered adverse or taxation that he considered unfair. Wingfield did not always get what he wanted, of course, but he invariably used the threat—either implicit or overt—of withdrawing his money from the state altogether to insure that no inimical measures would succeed. In 1914, for instance, when Nevada was debating a constitutional amendment granting women the right to vote, George Wingfield was not at all subtle about his opposition. In an interview in the *San Francisco Chronicle*, which was widely reprinted in Nevada, he declared "that if women are allowed to vote in Nevada by the adoption of the suffrage amendment at the coming election, he will close up his interests, including farming, banking and mining and leave Nevada." [33]

Purportedly, Wingfield feared that the votes of radical women would undermine Nevada's "conservative and consistent development," while their conservative counterparts, "matching the same vote among the men," would stay home. In this particular case, ridicule rather than recanting greeted Wingfield's pronouncement. Nevada's *Manhattan Post* printed a poem entitled, "Where You Goin', George?" which noted sarcastically that no place was safe for a man of his peculiar opinions now that women were voting in other states. A suffrage supporter in Carson City archly inquired, "What on earth can Mr. Wingfield want that he thinks the women of Nevada might refuse him?" Some hint of the latter can be found in the political alliances that Wingfield formed with other opponents of suffrage. He contributed to pay the expenses of Minnie Bronson, general secretary of the National Association Opposed to Woman's Suffrage, who toured the state to speak against suffrage; and he counseled Clarence Sage, then at the Buckhorn mine in Eureka County, to "see John Swan, Snider and all the other saloon keepers and get them to plug against this suffrage proposition. Also talk to anybody else you can without getting them to go in the opposite direction." In the end, while suffrage was defeated in the major Nevada cities, the votes in the small towns and mining camps such as Buckhorn were enough to carry the proposition for the state as a whole. The force of Wingfield's threat diminished considerably when he did not immediately depart; but the reasoning behind it remained the foundation of his political thinking in the 1910s.[34]

Yet, despite his emphatic and well-publicized stands on political issues such as suffrage, George Wingfield saw himself in the 1910s as an influential businessman, not a politician. He summarized his position in 1912, for the *Reno Evening Gazette*: "Politics doesn't interest me anyhow, except in the aiding of my friends and in furthering the interest of men and policies which I believe to be right." Generally, these men were Republican friends from Tonopah and Goldfield, such as Nixon and Oddie, and the policies were those to be expected from any conservative businessman. In 1910, for instance, when Nixon was running for reelection to the senate against Tonopah attorney Key Pittman, Wingfield confided to Bernard Baruch, "I am doing everything in the world I can for the Senator and do not think there is any question about his election."[35]

Continuing the pattern they had developed in Tonopah, Wingfield still served as the senator's local eyes and ears, although now on political matters. In March 1912, for instance, Wingfield consulted with Nixon about the political chances of Republican president William Taft. He sent Nixon an extended analysis of former president Theodore Roosevelt's popularity in Nevada and of local resentment of the conservation policies ordered by Roosevelt's Forest Service appointee, Gifford Pinchot. Yet Wingfield's political interest was not a simple matter of party allegiance, either. In 1910, Wingfield wrote to his friend George Bartlett, then Democratic congressman from Nevada, urging him to run again for the office: "All your friends in both parties want to see you go back to Congress and not get into this other fight [for governor] . . . of course I am not in politics and am a free lance and can split my ticket any way I see fit as I am not with the ring on either side."[36]

His political beliefs were conventionally Republican, no doubt initially gained through his association with Nixon but then reinforced by the acquisition of his own economic empire. Wingfield elaborated on these in a 1914 speech in Fallon, where he condemned professional politicians and the indiscriminate mixing of politics and business. Wingfield clearly recognized the interdependence of the two; but in his mind, private economic initiative such as his own offered a greater and more reliable stimulus for social renewal than any government initiative:

> We have gone too far and too fast and with too much politics mixed in with our business affairs. . . . Our economical questions should not be looked upon from the personal standpoint but wholly from the point of the public good. . . . We want a legislature that will pass laws which will tend to build up our state and not to tear it down.

Skeptical listeners might have questioned the extent to which George Wingfield identified his own personal interests with the "public good"; but this was standard Republican rhetoric of the period, advocating rational and efficient administrative practices in government as in business.[37]

The sincerity of Wingfield's commitment to business rather than politics was confirmed after Nixon's sudden death in 1912, when he was offered the chance to assume national political office and turned it down. George Nixon died unexpectedly in Washington, D.C., on June 5. A state holiday was declared for the day of his elaborate funeral in Reno, on June 11, at which Wingfield served as an active pallbearer. On June 12, Governor Tasker Oddie, an old friend to both men, although a sometime political opponent of Nixon, appointed Wingfield to fill Nixon's vacant senate seat until the general election that fall. Oddie's reasons went well beyond the fact that Wingfield had been closely identified with Nixon:

> He possesses a wonderfully strong and pleasing personality, an iron nerve, unexcelled business ability and integrity and an intimate knowledge of the general conditions and needs of the State. He is largely identified with many of its most important industries, and is constantly endeavoring to start new ones. In fact, I consider him one of the strongest and ablest men in this Western country. . . . He is fundamentally a man of action and accomplishment, broad-minded and possessing clear, cool judgment.

Although the appointment was generally lauded by the Nevada press, Wingfield surprised the world by asking for time to consider it. He wanted, among other things, to weigh the conflicting demands of other obligations to business associates:

> I am loath to accept a public office without feeling assured of my ability to give it an attention, untrammeled by personal concerns, which the public have a right to exact. . . . Another phase of the question which

demands serious thought on my part is the consideration as to whether I can serve the state as well in official capacity in Washington as by private business activity within its borders. From the state of Nevada I have derived much of success and material welfare, and I feel a deep sense of obligation to the state and to its people.[38]

True to his word, he began consulting prominent eastern investment partners. His correspondence with steel baron Henry Clay Frick is representative. On June 14, George Wingfield wrote a general letter reporting on conditions in GCMC and Nevada Hills and then explaining his ambivalence about the appointment:

> I realize perfectly that it is a great honor and I am quite sure that I would have no trouble in being reelected. Still . . . my business judgment tells me that I should decline the appointment as I believe I owe that much to my friends who have placed the confidence in me . . . relying entirely upon my personal recommendations. . . . I realize too, that a public office is a thankless job.

Frick wired him on June 19: "my advice is to continue as you are. You will be happier thus and will stand even higher in every one's esteem than you do now." He cautioned in a letter the same day, however, that Wingfield should decide the matter for himself and that "very few men would have the courage to decline it." Within the state, others were counseling him to accept the appointment. A petition from Churchill County asked Wingfield to accept the senatorship: "You are personally interested in the principal industries of our County and State and from personal knowledge know our needs." Even his critics expected him to succumb to temptation. One of Democratic U.S. senator Key Pittman's political lieutenants reported his reading of the situation: "It looks to me as though Wingfield will get it if they can drag him into the game. I understand he is not anxious to get in, but there is an awful pressure being brought to bear on him and Governor Oddie." Wingfield announced publicly that he was going fishing to think things over, but by June 27 the decision was made and he told Frick casually that "I have never yet given the matter very serious consideration."[39]

On July 1, 1912, he publicly disclosed his decision to Governor Oddie: "My survey of the wide field of thought which your tender of the office thus opened has led me to the conclusion that I can not accept this great office at the present time, in justice to the state, to its people, or to myself." His reasons were the ones he had advanced earlier, that many men of wealth depended on his supervision of their Nevada investments. As a private citizen, Wingfield was able to direct substantial capital into the development of Nevada. As a senator, he could offer less to his state:

> The satisfactory performance of the duties of a senatorship may be found in many directions, but the development of the industries of an empire of 112,000 square miles is reserved to few. . . . Were I to accept the office, whatever might be the character of my senatorial service, the state would inevitably lose something which I can give only by remaining for a time in private life.

In the national press, George Wingfield instantly became "The Cowboy Who Refused a Toga," hailed as "the only man in American history who refused a seat in the United States Senate. . . ."[40]

Frick was right. Declining the senate appointment brought George Wingfield squarely into the national limelight and greatly increased his stature. The friendly *Goldfield Tribune* summarized his decision in complimentary terms: "The battle was between personal ambition and the immediate interests of the state of Nevada. The latter won." The *New York Mining Age*, however, a paper with no motive for flattery, was equally adulatory:

> [Declining] shows pretty conclusively that Mr. Wingfield is a man built on the broadest possible lines of business activity. It is possibly a rare occurrence nowadays to hear of an American citizen being offered so high an honor and still possessing sufficient tact to decline to accept it realizing that by so doing he would throw in a jeopardy the resources of his adopted state.

The consensus in the national press was that "a man who is strong enough to refuse a United States Senatorship is worth while inquiring about." And inquire they did. In the months and years immediately after his refusal of the senate appointment, George Wingfield appeared in feature articles across the country, and the story of his rise to riches was repeated in endless, mostly garbled versions. That this rush of national media attention did not turn his head truly was remarkable and suggested the accuracy of the observation: "For a man of his years and training [Wingfield] has remarkable poise."[41]

It was not false modesty that led Wingfield to refuse Oddie's appointment, however. The former cowboy and gambler was neither prepared nor ambitious for public office. The laconic Wingfield was as keenly aware of his limitations as he was of his abilities. Some of the former were remarked by Nixon's democratic opponent for the senate seat, Key Pittman, in 1912. Writing to a political lieutenant several months before Nixon's death, Pittman sagely observed:

> I think that George Wingfield has in mind running for Governor. I do not believe that he is weak enough to be induced to run for the U. S. Senate. His observations of Senator Nixon's career must have convinced him that he is not equipped to gain any reputation as a United States Senator.

Always more comfortable behind the scenes than in the limelight, Wingfield shunned the publicity that would inevitably haunt a typecast Horatio Alger senator from Nevada. Wingfield was also such an inveterate westerner that he was unhappy being away from his high desert home, immersed in eastern humidity and humanity, for any length of time.[42]

If these considerations weren't enough to dissuade him, there was always the threat of embarrassing exposure by his foes. In July 1912, the memory of May Baric's public suit in California was not long distant, and the list of George Wingfield enemies certainly hadn't shrunk. Perennial adversary George Graham Rice was apparently still actively combating Wingfield. Shortly after the latter declined the senatorial appointment, Governor Tasker Oddie passed along a state police report about the source of "the several viciously unfair and untruthful writeups of you in some of the Eastern press." Not surprisingly, "the source of all writings after investigation has been traced to George Graham Rice."[43]

Something of their flavor is suggested by an editorial in the *Washington, D.C. Pathfinder,* which expressed approval that Wingfield had declined the senate seat because: "He is a notorious gambler and mine speculator and it is a disgrace to all concerned to have men of that stamp in the senate." At roughly the same time, an unsigned article in the *Literary Digest* quoted a *New York Press* account of Wingfield as "a true representative of what remains of the 'wild and wooly' West." Classifying George Wingfield as "one of the best known gun men and gamblers in the Golden West," the *Digest* depicted him atmospherically, in terms vaguely reminiscent of Rice's own prose:

> Wingfield's gaze never was steady. It continually shifted to and fro, perhaps a matter of habit. A man who deals or works as a lookout in a gambling-house has to keep a swiftly-shifting eye on every part of the board. Wingfield was cold of manner and taciturn of disposition. He was noted for his secretiveness.

In any event, it was not a description likely to reflect credit on the new senator.[44]

And Rice wasn't his only worry. By 1912, Wingfield had fallen out with infamous Goldfield mine owner and gunman "Diamondfield" Jack Davis, who had been a valuable henchman during the violent labor confrontations in 1906 and 1907. Davis was angry because he thought he had been "skinned" by Wingfield in a business deal, accusing the latter of having a policy "to use any one he can and then throw them aside like a broken branch." In an emotional 1913 letter to Governor Oddie, Davis accused Wingfield of having driven him out of Nevada and warned ominously, "Had he tried to take his seat in the Senate I would have fought him off the cross. . . . I can show him that men who live in glass houses had better not throw stones." In view of the many good practical reasons not to accept the senate appointment, it is tempting to suspect George Wingfield's official reasons for doing so; but they are entirely in keeping with his evolving philosophy of public service in the 1910s.[45]

He thus remained in private life, with a family now enlarged by the birth of a daughter Jean on February 6, 1912, and relocated to the comfortable four-bedroom residence that would remain his lifelong home, at 219 Court Street in Reno. Nixon's death left an economic as well as a political void, however, and Wingfield moved quickly to fill the former. By October 1912, the 36-year-old George Wingfield had assumed the presidency of three former Nixon banks: First National Bank of Winnemucca, Nixon National Bank in Reno (and its savings affiliate, the Bank of Nevada Savings and Trust Company), and Carson City's Carson Valley Bank, which Nixon had acquired in 1910. In cooperation with Nixon's longtime bank vice-president, F. M. Lee, Wingfield took over active management of the banks, a move that prompted conjectural headlines in the *New York Curb*: "Will Goldfield Con.'s President Quit Mining for Banking?"[46]

In truth, something of the sort seemed to be happening. Wingfield was now president of four Nevada banks, including John S. Cook & Co. in Gold-field. In 1914, he purchased the Nixon estate's stock in the two national banks, at Winnemucca and Reno. In that same year, he was named vice-president of the American Banker's Association for Nevada and began to give newspaper interviews on federal banking legislation. It was not a role he assumed easily. He initially took over the banks to help Nixon's widow, but found that they occupied more of his time than he wanted. By September, he was complaining to her that, "could I sell my stock even at a loss, I think I would be willing to do so and retire from the banking business in the city of Reno, as going into this bank has taken up so much of my time that I have neglected my own affairs to a great extent."[47]

By 1915, however, George Wingfield was firmly entrenched in his new role as Nevada's banker. Having taken over the Nixon interests altogether, he announced plans in that year to build a splendid new building for his flagship Reno bank. When the $250,000, four-story building on the corner of Virginia and Second streets was completed in 1916, the institution it housed was no longer the Nixon National, but the Reno National Bank. By 1918, as a new mining boom near Tonopah began attracting attention, he had taken over another former Nixon property, the Tonopah Banking Corporation. After two cashiers defaulted on loans they made to themselves, Wingfield came to the aid of his friend and fellow mine investor, Cal Brougher, by providing new capital and assuming the presidency of the bank.[48]

Although mining continued to occupy a considerable portion of Wingfield's time, the fortunes of GCMC were clearly in decline by the middle of the decade. As early as 1912, the company was having trouble arriving at any reliable estimate of its ore reserves, which were increasingly spotty and intractable at the lower depths. In 1913, in a move that provoked controversy, GCMC stock was removed from the New York Stock Exchange and returned to being traded on the less stringent New York Curb Market. At the time, there were unsavory charges that GCMC management wanted to manipulate the market in their own stock in order to boost a number of other cheap Wingfield mining stocks, which would then be sold before the market collapsed altogether. In 1914, GCMC general manager Albert Burch frankly acknowledged, "So far as the Goldfield Consolidated is concerned, everyone knows that the cream has been skimmed and that we are now doing our best to subsist on skimmed milk. . . . We are now working a low-grade mine." Seeking alternatives to restore GCMC's fortunes, the company that year purchased a controlling interest in the old gold and silver mining properties at Aurora, Nevada, the Aurora Consolidated Mines Company. Attempts to revive mining there resulted in a loss by 1916, however, and company reports after 1915 were increasingly negative in tone.[49]

The company won a gold medal in that year for its display of gold quartz ore at the Panama-California Exposition in San Diego, California, but specimen ore was becoming scarce in the ground by then. Indeed, 1915 was the year that GCMC general manager Joseph W. Hutchinson first suggested that the company establish a separate branch to find new mining properties. By 1916, GCMC had established such an office in San Francisco, "for the purpose of investigating, with a view to purchase, some of the many hundreds of properties which have been submitted during the past few years." In 1917, this operation, headed by newly promoted consulting engineer Estey A. Julian, was incorporated as a GCMC subsidiary, the Goldfield Consolidated Mines Exploration Company. Julian and occasional contract engineers fanned out across the West and even into South America, in search of likely looking prospects to replace the erstwhile colossus at Goldfield.[50]

The annual report for 1917 cited "particularly discouraging conditions" in explaining net profit for the year of only $128,500. By 1918, the end was in sight. The much-heralded 100-stamp mill shut down operations on January 31, 1919. Closure of the mill marked the end of an era, both for the waning desert community and for the man who had gotten his start there. As Wingfield sadly explained to former GCMC detective Clarence Sage, it was no longer economical to maintain the company's Goldfield headquarters: "I had hoped to strike something new so as to be able to keep up the organization but it has come now to a stage where that seems impossible." Sage was advised to find other work by January 1, 1919, and Wingfield prepared to move the GCMC records to Reno.[51]

There he turned his attention increasingly to other matters. Already in 1913, there were some signs of strain in his marriage. Claiming that he gave his wife a more than adequate allowance, Wingfield canceled all of her charge accounts and insisted that she pay cash for any orders that she placed. Apparently there was a disparity between their respective styles of living, as the *San Francisco Examiner* inadvertently revealed in January 1913, when it heralded daughter Jean's first trip to California, with her mother and a retinue of maids and nurses, under headlines announcing "Lavish Suite for Millionaire Baby." The man who rolled his own cigarettes and answered his own correspondence had little sympathy for his wife's elaborate tastes. The *Salt Lake Tribune* described him in 1913 in familiar terms: "open and above board, plain and unpretentious, easily approached and differing in no particulars in his personal appearance from the thousands of fellow citizens in Nevada who know him intimately." His own luxuries were less conspicuous, and his wife's extravagance was a constant source of friction. It became an issue again in 1916, when Wingfield advertised in the San Francisco newspapers that he would no longer be responsible for any bills that she incurred.[52]

In the meantime, another child, George Wingfield, Jr., was born to the couple in 1914, in Reno. The couple separated again in 1915, when Maude Wingfield took the two children to live in San Francisco. During the next few years, there were reconciliations and further separations. Finally, in July 1917, George Wingfield filed suit for divorce in Reno, charging his wife with extreme cruelty and seeking custody of the children. In the complaint he alleged, among other things, that she had been extravagant and that she regarded Reno as too small. A 1916 contract between the two had settled all questions of property and granted Maude Wingfield an allowance of $9,000 per year, so only the custody matter was in dispute. The suit was heard in

Maude Murdoch Wingfield and her children,
Jean and George, Jr., ca. 1916.
(Courtesy of Nevada Historical Society)

September 1917; but the Wingfields ultimately reconciled again after she suffered a nervous breakdown and it was dropped. After 1917, however, they rarely lived together.[53]

In May 1918, during a period of their joint residence at the St. Francis Hotel, the San Francisco papers reported a "mysterious accident" to Maude Wingfield's nose, which required the attention of a physician. George Wingfield left for Reno the day after the accident, and his wife filed suit seeking both divorce and separate maintenance shortly thereafter. In June, the two of them were in Reno, she at the Court Street house and he in a hotel, still negotiating. As George Wingfield confided to his attorney at the time, "I can not see any chance for any satisfactory arrangement being made whereby we could occupy the same house as it is simply a fuss every few minutes . . . but at the present time I can see that her intentions are simply to stock [*sic*] around here and be as disagreeable as possible." Nonetheless, they were reconciled again by October 1918, and he nursed her through the pneumonia that developed in November after she contracted Spanish influenza. Thereafter they lived apart, she in San Francisco and he in Reno, with custody of the children divided between them. It was another decade, until 1929, before they were finally divorced.[54]

Meanwhile, Wingfield also embarked on a number of other new ventures. In 1914, reviving an old love from Golconda on a new, opulent scale, he announced plans to establish a thoroughbred racing stable on 100 acres of land south of Reno, formerly part of the Alamo Ranch of Governor John Sparks. The purchase was described by the *San Francisco Examiner* as laying the groundwork for making Reno a major center of horse racing; and Wingfield clarified his intentions to a Reno newspaper reporter in February: "I am not going into the racing business, but I do admire thoroughbred horses in this state." He clearly approved, however, of an anticipated revival of horse racing at Reno: "If this can be done there will be a large attendance at every meeting and an immense amount of money will change hands." Always enthusiastic about anything that might promote the state, George Wingfield saw racing as a potential boon, although he specified that he favored only the pari-mutuel system of betting, "which is fair and gives the patron a chance."[55]

Horse racing was sternly regarded as unsavory by some elements of the community; but it was generally supported by breeders, who proclaimed themselves "anxious to re-establish racing not for the benefit of the race track promoter, but to encourage the raising of good horses." Wingfield's ranch background had given him an abiding interest in livestock, and he began to carry through his horse farm scheme in August 1914. He instructed his attorneys, the Reno firm of Hoyt, Gibbons and French, to incorporate the new company as the Nevada Stock Farm. Significantly, the owner specified,

"I also want the charter to include the power to race or run horses in all states but would rather that this be not mentioned in the articles of incorporation unless you think that it is necessary and will not come under the general powers." He began to purchase blooded stock for the operation, and in 1915, "hoping to benefit by a marked reduction in the price of thoroughbred horse-flesh on account of the European war," he sent his stock farm superintendent and a veterinarian to England to buy "equine bluebloods."[56]

Meanwhile, Wingfield secured from the 1915 Nevada Legislature a bill legalizing pari-mutuel betting on horse races, thus insuring local race meetings for his horses. By August 1915, scarcely a year after incorporation of the stock farm, Wingfield hosted over 200 people at a barbecue to celebrate the first running of the Nevada Derby. Fittingly, his horse, racing under the Nevada colors of silver and blue that identified the Nevada Stock Farm, won the event. In coming years, there were to be many more such winners, and George Wingfield became prominently identified with horse racing in Nevada. In 1916, he was appointed by Governor Emmet Boyle to the Nevada State Racing Commission, which had been established to oversee state-sanctioned betting. He held that office until 1946.[57]

Even more than Meadowbrook Ranch, the racing stable was a plaything for the man who had always appreciated the beauty of fine horseflesh. The Nevada Stock Farm allowed Wingfield to hone and then test his considerable skills as a breeder. He assembled a large library on the subject of horse breeding and read assiduously in it. His trainer, Preston Burch, a member of the Thoroughbred Racing Trainers Hall of Fame, later reported that Wingfield "knew more about horses than anyone he had ever worked for." Wingfield also amassed large numbers of animals. When the United States prepared to enter World War I in April 1917, he offered horses from Nevada Stock Farm for use by the cavalry. The entire stable then numbered more than 100 purebred and 500 mixed breed horses. As was the case for his other ventures, George Wingfield was willing to spend money for skilled help, including jockeys and trainers. His horses ran and won at meets throughout the country and in Mexico. Eventually, as his animals became national contenders in the 1920s, he expanded the Nevada Stock Farm operation to a second breeding farm in Louisville, Kentucky. There Burch produced famous winners like Hygro, which set a world speed record, and General Thatcher, which was briefly expected to win the Kentucky Derby and placed third at the Preakness Stakes in 1923. Until 1932, when financial disaster forced him to sell his stable at auction, operation of the Nevada Stock Farm and attending race meetings remained Wingfield's principal hobbies outside of hunting.[58]

In October 1915, as GCMC's decline was accelerating, George Wingfield symbolically completed his economic transition out of mining with the organization of the Reno Securities Company (RSC). This corporation, which Wingfield would own until 1955, began modestly, as a holding company devised by Clarence Burton to organize the purchase by several investors of Reno's Hotel Golden. It grew into something bigger, however, eventually building and operating the luxurious Riverside Hotel in the 1920s and owning the Spanish Springs Ranch in the 1930s. Over the years, RSC would prove to be one of Wingfield's most dependable investments, more durable if less spectacular than any of his mines. Along with the growing network of banks, it formed the centerpiece of a second Wingfield empire based on real estate and business. George Wingfield certainly didn't abandon mining. He remained emotionally identified with "the mining game" throughout his life, and he owned and operated various mines until his death in 1959. But with the formation of RSC, he began to move his fortune increasingly into commerce.[59]

This company was certainly compatible with Wingfield's professed philosophy of making investments that would expand Nevada's economy. Yet it also marked a new direction, implicating him in a business that depended for growth not just on soliciting outside dollars from anonymous investors, as mining did, but on the ability to attract a steady stream of newcomers to an isolated location. Outsiders would have to fill the hotels and buy the real estate in order to make them lucrative and incidentally help promote the diversification that Wingfield had been advocating since he left Goldfield. By investing in RSC, he made himself, perhaps unwittingly at first, a major force in that campaign to lure newcomers. George Wingfield's economic involvement in Reno's hotel business gave him an abiding interest in attracting tourists and thus implicated him politically in the development of Nevada's divorce industry and later in its legalization of casino gambling.[60]

This new stage of Wingfield's economic empire was symbolized by his move in 1916 to new offices on the second floor of the Reno National Bank Building. His suite of rooms there overlooked the small city of some 11,000, whose fortunes—in Wingfield's eyes—were synonymous with his own. From his mahogany rolltop desk in room 203 he presided not simply over his money, but also over the growth and development of the state. The visions that Wingfield entertained in these offices, which came to be known as "the cave," had profound consequences for the entire state of Nevada. Whether the power that emanated from the bank building was ultimately a beneficent or malevolent influence, its existence was real and undoubted, both within the state and beyond its borders.

SEVEN

"Probably the Wealthiest Man in Nevada"

I N 1916, George Wingfield turned forty. A mature man, he was now in full and undisputed command of an emerging economic empire he erected around the banks and hotels that gradually replaced GCMC as his most lucrative investments. This second Wingfield empire was more diversified than the first. In addition to the centerpiece Reno Securities Company and the banks, there were myriad smaller undertakings of which Wingfield might be only a partial owner. In 1915, for instance, he invested in the Lundy Gas Engine Company, which needed capital to develop a new automobile engine designed by engineer C. A. Lundy. In 1916, in a move intended to reduce expenses for Nevada mineowners, Wingfield financed a Reno machine shop and foundry, Nevada Engineering and Supply Company. This varied pattern of expansion, on top of his existing ownership of mines and ranches, involved him in virtually every aspect of Nevada's economy. As a tireless promoter of these ventures—and others he founded in the 1920s—he became, in fact, a kind of economic overlord of the state. Until the collapse of his banks in 1932, George Wingfield reigned from his Reno National Bank office as an insistent but doting emperor over an expanding realm.[1]

In middle age, the contours of his life gradually smoothed as its routine became fixed. Certain characteristics were clearly established and persisted for the rest of his life. Among them was his notoriety. At least since the time of his appointment to the U.S. Senate, Wingfield's exploits had been covered in the national press. Inevitably, this publicity imparted celebrity. It made him a public man whose actions and beliefs were a matter of curiosity to others. Wingfield's movements and decisions were newsworthy and his plans and motives were a matter for conjecture. In the splendor of his spectacular rags-to-riches career, George Wingfield acquired public status as an icon.

He even plagued the dreams of other men, as in the bizarre case of Nevada's Democratic attorney general, C. H. Baker. The latter died at a young age, in 1912, of a cerebral hemorrhage that struck after a nightmare in which he dreamed he had been shot by George Wingfield. The *San Francisco Call* covered the incident in the context of an unrelated, purported Wingfield plot to win a U.S. Senate seat in the 1914 election.[2]

The attention that his prominence brought was unwelcome, for the most part. George Wingfield thoroughly enjoyed the exercise of economic and political power, but he never relished the limelight. His experiences with May Baric and George Graham Rice undoubtedly had something to do with this reticence, but he was also a reserved man by nature. After the first flush of success at Goldfield, he had little to gain by further publicity of his exploits. Indeed, he risked attracting unwelcome attention. In July 1915, for instance, he received two threatening letters from "The Organization." The letters demanded $15,000, later reduced to $10,000, or else Wingfield and his property would come to harm. While no incident resulted, the experience clearly unnerved him. Nonetheless, public interest in and media coverage of his actions was unflagging.[3]

Although there were still isolated episodes of personal violence, as in a 1915 quarrel with Reno newspaper editor Boyd Moore, when Wingfield broke the latter's nose, they were less frequent and usually associated with alcohol. Wingfield reportedly swore "like an old rancher"; but drinking was his major vice, one which he indulged frequently and often excessively. He periodically vowed to quit but succeeded only at the age of fifty-five, in 1932. In the meantime, his public deportment was not uniformly dignified. Clarence Burton observed one lapse in San Francisco in 1915 and reported it with some trepidation to his boss:

> I understand that you have resumed your seat on the water wagon. I do not want to be presumptuous but if you had seen yourself tacking across the St. Francis lobby as I did last Sunday a week ago and the comments that followed you, I think booze would be a stranger thereafter. This is not advice, which I am not in a position to offer, but a statement of a fact in my knowledge which I think I should tell you.[4]

Despite occasional periods of forswearing alcohol in the intervening years, Wingfield's behavior was essentially unchanged twelve years later. In 1927, when another Wingfield business associate was lecturing about an employee's drinking problem, and the problems of public perception, he observed sanctimoniously that Wingfield could afford to behave the way that he did only because he had a network of trusted employees to attend to his business:

"Mr. Wingfield does these things himself but you don't find Julian, Laurie [Arthur H. Lawry, mine superintendent], Zobel [William Zoebel, office manager], Sheehan [J. A. Sheehan, bank vice-president] and others in whome [*sic*] he has confidence doeing [*sic*] them, its [*sic*] because they do not that he has that confidence in them otherwise they would not stay with him two minuets [*sic*]." That same year, after numerous predinner cocktails with his attorneys, George Thatcher and William Woodburn, and their wives, George Wingfield began telling a story to Mrs. Woodburn, who was his dinner partner. He emphasized the high points by poking her in the ribs with his pistol. Mrs. Woodburn was rescued by her husband's observant partner, George Thatcher, who disarmed his host while muttering that he was "a damned old fool." Wingfield later apologized profusely and ordered Chevrolet sportsters delivered to both William Woodburn, Jr., and Thatcher's daughter, Ruth, to make amends for his behavior.[5]

Possibly linked to his drinking, George Wingfield was also prone to illness. The local superintendent of the Virginia and Truckee Railroad candidly described Wingfield's personal habits to railroad owner Ogden Mills: "while he travels the straight and narrow most of the time when he relaxes he stays at home and makes a business of drinking which is always followed by a sick spell." Chronically afflicted with colds, Wingfield frequently battled cases of flu that he couldn't seem to shake. In 1915 and 1916, he had tonsillitis; his tonsils were finally removed in February 1917. He had some kind of cold or flu most every winter, and a bad case of hay fever most summers.[6]

When he wasn't sick, he traveled frequently, typically combining business with pleasure. Quarterly directors' meetings at his various banks and businesses took him throughout the state of Nevada and were sometimes extended to include a hunting trip. In San Francisco he visited his family and his personal bankers at Crocker National Bank and sought relief from illness. Political and company affairs took him east to Washington, D.C., and New York, and sometimes on to racetracks in the United States, Canada, and Mexico, where his Nevada Stock Farm thoroughbreds were running. A Lexington, Kentucky, branch of the Nevada Stock Farm was also a regular destination.

George Wingfield's pattern of leisure activity had been set during this younger days. The saloon keeper who raced horses in Golconda still enjoyed betting on the national champions that he now bred and trained at this stables. The crack shot carried throughout his life a .48 caliber revolver he fondly referred to as "Betsy" and greatly enjoyed hunting. Never a socialite, Wingfield remained aloof from the social whirl. He didn't dance and didn't care for formal parties. A member of numerous private clubs throughout the

West, he participated in few except the prestigious Bohemian Club of San Francisco. He remained separated from his wife and family, who lived in San Francisco while he resided at the house on Court Street. There he hosted small dinner parties prepared by the cook and butler that he kept on staff. Frequently, though not exclusively, the guests were all men, a reflection of the male social world of the saloon. Although he prided himself on the contents of his wine cellar, he customarily shared them only with close friends and associates. To the latter he was exceptionally generous, but after the Goldfield banquets George Wingfield never again ostentatiously displayed his riches through elaborate entertaining.[7]

Indeed, his was a life with relatively little opportunity for recreation. In 1918, Wingfield rode the hectic crest of another Tonopah mining boom, this one in the Divide district approximately four miles south of the town of Tonopah. Joining an old Tonopah associate, H. Cal Brougher, he took over a controlling interest in both the Tonopah Banking Corporation and the Tonopah Divide Mining Company. The latter company had belonged to Wingfield and Brougher earlier in the decade and had been mined from 1912 to 1915. In 1916, however, he sold his interests to Brougher, when the veins appeared so slim as to be unprofitable. When the company struck rich ore again early in November 1917, Brougher offered Wingfield an opportunity to buy back in. At the same time, in January 1918, Wingfield invested in the Tonopah Banking Corporation, in a deal that saved the bank and also supplied capital that was needed to develop the Divide mine. In the following two years both partners made millions from the deal, as the stock soared from 30 cents a share to almost $2.00, and they formed a pool to sell their interests in the subsidiary Divide companies for which the main strike had created a market.[8]

The Divide boom lasted just two years, killed in part by falling silver prices after World War I and more immediately by a strike in August 1919. On that occasion the state police were called in when George Wingfield ordered the mines closed rather than give in to the miners' demands for a wage increase. Prices for Divide stocks declined as a result, and, although the mines continued to produce into 1921, the frenzy subsided. At the time, however, the Tonopah mining revival seemed just another instance of the phenomenal "Wingfield Luck." Just as Goldfield entered its final decline, with the GCMC mill closed for good in 1919, George Wingfield struck it rich again in another southern Nevada mining boom. As the *San Francisco Examiner* reported in May 1918, everything Wingfield touched seemed to turn to gold. Sitting at lunch in San Francisco, according to this story, Wingfield made $50,000 without even knowing it. When his companion Zeb Kendall mentioned that Simon Lead stock was selling well, Wingfield remembered that

As a prominent and prosperous businessman,
George Wingfield was invited to join a number of western men's clubs,
among them San Francisco's elite Bohemian Club.
Here the mining magnate is pictured at left,
enjoying a drink at the Bohemian Grove, ca. 1912–1918.
(Courtesy of Polly W. Kline)

he had once owned some. Consulting his vest pocket notebook, he discovered that he still held shares that he had purchased for 30 cents, which were selling that day for $7.[9]

Goldfield, meanwhile, continued its decline into stagnation, as the population sank from perhaps 15,000 to only 1,558 in 1920. In that year a discouraged George Wingfield announced plans to sell the unprofitable Goldfield Hotel. Once the pride of the prosperous southern Nevada town, the luxurious four-story hotel was now too grandiose, out of scale for the area's diminished mining expectations. The decision marked the end of an era, as Wingfield's emotional identification with the community where he had made his greatest fortune dwindled. The mill was closed, GCMC's properties were leased to the Goldfield Deep Mines Company, and the hotel had become a financial drain. Ultimately, however, harsh economic prudence did not prevail. In response to public outcry George Wingfield relented and agreed not to sell the property, in exchange for community investment of $25,000. The amount was too ambitious, and by 1923, in the aftermath of a disastrous fire that destroyed most of Goldfield's major buildings, Wingfield finally carried out his threat and sold the town's most significant landmark. When the purchaser defaulted on his payments, the hotel was sold again in 1925, with no better luck. Failure to get out early enough left George Wingfield saddled with an expensive property that couldn't be rescued by goodwill alone.[10]

The fortunes of GCMC were only slightly better. After establishment of the subsidiary San Francisco office, the Goldfield Consolidated Mines Exploration Company, Wingfield's staff of mining experts was occupied in the search for new properties. Hundreds of prospects were submitted for consideration; dozens were thoroughly investigated. In 1922, through default on a loan, the company acquired the Dolly Varden silver mine in British Columbia; but the returns were disappointing. Later in the decade, in 1929, the company once again acquired a majority stake in a promising Canadian property, the Base Metals Mining Company, which it held until 1933. GCMC operated an office and paid its staff, and its stock continued to be traded; but prices fluctuated in the range of cents, rather than dollars per share, as in the halcyon days of 1906. By the end of the decade the company held, by Wingfield's estimates, between $600,000 and $700,000 in cash and liquid assets, including some oil royalties from California; but active mining was limited to its fifty-five percent share in the new Canadian company.[11]

George Wingfield thus began to focus his attention and his finances on new and ideally more profitable realms in the 1920s. Among his most ambitious endeavor was the Trent Process Corporation, formed in 1921 to finance the commercial development of a fuel treatment invented by Reno engi-

Once his engineers had located promising mine prospects,
Wingfield often visited them personally to inspect,
a practice he retained from the early days in Tonopah and Goldfield.
Here he is shown in a casual camp outfit, second from the right.
(Courtesy of Polly W. Kline)

neer Walter E. Trent. Trent had devised a process based on purifying coal by removing the ash, but it required substantial capital to try it out on a large scale. Trent determined to experiment with his process near large eastern markets and sought assistance from investors. After dispatching Estey Julian to appraise Trent's design, George Wingfield became identified with the work in 1919, when he owned thirty percent of the capital stock in the venture. Among other investors was Nevada's Democratic U.S. senator Key Pittman, who had won election to the Senate in 1912, filling the seat that had been George Nixon's. Pittman was another associate from Tonopah days and eventually became vice-president of the company that was organized to develop and market the Trent process in 1921, after initial tests proved promising.[12]

Wingfield's office manager, Clarence Burton, clearly expected great things from the Trent process. Although he left Wingfield's employ in 1920, he remained captivated by the glittering possibilities of the embryonic company:

> You know that I have never been inclined to be much of an optimist but this thing has certainly got my goat and undoubtedly you can afford to give it your most able attention. In some one week the whole thing is going to jump onto another plane and pass from the possible to the positive.
>
> With all of your other affairs in such excellent shape you can certainly afford to play with this one to the limit.

Although Wingfield never became quite so breathless, he did, indeed, "play with this one." In addition to his stock purchase, he loaned money in succeeding years to the corporation and to Walter Trent personally, as one obstacle after another interfered with ultimate perfection of the process. George Wingfield spent considerable time on the affairs of the company in Washington, D.C. (initial headquarters of the Trent Process Corporation), and later in New York, dispatching trusted emissaries when poor health prevented his personal attendance. Typically guarded, Wingfield fairly glowed in 1922, when he hazarded his own opinion that "with a fair chance this thing has great chances."[13]

Ultimately, it took longer than anyone expected, and there were many pitfalls along the way. Early experiments with the refinement process proved disappointing, and a Georgetown demonstration plant to produce natural gas was abandoned by 1923. Wingfield dispatched the best engineering talent he knew, including J. H. Mackenzie and J. W. Hutchinson from Goldfield days, but the problems were considerable. A French licensing agreement designed to raise funds to continue U.S. experiments did not bring in the expected infusion of cash, and Wingfield and his partners were increasingly unwilling to make further loans. By the beginning of 1926, Pittman was anxious to sever his connection with the company, which then seemed far less promising financially than it had in 1919. As he assured George Wingfield, however, "I won't do it unless you feel absolutely protected." Later that year the company turned to making a substitute for anthracite coal out of reclaimed waste coal, and its affairs gradually turned a corner. As others were convinced of its potential profitability, a modest market developed for the previously unsalable stock. The first options were exercised at $1 per share and they eventually climbed as high as $4. By 1929, George Wingfield had sold most of his Trent Process stock, having made a tidy—if long-delayed—profit in the process.[14]

The saga of the Trent Process Corporation suggests the extent and the nature of Wingfield's active involvement in the details of administering his business empire. Even with his coterie of experts, fundamental responsibility still rested on George Wingfield, who assimilated their advice but then made up his own mind about what should be done. Particularly after the departure of Clarence Burton in 1920, and his replacement as office manager by Stanislaus C. Mitchell, Wingfield had less reliable central office personnel to assist him in this process. Mitchell was a former Internal Revenue Service field agent who had been employed by the Tonopah Divide mining companies before he joined the Reno staff. Evidently an alcoholic and a compulsive gambler, he was gone from the office, under some duress, by 1924 and committed suicide in 1927.[15]

Mitchell was particularly attractive to Wingfield because of his IRS experience, which gave him the background for arguing the numerous tax appeals in which Wingfield and his companies were perpetually involved. As an extremely wealthy man, Wingfield availed himself of every favorable provision in the tax regulations, and his tax returns were accordingly scrutinized with particular care. His returns were prepared by Burton, and later Mitchell, then reviewed by his longtime accountant and auditor, George K. Edler. Many of the interpretations he made on their expert advice were controversial and were later challenged by the federal authorities. IRS audits of his finances were common. Mitchell represented George Wingfield in Washington, D.C., on one such occasion, in 1921, to appeal the decision on a series of income tax cases related to RSC. In other respects, however, he was no match for Clarence Burton, whose steadier habits made him a more reliable office manager, and whose training and background made him more of a peer to his employer.[16]

Indeed, it took two men to replace Burton. In addition to Mitchell, Wingfield also hired William E. Zoebel, a former deputy county recorder from

Goldfield who had been employed by GCMC in Goldfield from 1910 to 1918. Zoebel was born in Germany and attended business college in Denver before arriving in Nevada in 1907. As Wingfield's private secretary, Zoebel attended to office management while Mitchell concentrated on financial matters. Less volatile than Mitchell, Zoebel remained in Wingfield's employ until tuberculosis forced him to seek medical treatment in 1932. In the interval, however, he had become a trusted business and political confidant of Wingfield. His discretion and loyalty were such that Wingfield continued to pay him throughout his illness until his death in 1946.[17]

Burton's resignation and the consequent change in Wingfield's office staff facilitated the expansion of George Wingfield's second economic empire and his assumption of a new, more prominent leadership role in politics. In 1920, in a political contest covered in the next chapter, Wingfield became the Republican national committeeman for the state of Nevada, a position he was to hold until 1936. Meanwhile he put his mining profits to work in real estate and banking by purchasing the ranches, Reno real estate, and the bank stock of H. G. Humphrey, his former partner in RSC. In the early 1920s, Wingfield was cautious about economic prospects: "I don't like conditions as they look at the present time and I don't like to spread out too much." But he continued to invest in familiar areas where he had both expertise and previous success. In August 1921, George Wingfield merged two small country banks to form the Churchill County Bank in Fallon and also organized the Virginia City Bank. Earlier that same year, he took over the Bank of Sparks, thus making him the owner and president of eight financial institutions. The previous year he had built a new hotel for Winnemucca that also provided new quarters for the First National Bank there.[18]

Since his days as George Nixon's younger partner, Wingfield had observed both the pitfalls and the possibilities of banking. His experience in Tonopah and Goldfield had taught him that a reliable source of capital was absolutely crucial if Nevada were to grow and flourish. Banks were thus a natural investment choice for the man who had devoted himself to the economic development of his state as well as his own profit. Over the coming decade, he bought or established several more. To manage them, George Wingfield relied heavily on the advice of experts, as was his common practice. In the case of the banks, a single man served as vice-president of all the Wingfield institutions, overseeing day-to-day operations and keeping Wingfield informed of trends. This was a system he had inherited from Nixon, whose capable vice-president had been F. M. Lee. Lee continued to work for George Wingfield after the latter took over the Nixon National Bank and was subsequently succeeded in the position by W. H. Doyle, L. W. Knowles, and, in 1923, by Winnemucca banker Jerry Sheehan. These vice-presidents attended the quarterly bank meetings with Wingfield and oversaw matters during his increasingly frequent travels to the East.[19]

Beginning in the 1920s, however, George Wingfield also insisted that weekly reports be sent directly to him from the cashiers of each of his outlying institutions, along with customary quarterly balance sheets that were prepared in advance of each meeting. Although the successive vice-presidents exercised considerable discretion in the daily management of the banks, George Wingfield was not a figurehead president. He personally approved large loans, directed his cashiers how to invest their excess funds, and generally superintended all their activities.[20]

On the whole, despite Wingfield's caution, his banks were in excellent shape in the 1920s. He himself admitted as much to his own bankers, at Crocker National Bank in San Francisco, when he noted that there were only "four or five slow trains in them all put together, which I consider a wonderful showing these kind of times." In 1921, he was taking steps to remedy the only situation he saw as potentially dangerous (a sheep loan at Winnemucca) by slashing dividends (which were his profit) in order to establish a fund to cover potential losses. His friends at Crocker, presumably in a position to know, agreed with Wingfield's assessment of his affairs:

> It is a pleasure to me to know that your banks are in such good financial condition, and I know that with your ideas regarding the business, you will keep them that way. Should you wish to use additional money for the purpose of buying the shares of the different banks mentioned by you, we will be glad to advance it to you.

George Wingfield took them up on their offer of a loan and continued to buy bank stock, but his personal life soon interfered with his expansion plans.[21]

In the autumn of 1921, George Wingfield slipped on a rug in his Reno home and fell awkwardly. At the time, he got up again and went on about his business, with only occasional twinges in his neck. By November, however, the pain had become persistent and severe. Early in November 1921, he had to be rushed by train from Goldfield, where he was attending a bank meeting, to the Adler Sanitarium in San Francisco. There he was diagnosed with several fractured vertebrae—a broken neck. Hospitalized for several weeks with his head immobilized in a brace, Wingfield was "disturbed and restless," and his recovery was complicated by the distraction of too many visitors. When he finally returned to Reno in late December, he was still under a physician's care, and the injury continued to pain him well into the next year. As late as July 1922, he was reporting to friends that "on account of the accident I had to my neck I am unable to ride around in automobiles to any extent," and the injury figured heavily in his temporary resignation that June from his position as Republican national committeeman. He was still suffering pains in his neck in December 1922 and was again hospitalized in San Francisco for another one-month stay. Although Wingfield continued during this period to correspond widely, and to confer on political matters, he traveled little and undertook no significant new business ventures during 1922.[22]

By the time he regained his health and his customary mobility in 1923, there were new opportunities to be pursued. Now thoroughly immersed in political matters, George Wingfield spent much of his time conferring with various state and local officials about political appointments, campaign financing, and pending legislation on all governmental levels. No longer merely a private citizen, George Wingfield had emerged as a power broker, a man in a unique position to bring his economic and political visions for Nevada to fruition. He had even less time for relaxation. In 1923, after years of declining use, he sold his country retreat, Meadowbrook Ranch. Coordination of his political activities involved him in an entirely new kind of management by consensus and introduced him to new complications of power. His duties as national committeeman were numerous and delicate, requiring him to exercise a certain statesmanship. His business, meanwhile, continued to pivot around the banks and hotels. On November 11, 1924, Wingfield took the first step toward a significant expansion of the latter by purchasing the lots at Virginia Street and the Truckee River formerly occupied by the recently burned Riverside Hotel. Speculation about his intentions built, but Wingfield made no immediate announcement of his plans for this important Reno site.[23]

Initially, he was undecided about what to do with the property. At the time the site was somewhat removed from Reno's main commercial axis, located several blocks to the north at Commercial Row along the railroad tracks. One proposal was to build an elegant apartment house that would cater to the society men and women who were seeking divorces. A luxurious establishment would require substantial money to build, however, and there was opposition from other apartment owners. Another thought was simply to subdivide the land and sell the pieces to the city, county, and state governments. The city would use its section of the property for a second Truckee River bridge and to extend Island Avenue along the river. The county would want room for expansion of its courthouse, located adjacent to Wingfield's lots. And the state would use the remaining ground for public exposition buildings. Ultimately the first two sales were made, after a carefully orchestrated 1925 bond campaign to approve the money to finance construction of the Center Street

Bridge. With some of his initial $70,000 purchase expense defrayed by these sales, George Wingfield felt justified in proceeding in 1926 with construction of a $750,000 hotel-apartment building.[24]

The new hotel, also called the Riverside, would be something distinctive in Reno. Unlike the Golden, or the Golden's major competitor, the Overland Hotel, the Riverside was planned as a luxury establishment, intended to cater to travelers who sought amenities that the commercial hotels didn't offer. The Golden had a merely functional lobby, a bar, slot machines, and a pool room on its premises. Plans for the Riverside, by contrast—which were drawn by eminent Reno architect Frederic Delongchamps—called for an elegant dining room, a beauty parlor, a bank, and retail shops. The upper floors mixed standard hotel rooms with apartment suites designed for the longer sojourns that divorce-seekers were forced to make while establishing legal residence. The building positioned George Wingfield to take advantage of Reno's burgeoning divorce trade, especially its upper echelons, where men and women were willing and able to pay for gracious surroundings while they put in their time.

Wingfield's purchase of the Riverside lots tied him even more closely to Reno's peculiar development in the 1920s as a tourist destination and entertainment center for captive divorce-seekers. By 1924, mining and ranching were declining in importance as sources of economic support for Nevada as they were for George Wingfield personally. Although he still sought out promising mining properties, and still lobbied hard for federal funds to support traditional agricultural developments, Wingfield recognized in the 1920s that Nevada would never grow on the strength of those industries alone. Along with many others in that decade, then, he sought economic diversification and turned increasingly to outsiders as a potential resource. In a somewhat haphazard fashion, and without any overt coordination, the pattern of Wingfield's investments involved him economically in securing and pleasing tourists. This new direction had implications both political and economic, culminating in 1931 in Nevada's relegalization of open casino gambling and reduction of the divorce residency requirements to an unprecedented six weeks. Wingfield's role in that campaign is considered later; but the foundation for that flagrant legislation was laid much earlier, in political and economic decisions made in the 1910s and 1920s.[25]

Divorce had been raised to the status of an industry in Nevada after a few celebrity divorces early in the century revealed the potential for publicity and attendant profit. Legislative and judicial cooperation were required to establish divorce as a business. Nevada's legislature had defined relatively liberal grounds for divorce and required only six months' residency to qualify. Enlightened judges like Reno's George Bartlett, the former congressman and good friend of Wingfield, interpreted "cruelty" so broadly as to produce what moralists referred to disparagingly as "divorce by mutual consent." A supporting industry of hotels, apartment houses, witnesses, and resorts sprang up to cater to the special requirements of the waiting divorce-seekers.[26]

Initially, George Wingfield was neither a participant in nor a supporter of this divorce trade. In 1913, for example, he approved when a progressive Nevada legislature, concerned over its reputation, raised its residence period from six months to one year. Wingfield explained his position in a speech to a cattlemen's banquet:

> It has frequently happened that some person comes to Nevada for a divorce, and after a residence here of about seven months, comes out for public office, and especially is this true in the men aspiring to the state legislature. . . . Seven members of the last legislature left the state within ninety days after the session ended. . . . You cannot get results by sending men of this class to Carson to make your laws.[27]

Although the 1913 legislation had cut down on Reno's divorce trade, Wingfield did not favor its repeal in 1915.

George Wingfield had also opposed any significant changes in the 1909 statute prohibiting gambling, although he advocated allowing private card games to be played for money, "provided no percentage is taken by anyone for conducting the game." His reasoning was that the prohibited games were being played openly anyway and that "the public does not demand or desire the punishment of those so playing. Any law that is not enforced should be repealed, as open violation of a law when sanctioned by the people breeds a contempt for all laws." Never one to encourage lawlessness in spite of his unorthodox background as a professional gambler, George Wingfield in 1914 had none of the hallmarks of the man later blamed for Reno's development as a lurid "whirlpool of vice."[28]

In fact, however, his economic interests soon led him in new directions. In 1915, the legislature made changes in the laws governing divorce, gambling, and horse racing. The latter two were measures that Wingfield favored, allowing private card games to be played for money and legalizing state-supervised betting on horse races. The divorce bill decreased the required residency period from the reformers' one year back to the six months that had prevailed previously. As one of Key Pittman's advisors reported to Washington, "The divorce bill passed the Senate today and now goes to the Governor. Reno is a wild town today and will be for several days and nights." Although George Wingfield initially opposed this change, he conceded in

The Riverside Hotel, shown here in May 1927, shortly before opening,
was a luxury establishment. Its location was peripheral to Reno's
central business district but well chosen for the divorce trade.
The Washoe County Courthouse can be seen directly behind the hotel to the left.
(Courtesy of Nevada Historical Society)

order to secure passage of the horse racing bill, which he was quite eager to have because of his Nevada Stock Farm. As it turned out, however, he benefited from the divorce bill as well as the racing and gambling measures.[29]

His gain from the racing bill was obvious. When the 1915 Nevada Legislature legalized pari-mutuel betting on horse races, and provided for a State Racing Commission to license it, George Wingfield not only secured local race meetings for his horses, but also a substantial attraction for outside visitors and a source of revenue for the state. From 1915 through 1929, there were race meetings every year except two, which brought in a total of over $161,000 to the state treasury. The races also brought people into Reno, as Wingfield routinely noted to his correspondents. In 1929, for instance, he commented knowledgeably to a friend in Chicago: "We are having a fair little race meeting here, a lot of people in town, but not as much money as usual on account of California having had a very bad season."[30]

Ironically, even the divorce legislation that he initially opposed turned out to be in Wingfield's interests. By 1916, George Wingfield, too, was the owner of a hotel, after his purchase of the Golden. His new business naturally fostered an interest in any laws or occasions that would attract visitors to the city. So the residency reduction to six months, which made Nevada once again attractive as a destination for the unhappily married, now meant to George Wingfield not irresponsible political vagabonds, but potential customers. Some of the divorce-seekers, many of whom were women, would undoubtedly seek temporary quarters in his hotel. Others would need to work for relatively low wages, perhaps as maids or elevator operators, in order to support themselves while they established legal residence. Almost all of them would need banking services. Like horse races, then, divorce turned out to be another stimulant of Nevada's incipient tourist industry, and thus a boon not only to the city and the state, but also to Wingfield. As Wingfield summarized the matter to a political ally in 1916, he was against "any change in the laws which were passed by the last Legislature on the subjects of gambling, racing and divorce. I know you will agree with me that the State is better now than it ever has been, and that we want to let well enough alone."[31]

In 1927, then, when the legislature further reduced the residency requirement, from six months to three, there was no question about Wingfield's support. That reduction had been proposed in 1925, evidently without Wingfield's active involvement, but made no headway. In 1927, however, a year during which Wingfield was personally attending the legislature, the three-month bill was successful. Nevada shortened its residency in the final hours of the session, in an obscure bill, and without the usual committee approvals. The whole thing had every appearance of collusion. Governor Fred Balzar,

Wingfield's political ally, signed the measure immediately despite public condemnation of "indecent haste." The bill was publicly backed by Reno mayor E. E. Roberts, another Wingfield associate, who had campaigned for office on a promise to make Reno "the playground of the world," but also by Democrat Patrick McCarran, at the time a private attorney but later to be Nevada's U.S. senator, succeeding Tasker Oddie. But rumor also strongly linked it to George Wingfield, whose Riverside Hotel was then in the final stages of construction, and who now clearly stood to gain by any measure that would boost visits to Reno. This version was reported by one local political observer to his boss in New York:

> The legislature adjourned without doing any particular damage. . . . The high license gambling bill was defeated but a three month's divorce bill was rushed through at the last minute to assuage Wingfield's wounded feelings; this should keep his apartment-hotel building filled—this building is nearly completed and is much of a credit to Reno.[32]

Tourism depended on more than attractions and facilities, however. Transportation was also a key factor. As automobiles became increasingly common, motorists demanded improved roads. In this regard, Nevada was particularly backward. Federal highway aid began as early as 1916, but Nevada, with its tiny 1920 population of 77,000 spread out over 110,000 square miles, was not in a position to make the required federal match of one-half the cost of construction. The state created a highway department in 1917, but little road building was done until the 1920s. By then a combination of state gasoline taxes and bonds with more liberal federal financing produced annual road-building appropriations of about $1 million.[33]

Here, too, George Wingfield placed himself in a position to benefit. In 1924, he helped finance the partnership of Dodge Brothers and Dudley Construction, which bid on and secured numerous road building contracts awarded as the paving of the Lincoln Highway progressed across the desolate miles of interior Nevada. A portion of their profits, of course, went to George Wingfield, who simultaneously launched a program to promote the building or improvement of other roads. In 1926, for instance, he was especially interested in the improvement of the Mt. Rose highway, the most direct route between Reno and the nearby mountain tourist attraction of Lake Tahoe. He was lobbying at both the state and national levels to include this route on the list of roads to be built on U.S. Forest Service lands in Nevada.[34]

In George Wingfield's mind, road improvement was clearly linked to tourism, and it was all part of the decision to build the Riverside Hotel. As he reported to his San Francisco bankers in July 1926, "The town has built up most wonderfully in the last year and with the good roads and the development of the Southern Pacific at Lake Tahoe and other improvements, I am satisfied that I have a wonderful proposition." To insure that it remained wonderful, Wingfield also did his part to promote travel to the desert oasis of Reno, contributing to promotional booklets "boosting Reno and Washoe County" and "designed to reach the tourists through the country." He participated enthusiastically in promoting the Nevada Transcontinental Exposition held in Reno in 1926, to celebrate completion of the Lincoln Highway. He also sent Senator Oddie colored panoramic pictures of scenic local lakes Pyramid and Tahoe: "Mr. Wingfield believes these will be quite an addition to your office walls and help to dispel the idea that Eastern people have that the great State you represent is nothing but sagebrush and desert." And he was pleased when an associate reported seeing an advertisement for the Hotel Golden in the 1928 movie *French Dressing*, in the form of a conspicuous luggage tag from that establishment displayed on a suitcase.[35]

George Wingfield could and did justifiably take credit for Reno's emergence in the 1920s as a growing desert resort. In 1927, in the midst of legislative debate on the licensed gambling bill, his pride was palpable, if characteristically indirect: "It is quite true that Reno would still have been a whistling post if it had not been for some of those who stepped in behind the situation and dragged some of those old moss backs through the river a few times backward." There may not have been universal agreement on the direction that Reno was taking, but in Wingfield's mind, there was no doubt about its propriety.[36]

Another facet of George Wingfield's new economic empire was the Nevada Surety and Bonding Company, which he established in 1924 to write the bonds required of public officials, contractors, and others. Created just in time to take advantage of the building boom, the bonding company had a ready-made client base. Among its first clients was the Dodge Brothers firm. Others included the many public officials whose bonds Wingfield had previously been asked to guarantee personally. A logical extension of George Wingfield's standard investment objectives, the bonding company was a way to relieve himself of the risk of personally underwriting performance bonds and to assist in the upbuilding of the community, while simultaneously making a modest profit and keeping in the state money that otherwise would have gone outside to other bonding firms.[37]

Meanwhile, Wingfield also continued his expansion in traditional arenas. In 1925, he added to his string of banks by acquiring a seventy percent interest in the Henderson Banking Company of Elko. The next year, as he turned fifty years old and began construction of the Riverside, he also made another major mining investment, in a group of silver claims in the new Quartz Mountain district sixty-five miles from Fallon, Nevada. Through the Reorganized Booth Mining Company, a Goldfield company he had reorganized as a holding company, Wingfield bought a controlling interest in four different mines, as well as the San Rafael Development Corporation. The latter was owned by mining engineer Lou Gordon and Salt Lake City stockbroker Arthur Thomas. Astute promotion by Thomas, combined with efforts by Wingfield's San Francisco broker, James Gartland, created a minor boom in the stock and enabled the three principal stockholders to dispose profitably of some of their holdings. In 1927, in order to organize the various holdings, George Wingfield and his partners created the San Rafael Consolidated Mines Company. Profits from the mines were short lived, however, and by 1931 George Wingfield had sold all of his interests in the operation.[38]

Much of this expansion, as was the case with the banks, was financed by George Wingfield's San Francisco bankers, the Crocker First National Bank. Throughout the 1920s, Crocker routinely carried his personal note for $225,000, at interest rates of five or five and a half percent. At times, as with the bank purchases, the financing of the Riverside, or the 1927 emergency of the Cole-Malley scandal, the total rose higher, to a peak of $850,000 in 1927. Wingfield's relationship with this bank dated from the days in Goldfield when William H. Crocker had been instrumental in helping Nixon secure the funding for GCMC. Although George Wingfield had had other San Francisco bankers, particularly after he first came to Reno, when he conducted business through his father-in-law's bank, he returned before long to the institution where his loyalties were longest.[39]

Most of the time, Wingfield dealt on routine matters with a bank vice-president, but he was also a personal friend of the man whom he always addressed respectfully as "Mr. Crocker." The two men conferred somewhat formally on national politics (Crocker was the Republican national committeeman for California, and thus Wingfield's counterpart) and finances. Later, when Wingfield's financial circumstances became desperate in 1932, the discussions became much less theoretical and quite personal in tenor. Yet the association had been a cordial one for many years. In 1929, for instance, when Crocker was not feeling well, George Wingfield wrote to invite him to Reno: "If you were to come up here yourself and loaf around for two or three weeks it would do you a world of good. I have a good sized house and it goes without saying that you can have any part or all of it. . . . Incidentally

I have some vintages of 1885 and 1893." This was a banking relationship that extended beyond the traditional formalities, and one which would prove extraordinarily consequential when George Wingfield needed it most.[40]

In the 1920s, however, Wingfield's activities were still making plenty of money, both for himself and for his San Francisco bankers. His income came from dividends (principally from his banks, but also occasionally from other companies including mines, and from bonds issued by the Sutter Butte Canal Company and RSC), from interest on personal loans he made, from rents on properties he owned, and from salaries paid to him as president by all his principal companies. In 1925, not a particularly remarkable year, these salary payments totaled $125,000. In addition to his other holdings, Wingfield also set aside substantial property, beginning in 1919, for his two children. The Wingfield Trust Fund held bank stock, bonds of the Sutter Butte Canal Company, and numerous demand notes and mortgages. This fund, too, was controlled by George Wingfield as trustee for his children, although he did not receive the income from it. The businessman estimated his net worth in these years as $5 million. In 1927, his office was responsible for thirty-five different companies, not including any of the banks. All in all, the management of this second empire made for a hectic, but financially comfortable life.[41]

As was his long-established habit, George Wingfield continued to live relatively modestly. Although he kept a car and driver, he walked to work most days. On his way to the Reno National Bank Building each morning, he stopped by the Hotel Golden, and later the Riverside, to check up on everything from the occupancy rate to the deportment of the elevator operators. Wingfield supported his wife and family somewhat more elaborately in northern California, first in a house in the San Francisco suburb of Burlingame, and later at a large home in the city on Pacific Avenue. These luxurious establishments, however, reflected his wife's taste rather than his own.[42]

For himself, George Wingfield had few indulgences beyond good food and drink and betting on horses. A good portion of his personal expenditures, therefore, went to gifts for relatives and friends. His support of his deceased brother's family has already been mentioned, and he continued to support and care for his mother. In 1919 he took into his household a 14-year-old runaway orphan from Sacramento, Walter Hawkins. Hawkins apparently reminded George Wingfield of himself as a youth, a bit rebellious and fond of both rodeos and horses. During the 1920s, Walter Hawkins lived in the house on Court Street, did odd jobs for his benefactor, vacationed (and worked) at Meadowbrook Ranch, and ultimately attended the University of California at Wingfield's expense. The millionaire indulged him by finding him ranch

*Wingfield rented this elaborate suburban Hillsborough house
for his wife Maude and the children after their separation.
The house, considerably larger than his Court Street house in Reno,
was later followed by one that he purchased for Maude on
Pacific Avenue in San Francisco. (Courtesy of Polly W. Kline)*

jobs in the summer, but made sure he was back in time for school again each fall. At Berkeley he urged Hawkins to study geology and become a mining engineer. This kind of personal generosity was legendary among Wingfield intimates, who reported numerous examples of his kindness, including gifts of purebred animals, hunting rifles, fur coats, and even automobiles.[43]

George Wingfield was also generous within the community where he lived. He supported virtually every local charity effort, including among others the Salvation Army, YMCA, Community Fund, and St. Mary's Hospital. He advanced money under the polite fiction of "loans" to old friends and associates who were down on their luck, both where there was some prospect of helpful influence in return, as in the case of Senator Tasker Oddie, and where there was absolutely no such hope, as with Joseph Hutchinson of Goldfield, or his old partner, J. P. Hennessy, now of Smackover, Arkansas. Renowned as a soft touch since his days in the Tonopah Club, Wingfield nevertheless distinguished worthy from undeserving supplicants. He did not act favorably on all personal requests that reached him, and in 1925 he counseled his former gambling partner Hennessy to be similarly cautious:

> don't give away everything you have to a bunch of bums that are always after people and I don't suppose you have changed your good heartedness since I last saw you. A fellow has really got to look out for himself these days and if he doesn't, these beggars will eat him up.[44]

In 1920, George Wingfield gave the city of Reno its first public park, site of a former amusement park on Belle Isle in the Truckee River at present-day Arlington Avenue. Wingfield had acquired the property from John S. Cook & Co., who in turn had foreclosed on it in 1914, when the owners defaulted on a mortgage. A grateful city council named the site in his honor, "George Wingfield Park," although the local chapter of the Women's Christian Temperance Union had somewhat puckishly proposed naming it for his mother, Martha Wingfield, a lifelong member of the temperance organization, who prided herself on never having tasted alcohol. In 1928, when a spring flood seriously damaged "the city's finest beauty spot," Wingfield immediately offered to pay all expenses of restoring it to its previous condition. His gesture in this case attracted favorable attention throughout the city, including the president of the University of Nevada, Walter E. Clark:

> As one of the citizens of this community, I thank you very sincerely for your gorgeous generosity in sending word to the City officials, while the flood was still in progress, that you desired them to have Wingfield Park not only repaired but made better than ever and the bill charged

to you. This Park makes a most beautiful centerpiece for the whole expanding, progressive Reno.[45]

George Wingfield made other public gifts, as well. In 1928, for example, a year when the combined net profits of his banks exceeded $500,000, he poured thousands of dollars back into Reno. In May, he donated $3,000 to the First Methodist Church (his mother's church) to enable it to finance the remainder of its construction debt on a 20-year mortgage. In June, he pledged $5,000 one day toward the construction of a new building for St. Mary's Hospital and $7,000 the next for a Lake Tahoe summer camp. In October, he offered the school board a block of land in the new southwest Reno subdivision he was selling, as the site for a new school, later Billinghurst Junior High. Although Wingfield generally shunned publicity for his gifts, a grateful city council the next week offered him a vote of thanks. His record of public generosity bespeaks a man who was devoted to his community, as well as to his friends and associates.[46]

It was also true, however, that in 1928 George Wingfield was running for public office, as a regent of the University of Nevada. He had been appointed to that nonpartisan 5-member body in 1927 by his friend and political ally, Republican governor Fred Balzar. The appointment to replace a deceased member expired in 1929, so Wingfield sought election in his own right in November 1928. Although he was unopposed and won a 10-year term handily, his conspicuous donations in 1928 may have been a way of currying public favor, especially in the light of the unpopular settlement earlier in the year of the Cole-Malley case. In January 1928, Governor Balzar convened a special session of the legislature to settle the issue of responsibility for the $516,000 loss sustained by the state due to embezzlements by its treasurer and controller, aided and abetted by the cashier of Wingfield's Carson Valley Bank. The final arrangement, whereby George Wingfield was held liable for only thirty percent of the total loss and the state sustained the remainder, was controversial, and Wingfield was well aware of it. In any event, he had a number of reasons to emphasize his public-mindedness in 1928, and in due course the university, too, became a beneficiary, both of his dollars and of his considerable administrative experience. Indeed, the latter may have been as valuable as the former.[47]

As the decade of the 1920s drew to a close, then, George Wingfield was at the peak of his career, a rich and powerful man at the center of a complex network of business and political relationships that gave him not only an interest, but also a voice in most of what went on in the state of Nevada. The extent of that power would be most evident to the general public, perhaps, in the events surrounding the Cole-Malley scandal of 1927–1928. It was also apparent, however, in the 1927 divorce legislation and the fanfare that surrounded the opening of the luxurious Riverside, with *another* new Wingfield bank, also called the Riverside, in May of that year. Looking around him earlier in the year, George Wingfield was supremely satisfied: "The banking business in this state is the best it has been in its history. This is a good town and has grown considerably the past year." It went without saying that he could take considerable personal credit for that fact. Despite setbacks, and occasional criticism from men he characterized as " 'old hens' who are not for the upbuilding of the town," Reno was growing and George Wingfield's money was doing double duty, both for himself and for the community of which he was a part.[48]

In 1927, also, Wingfield publicly joined the battle over gambling in Nevada, by supporting a licensed gambling bill similar to the one that was eventually enacted in 1931. George Wingfield championed this measure, which failed to pass in 1927 by only one vote, on the grounds that the existing situation was hypocritical. As he explained to Senator Oddie:

> the whole State seems to be for it but the federated churches of Reno sent over a petition containing 258 names and we are sending in one today containing over a thousand. They don't object to the rotten conditions of the town as it is now with law breaking going on all around in every respect. However, I think we will clean them up on that too and then I expect I will become as popular as a pet skunk with that element but that doesn't concern me as they are just as popular with me as I am with them. . . .

This concern for flagrant law-breaking was characteristic. It was the same reason he had advanced in 1915 for wanting to see the laws regulating card playing relaxed. It was also the case, however, that his own Hotel Golden featured slot machines that added modestly to its profits. If gambling were legalized and licensed, his slot machines would be left in peace.[49]

More generally, gambling was another element in the tourist-based economy that Wingfield was so proud of cultivating in Reno. After the state allowed small stakes gambling in 1915, enforcement of antigambling laws slackened. Back-room games for higher stakes gradually moved into more elaborate settings, patronized by the crowd of thrill-seeking marital refugees. The Golden Hotel had both legal slot machines (those not played for money) and a pool room, for instance, in addition to backroom card games. Eventually Wingfield leased basement space in his hotel to Reno underworld figures William Graham and James C. McKay, the latter a close personal friend, for their Bank Club saloon and casino. Graham and McKay also catered to a select trade at the Reno Social Club, the elegant Willows on the road west to Verdi, and later the Cal-Neva Club on the California border at the north shore of Lake Tahoe. No longer a professional gambler himself, George Wingfield was well aware of the potential profits to be made and had no objections to games that were fairly operated. As he told one interviewer:

"A man gambles when he marries, and he gambles at whatever business he is engaged in," Wingfield told me, in justification of his attitude. "There's no difference between putting a pile on the wheel and buying a stack of stocks—except you have a better chance and bigger odds at the wheel."

To such a man, clearly, gambling deserved toleration, offering as it did both healthy recreation and potential profit.[50]

The new Wingfield-sponsored economy was not universally popular, of course. Campaigns were waged and sermons were preached warning "that the town was being turned over to a group of men that wanted it run wide open and advertised as such." In 1928, editor Harold P. Hale of the *Elko Independent* looked forward to the day "when Reno begins producing something besides recreation and ceases to rely for performance upon divorce laws, scofflaw gambling and protected speakeasies. . . ." But such resistance, though heartfelt, was ultimately doomed by the strength and undeniable prosperity associated with the opposing forces. In Nevada in 1927, George Wingfield was a force to be reckoned with. Even though *Reno Evening Gazette* editor Graham Sanford was said to be "fighting it very bitterly," some thought the gambling bill "likely to pass," simply because "it is said Wingfield is back of the bill." Although they were unsuccessful in 1927, Wingfield and his associates eventually secured public legitimation of the new Reno they had done so much to build.[51]

By much the same logic he applied to gambling—of legalizing the status quo—George Wingfield also opposed both state and national prohibition. Himself a dedicated imbiber, Wingfield never saw alcohol as a moral issue, and he gave financial support to state antiprohibition groups working to defeat passage of Nevada's 1918 legislation. In 1924, in the midst of political controversy in Reno about the enforcement of prohibition laws, Wingfield wrote candidly about his position:

I have been helping out the parties who came up on the Anti-Prohibition work, but, of course, I hardly feel that I can go outside of my own state to help out the work, but am willing to give them every assistance here. Of course, being National Committeeman for Nevada I have got to be pretty careful on this work as I don't want to involve the party which I represent or lead anyone to believe that I am trying to use them in regard to this work, but, of course, I feel that I have a right to express my personal opinion, which I have done.[52]

As with gambling, George Wingfield was both a personal enthusiast and an economic beneficiary of protected drinking in Reno. His friend Jim McKay was a bootlegger. In 1923, McKay's home south of Reno was raided by federal prohibition agents from Los Angeles and alcohol worth more than $100,000 was seized. This was obviously no private stockpile for personal use, although both McKay and Wingfield kept such reserves. Wingfield even appropriated the good whiskey that was left at the Hotel Golden when Nevada's prohibition statute took effect, although he was more successful than McKay in avoiding detection. When prohibition agents showed up at Wingfield's house with a search warrant, they found nothing unlawful. The illicit gambling establishments run by Graham and McKay all served alcohol, as did a number of other nightclubs. Making alcohol available despite prohibition was just another part of the tourist package, part of Reno's appeal for visitors and locals alike. By 1930, George Wingfield was confidently advising Senator Tasker Oddie that "there is a great wet sentiment in this State." He was in a position to know, having worked hard to foster it, even in the bleakest days of prohibition.[53]

As was also the case with gambling, however, George Wingfield did not approve of lawbreaking or the disorderly provision of alcohol. In 1923, he was explicit about the matter in a letter to Senator Oddie: "I am not upholding any of the bootleggers or lawbreakers, as I am for law enforcement and law and order, and I realize that Springmeyer [U.S. district attorney, charged with prosecuting prohibition violations] has got to do his job. . . ." But he was equally forthright in more private forums. In 1925, Wingfield warned his former Tonopah poker partner, J. P. Hennessy, now part owner of a restaurant and gambling house in Arkansas, against the dangers of bootlegging. Three years earlier, he coldheartedly evicted one of his own tenants who was discovered to be keeping alcohol on his premises despite promises to the contrary, ordering in a handwritten addendum to his instructions that "should Panama take it the place has got to be somewhat deacent [*sic*], and no booze." Wingfield had clear standards about what kind of drinking was acceptable, and it was definitely not the disruptive kind. After all, he was the ultimate recipient of complaints from Hotel Golden guests, "whose sleep is disturbed by patrons of the two boot-leg joints across the way," who checked out because they couldn't get any rest.[54]

George Wingfield suffered economically when this happened. Consequently he and his employees sought a delicate balance, whereby speakeasy patrons, who also gambled and bet the horses, could be accommodated, but hotel guests would not be annoyed. In 1926, his staff puzzled over how to regulate the illegal liquor trade so that hotel guests would not be discommoded. After a notorious incident in which a visiting judge "staged a party in his room" for thirty people at 1:30 A.M., and "put it on proper, fortifying himself with two one-gallon jugs of moonshine," they despaired: "We haven't been able to learn who brings in the whiskey or we might stop it that way. Have you any suggestions?" The problem was a perennial one, and it was at least part of the reason that George Wingfield favored some legitimate controls over alcohol, rather than the notorious wide-open situation that prevailed in Reno throughout most of the 1920s.[55]

In the meantime, however, he had personal problems as well. In the spring of 1927, he had a badly infected toe, which almost had to be amputated in June. In that same month, in the midst of the growing public scandal surrounding the revelation of the defalcations of state officials Cole and Malley, George Wingfield once again filed suit for divorce against his estranged wife Maude, charging extreme cruelty and seeking custody of their two children, then ages fifteen and thirteen. The allegations were not particularly surprising—that Maude had been insulting, disparaging, and sarcastic, often in the presence of others; that she called him names; that "on numerous occasions [she] told [him] that she no longer loved him" and threatened to bring action for divorce "in such form as would humiliate and embarrass the plaintiff, irrespective of the truth of her allegations." As a consequence, George Wingfield found life with his wife to be miserable and further cohabitation with her "unsafe and dangerous." Maude Wingfield's attorneys cross-filed alleging desertion and sought joint custody of the children.[56]

Like the divorce action of a decade earlier, the 1927 suit was also allowed to lapse. In March 1928, apparently reconciled, George Wingfield maintained a vigil at his wife's bedside in San Francisco during her critical illness. By December of that year, however, George Thatcher was once again negotiating with her attorney over property rights and alimony, eventually declaring in disgust that the two parties would just have to settle matters in court. In May 1929, after twenty tempestuous years of marriage, the Wingfields were finally divorced. Judgment was awarded to Maude Wingfield, on the grounds of extreme cruelty. She received the Pacific Avenue house in San Francisco,

$2,500 monthly for alimony and child support, and a lump-sum payment of more than $58,000 to pay outstanding bills. They shared custody of the children.[57]

In the intervening years, George Wingfield's already flourishing business affairs simply got better. In 1927, the Sutter Butte Canal Company realized its highest net profit ever, over $30,000. The Henderson Bank in Elko paid a dividend of $100,000, seventy percent of which belonged to Wingfield personally. As a group, his banks had net earnings of about $450,000. In 1928, even after substantial charge-offs to cover doubtful loans, they had earnings of $513,000. In 1929, Wingfield wrote triumphantly to his friend Senator Oddie:

> 1928 was the best year I have ever seen in Nevada. Bank deposits increased wonderfully and business was put on a very sound basis; everything is steady. The banks are in a healthier condition than I have ever seen them. The hotels did much better than they did through 1927 [a year when Wingfield's banker in San Francisco thought their showing was "splendid"].

In February 1929, Wingfield opened a luxurious new bank building at Elko "in a blaze of glory" and triumphantly reported Reno to be "crowded with people and the hotels are overflowing." In the generally affluent final years of the 1920s, his luck seemed better than ever.[58]

To be sure, there were a few setbacks. In 1927, for example, he had once again set out to make beet sugar a viable crop for the agricultural area around Fallon, Nevada. With a group of local investors, Wingfield had purchased the sugar beet factory there in 1926 and secured growing contracts for the 1927 season. Expenses proved greater and contracts fewer than the group expected, however, and the unprofitable factory was closed again in 1928. Eventually it reverted to the Michigan company that had originally sold it to the group of Wingfield associates. For the most part, however, such incidents were merely minor disappointments in a general picture of constantly increasing prosperity. More symbolic of George Wingfield's investment activities at the end of the decade were two 1929 undertakings.[59]

In its own way each was symbolic of the investment philosophy that Wingfield had consistently espoused since coming to great riches in Goldfield, of using his money not only to profit himself, but also to develop the economy of his state. One was undertaken in a spirit of profit-seeking expansion, and the other as a sort of incidentally profitable public service. In the end neither was successful. But at the time each confirmed George Wingfield's status as Nevada's principal capitalist, the man who could be looked to whenever a situation demanded initiative, influence, cold cash, and the willingness to risk it. The first undertaking was his expansion into extreme southern Nevada, with the purchase of prime lots in downtown Las Vegas to build another hotel. The second venture was his "rescue" and consolidation of two failing Reno banks.

The hotel project actually began in 1928, after an exploratory trip south to Las Vegas following the bank meetings in Tonopah and Goldfield. Extreme southern Nevada had never been of particular interest to George Wingfield, but road improvements had reduced the physical isolation that he remembered from the days "when it would take a week to go from Tonopah to Las Vegas." Now, he commented, though it was somewhat rough, "with a little work on the road, the trip could be made from Beatty to Goldfield easily in two hours." This gave him ideas. Mindful of the pending passage in Congress of the Boulder Canyon legislation that would ultimately lead to the building of Hoover Dam, Wingfield was contemplating building a commercial hotel. The dam, as everyone knew, would bring construction workers and others flooding into Las Vegas. In light of his encouraging Reno experience Wingfield believed it was a viable project regardless of the outcome of the bill. Accordingly he met with Walter R. Bracken, vice-president of the Las Vegas Land and Water Company and local agent for the Union Pacific Railroad, to look at likely property. They settled on two lots at the corner of Second and Fremont streets in Las Vegas, which George Wingfield purchased on behalf of RSC in December 1928. The total cost was $45,000.[60]

By March 1929, Wingfield was sending Bracken drawings of the proposed 100-room Hotel Fremont that he planned for the site and inquiring about other Las Vegas possibilities: "I would be glad to investigate the situation further with a view of doing some real development in that section, which would include a very substantial interest in the bank of say at least fifty percent, if it could be had." His curiosity about southern Nevada was clearly piqued, and there were those in the region who welcomed his move and all that it represented. As one potential Las Vegas investor confided to Bracken, Wingfield's presence alone was of tremendous symbolic value to the community:

> I may say quite confidentially that I have a deep seated conviction, that for Las Vegas to come into her own needs above and beyond all other influences George Wingfield, not necessarily for his money, but for his name and his leadership. Our one outstanding need is a leader upon whom we can combine and follow, and I feel sure we could combine on following Wingfield's direction both politically and financially. His standing for wisdom, vision and square dealing together with his

national reputation would give us the one notable factor lacking for our ultimate success. . . . I believe you agree with me that your ultimate goal is an industrial city. With cheap power at the switch board and nearness to water transportation all we lack is the advice of a directing genius such as George Wingfield.[61]

Such directing genius, alas, was not to come. By June, Wingfield was writing to Bracken, explaining that building costs for the kind of hotel he envisioned were too high and that he might need the money instead for extension of the Riverside. Las Vegas had not turned out to be as cooperative as the millionaire investor might have hoped: "Another thing is the high tax rate and the numerous factions that exist there that are continually fighting among themselves." Unwilling to get involved in the local politics, and with other uses for the money, including the Washoe County bank reorganization that came up in the summer of 1929, George Wingfield withdrew from his Las Vegas venture. By September, RSC was trying to sell its Las Vegas lots, marking the end of Wingfield's brief flirtation with a southern hotel. The flurry which even an aborted venture had caused, however, confirmed his public position as Nevada's wealthiest man.[62]

In July, when he took over the failed Washoe County Bank in Reno and combined it with another institution to form the new United Nevada Bank, Wingfield was living up to the substantial responsibilities of that position. The United Nevada Bank, which was organized in August, was not his idea. In fact he resisted it strongly, complaining to the cashier at Crocker, "I hardly think I want to be bothered any further with it as it means a lot of hard work and I have just got all of our concerns in first class shape and have no worries on my hands whatever and I dislike to start in on a mess like that, that would take two or three years to clean up." The next day, with his own banker at Crocker, he was even more direct: "After going through nine years of house-cleaning, I hate like H- to clean up an old rotten carcass like this one that just closed up." Taking over the failed bank was a public service, one that Wingfield undertook less because of the chance for profit than because he was in a position to do so, and because he felt an obligation. As the *San Francisco Bulletin* melodramatically summarized: "When things looked blackest and almost before the ink was dry on the notice of closing posted on the bank door by Examiner Seaborn, George Wingfield began to work to save the depositors."[63]

Wingfield would never have described his activities quite so colorfully, but he wouldn't have disagreed with the depiction of them as heroic. The Washoe County Bank failure was a debacle exacerbated, in his view, by the personal cowardice of the officers: "I consider them a bunch of welchers anyway as they never attempted to raise any of their personal funds to protect their institution." For George Wingfield it was a matter of honor to be personally accountable for the safety of banks he presided over. In an era before government insurance of bank deposits, this self-imposed responsibility was virtually the only security for depositors in banks impaired by mismanagement or financial crisis. As he had done in Goldfield in 1907, in the Carson Valley Bank during the 1927 Cole-Malley scandal, and would do again during the depression-caused crisis of 1931–1932, George Wingfield threw his personal credit into the breach to protect his banks. It was the essence of his fiduciary responsibility for other people's money, and part of the reason he was so reluctant to take on the burden of a new bank with a portfolio of bad loans to be liquidated. As it happened, he rescued the Reno banks in concert with Herbert Fleishhacker, president of the Anglo & London Paris National Bank in San Francisco. The Fleishhacker bank already had interests in the Scheeline Banking and Trust Company, which was the second bank in the combination, and took a one-third interest in the new institution.[64]

After securing agreement from the depositors and the stockholders of the old companies, the United Nevada Bank was organized in August 1929. Only the sound assets of each bank were absorbed by the new institution. Wingfield offered the Washoe County depositors 75 cents on the dollar, although ultimately he hoped to be able to pay them as much as 90 cents as the bank's assets were liquidated. The questionable assets were segregated into separate realization companies for each bank, which would try to recover something from them. In the case of the Scheeline bank, those proceeds would accrue to the stockholders of the former bank. The Washoe proceeds would go to the depositors. The new bank would take over the deposits of both institutions, amounting to nearly $4 million. Its capital and paid-up surplus was $750,000. Wingfield borrowed his two-thirds from Crocker on a personal note, which he thought could be reduced as the affairs of the old institutions were straightened out. In fact he began to make payments on it almost immediately. The names of George Wingfield and Herbert Fleishhacker were sufficient to calm the fears of most depositors, and the new bank experienced no drain of cash.[65]

In the end, Wingfield could feel justifiably good about his bargain. The United Nevada Bank was a strong institution, and, as he confided to Senator Oddie, "I think the people here in general appreciate being saved, outside of a few hoodlums that nobody cares much about, but even a lot of them have shut up." He had acted in accord with his principles to salvage something for hundreds of depositors. Even though it also offered him a potential profit, there was no guarantee of any such happy ending. In agreeing to rescue the failing banks, George Wingfield was saving his fellow citizens, not himself. In truth, as the caption on the *San Francisco Bulletin* read, he acted in this situation as "a friend in need," a benevolent capitalist "always ready to aid his state when it needs assistance." The bank deal was further testimony to Wingfield's absolute centrality to the economy of the state, and his genuine sense of responsibility for it. His ever-expanding empire brought him enormous profits, but it also brought obligations. In the years of his zenith, George Wingfield tended scrupulously to both.[66]

EIGHT

Playing the Game

ALONG WITH great wealth, influence also inevitably accrued to George Wingfield in the 1920s. No longer did he threaten, as he had during the 1914 suffrage campaign, to leave the state if he didn't get what he wanted. For one thing, he was now too thoroughly enmeshed in Nevada affairs for such a threat to be credible. For another, it was widely assumed in the 1920s that he was in a position to dictate exactly what he wanted anyway, so public threats were gratuitous. As one Reno politician remembered those years, "It was a well-known fact and no one denied it, that George Wingfield became stronger and stronger." Her claim was confirmed by the passage of liberal legislation supporting Reno's new tourist-based economy, and in events like the favorable financial terms extended by the legislature to Wingfield in the 1928 settlement of the Cole-Malley scandal. By the end of the decade, allegations were rampant that George Wingfield ran both of Nevada's political parties and that the state operated as his personal fiefdom. A typical interview of the period described him simply as "the man who is Nevada." No longer notable simply for his fortune, as had been the case in newspaper articles of the 1910s, Wingfield was now portrayed as the "venerable boss of Nevada" and the "uncontested ruler, politically, of the northern and central part of the state." During the decade of the 1920s, Wingfield had gone beyond mere wealth to acquire and exercise political power.[1]

The means are clear. Once the early-twentieth-century mining booms at Tonopah and Goldfield subsided, Nevada resumed its customary status as a small and impoverished state. Its population actually fell to 77,000 in the decade from 1910 to 1920 and rose by only 14,000 over the next ten years. Reno, the largest town, had 12,000 residents in 1920 and over 18,000 in 1930. In such a small state, the economic impact of a man willing to invest a substantial part of a $5 million fortune was considerable. As Wingfield accumulated banks, hotels, and other companies, influence and power seemed to follow naturally. His Nevada contemporaries astutely described the intersection of Wingfield's economic and political authority:

> Wingfield was a very, very strong character; he had very, very loyal friends. The sense of power this gives is something that grows on people; they love the power that it gives them, and you acquire political power by having other types of power. You have a big interest in this kind of a business and that kind of a business. You have all these men. The men are the employees and they value their jobs. . . . Then they are influenced by what the boss says, very much influenced by what he says, because it means bread and butter for them.[2]

Wealth did not automatically lead to political power, but it did bring a nebulous influence that could with skill be transformed into political leadership. George Wingfield had the necessary skill. In the years after Goldfield, he mastered the uses and potential benefits of such influence and adroitly translated his economic eminence into a political sphere.

He did so, initially, by limiting his ambitions. By refusing appointment to public office in 1912, and remaining in Nevada, he not only gained national prominence, but also positioned himself as a permanent player in the arena most sensitive to the nuances of his power and his money. In the desolate desert state that was his adopted home, George Wingfield's wishes and even his whims were regarded respectfully not only by his employees, but by his actual and aspiring business associates, and by many elected officials as well. The men in power, most of them, were friends or acquaintances from his youthful days in Tonopah and Goldfield. They had seen Nevada's mining boom towns come and go, and their populations blow on to other places. They were aware of the manifold difficulties of governing and developing a transient state, and they gave Wingfield full credit for the personal dedication to Nevada that made him stay when so many other rich men had gone. Some of them also owed him money, either personally or through his banks. Beginning in the 1920s, Wingfield began to draw on that common history and their regard for him in an attempt to shape events according to his own particular vision of a more stable future for the state of Nevada.[3]

That vision was unquestionably influenced by self-interest. Wingfield, in common with most mortals, had a virtually infinite capacity to see the justice of measures that would benefit him personally. As he wrote forthrightly to Senator Key Pittman in 1917, "I feel very grateful to you for the interest you have taken in matters concerning my interests, and in my opinion were for the best interests of all." Yet Wingfield had also learned good, conservative Republican political principles from George Nixon. He outlined these succinctly in 1914: "I am in favor of all proper measures aiding any legitimate industry or decreasing taxation."[4]

Wingfield's political philosophy was not complicated. He assumed that economic growth was a necessary foundation of the good society. It was a belief that undoubtedly took on added resonance for him because of his early experiences in isolated Lakeview and Golconda, as well as his career in banking. Over time this faith led him to support some measures, such as lenient regulations on gambling, that were clearly personally profitable. But it also led him to support measures, such as an increased tariff on hides or the Boulder Canyon Dam project on the Colorado River, that would presumably contribute to Nevada's economy while affecting him only indirectly, if at all. Wingfield's political program during the 1920s was thus an amalgam of blatant self-interest and a more statesmanlike Republican promotion of limited government and economic diversification. He enjoyed making money, and he was quite good at it. Yet he was also sincere about the benefits that he assumed his activities would bring to Nevada.

This political program was customarily implemented from behind the scenes. The man who hated publicity and shunned the limelight never sought partisan political office, although he came close in 1914. In July of that year, he announced his candidacy for the state senate, having "been strongly urged by many republicans to do so." This was the year he sought horse racing legislation for his new Nevada Stock Farm, opposed woman suffrage, and supported the controversial one-year residency for divorce. George Wingfield had plenty of reasons, therefore, to seek an active political role, though it surprised many political insiders, who had predicted that he would run for governor or U.S. senator, that he did not aim higher. Indeed, Wingfield's friend Republican congressman E. E. Roberts reported the opinion of national leaders in Washington, D.C., that "a man who would turn down the offer of a United States Senatorship without opposition and make a race in his home county for the State Senate for the purpose of upbuilding the State by the enactment of sane business legislation, was too big a man to be overlooked in national affairs." Wingfield had revealed his reasons for choosing the state senate in February, however, when he declared:

> It would not be a bad idea if the next legislature should repeal at least one-half of the laws now on the statutes and then adjourn not to meet again for twenty years. All business interests should stand together and

labor for the common good of the state. . . . The state was fortunate last year in having a good senate or we would have received the worst warping of our lives.[5]

George Wingfield had for some time championed the need to apply sound business principles in government. In March, he suggested to a Fallon audience that "we all put our shoulders to the wheel and boost for a greater Nevada," claiming, "We want a legislature that will pass laws which will tend to build up our state and not to tear it down." Wingfield was genuine in his determination to rally the state's business interests by seeking public office. As he summarized his political philosophy for the *Reno Evening Gazette* in August, "In short, anything that will improve or better Nevada has my hearty support, as service to the state of Nevada has become a religion with me." At about the same time he replied excitedly to Congressman Roberts, "It looks like I am to become a real politician as there are three candidates in the field including myself; still I think I will win the race. However, I am not particularly anxious for the job."[6]

By mid-August, scarcely three weeks after his initial announcement, Wingfield proved the truth of the last statement by withdrawing abruptly from the race. He explained that the press of business now required that he spend five or six weeks out of the state, which he had not foreseen at the time he became a candidate. It was true that 1914 was a busy year. Later that fall, Wingfield purchased most of Nixon's bank interests, which required substantial capital from San Francisco banks. However, it also seems that Wingfield had discovered in the interim a more congenial style of accomplishing political tasks. Instead of undertaking them himself, he could find others of like mind who were willing, or could be convinced, to do the hard political work of attending sessions and securing support. By December, Clarence Burton was conferring with the man who ultimately won the Washoe County senate seat, Walter Huskey, and reporting happily to Wingfield that Huskey "is all ready to go to the bat and swing the whole Washoe County delegation behind him," in support of "all of these so-called liberal measures."[7]

This was a style of politics that was more comfortable for the reticent Wingfield. Instead of following in the footsteps of Nixon, Oddie, and Pittman and seeking political office, George Wingfield contented himself thereafter with exercising political influence. His political principles did not change, but his methods did. He developed persuasion to an art, consulting with national, state, and local legislators and policy makers, making his opinions known and giving unsolicited advice on matters close to his heart. This was a politics without the day-to-day drudgery of public office and with no constituents other than himself to please. It was politics, in short, that grew out of and depended heavily upon lobbying.

Wingfield understood lobbying from the beginning. Pressuring elected officials in support of measures he wanted was a tactic he learned at least as early as the 1907 Goldfield strike, when Governor Sparks was persuaded to issue a call for federal troops. Thanks to his connection with Nixon, Wingfield was a man unabashed by U.S. senators and representatives. He understood how to get things done. Throughout the 1910s, he contacted various officials such as Governor Oddie and senators Newlands and Pittman, whenever the circumstances warranted. Wingfield thought it only natural that his opinions would carry special weight by virtue of his wealth and prominence, and he did not hesitate to make them known. As time went on, he also did not hesitate to organize others to help secure measures he supported. At each biennial session of the Nevada legislature there was someone designated to look after his interests. Often this was the cashier of the Carson Valley Bank. Sometimes it was a newspaperman or legislator who had been requested to let Wingfield's staff know about any proposed legislation of potential concern.[8]

If action was called for, George Wingfield and the Reno office took over. In 1916, for instance, they anticipated more reform efforts directed at the horse racing, gambling, and divorce bills passed by the 1915 legislature. Wingfield thus organized carefully for the November election, contacting Republican allies throughout the state:

> Our only hope of keeping the present liberal laws in effect is to block any attempt at legislation in the Assembly, because we cannot hope for much in the Senate. Therefore it will be greatly appreciated if you will use some effort to see that proper men are nominated in each party who will stand with us to block any change in the laws which were passed by the last Legislature on the subjects of gambling, racing, and divorce. I know you will agree with me that the State is better now than it ever has been, and that we want to let well enough alone. We are working on this very quietly, so as not to raise any public issue that will antagonize the so called reformers.[9]

Once suitable candidates had been secured, he advised his mining superintendents of his choices, enclosing sample ballots that were marked with the appropriate names—not invariably Republicans—in each race. When the results were in and the legislature convened, it was a matter of careful daily monitoring. In February 1917, for example, Wingfield admonished Clarence Burton for failing to attend to this job: "See old Booker has put in a bill to stop racing how did they get it in the Committee on Education Some one should watch out for those things and see they fall in the hands of the proper committees. Things will have to be watched carefully over there for the balance of the session [all punctuation and spacing *sic*]." [10]

This pattern of lobbying was repeated for each session, with greater vigor in years of controversy, and less fervor in years when there was no legislation of particular interest. If necessary, Wingfield attended sessions personally. Generally, though, he had representatives to make his views known. The key was keeping friendly control of the 17-member state senate. In 1926, in another important addition to his staff, George Wingfield hired the man who was to do that, among other things, John V. Mueller. Mueller was born in 1893 and was a Democratic associate of Governor James Scrugham. An expert on water issues, he served the latter's administration as assistant state engineer. He was recruited by Wingfield in April 1926, the same year that Scrugham was defeated in November by Wingfield's Republican political ally Fred Balzar for the governorship. Mueller converted to Republicanism and became Wingfield's close personal friend as well as his lobbyist. The age difference between the two men was almost exactly that between Nixon and Wingfield, and their relationship was described as that of father and son. A big man who smoked cigars, Mueller was widely respected as a lobbyist and regarded by legislators as extremely effective in his work. [11]

In later years, after Wingfield's economic collapse, Mueller was associated in Republican politics with Noble Getchell. During the late 1920s, however, John Mueller kept tabs on the legislature and on water issues for George Wingfield. His job was described by Clark County political observer A. E. Cahlan:

> John Mueller . . . was charged with the responsibility for making certain there were at least 10 Wingfield senators and he spent much of his time at that task. He would visit the various counties, except Clark, several times each year to keep his finger on the pulse and always saw to it that a Wingfield man was in the race and amply financed. Mueller always attended the legislature to ride herd on the organization's members and keep them in line on legislation important to the clan and also to the economy of the state.

It was a perfect marriage of Mueller's deftness with Wingfield's need for careful cultivation of legislative contacts. His selection of Mueller had a great deal to do with George Wingfield's efficiency at the state level in the years of his political ascendancy. [12]

His later dominion was not achieved instantly or effortlessly, however. Despite his burgeoning economic empire, Wingfield never felt that he was in a position simply to issue political orders. Instead, he consulted and coaxed, laboriously currying favor for his positions among the relevant players and repaying their loyalty, in turn, with his gratitude and the prospect of future favors. This hands-on process involved him not only at the state level, but also in national and in local politics, always behind the scenes, and always in the name of boosting Nevada. It was an intimate politics of friendship and influence, pursued by Wingfield among a relatively small circle of insiders who, though they differed as to means and measures, were nominally united in having the economic interests of their state at heart.

By the 1920s, in an analogy that must have resonated for the former professional gambler, Wingfield had come to think of this complicated operation as "playing the game." Whenever he wanted to refer to a reliable, right-thinking man who understood the pragmatic demands of politics, Wingfield described him as "playing the game right." He meant by this loyalty, dependability, fairness, and a sensible recognition that politics entailed losing as well as winning—in short, the same collection of traits that had served him well in the Tonopah Club in 1902, when he took his losses with equanimity and treated the players whether he won or lost.

Playing the game invoked the social world of the saloon, with its standards of personal loyalty and camaraderie, qualities which George Wingfield deeply valued. Violation of its standards of fairness was a serious breach of etiquette and called for retaliation. Once when he felt that Senator Oddie was being ignored on a local political appointment, he exploded:

> If I were in the United States Senate and told them to get rid of one of those birds in my jurisdiction and they did not do so, I would give them a fusillade that would last them for quite some while by upsetting every damned thing they proposed. In other words, I would turn with the insurgents occasionally until they treated me fairly. I think you are the biggest sucker in the world for standing for any such stuff as this and you should assert yourself as there is only one way to get anywhere with that gang and that is to hit them in the ribs every time you get a chance when they don't *play fairly with you* [emphasis added].[13]

Reciprocity was an important facet of playing the game, one which Wingfield prized. Though he might not reasonably expect to win every contest he entered, he did anticipate that both allies and opponents would conform to his basic standards: fair play and paramount devotion to a common goal of economic development for the state. Wingfield envisioned a smooth, efficient political process unimpeded by any genuine difference in beliefs. As he explained to one political ally after the 1926 election: "I would have liked one or two more Republican Senators. However, with Fletcher playing the game right, which I am sure he will, there will be nothing to it anyway as there are several Democratic Senators that will play decently on any bills that are aimed for economy." Those politicians, by contrast, who did not play the game—men who developed an independent vision that wasn't congruent with Wingfield's own—inevitably became his enemies. They were unpredictable and unreliable and their very existence undermined the stability that Wingfield labored to achieve in Nevada.[14]

In this context, of a chummy politics dominated by personality rather than principle, the highest accolade that Wingfield could give a political ally was to proclaim, as he did in 1926 of governor-elect Fred Balzar, "Fred will absolutely play the game." It meant not simply personal allegiance, but also a common bond of shared attitudes and purposes. With someone who played the game, Wingfield would not have to pull strings or blatantly exercise his power. From someone who played the game, he could count on a certain automatic sympathy and understanding, if not invariably on support. Players, in sum, could be relied on to do their jobs and not to rock the boat. If Nevada politicians played the game right, then George Wingfield would never have to threaten to leave.[15]

He became a political player himself in 1920, when he was chosen as Nevada's Republican national committeeman at the state convention in Reno. By then, Wingfield's brief early flirtation with the Democrats had been forgotten, and he appeared in the guise of a Republican statesman. The office of national committeeman had earlier been described by the editor of the *Goldfield Tribune*, a Republican paper financed by Wingfield, as a position of party service rather than political ambition. In the absence of a Republican senator, the national committeeman would be the party's leader in the state and had to be, therefore, "the man above all men to whom all could appeal with full confidence of a 'square deal.'" But the job also required executive ability, deep pockets, and a certain instinct for political horse-trading. These Wingfield had in abundance. The biography that he prepared after his election, for the national office of the Republican party, described him, with a candor that was probably unintentional, as a man who "has always placed his faith in the principals [*sic*] of the Republican Party and has been an ardent worker for its success." Upon election he redoubled his efforts. Along with the Nevada delegation, he attended the Chicago convention, where he traded the state's votes in support of Leonard Wood for a substantial donation of $5,000 in campaign financing for Republican senatorial candidate Tasker Oddie.[16]

Election of Oddie to replace Democrat Charles B. Henderson became Wingfield's immediate priority. Upon his return from an extended two-month sojourn in the East, in June 1920, he went to work, issuing a statement urging Republican voters to stick together so they could increase the party's majority in the U.S. Senate. In the nationwide repudiation of Woodrow Wilson's postwar policies, Nevadans elected a Republican congressman, Samuel Arentz, and elevated former governor Oddie to national political office. It was a position he occupied through two terms until George Wingfield's economic downfall in 1932 marked the end of his political career. In the meantime, Oddie's election gave Wingfield once again the kind of intimate access to Washington that he had enjoyed during Nixon's incumbency. Wingfield, in turn, served Oddie as he had Nixon, dutifully reporting local sentiment on various issues.[17]

With Tasker Oddie, however, Wingfield's relationship was collaborative. No longer the junior partner of a U.S. senator, Wingfield functioned as Oddie's political ally. The two men were old friends who worked well together despite occasional disagreements. Ex officio, they cooperated in decisions on patronage appointments, with Wingfield making suggestions or testing the Nevada waters before Oddie actually made his recommendations in Washington. Oddie and Wingfield consulted exhaustively on the most minor details of matters having to do with Nevada, from pending tariff legislation to appointments to the naval academy or proposed changes in post office routes. As he had done at least since 1908, Wingfield continued to extend loans to the chronically impecunious Oddie. He also provided or secured substantial campaign funding for each of Oddie's three runs for office.[18]

Yet despite their financial involvement, the two could and did disagree. In the days when Oddie was governor, shortly after Wingfield had declined the U.S. senate appointment in 1912, they differed over the Progressive party candidacy of Theodore Roosevelt. Wingfield was bitterly opposed to Roosevelt, whom he blamed for a wide range of ills, including the Panic of 1907, which had cost Nixon and Wingfield $5 million. Roosevelt was also responsible for the appointment of Gifford Pinchot as head of the U.S. Forest Service, and Wingfield condemned Pinchot for the "conservation blight" that was hampering western industry by prohibiting mining development. Perhaps equally important, Theodore Roosevelt had snubbed George Nixon during an earlier Reno visit, by mentioning Nevada's Democratic U.S. senator Francis Newlands, a man of progressive vision, but not the Republican Nixon. In any event, Wingfield had no use for Theodore Roosevelt, and in August of 1912 he made his position clear to Governor Oddie:

> The "Big Noise" will be here the 14th and I think it would be a sad mistake for any of us fellows to get on the platform that night. I am

going to be at Sacramento that day, and hope *sincerely* that you will not let them get you up on the stage for it would lend them ammunition and we have a hard fight this fall . . .

The insurgent Oddie, who had earlier campaigned against George Nixon on a progressive platform, was not in this case willing to be one of "us fellows." He went to Reno anyway and appeared with Roosevelt.[19]

In 1927, with Oddie now in his second U.S. Senate term, they again publicly disagreed on political matters. This time it was the licensed gambling bill being considered by the Nevada legislature, which Wingfield enthusiastically supported and Oddie opposed. Explaining his stance to the national committeeman, Oddie was not apologetic. He assessed the matter from a national perspective: "I personally feel that should this bill pass it will react unfavorably on the State, because I am in a position to see things from many angles, and think from the party standpoint, it would be a mistake to have this law enacted." Wingfield, on the other hand, concentrated on internal Nevada factionalism in his irate response:

I think you made a mistake by having anything to do with the anti-gambling bill as you are playing right into the hands of Sanford and a few of the "long hairs." While it is not hurting my feelings any, I would try and have that matter kept quiet as it certainly will not do you any good and I think you are clear out of your territory when you mix up in it and used very poor political judgment.

In this case, for reasons each man saw as compelling, neither changed his mind. It did not affect their congenial working relationship, however. The bill was defeated, the tempest passed, and they continued business as usual. The two men consulted on the numerous patronage jobs to be filled in a decade of Republican domination, on the sale of some of Wingfield's Truckee River property to the federal government for a new Reno post office, and on the intricacies of local prohibition enforcement. All in all, Tasker Oddie and George Wingfield could both be counted on to play the game.[20]

Wingfield's advice as national committeeman tended to keep Oddie firmly focused on local Nevada political issues. Such resolute localism was the essence of Wingfield's worldview. Once he made the crucial decision in 1912 to remain in Nevada, he became a dedicated provincial. His tenure as national committeeman was just one more example of his lifelong faith that he served his state best by remaining in it. Allowing for a certain willingness on Wingfield's part to identify Nevada's interests with his own, and wise public policies with his personal Republican principles, it was nonetheless a creed to which he was remarkably faithful. Being the Republican national committeeman was not a position of power and glory. It involved him in multiple obligations: to organize the party mechanism within the state, to procure harmony among the various factions, and to provide a considerable amount of the financing for campaigns. As Wingfield complained in 1926:

> The people here, as long as I am National Committeeman, will not make any donations as they expect me to carry the load and it is impossible to get anything out of them to speak of. Our state candidates are all poor men and have to be carried in their battle.[21]

Ultimately there were as many demands as there were satisfactions. Wingfield was constantly approached for contributions to the national campaign, and he was expected to organize and fund the local events that stirred up political interest in Nevada's tiny outlying towns. Campaign workers and bands alike were arranged for and paid out of Wingfield's office. As the perpetual power behind the throne, recognition of his role in the political successes of Nevada Republican candidates in the 1920s was not widespread. In 1922, Wingfield complained to Grant Crumley of Tonopah, "There are always so many 'politicians' keeping after me for one thing and another that I feel sometimes that I would like to take a flying machine and go to China."[22]

Despite the frustrations of the position, however, Wingfield retained it throughout the 1920s, until his financial difficulties in the 1930s forced his withdrawal from politics to concentrate on business. Being national committeeman may have been a chore, but it was also an ideal opportunity for someone of his political interests and abilities. It offered authority and influence in exchange for money and the occasional headaches of partisan attacks or interparty squabbles. For a reserved man who was intrigued by politics, it was the perfect way to play the game.[23]

As a political insider George Wingfield tried to remain scrupulously neutral among competing Republican factions, seeing his proper role as that of a mediator. He described his vision to Oddie in 1924, when recommending an appointment he knew the latter would not like: "I know how you feel toward that crowd. However, it takes all crowds to make a party, and they must be given consideration to hold them together." Within limits, Wingfield abided by his own rules. When former congressman and mayor of Reno E. E. Roberts announced that he would oppose Tasker Oddie in the 1926 primaries, Wingfield was annoyed, but his public course was clear. He explained it to Oddie in a personal letter: "I have told him that I could not, under any circumstances, get mixed up in any of the Primary rackets as I was simply National Committeeman and was acting for the party as a whole . . .

and that I would do everything I could for the Republican Candidate in the General Election."[24]

Appearance and reality were two different things, however, and Wingfield could not help having preferences. In 1926, for instance, he secretly contributed to Oddie's primary campaign and encouraged others to do so, "even though he is technically to remain neutral." This was another aspect of Wingfield's politics—that it seldom remained absolutely pure. His vast and growing business interests and his economic visions for Nevada's future all became entangled, more or less inevitably, in his politics. Putting his plans into effect depended on the right kind of support in Washington, in Carson City, and in Reno.[25]

For Wingfield, politics and business were inextricably intertwined, as in the case of gambling and divorce legislation and the tourist economy they helped promote in Reno. When lobbying on behalf of a proposed extension to Nevada's Newlands Reclamation Project, known as the Spanish Springs Project, he enumerated the economic benefits, including producing more winter feed for the livestock industry and bringing more "landed home-owners" to the state. But he also put the argument in strictly political terms when he wrote to President Coolidge's secretary, C. B. Slemp: "should we be successful, which I hope we will be, it will mean that it will bring at least five thousand more people into this section, which would offset the past democratic majority in this State." Wingfield clearly believed that the two perspectives—economic and political—could not be separated. As he wrote to his friend Senator Oddie, "There is a legitimate relationship between material success and meritorious legislation." Significantly, the question of which was cause and which effect was left unanswered.[26]

The matter was especially difficult to explain to suspicious outsiders. Wingfield's economic domination of Nevada was obvious to all. When he began to dabble in politics as well, it strained credulity to suggest that his purposes might be innocent. Regardless of what he did or said, there were many in Nevada who feared and mistrusted him and suspected that his power was nefarious. Even his supporters acknowledged the problem, which the sympathetic wife of a former bank cashier explained in her oral history:

> Of course, power, political power and financial power, are two hard masters to rule you. That, I think, was the only criticism that I can make of George Wingfield, he had too much power. . . . He was the only millionaire Nevada had that was truly a Nevada millionaire and stayed here, and that gave him all this political power that he could

almost wield the state in any direction that he wanted, and he could get most anything he wished politically.

From Wingfield's own perspective, inside the Reno National Bank building looking out over the booming little town, politics was a game which he sometimes won and sometimes lost. The outcome could never be taken for granted, and lots of hard work was always required. His Republican partisanship was absolute and unwavering.[27]

From outside the bank building looking up, however, the view was much different. Many outside the privileged circle of associates saw George Wingfield as part of an elaborate political conspiracy, in which both political parties were cynically manipulated to serve the collective interests of the Wingfield empire. In this view, Wingfield was not simply a rich Republican functionary, but the uncontested boss of both parties, the owner and operator of virtually the entire state of Nevada. The classic depiction comes from John Sanford, the son of *Reno Evening Gazette* editor Graham Sanford, who portrayed Wingfield's power as all-encompassing:

> Well, that George Wingfield machine, certainly it dominated almost every phase of life around Reno and western and northern Nevada, economic, political, and even social. And it controlled every phase of politics there were [*sic*], from the city hall up through the state legislature and into the governor's office, and even into our representatives and senators in Congress. They just all had to have that blessing. And nearly everybody knew it and respected it, and not very many people stood up against it.[28]

Allegations of such bipartisan political orchestration peaked at the end of the decade, especially during the 1928 election following the Cole-Malley settlement. But they began earlier in the decade, once George Wingfield began his long association with two Democratic attorneys, George B. Thatcher and William Woodburn. Thatcher was born in Colorado and came to Tonopah as a young attorney in 1904. A former law partner of congressman and judge George Bartlett, Thatcher served as Nevada's attorney general from 1912 until 1918, when he returned to private practice in Reno with former Nevada Supreme Court chief justice Frank Norcross. In April 1918, Thatcher and Norcross were joined by William Woodburn, who had been born in Virginia City and served two terms as U.S. attorney. At the time, George Wingfield's attorneys were Hoyt, Gibbons, French & Henley, particularly senior partner Benjamin Hoyt.[29]

When that firm dissolved in 1919, Hoyt and Henley joined forces with the Thatcher firm, to form what Woodburn later described as "the first '5-storied firm' in the State," Hoyt, Norcross, Thatcher, Woodburn & Henley. The Thatcher firm had trial experience that Hoyt and Henley lacked and the new combination at first seemed promising. Beginning in 1922, however, the firm went through some chaos. Senior partner Benjamin Hoyt, Wingfield's long-time attorney since Goldfield, abruptly resigned from his office in the Trent Process Corporation, which he held as Wingfield's representative during the period when the latter was unable to travel because of his broken neck. Hoyt's failure to consult with him about this move enraged Wingfield, who fumed to Stan Mitchell, "Still have no letter from Hoyt. He is about the limit, and I can never forgive him." When Henley moved on to a position in San Francisco, Hoyt and Norcross formed a new partnership, and the remaining two attorneys formed the new firm of Thatcher & Woodburn. Sharing with Wingfield an interest in politics and a passionate devotion to Nevada, Thatcher & Woodburn became his principal legal advisors. Their firm represented his extensive business interests until Wingfield's death in 1959.[30]

During some of this period, they were also the major Democratic party powers in the state. Thatcher held the office of national committeeman corresponding to Wingfield's from June 1932 to April 1934, and Woodburn chaired the Democratic State Central Committee. Both men were influential in dispensing political patronage in Nevada. The Thatcher & Woodburn firm had offices on the second floor of the Reno National Bank Building and shared with George Wingfield a common reception area and telephone number, 4111. Thatcher, in particular, was a close confidant and advisor of Wingfield, and all three men socialized together. In the eyes of their contemporaries the relationship was a bit too close for comfort, and they began to see in the circumstances of Nevada's national representation more than the mere happenstance of politics. Nevada historian Russell Elliott summarized the accusation:

> The general thesis of Nevada bipartisanship is that the two major parties agreed to keep one Republican and one Democratic senator in Washington in order to ensure proper patronage and representation for the state no matter which party was in power in Congress. The machine was supposed to operate on the local level by supporting candidates for the Nevada legislature from each party who could be depended upon to vote for the establishment. Thus, no matter who controlled the legislature, business interests such as those represented by Wingfield would benefit.[31]

*The Reno National Bank building was the capitol of Wingfield's empire.
His office, located in the right-hand corner on the second floor,
was sometimes referred to as "the cave." Its telephone number, 4111,
became a symbol for George Wingfield's reputed bipartisan control in
Nevada politics. (Courtesy of the author)*

Allegations of collusion began to be whispered during the 1922 senatorial campaign, when Wingfield briefly resigned as national committeeman in June. This was the year of his broken neck, and he claimed, both publicly and privately, that ill health was the reason for his resignation: "I could not do anything else but resign from the National Committee, as I could not give it the proper attention this year owing to my health. . . . some of these office-seekers have certainly run me ragged within the last few days, but I have been unable to see them." [32]

The San Francisco papers immediately claimed that the resignation "brings to a head the constant friction that has existed between Wingfield and Senator Oddie," especially over Oddie's appointment of U.S. attorney George Springmeyer; but both men were at some pains to deny this version. In a formal letter evidently intended for publication, Oddie reassured Wingfield: "You and I have worked so well and successfully together in political matters that I want you to know that I consider your resigning not only a serious loss to our party but to me personally." Wingfield privately reassured his former attorney, William Metson, now living in San Francisco: "Oddie and I have gotten along together fine, and so far as that is concerned there is nothing in it whatever." And he wrote directly to Oddie: "I shall be very glad to help out the game any time that I can." [33]

Another version soon surfaced, however. In 1922, Key Pittman was running for reelection to his senate seat, and he and Wingfield were known to be business partners and associates from twenty years earlier in Tonopah. As prominent Nevadans with a common background, they ran in the same circles. Both men, for instance, were members of the Pacific Coast Bear Club that initially brought Wingfield to the Lassen County area where he later purchased the Meadowbrook Ranch. Wingfield's resignation from the national committee position was thus plausibly rumored to be an attempt to insure Pittman's reelection. This was an interpretation confirmed by William Woodburn, who wrote privately to Pittman to take personal credit for convincing Wingfield to resign "after weeks of perseverance." Unfortunately, the resignation didn't stick. Before the end of the month, Wingfield had received petitions from delegates to the Republican State Convention urging that he "continue to perform the high public service he has so faithfully and successfully rendered in the past." As Woodburn disgustedly recounted, "a committee of seventeen members, one from every county in the State, waited upon him and asked that he withdraw his resignation. In view of this request it was very difficult for him not to accede." [34]

Nevertheless, the sincerity of Wingfield's subsequent support for the Republican senatorial candidate, Charles S. Chandler, was always suspect. It was a suspicion that William Woodburn did everything possible to encourage, boasting to Pittman, that "[Wingfield] felt that you were as good as elected, and that, any report to the contrary, he proposed not doing a single thing against you; that hundreds of Republicans had told him that they were going to support you, and that he said nothing which would make them change their opinion." Wingfield, not surprisingly, had a slightly different slant on the matter, confiding in the Republican National Committee chair that "our candidate for Senator, Hon. Charles S. Chandler, is a very fine man, but does not seem to be a mixer, and I am afraid he is going to be hard to carry over." When the inevitable happened, and Pittman defeated Chandler by more than 7,000 votes out of fewer than 29,000 cast, Wingfield wrote a good-natured note to the victorious Democrat, which read in full: "Congratulations, Mr. Exterminator! It is a great feat to go around the track three time [*sic*] to your opponent's once, and no doubt by doing so you carried a lot of lame nags along with you." To his political superior on the Republican National Committee, he reported philosophically, "There was no chance whatever to beat Senator Pittman on account of the Silver Bill and several other things that he has done which the people think are of great interest to this State." [35]

No doubt the outcome was not unwelcome to Wingfield. The well-connected Democrat Pittman could be of more service both to Nevada and to Wingfield personally than could the inexperienced Republican Chandler. Some years later, in 1926, Pittman reported that Wingfield had publicly admitted voting for him. But subsequent charges of partisan perfidy seem unnecessary to explain the election results. Pittman was the stronger candidate and he won. Wingfield expected it from the beginning and didn't spend undue time and energy promoting a candidacy he saw as doomed and probably unfortunate. Even the partisan Woodburn admitted that Wingfield would work hard on behalf of those Republican candidates that *might* have a chance. It was simply, in 1922, a Democratic year. In subsequent years, as the Republicans under Wingfield perfected their state organization, that would change. [36]

Meanwhile, relations between Pittman and Wingfield continued to be cordial, which further contributed to the incipient perception of bipartisanship. Their business association in the Trent Process Corporation gave them frequent occasion to consult during Wingfield's eastern trips, and the two men clearly respected each other. Just before the 1922 election, for instance, Key Pittman was in Reno, but he decided against visiting Wingfield, for fear that his presence would prove embarrassing. Pittman and Wingfield never conferred about partisan political matters as Oddie and Wingfield did, but they did cooperate on legislative matters of common interest. Sometimes Wingfield asked for Pittman's support and sometimes the roles were reversed. In either case, each man sought from the other only the kind of help and support that he would feel comfortable giving. As Pittman put it to his brother, this was just the nature of politics in a small state: "Of course, I have got to oppose Oddie if he is nominated, and I have got to support the Democrat that is named, and I will do it sincerely and actively. I trust, however, that Wingfield will be broad enough to understand that I have got to do these things, and that I will not gain his enmity." Key Pittman, too, knew about playing the game.[37]

In 1923, the locus of the game shifted from national to local politics, as Reno elected its mayor. Here, too, Wingfield had a vested interest to protect, as the city's new, tourist-based economy was threatened by would-be reformers led by Mayor H. E. Stewart. The combination of legislation and lax enforcement that served Wingfield's purposes so well was by no means universally popular. The new Reno was deplored by progressive-minded citizens like Anne Martin, who described the unsavory results in a 1922 article in the *Nation*:

> Reformers know her as perhaps the most "wide-open" State of the West, where prize-fighting, gambling, and saloons have been encouraged greatly to flourish, and where the six-months' divorce still reigns, backed by legal and business interests of Reno.

Martin was a prominent supporter of woman suffrage in 1914 and had tangled with Wingfield before. She knew firsthand the power he wielded and despaired of making any changes for the better in a state where "politicians, irrespective of party, cynically combine every campaign to elect congressmen and legislatures pleasing to the 'interests.'"[38]

When Stewart ran for reelection in 1923, he advocated measures displeasing to those interests, including closing down brothels and strengthening prohibition enforcement. He was opposed in a three-person race by another reform candidate, Frank Byington, and by a staunch advocate of the status quo, former Republican congressman E. E. Roberts. When the votes were counted in May, Roberts handily outdistanced both of his opponents combined, to the palpable relief of George Wingfield, among others. The latter reported gleefully to his friend, James C. McKay, then in New York: "The town has picked up wonderfully since the change [election of Roberts], and it is really pretty good now. There are more working men on the street than I have seen for many months. There are a great many horses here for the race meeting, and there will be no shortage." E. E. Roberts, who served as Reno's latitudinarian mayor until his death in 1933, was a man who could be counted on to sympathize with those who had invested in the new, leisure-based Reno economy. He was another who, by Wingfield's lights, at least, played the game right.[39]

George Wingfield supported Roberts for mayor in part because of this affinity. But there was also a more strictly political aspect to the campaign, as he explained to Senator Oddie. Stewart was a renegade Republican, whose reform notions jeopardized the party line in support of Nevada's economic development. As national committeeman, Wingfield abhorred factionalism, which could conveniently be defined as any opposition to his chummy vision of get-along politics. When he heard that Stewart was spreading rumors that Roberts wanted to be mayor simply as a stepping-stone to higher office, so he could build up a machine that would enable him to challenge Oddie in 1926, Wingfield wrote Oddie angrily to counter the rumor. The letter revealed another side of his animus against Stewart: "The truth of the matter is that Stewart has made an ass of himself, and Roberts has come out and will win, as I do not propose to sit here and turn over the only organization we have left in the State to our opponents. . . ." So Roberts's election in 1923 was important to Wingfield in two respects, not only for the protection of Reno's liberal and lucrative social practices, but also for the defense of his own laboriously nurtured Republican political organization.[40]

His support for Roberts did little to bolster Wingfield's local reputation, however. As he was well aware, Wingfield was unpopular with "the reform element." Anne Martin was not the only one who detested the raucous Reno that emerged in the 1920s, where "the city police force increased in size, improved in equipment, and vanished from the scenes of any important misdoings. The average citizen became wary of what he said publicly. He was living in a community of gangsters, bought politicians, thugs, and bootleggers. . . ." Many people blamed this moral laxity on Wingfield and sinister associates like Jim McKay and Bill Graham. The latter two were well-known Reno gangsters—Graham a loud and gregarious man who mixed easily with "the boys" and gave away money and drinks, McKay smoother and more reserved. The two began their association in the 1920s. They were, variously, bootleggers, fight promoters, gamblers, racetrack operators, and owners of the notorious "stockade" brothel on the eastern fringes of Reno. Until 1952, they operated Reno's biggest casino, the Bank Club, in space they leased in Wingfield's Hotel Golden. In 1939, after two previous mistrials, they were convicted of mail fraud in connection with a horse-racing swindle. One of the men who gave key grand jury testimony against them in 1934, Riverside Bank cashier Roy Frisch, mysteriously disappeared from the streets of Reno and was presumably murdered before he could testify at the first trial.

For their misdeeds Graham and McKay were fined $11,000 each and sent to the federal penitentiary. Several years later, they were pardoned by President Truman, through the intercession of Nevada's Democratic senator Patrick McCarran, and they both returned to Reno to live out their lives among friends. Graham was said to have referred jokingly to their incarceration as the time "when he went to college."[41]

Opinions about Graham and McKay were divided and neatly reflected varying attitudes toward the wide-open Reno they represented. Graham, in particular, was well liked. As Reno postmaster Pete Petersen remembered, "Those people that knew Graham said they could overlook all of the things he had done because he was a terrific guy in any other way." It was the quieter, more subdued Jimmy McKay, however, who was George Wingfield's particular friend. The two men shared a passion for thoroughbred horses and prize fighting, and they owned property next to each other on the South Virginia Road, where the Nevada Stock Farm was located. They invested together in mining ventures and also saw each other socially. Both were members of the Nevada State Racing Commission. Over the years, their relationship subjected Wingfield to much criticism from people who were uninclined to view the two Reno gangsters simply as benign local color. Loyalty was a central value in Wingfield's world, however, and he never disavowed his friend, regardless of the personal or political costs of their association.[42]

Naturally, the illegal activities that Graham and McKay were known to engage in were attributed to Wingfield as well. Although there was no actual evidence to that effect, rumors circulated that Graham and McKay were operating the posh speakeasy known as the Reno Social Club for Wingfield, or that Wingfield was a partner in the company that owned the notorious Stockade, the Riverside Securities Company. Wingfield himself attributed such rumors to Democratic party operatives, and in 1929 he stoutly denied any such connection: "I wish to state that I have no interest whatever in the Riverside Securities Company and that I think you know as a bunch of politicians were trying to work me into that some way or other just before the election and I certainly resent this as you know what business the Riverside Securities Company is in." Wingfield's Reno National Bank had loaned Graham and McKay money on their stock in the Riverside Securities Company; but Wingfield himself had no financial interest in any of the shady concerns. Such rumors continued to circulate, however. In 1923, for instance, in the midst of a heated city council fight about licensing brothels, Wingfield's office manager reported that "the Rev. Pendleton preached a morning and evening sermon which was directed primarily against you, although your name was not mentioned." In the public mind, George Wingfield was culpable simply by association with Jimmy McKay.[43]

At heart, of course, Wingfield probably never disapproved of most of the things that McKay was involved in. The sporting world of the racetrack and saloon had been Wingfield's own; and he was certainly not opposed to gambling or drinking, if they were regulated. As he became a political figure, however, Wingfield negotiated unaccustomed territory. His prominence subjected him to increasing scrutiny, despite a careful and conscious effort to segregate his personal beliefs from his public life. People who were critical of the direction that Reno was taking could not help seeing Wingfield's hand in everything that occurred, whether or not it was actually there. Despite his disgust at being vilified, however, Wingfield would not sever his ties to men like McKay or Roberts. Taking the public criticism that resulted became, in his mind, just another cost of playing the political game.[44]

In exchange for enduring the public disapproval, Wingfield enjoyed the prerogatives of political power, one of which was getting his own way. As a major economic and political force in the state of Nevada, Wingfield was accustomed to respect for his wishes. When opposition developed in 1927 to his proposal to sell some of his Riverside lot to the federal government for a new post office south of the Truckee River, he was firm:

> Concerning the stage fright some of the boys had about putting up a Government building here, I will say that about ninety per cent of the people of the town would prefer to see it on Mill Street between Virginia and Center Streets [Wingfield's proposed site]. Those who belched did so for personal reasons. I think I treated them pretty well on Virginia Street by building the Riverside Hotel but the more they get, the more they want.[45]

A year later, in 1928, Wingfield was adamant about the post office route for the new mining boom town of Wahmonie. Perhaps reflecting his unhappy experience with Las Vegas factionalism when he was briefly considering building the Hotel Fremont, Wingfield was bitter about a proposal to bring mail into Wahmonie from the southern city. Instead he wanted the mail route to come from Goldfield and Beatty, to the north. When he wrote to Oddie about it, he made no attempt to conceal his biases against the southern part of the state:

> The ground is owned by Nevada people [including George Wingfield] and they live North of the Mason-Dixon Line and as all business matters pertaining to that camp are transacted in the Northern part of the

State, I don't feel we are going to let Las Vegas benefit to any great extent by our efforts.

It suited Wingfield's convenience, and his notions of propriety, to have the route run the way that *he* wanted it to go. Anything else, he assured Oddie, "would not do the State any good and would only benefit the orange pickers from Long Beach and Santa Monica." And lest Oddie have any hesitation about which way the prevailing political winds blew, Wingfield assured him "a petition will be sent in soon signed by practically everybody in the camp."[46]

By the 1920s, Wingfield had acquired the habit of command in the political as well as the financial realm. There were definite limits to his power, and he didn't always get his way; but he had assembled a network of men throughout the state who listened respectfully to his proposals. Most of the time, that was all he asked. Whether he won or lost on specific issues, Wingfield was willing to play the game. But with those who refused to adhere to his rules he had little patience. One notable case was U.S. district attorney George Springmeyer, a progressive Republican appointed to office at Tasker Oddie's recommendation in 1922. Wingfield had not supported the appointment initially, explaining to Oddie, "While I like George personally, I know that he would be in a row with everybody he disliked should he be appointed. . . ." In short order, trouble resulted, as Wingfield had predicted. Never an imbiber himself, Springmeyer was a scrupulous advocate of prohibition enforcement. To that end he began interfering with the work of prohibition director John P. Donnelley, another Republican appointee. By July 1922, Wingfield was reporting the problems to Oddie:

> I understood when Springmeyer was appointed he was appointed United States District Attorney and not a policeman, but I see that he is personally conducting raids and taking one or two of Donnelley's men without Donnelley knowing anything about it until after it was done. I was afraid of just such things as that, because we know George so well that he has got to blow up once in awhile. While I have not said anything to him about this, I don't think such affairs as that are doing us any good.[47]

Over the next few years, Springmeyer became an increasing annoyance to the Republican bosses. His public quarreling with Donnelley, whose office he insisted on investigating officially, was dividing the Republican party ranks just as Wingfield was endeavoring to unify them. It seemed to the disgusted national committee man that Springmeyer was blatantly refusing to play the fame. He "has been trying as hard as he can to get Donnelley's scalp," but

When this picture was taken, in 1928, Wingfield was investigating the recent mining excitement at Weepah, Nevada. Although he decided not to invest there, this photograph was widely circulated by promoters as a means of attracting other investors. (Courtesy of Nevada Historical Society)

as far as Wingfield could see, Donnelley's office was doing its job, and Reno was "much drier than Washington, D.C.":

> While probably there is some bootlegging going on in most every county in the State, I think the same condition exists in all other counties in every other state. I think Donnelley has handled the matter very well and he has certainly made a lot of raids.

A frustrated Oddie tried to have Springmeyer reigned in by Justice Department officials in Washington, but without much luck. The U.S. district attorney declared in the press that, while enforcement of prohibition was not his concern, "you can say for me that if Nevada is dry, then the Pacific Ocean is a desert."[48]

Eventually the two sides came to a predictable parting of the ways. By December 1923, Wingfield was thoroughly disgusted with what he saw as Springmeyer's publicity seeking. No one, he complained to Oddie, wanted George Springmeyer not to do his job:

> However, all he wants is a lot of cheap advertising for himself, and to have it gotten out in a manner to injure other officials. I cannot stand by and see things shot to pieces while I am wasting my time and funds trying to build up an organization and have someone in our ranks who is tearing it down.

For Wingfield, it was a matter of politics, not principle: "I have talked to a number of our Republican friends who always play the game, and I have found only one who has not condemned Springmeyer in the harshest of terms." Springmeyer's actions were alienating Reno mayor E. E. Roberts and the gambling and saloon elements who had backed the latter's election over Stewart. The district attorney's quarrel with Donnelley divided the Republican ranks and injured a man who was Wingfield's friend. By January 1924, Oddie and Wingfield were both seeking Springmeyer's resignation. They arranged that Springmeyer would be offered a federal appointment in the Veteran's Bureau in Washington, D.C.; but he declined the job.[49]

Despite their collective clout, the two political leaders were unable to dislodge George Springmeyer from office. Matters dragged on in the same fashion for two more years, until Springmeyer's appointment came up for renewal in 1926. Oddie and Wingfield were alternately reassured by Springmeyer's promises of cooperation and then furious at his badgering of Donnelley. By 1926, the U.S. district attorney's animus had extended beyond the prohibition director, whose case was still dragging through the court system, to include the two Republican leaders. Wingfield reported to Oddie that Springmeyer "has told others, so I understand, that he would seek re-appointment to embarrass some of the Republican Politicians, referring to you I suppose and possibly me. However, he can give me no embarrassment and it would be a crime to re-appoint him under the circumstances, especially after he has made those remarks." Since 1926 was an election year for Oddie, Wingfield was anxious above all to protect him from internal party squabbling. Springmeyer knew this and threatened to cause trouble if not reappointed. Oddie and Wingfield nonetheless lobbied the Justice Department for the appointment of Harry H. Atkinson in his stead, a man they compared with obvious relief to the volatile Springmeyer:

> [Springmeyer] could be a pretty good fellow if he would try but he doesn't seem to be of the type that can be relied on in any manner, shape or form and we always know where Harry stands and he can be of a whole lot of good to us up here. He has ability and some sense along with it.

Atkinson's appointment to succeed Springmeyer in April 1926 put a belated end to the problem, but the Springmeyer imbroglio demonstrated that there were clear limits to Wingfield's political power, even at its zenith.[50]

Intensely aware of these limits, as outside observers never were, George Wingfield was careful to take nothing for granted. Because he knew that he was not omnipotent, as the Springmeyer incident painfully reminded him, Wingfield worked through regular political channels when he wanted to accomplish something. Even a relatively minor task, such as sale of some of his Riverside property to the city of Reno for construction of a bridge across the Truckee River at Center Street, required careful coordination. The campaign that culminated in passage of a $70,000 bond issue for this bridge, in December 1925, began a year in advance. There were other competing sites for a bridge, at Lake Street to the east and Sierra Street to the west of Center. Each site had its own political constituency. Office manager William Zoebel began lobbying the newspapers, other Reno bankers, and prominent property owners about the Center Street location in January 1925. By June, he was discouraged, as he reported to his boss:

> At the hearing last night the Lake street property owners were unanimously for a bridge at Lake street and the Sierra street property owners were unanimously in favor of a bridge at Sierra street, but the Center street property owners were not so unanimous . . .[51]

Mayor Roberts and the city council took the easy way out and approved all three sites, then put pressure on the three groups to get together and agree on one. If they failed to agree, Roberts feared that the three-bridge program would be turned down by the voters, "which would be tantamount to a repudiation of the city government." Neither Roberts nor Wingfield wanted that, so Zoebel went to work. He proposed lobbying "regular residents," but also providing some insurance by persuading two hundred "of our sporting element" to pay a poll tax, personal property tax, or dog license so as to qualify to vote on the issue. By November, he was urging his employer to give a newspaper interview "to rouse them out of their apathy" and proposed a comprehensive campaign for the final phase of the operation:

> Have it brought into the Rotary, Kiwanis and Lions Clubs and Chamber of Commerce as a matter of civic necessity; have Burns and Clinedinst spread it among the labor as a union proposition; pass the word to the police and fire departments; appeal to the Lake and Sierra street people "We asked for ours first, and wont [*sic*] stand in your way when you ask for yours"; and to the liberal element can be said "We helped you, and now you help us" and to the general community "We pay the taxes and are entitled to it."[52]

The final days before the December 30 election were a frenzy of getting voters registered, contacting various ward organizations, seeking support from former governor Boyle, and otherwise keeping the political operatives in order. This last was by no means an easy task. Both Reno newspapers agreed to support the bond issue, for example; but the Republican *Gazette* was fearful of "hurting the feelings of some of the Christmas advertisers" and thus reluctant "to open the publicity guns until December 26th." In addition, there was continuing resentment of Mayor Roberts and the new Reno he represented, "the longhairs against the liberals," as Roberts put it; and "the additional ambition of Ben Barbash to be the biggest man in town thrown in." Zoebel reported to Wingfield "Barbash's cracks that he has built up south Virginia Street and that he will have a hotel before Wingfield ever gets started," theorizing that Barbash opposed the bridge for the sheer joy of being able to boast that he had defeated Wingfield's proposal. Wingfield made lists of people to be consulted personally, and Zoebel drafted a letter for the newspapers. When it finally appeared, it repeated Wingfield's familiar development theme: "One street might make a town from a village but a one street city is impossible, and if the people expect Reno to become a city there must be more than one way to get in and out of town." Wingfield himself returned home immediately after Christmas to deliver in person the inspirational message of his letter: "Why not work together for a population of forty thousand people and forty millions in bank deposits, which is easily probable if our citizens will only realize the value of united interest and intelligent action. Lets [*sic*] get together and have further reason to be proud of our own home town."[53]

In the end, they were successful and the measure passed by 158 votes out of 1,569 cast. But George Wingfield and his associates had assumed nothing in their crusade to achieve this outcome. Zoebel related with some pride, for instance, that "Father Tubman spoke in favor of the bond issue at all three masses yesterday and said he would mention it more strongly tomorrow." They worked assiduously to create support for their measure at every level of society and to sustain it until the crucial moment of decision. After the contest was over, they were careful to thank their constituents, both high and low. Wingfield's letter to Governor Scrugham was more formal than others, but it demonstrates the attention to detail that characterized the entire undertaking. Wingfield wrote graciously to the Democratic Scrugham:

> It was a source of great gratification to me to have had your whole-hearted support on the bridge bond issue. While I appreciate the fact that it was a matter in which all progressive citizens of Reno were interested, nevertheless, I feel that in some measure, at least, your support was due to your friendship to me, for which I wish to thank you very deeply.

The Center Street bridge campaign was a prime example of how Wingfield played the game. A major victory in a minor cause, it was an example of the personal politics to which Wingfield was uniquely suited by virtue of his wealth and sensitivity to local circumstances.[54]

The election year of 1926 was a supreme test of Wingfield's political skill, as he sought not only to reelect his Republican friend Oddie, but also to secure a Republican state administration in Carson City. It was by no means an easy task. Oddie had opposition from Mayor E. E. Roberts in the Republican primary, and Roberts was liberally funded by "the gambling interests of Reno." Although Roberts eventually lost and pledged to support the Republican ticket headed by Oddie, he was resentful. When Wingfield's office manager William Zoebel approached him in October to preside at a campaign rally, Roberts was difficult to deal with:

> I made the request on Hizzoner as directed. This before I discovered he had been drinking. . . . He very promptly declined, saying that he wouldn't humiliate himself by presiding, for anybody. And before I got away he mentioned that McCarran was getting $500 for every speech he made, whereas Ed Roberts wasn't given a chance to make a nickel;

that within 15 days the "line" [brothels] would be closed and there wouldn't be any slot machines in operation. . . . My theory is that someone is looking for grease.[55]

Meanwhile, Oddie also had Democratic opposition, in the person of Democrat Ray Baker, who had substantial financial backing from the Herbert Fleishhacker banking interests in San Francisco. George Wingfield supported Oddie with his own funds, but these were not infinite and had to be contributed through a third party. By October, Wingfield claimed to have contributed $20,000 to the Republican campaign, but more was always needed. As national committeeman, solicitation of campaign funds was a big part of his job. And money was not the only issue. Wingfield also tried to keep the Republican ranks unified and to neutralize Democratic senator Key Pittman's potential influence on behalf of Baker. The latter was a constant battle. Pittman was obliged to oppose Oddie's candidacy, but he and Wingfield supposedly had an understanding that Pittman "would not interfere with the present campaign." After some speeches that violated the agreement, Wingfield was at pains to convey the message "that it will be policy for him to go rather easy." Despite all Wingfield's efforts, Oddie's reelection was by no means assured. The fact that it was achieved by a margin of more than 4,000 votes out of 31,000 was in no small measure a tribute to Wingfield's political skills. As Zoebel reported the day before the election, prevailing opinion was that "if your friendship for Oddie was out of consideration, Oddie would be duck-soup for [the Democrats]." His influence apparently extended to Republican congressman Samuel Arentz, as well, who was reelected by a similarly large margin.[56]

Oddie was not Wingfield's only worry, either. In 1926, the Republicans were also trying to defeat the incumbent Democratic governor Scrugham and replace him with the Republican nominee, Fred Balzar, a former state assemblyman and senator. The party had first offered the nomination to Wingfield, but he refused. It went instead to Balzar, a congenial former railroad conductor and county sheriff, who knew all about playing the game. Against the popular Scrugham he was deemed to have little chance, so steady political pressure applied at the local level was crucial. Campaign workers reported the Republican efforts as a model of political organization, all run from party headquarters in Reno: "Every two or three weeks someone would be coming through our county, and 'Have you gone here? Have you gone there? Have you contacted this person? Have you gotten out these letters?' And you just had to be active. They insisted you get moving."[57]

In the final stages George Wingfield himself took "a turn around the circle," touring the state on a political mission to check on the workings of the party machinery. The result of all this careful attention to detail was that Balzar, too, was elected, although by a much smaller margin than Oddie, only 1,800 votes. Wingfield was characteristically generous in sharing the credit for this victory. His letter to Noble Getchell was only one of many: "You certainly delivered the goods in your neck of the woods and everybody is very jubilant." To the Republican chairman in Eureka County, a banker, he wrote expansively, "Please tell all the boys that I appreciate the great work they did, most wonderfully." In addition, he promised, "We will try and have an organization that the State will feel proud of," which meant, as it always did to Wingfield, that "I look for a great cut in State expenses." [58]

With the 1926 Republican victories, Wingfield's years of political labor finally bore fruit. For the first time, at all levels of government, there were men in office who shared the cardinal precepts of his particular political creed: economic diversification and social toleration. While they did not agree with him in every respect, and Wingfield did not directly control their actions, he had put them in a position of being to various degrees indebted to him for their election. As a result, they were all willing to attend carefully to his view of matters. As it happened, though Wingfield could not have anticipated it at the time, this amenability was to prove particularly important to him during 1927 and 1928: 1927 was the year of the proposed gambling bill described earlier and of the reduced divorce residency. It was also the year of the breaking Cole-Malley scandal, which involved George Wingfield both as an officer of the Carson Valley Bank and as a bondsman for the two state officials.

George Cole and Ed Malley were, respectively, Nevada state controller and treasurer. Both men were Democrats who had initially been elected to office in 1914. In 1926, as part of the Republican victory that Wingfield engineered, Cole was defeated in his race for reelection. In April 1927, the two men journeyed to Reno to see George Wingfield and revealed an elaborate story of financial defalcation that they had committed in collaboration with the former cashier of Wingfield's Carson Valley Bank, H. C. Clapp. The latter had only recently been dismissed because of heavy drinking on the job, and the state officials were convinced that the shortage, then amounting to over $516,000, would soon become public knowledge. On April 27, in desperation, they sought out George Wingfield to see if he would help them cover their losses and avoid the public scandal. Wingfield at first thought the men had come to ask for a loan to help Cole go into business in Las Vegas. Confined to bed with his injured toe, Wingfield was visiting with Jimmy McKay and hospitably offered everyone a drink. When McKay departed, however, Cole and Malley's true mission became clear, and Wingfield summoned George Thatcher.[59]

The full story was eventually revealed, how Malley, Clapp, and Cole had invested in mining stocks beginning in 1919, with the Tonopah Divide boom, and later in oil stocks, all with money belonging to the state. In addition bank cashier Clapp had allowed state bank examiner Gilbert Ross and others to carry overdrafts amounting to several thousand dollars, and Malley had advanced cash to cover them so the bank wouldn't lose and co-conspirator Clapp wouldn't be fired. Cole became involved when he used money from the state insurance fund to try and recover their collective losses in the stock speculations. These illegitimate borrowings were concealed by means of false cashier's checks, issued by Clapp against the Carson Valley Bank and credited to the state treasury or insurance fund whenever these were to be audited. Three separate cashier's checks were carried on the bank books for small amounts, but actually totaled $516,322. They covered Clapp's shortages at the bank, the amount that Cole had borrowed from the state insurance fund, and the amount the three men lost in their speculations. Whenever the bank was scheduled to be audited, and Clapp's discrepancies had to be concealed, Malley issued receipts for state money ostensibly received by him. By this means, the three men had successfully hidden their shortages for eight years. With Cole's defeat and Clapp's firing, however, exposure was inevitable. Cole and Malley came to Wingfield in hopes that he would help them avoid public humiliation, for the sake of protecting his own Carson Valley Bank.[60]

Wingfield was shocked by the disclosures, and particularly by Clapp's role, but he said nothing initially about his plans. Cautioning Cole and Malley to remain silent about the shortages, he had Thatcher and Woodburn interview them extensively in the next few days. Meanwhile he went to work to safeguard his bank. The most immediate problem was the half-million-dollar shortage in the accounts of the Carson Valley Bank. If it were not replaced, then a run on the bank would result as soon as the embezzlement was revealed. Regardless of where the fault ultimately lay, Wingfield wanted to avoid that. He therefore sent his bank vice-president, J. A. Sheehan, to San Francisco to negotiate with officials at Crocker First National Bank about a loan to cover the shortfall. William H. Crocker sent the bank's attorney, J. F. Shuman, to confer with Wingfield, Thatcher, and Woodburn about the legal liability; but he also responded immediately to the loan request: "There is really nothing more to say than we are at your service."[61]

Wingfield himself was not certain where to place the blame, but he was prepared to absorb the entire loss himself if need be. He mortgaged the brand-new Riverside Hotel and turned over much of his bank stock to cover the loan. As he acknowledged to Crocker, "we may lose this money, but your attorney questions any liability on the part of the Carson Valley Bank. However, we never can tell about these things and I want to be loaded as we are going to start the fur flying." No welcher, as he accused the officials of the Washoe County Bank of being in 1929, Wingfield used his personal credit to guarantee solvency of his institution.[62]

Financial backing alone didn't solve the problem, however. After securing the loan from Crocker, Wingfield carefully orchestrated the public announcement of the scandal. In order to minimize panic, he determined to publicize it in a story to be released simultaneously to all banks after the close of business at noon on Saturday, May 7. He had informed state officials including attorney general M. A. Diskin of his plans at dinner at his home on May 6. When the news appeared, it was accompanied by a statement from Wingfield announcing his deposit in the Carson Valley Bank of "the full amount of money involved to be there held to meet and liquidate whatever liability may be legally imposed upon the bank." By this action, he guaranteed to meet the bank's obligations, whatever they might ultimately be, "without a cent of loss to any one, other than to myself." Privately, he was convinced that the bank would not have to absorb the full loss. Cole and Malley were desperately trying to repudiate their confessions and place all the blame on Clapp and the bank, but by May 10 Wingfield had secured Clapp's confession and was expecting the latter to testify against them. As he wrote grimly to Oddie, "This is a H— of a mess and I think in the wind up you will find a good many people in jail."[63]

In the next few months, throughout the summer of 1927, he was preoccupied with that goal. He sent his accountants to go through the records of the Carson Valley Bank and conferred with Crocker's attorney, Frank Shuman, both to prove the criminal involvement of Cole and Malley and to determine the extent of his own liability for Clapp's misdeeds. At Shuman's suggestion, he hired a private investigator to pose as a divorce-seeker in Carson City and ascertain local sentiment about the case. As he had remarked to William Crocker, with characteristic understatement, "I believe in being prepared so that things can be taken care of promptly, if necessary."[64]

The situation was further complicated by the fact that George Wingfield was one of the guarantors on Malley's performance bond. He thus owed $75,000 if Malley should be found guilty. Unraveling the various strands, and tracing the illicit transactions, took months. Cole and Malley were arraigned on May 21 on charges of misappropriating state funds. Clapp pleaded guilty in June and was sentenced to prison. The state officials maintained their innocence and retained prominent Democratic attorney Patrick McCarran to conduct their defense. As both sides prepared for the trial, Wingfield no longer had time for betting on horse races, his favorite recreation. He complained to a friend in Chicago that "this thing has got me tied hand and foot," but the efforts paid off in September, with the conviction of Cole and Malley after only three hours of deliberation by the jury.[65]

McCarran had sought to divert the jury's suspicion to George Wingfield, by hinting ominously that the charges against Cole and Malley were part of an elaborate plot to minimize Wingfield's own losses in the case. Since there was a separate state suit under way to determine the bank's liability in the matter, McCarran played on fears that Wingfield was using his enormous power to victimize Cole and Malley and thus avoid all financial responsibility for the huge loss. Melodramatically, but somewhat muddily, he depicted Cole and Malley as heroes, brave and honest men who could have fled from prosecution, but returned to "stand for right even when the headman's axe hangs above them." By means of irrelevant questions about Wingfield's origins as a gambler, and by emphasizing his association with Graham and McKay, McCarran insinuated that the millionaire was the evil genius of a corrupt operation designed only to protect his money. As the defense attorney constantly reiterated, Wingfield had a network of collaborators, men who did his bidding without having to be told because "they know what I want":

> Can human liberty go into bondage and come out? Can liberty of state go into bondage of gold and come out? If so, free men, where is your blood? I want wealth in this state, but I want liberty more—even if there is not a dollar in the state.[66]

Wingfield recognized McCarran's rhetorical strategy for what it was, and enthusiastically recounted his own combative response in a letter to Frank Shuman: "[McCarran] started off in his boisterous manner trying to bulldoze some one but he put his questions in such a manner that it was possible for me to explain my answers so I gave him good and plenty. The audience were in applause several times." At first the contest of wits was something of a game. As the special state prosecutors, Lester Summerfield and M. A. Barry, pointed out, however, it was Cole and Malley, not George Wingfield, who were on trial. By the end of the trial McCarran's personal attacks had become obnoxious, and Wingfield was no longer feeling so smug. In a burst of temper after reading the newspaper coverage of the closing arguments, he exploded to Shuman about the defense attorney, "To say the least, he is miserable trash." Still, the verdict was the one Wingfield had sought. "It was a personal vindication for you," as William Crocker immediately telegraphed him. Now he could go to work on the matter of parceling out the respective responsibility of the state and the bank for the missing half million.[67]

In a separate suit, the state of Nevada was seeking to recover from the Carson Valley Bank on the three fraudulent cashier's checks, although arguing at the same time that it would not pay a $392,000 state warrant issued by Cole that was in the custody of the bank. Feeling that "a protraction of this controversy is detrimental to the State and the business of the State," Wingfield went to work to secure some kind of legislative compromise. In a public letter to Governor Balzar, Wingfield explained his reasoning:

> The bank as an institution was absolutely innocent of any wrong doing or misconduct. The State of Nevada stands in the same position. We have, therefore, two innocent parties the victims of the criminal acts of their servants. . . . If the State was a private person, there would be no difficulty in arranging for a discussion of this matter, to the end that some settlement, that would be fair to both sides, would be made.

Failing that, however, the only solution was a special session of the Nevada legislature, which ordinarily would not have met until 1929, to consider the matter.[68]

Wingfield supported his call for the special session with a thorough canvass of public opinion around the state. His bank cashiers and political associates talked to people on the street and to local politicians, reporting back, in one instance, that "the substantial men I have talked to are for it, while the ordinary run, have not paid much attention to it, many not having even read the letter." Thus reassured, Wingfield reported to his San Francisco bankers, "The sentiment of at least eighty per cent of the people is with me as I have had lines out over practically all sections of the State to see what was going on." To be sure, there were some flies in the proverbial ointment, including "some Democratic politicians who do not relish the idea," and a Singer Sewing Machine representative who declared in no uncertain terms that "[Wingfield] belongs out there with Malley, Cole & Clapp he must be pretty crooked as he knew all along that they were pulling those crooked deals and he never said or did a thing about it and then he railroaded those fellows to the pen." Wingfield was encouraged, however, by a missive from Governor Balzar's secretary, J. H. White, enclosing a favorable editorial from the *Carson City News*. The latter observed that both Wingfield and the state held spurious documents, and "if the warrant is to be regarded as a scrap of paper, fraudulently issued, the cashier's checks should be treated likewise." Given the culpability of both sides, the editorial writer advised compromise. As long as Wingfield's offer exceeded the amount of his legal liability of Malley's bond ($75,000), "we would say that such offer should be accepted, rather than await the uncertain outcome of long-protracted litigation. Any effort to 'shake him down' for more would be not only unjust but dishonest. . . . It is a situation in which he has 'laid his cards on the table,' and in which he is in turn entitled to fair treatment."[69]

Just in case, Wingfield also arranged for dozens of supportive letters to Governor Balzar from influential Nevadans. One typical example, from Tonopah Extension Mining Company general manager John G. Kirchen, stressed his position "as a representative of mining and banking interests in this state, which interests pay a material amount in taxes to maintain our State government and they are, therefore, interested in conserving the State's funds." In the name of advancing that interest, Kirchen offered his advice that Balzar call a special session for the purpose of compromising the liability question:

> I have had sufficient business experience to know that this complicated matter will take years of litigation before it is definitely settled, and with doubtful outcome. The expense of carrying this litigation to a definite conclusion is an item that might amount to such a sum that the winner might also be a loser. It, therefore, appears to me to be good business to try to effect a compromise.[70]

The letters, and Wingfield's careful cultivation of public opinion, had the desired effect, and Balzar called a special session that convened on January 16, 1928. A subcommittee composed of members from both houses heard testimony and recommended acceptance of Wingfield's initial offer of $123,622.16 (the difference between the total shortage in the state treasury and the amount of the state warrant held by the bank). This plan was rejected after an assembly attempt to charge Wingfield with half of the total loss. Eventually, the two sides agreed on a figure of $154,896.65, which represented thirty percent of the missing funds.[71]

Both the *Sacramento Bee* and the Republican *Reno Gazette* railed about the injustice of a settlement that required from George Wingfield less than half of the total loss, and attorney general M. A. Diskin repeatedly advised the legislature that the whole amount could be recovered if he were allowed to pursue the state's suit against the bank. However, as Wingfield had pointed out in a letter to the legislature, he had the option of simply liquidating the Carson Valley Bank, taking a loss on the $45,000 of capital he had invested there, paying the $75,000 due from him as bondsman, and leaving the state to try and collect the remainder from Malley's other bondsmen, many of whom were dead. As he proudly maintained, when he voluntarily deposited the missing half million dollars in the Carson Valley Bank, "I did not stand upon legal technicalities or my legal right." From his perspective, then, the $155,000 that he did pay was already $35,000 more than he technically owed, and his actions ought to have been heralded as those of a public-spirited citizen. By early February, when the special session finally adjourned, the majority of the state probably reluctantly agreed with editor Graham Sanford of the *Reno Evening Gazette*, who declared, "The whole sorry mess should be cleaned up now." [72]

In retrospect, the Cole-Malley settlement was a pyrrhic victory for George Wingfield. Though he continued to believe that he had been generous with the state of Nevada, his opinion was not widely shared. Although there was condemnation of the State Board of Examiners for having failed to uncover the embezzlement, the case also stirred up overt criticism of Wingfield's diabolical influence and resentment of his control. McCarran had scored some points after all by directing attention to the fact that it was the capitalist Wingfield who told the state officials what was going on at the infamous May 6 dinner, rather than the other way around. Wingfield never entirely managed to cleanse himself of the lingering taint, which bubbled to the surface again during the 1928 election campaign. [73]

At first the Republican national committeeman approached that election, in which Democratic senator Pittman sought reelection and Wingfield's old friend Herbert Hoover was nominated for the presidency, as he had many others. A year before the election, he was already discussing it with Republican congressman Samuel Arentz, assessing the latter's chances for reelection as "perfectly safe," but speculating about whether the Republicans could find a candidate to defeat Pittman. In June 1928, Margaret Bartlett, the daughter of Wingfield's longtime friend Judge George Bartlett, commented breezily on what had by then become Wingfield's traditional role in Nevada elections: "Suppose you are busy as the devil with everybody in the blooming state expecting you to elect them. But that's what you get for being smarter than anybody else. You shouldn't blame anyone for depending on you. It's just natural." [74]

Yet the election of 1928 was not just like the others. In this campaign, George Wingfield was unable to maintain his preferred position behind the scenes and found himself instead embroiled in public controversy. It started innocently enough, with the usual strategy to find a viable Republican candidate to defeat Pittman for the senate seat. Wingfield wrote to Tasker Oddie in February, requesting the records of all of Pittman's votes "on different matters that might be beneficial this Fall in our coming election." He maintained official neutrality through the primaries, though Republican insiders reported that he was already supporting Sam Platt, the man who had initially sought the position as Republican national committeeman when Wingfield won it in 1920. Platt had narrowly missed election to the U.S. Senate in 1914, against Francis Newlands, and Wingfield was determined that he would triumph in 1928, against Pittman. At the same time, Wingfield was enthusiastic in his support for the Republican presidential nominee, Herbert Hoover. These twin allegiances determined his aims for the 1928 campaign, as he worked especially hard to elect the entire Republican ticket.[75]

Wingfield chose the Republicans' protective tariff as his point of attack on the Democrats. He distributed throughout the state a long circular letter dated August 20, in which he explained the history of the tariff issue and how a high Republican tariff had positively affected Nevada products and population. The argument was a simple one: "I urge upon the people of this state to vote the Republican ticket from top to bottom to help maintain the prosperity which we now enjoy." Not only did Nevada need Herbert Hoover, but it needed Sam Platt in the Senate and Sam Arentz in the House of Representatives. Leaving little to chance, he followed the letter up with numerous personal letters and visits, and with contributions to the various county central committees. To his old partner, Dick Vanetta, from Golconda, whose personal proclivities Wingfield knew well, he wrote at length, explaining why electing Al Smith would not put an end to prohibition despite Smith's public opposition to it. Lest there be any doubt in the matter, Wingfield appealed to personal trust, assuring Vanetta, "I am always for Nevada and America at all times, and I am sure that your Country's best interests lie with the Republican Party." That same day, he was busy combating a rumor that was current in the mining camps, "that Hoover had a sign painted on his fence at his ranch in Kern County, California, that 'No Whites need apply.'" Wingfield informed his mine manager that he had personally investigated the rumor and found it false, then instructed him to "get this passed around through your channels in Goldfield as well as Wahmonie." Summarizing his political activities, Wingfield reported that he had been "doing everything I could to hold our Party together and to get as many new recruits as possible."[76]

Defeating Pittman was an uphill battle, but one that the Republican committeeman thought he had at least a chance of winning. To the chairman of the Republican National Committee, Hubert Work, he wrote with cautious optimism: "I might add that Senator Pittman is scared to death and admits that Hoover will carry the State with a large majority which might defeat him—Pittman." There was the usual partisan sniping. When Wingfield gave a summer interview intimating that his plans for expanding the Hotel Golden would depend on the outcome of the fall elections, Democratic newspapers around the state responded predictably. The *Las Vegas Review* concluded that the veiled threat indicated Republican uncertainty about their strength in Nevada:

> It also indicates, so far as local politics are concerned, that Mr. Wingfield, whose unseen hand was the guiding spirit of the last campaign in communities where he controls the financial institutions, has grown in power to such an extent that he throws off all sham and is out in the open as a dictator of Nevada's politics.

The *Humboldt Star* of Winnemucca was gentler, questioning whether Wingfield had ever really made the statement attributed to him and ridiculing the threat: "One would think from such absurd propaganda that a hotel addition had a gender and could define its political affiliations. Why not carry it a little further and run the Hotel Golden on the republican ticket. The Star knows several good hotels that would accept the democratic nomination." To this kind of needling, Wingfield responded in kind, releasing a statement to the *Reno Evening Gazette*:

> It appears that some of the Democratic papers, who claim to be Independent in politics, are badly worried because I am not going to put up some buildings this Fall for them to tear down. While I don't think they have a chance to win, I am quite positive that if they did win, no buildings would be necessary for several years to come.[77]

By fall, the Democrats had launched a publicity initiative of their own. Late in September, the Democratic State Central Committee hired L. J. Blake as its campaign publicity manager. Blake was the publisher of the *Santa Clara Journal* in California and a former publisher of Nevada's *Carson City Appeal*. He launched an all-out attack on George Wingfield in an editorial entitled "Nevada, Wingfield and Smith" that was reprinted and widely circulated in Nevada. It downplayed the importance of the tariff and, echoing the earlier *Las Vegas Review* editorial, charged that Wingfield was using the issue to dictate the votes of the state, concluding: "It will be a happy day for both the Sagebrush State and the Republican Party therein, when they are rid of Wingfield." This blast was soon followed by a series of hard-hitting articles by Arthur B. Waugh in the Democratic *Sacramento Bee*. Waugh charged that Nevada politics was being dominated by an "unholy alliance for Hoover," made up of bootleggers Graham and McKay, the Ku Klux Klan, and the Women's Christian Temperance Union. The next day he went on to tie this group to Wingfield, "the most powerful of these, backed by the octopus-like influence of his enormous wealth and the stranglehold he has on the political and financial life of Nevada."[78]

In the year of Wingfield's most ostentatious public donations to charity, when he was also running for office as a university regent, Waugh revived and embellished Pat McCarran's insinuating rhetoric from the 1927 Cole-Malley trial:

> Of Wingfield's place in the line-up they speak only in whispers in Reno. For the Wingfield influence stretches far afield, reaching over the desert, through his chain of banks, into the mortgage-ridden homes of cattle and sheep men and filtering into the cash register of merchants and realtors through other loans and mortgages.
>
> Churches, institutions of learning, uplift organizations and semi-charitable bodies are not exempt from the Wingfield influence. Gifts and donations, discreetly placed, have served to still the voices that might have been raised against the Wingfield dictatorship, and protests of the righteous have been smothered by the weight of the Wingfield pocketbook.

At first, Wingfield was relatively calm under the attack, writing to Republican national chairman Work, "They are attacking me in every contemptible underhanded manner they can, but as it happens I am not running for office and I can take care of myself." He realized that the Democratic State Central Committee was behind the articles, which were being circulated and reprinted in Nevada. Like the local manager of the Virginia and Truckee Railroad, Frank Murphy, Wingfield predicted that the slurs against him would "have just the counter-effect of that intended." [79]

Life in the spotlight glare of this kind of negative publicity was uncomfortable, though, and Wingfield quickly came to resent it. Observers reported that the "attack on him has hurt his pride" and that "he has been keeping particularly straight, which evidences his earnestness in maintaining his political standing in Nevada." Protestations of innocence were useless, and fundamentally unbelievable. Wingfield, after all, was well known to be a personal friend of Jimmy McKay and to favor an end to prohibition. His power and influence in Nevada, however judiciously exercised, were undeniable. He had worked for over a decade to achieve them. He was proud of the way he used them, in his eyes at least, to benefit the entire state.[80]

Thus, although George Wingfield was not a candidate for partisan office, he became a major campaign issue in 1928. It was his vision of economic development based in part on tolerance of liberal institutions, and the tourism they attracted, that was under attack by Waugh and the *Sacramento Bee*, which pointed out that "never, even in its palmiest days was Reno so 'wide open.'" Eventually Wingfield abandoned even the pretense of remaining behind the scenes and responded in kind. As he thundered to the manager of his Elko bank:

The Democratic State administrations have cost me nearly two hundred thousand dollars through embezzlement of State funds. They have turned their guns loose on me in the Democratic Press, through their lieing [*sic*], underhanded tactics of which some of their tribe are responsible for [*sic*], so I am going to ask you to turn into them and ask every employee in the bank to do likewise as we are in politics now, and we are in it to win.[81]

This campaign was personal and partisan in a way that previous chummy electoral contests had not been. Wingfield's involvement was controversial at every level. Even in the Democratic party, Wingfield inspired factionalism. His attorneys, George Thatcher and William Woodburn, had been criticized by Pat McCarran, who was "spreading a lot of propoganda [*sic*] that we should surrender our leadership in the party on account of our close connections with Wingfield." The two defended themselves by pointing out, somewhat disingenuously, that "during the ten years that we have been with Wingfield he has never once mentioned politics or suggested a deal" and observed sardonically that Wingfield was subject to similar criticism within the Republican party.

The Sanford wing of the Republican party (opposed to Wingfield) complained that Wingfield is controlled by George [Thatcher] and me and that we are running both parties. While, of course, this is ridiculous, at the same time there is a whole lot more to this end of it than the other.[82]

Along with allegations that he was a political dictator with unsavory political associates, George Wingfield in 1928 was also combating persistent rumors that he operated a bipartisan machine. These charges clearly originated with political enemies of the alleged principals. Pat McCarran, a perennial aspirant for national political office, had been blocked by Woodburn and Thatcher on several occasions. Graham Sanford, publisher of the Republican *Reno Evening Gazette*, opposed Wingfield's local patronage choices and was a rival for the office of national committeeman. Yet they were not the only believers. At the height of the 1928 election campaign, San Francisco newspaperman J. J. McNeary was exploring the possible purchase of Reno's Democratic newspaper, the *Nevada State Journal*, from the Kilborn family who owned it. He reported to Wingfield, who was his backer, that he had met with Mrs. Kilborn, who "seemed more interested in what you were doing than in the sale of the paper." After observing that she was "far from a bonehead," he relayed her suspicions:

She wanted to know if you were sincere in advising voting for Sam Platt; she was almost sure that you and Key Pittman were the best of friends, and that you had befriended him in many ways in other campaigns. I assured her you were not only for Platt but that you were working night and day for the success of the entire Republican ticket. . . . [83]

Evidence suggests the truth of McNeary's assurances to Mrs. Kilborn. Wingfield may have voted for Pittman in 1922, but in 1928 he was positively frenzied in his support of Platt. In late October, he issued another public letter to the people of Nevada, denying all the Democratic charges and explaining the basis of his recommendations:

> I am seeking no favor; neither am I telling you how to vote. . . . For years I have been in close touch with the development and progress of our State. I am in daily contact with its people and business in every section, and I further call your attention to the fact that my interests are in Nevada.

Attempting to diffuse all the charges about nefarious influences, Wingfield represented himself simply as a knowledgeable, public-spirited citizen. Once again he reviewed the history of the tariff on Nevada products, with special reference to Pittman's misleading claims about his own role. Wingfield closed with a direct denial of the charges of bipartisanship: "I am convinced that this State would be more consistently represented by two Republican United States Senators voting in favor of the same ideals, than the election of one from each party naturally voting against each other on tariff and other partisan issues." [84]

Ultimately, it was not enough. While Nevada supported Herbert Hoover and Sam Arentz by large majorities, Platt was once again defeated. Key Pittman won by a comfortable majority of over 6,000 out of almost 33,000 votes cast. His margin was not as great as in 1922, but it was substantial enough to reprove George Wingfield. The Republican national committeeman was sympathetically reported as "very wrathy at the defeat of Sam Platt— some of his closest political friends betrayed him and it has hurt his pride." Wingfield understood well the personal nature of the message delivered by Nevada voters in 1928. In a state still reeling from the budget deficit created by the Cole-Malley defalcations, Wingfield's extraordinary combination of economic and political power had become controversial. The nature of that power hadn't significantly changed, but it had been displayed with special flamboyance in 1927, with the divorce legislation, and again in 1928, at the special session of the legislature. Political opponents like McCarran and Sanford also capitalized on growing resentment of the new, wide-open Reno economy that George Wingfield had helped to create and with which he was so prominently identified. [85]

The 1928 political campaign, by stimulating public debate over the character and extent of Wingfield's influence, ultimately operated to limit it. Nothing startling happened. Wingfield's influence didn't immediately wane; but his commanding position in the state began to be a matter of public dispute. Increasingly over the next few years, that dispute hampered his ability to exercise the considerable power he still retained, because it subjected his every action to scrutiny and attack. After 1928, playing the game became a rougher proposition.

NINE

"Thousands Hate Him"

A T FIRST, nothing seemed changed. After the 1928 campaign, despite the bitter aftertaste of the vituperative newspaper rhetoric, George Wingfield was riding high. Everything he touched still turned to gold, and the Nevada economy seemed proof against the depression that was spreading elsewhere in the country. When panicky friends in the East wrote him letters seeking investment advice in the aftermath of the 1929 stock market collapse, Wingfield replied almost jauntily that he was personally unaffected by the crash: "Some of the boys got trimmed a little on the stock market. . . . I went the other way and have been lending a lot of money on these high rates. I have no stock and have not had any." Characteristically, he blamed the country's economic troubles on politics and assumed that the financial losers had brought their problems on themselves. As he lectured his old friend and sometime bookie, Hoyt Smith: "the suckers who play the races or stock market with all the odds against them, either go broke or commit suicide. Never play the other fellow's game and you will always make money." It seemed at the time to be absolutely true.[1]

In the early 1930s, Wingfield was still playing his familiar economic game and making money at it. The price of GCMC stock was up to 62 cents. In 1930, in a speculative mood, Wingfield bought the controlling stock interest in the tiny Wells State Bank in northeastern Nevada, intending to liquidate it if there was no money to be made there. He assigned his banking assistant, former national bank examiner Charles P. Weigand, to manage it, meanwhile instructing his bank vice-president to investigate the State of Nevada bank deposits, to make sure that the Wingfield banks were receiving their fair share of the state trade. It was, in short, business as usual.[2]

All the signs pointed to good times. In June 1930, he wrote to Walter

Bracken, his Las Vegas agent, that he didn't want to sell his Las Vegas lots after all: "I hardly think if I were offered $75,000.00 for them today, I would take it." A few weeks later, he set the asking price at a phenomenal $150,000. If economic depression was affecting the rest of the world, you could scarcely tell it in Nevada. An exuberant Wingfield boasted in a confidential letter to Tasker Oddie, that, despite conditions in the East, "We have had the best year of our career [1929] and we have the banks in wonderful shape. We could stand some pretty hard knocks, but I hope we won't have to." Still a major borrower from Crocker National Bank, which carried his personal notes for amounts ranging from $300,000 to $750,000 during these years, Wingfield evidently had little reason to fear the future. As late as September 1931, he was still trumpeting his faith in the Nevada economy, confiding to a correspondent in Washington, D.C.: "Conditions in a business way here are very good and much better than in any other section of the country."[3]

Ever the promoter and protector of his home state, George Wingfield during the early 1930s further refined his vision for it. A good example was the federally financed Boulder Canyon Project, the interstate agreement to dam and distribute the waters of the Colorado River. Negotiations about division of the river's water, and the hydroelectric power it would produce, were pending in 1930. Wingfield was worried that short-sighted Nevada negotiators, in their haste to get the construction started, would allow insidious southern California power interests to steal water and power rights that Nevada couldn't use in 1930, but might someday require. He spent considerable time and energy advising Senator Oddie about the negotiations and explaining the Las Vegas factionalism that he thought was undermining Nevada's case: "The Las Vegas crowd don't care whether Nevada gets anything out of it or not as long as the Dam is built and they get a temporary boom." Wingfield, by contrast, urged caution, adopting the statesman's longer view: "I want to see this development carried on; in the meantime, however, I don't want to see Southern California steal everything that belongs to Nevada."[4]

Wingfield realized that Boulder Canyon represented the future of the state. The building of Hoover Dam, and consequent growth of southern Nevada, was one of the prime reasons he had purchased his Las Vegas lots in 1928. As a man well acquainted with both the potential pitfalls and the benefits of such large-scale operations, he gave unsolicited advice to all who would take it, including Governor Balzar. John Mueller spent much of his time consulting in Washington, D.C., and elsewhere about the proposed power and water allocations. Although Wingfield's subsequent tribulations ultimately distracted him from the Boulder Canyon Project, his enthusiasm for it never flagged. After visiting the site of Hoover Dam in 1932, he described it to a Chicago friend in terms that were, for Wingfield, almost impassioned: "Boulder City is a model one and the Hoover Dam is a wonderful piece of work. It is well worth going to see as it is the largest undertaking of man." Keenly aware of what this undertaking could mean for the state, Wingfield played his customary role with special fervor, urging Las Vegan Walter Bracken, for example, to take care about certain proposals and certain personalities, to guard against "these people trying to play a lot of petty politics as well as being a little greedy personally." In his own eyes, at least, Wingfield was long past that point.[5]

Indeed, in a series of long, expansive letters written in 1930, Wingfield came as close as he was ever to do to enunciating a leader's comprehensive vision for the economic development of his state. He lectured Oddie magisterially on Nevada's future, about the pressing need for upstream storage on the Truckee River, about ways to save the fish hatcheries at Pyramid Lake, on the Paiute reservation outside Reno, and about the need to secure passage of the Oddie-Colton bill to provide federal money for road construction and maintenance in states like Nevada, with high percentages of federal land and a low tax base. Less concerned now with questions of political patronage, he continued to promote road improvements, including paving the road to Pyramid Lake to attract more tourists. None of these measures had potential for immediate personal profit. In his own mind, however, Wingfield's interests had by now surpassed mere profit or politics. They had become indistinguishable from those of the state at large.[6]

He regretted only that he was so little able to serve them. In December 1929, Wingfield was taken seriously ill with the flu. He was in bed for three weeks and at home for more than a month, receiving serum treatments and seriously considering seeking hospital treatment. It was a continuation of his persistent problems with hay fever and asthma, only this time more debilitating than usual, possibly pneumonia. In late January 1930, he was still apologizing to Oddie for the crimp it put in his usual style. He wanted to spice his letters by sending along the political gossip: "It is going to be good and I am sorry I can not get around a little more to pick up a little of the side lights." The next month, in late February 1930, he had recovered sufficiently to be outdoors at the racetrack, only to be trampled by a group of stampeding thoroughbreds. The yearling horses badly lacerated his left leg, and Wingfield stayed close to home for a time to guard against infection in the wounds. He was beginning to show his age. In 1931, at age fifty-four, he spent two weeks in San Francisco to "go through a clinic" trying to diagnose his "spells." He reported to his friend Governor Balzar that his blood pressure was low, but the doctors were unable to explain exactly what was wrong. A month later, he was back in San Francisco in the hospital. Hay fever, severe colds, and stomach flu all plagued him increasingly as the decade wore on.[7]

Not all was bleak, though, and there were also reasons for celebration. In 1930, George Wingfield's 18-year-old daughter, Jean, made her social debut in San Francisco. That same year, on July 26, Wingfield remarried. His second wife, Roxy Thoma, was sixteen years his junior, the daughter of a Reno physician who had a lifelong interest in politics. A vivacious and strikingly handsome woman, she was the sister-in-law of Wingfield's sometime employee, mining engineer Roy Hardy. At the time of her marriage she was in her late thirties, living with her sister and brother-in-law, and their two children. Wingfield courted her at the Hardy house, after first observing the proprieties by seeking permission from her brother-in-law.[8]

The Hardy children remembered the courtship period fondly, when George Wingfield would call on Roxy Thoma and woo them as well by tossing them enough silver dollars to fill and refill their piggy banks. They were devastated when their aunt insisted that he stop the game. When the wedding occurred, after about a year, it was reminiscent of Wingfield's first one. The small, quiet ceremony took place without prior announcement. It was conducted by Reno minister Brewster Adams in the Hardy home, at the corner of Liberty and South Virginia. Wingfield gave his bride a breathtaking $6,000 diamond ring, but the couple honeymooned relatively modestly at the groom's Riverside Hotel. The wedding was covered by the wire service and congratulations poured in from Wingfield's old friends across the country. To them he replied, in a repetitive refrain, "I think I've got the right one this time."[9]

Apparently, it was so. Roxy Thoma and George Wingfield remained married until his death in 1959. They lived in the same Court Street house he had always occupied, although Roxy gave away Maude's things and entirely redecorated the interior. In November 1931, he deeded it to her. She kept house with the help of a small staff, and the couple entertained graciously, although not lavishly. Visitors recalled Roxy Thoma Wingfield as an elegant hostess who used finger bowls and expensive crystal, but she was also a woman content to live in Reno, one who fit comfortably into Wingfield's world. When hard times struck with the bank collapse of the mid-1930s, Roxy Thoma Wingfield helped her husband endure them. She was instrumental in encouraging him to stop his self-destructive heavy drinking, which he did, in an act of tremendous will, at age fifty-five, in the midst of the bank crisis. Thereafter he drank sparkling water and chided his weaker-willed associates who still looked forward to the cocktail hour. Roxy supportively served only one drink to dinner guests at their house. Later she also convinced her husband to give up smoking the hand-rolled cigarettes which had been his habit since boyhood. She shared his stories and his company and left him in solitude to enjoy hunting and horses as he always had. To all appearances, Wingfield's second marriage was a thoroughly satisfactory, companionable match.[10]

Meanwhile, Wingfield continued to wield Republican political power on all levels. In 1929, in the familiar Nevada tradition of personal politics, he invoked his Washington connections to head off a potential federal land fraud prosecution of rancher John G. Taylor, a friend from Wingfield's years in Winnemucca and also a very wealthy man and director of the Reno National Bank. In May 1930, Wingfield himself was in Washington, consulting with his old friend President Herbert Hoover. In June, he was pulling the customary strings to secure harmony at Nevada's Republican State Convention, jauntily assuring an out-of-state correspondent that "I don't look for any dissension or kicks whatever, maybe a little loud talk from one or two persons." Clearly a man in control, George Wingfield dispatched a constant stream of advice and gossip to Senator Oddie and urged Republican Governor Balzar, reelected in 1930, not to veto a bill that was sponsored by a friendly state senator who "has played the game all the way through and has asked for nothing." [11]

It was not quite entirely business as usual, however, as Wingfield was still squirming from the vehemence of the 1928 attacks on him. He stayed away from the 1929 legislature in order to give the campaign rhetoric time to die down, although, as he confided to Oddie: "I have seen a bunch of the boys and there seems to be a good lot on both sides and no partisan politics. The less they have of that the better it will suit me." The entire experience made Wingfield especially sensitive to the disruptive power of the media. In 1929, for instance, he reluctantly accepted a $56,000 mortgage on Reno's Democratic newspaper, the *Nevada State Journal*, then published by former governor James Scrugham. Not particularly anxious to own a newspaper, Wingfield insisted that the note be endorsed by his Democratic attorneys, Thatcher and Woodburn, and he eagerly sought a reliable purchaser on Scrugham's behalf. As he confided to a potential customer, however, he had had no choice but to make the loan, "as I was afraid the paper might get in bad hands." Later, to his comrade Senator Oddie, he was more explicit: "The McClatchey outfit from California are trying to horn in here. You will remember them as being the owners of the Sacramento and Fresno Bees, and I would fight them through H——— [*sic*] before I would let them come in here on any proposition I could prevent." His memories of the 1928 campaign obviously remained both immediate and painful.[12]

Meanwhile, controversy about his alleged bipartisan machine continued.

As always, debates about Wingfield's role in politics were inseparable from economics. A newspaper editor from rural Elko, Nevada, aptly summarized prevailing suspicions: "A man who owns ten banks can talk either language —Democratic or Republican—and will be heard and understood by both parties." The political costs of the 1928 Republican victory, which focused public notice and resentment on Wingfield's empire, had been high, and the underlying resentment never completely died away. Both Nevada insiders and outsiders continued to remark the politician-banker's omnipotence within the state. In a book published in 1933, one visitor observed that "Wingfield today is more powerful in Nevada than he would be if he had gone to Washington as a Senator." And a Goldfield contemporary characterized him in 1932 as "the richest man in Nevada" and "far more difficult of access than the United States Senators whose characters were being formed beside him in the early hardships of the mining camps." [13]

Long after the fact, when time and economic reverses had dismantled any machine that might once have existed, political insiders tried to explain the complex reality of Nevada politics in that period, as they had experienced it. They described an isolated state with a small population and very few political players, which fostered a peculiar kind of intimacy and interdependence among those who sought and wielded power. Republican governor and congressman Charles Russell in 1967 recalled the so-called bipartisan machine as a series of several loosely related groups that worked together innocuously "for the benefit of the state." Others pointed out that George Wingfield was always eminently fair, that he never used his power for selfish purposes, that he worked to insure a good government rather than for political control. But at the time, in the 1930s, few in Nevada or elsewhere accepted such a benign view of Wingfield and his political power. Spurred by the *Sacramento Bee*'s insinuating prose and by persistent condemnation from disaffected political outsiders like the McCarran wing of the Democratic party, or the Sanford faction among the Republicans, Nevadans became increasingly suspicious of Wingfield's intentions and critical of his undertakings. In 1931, when the state legislature both legalized casino gambling and further reduced the divorce residency, all their worst suspicions about Wingfield's dominance of the state seemed to be confirmed. [14]

The process was deceptively simple. With little fanfare, one day apart near the end of the session in March, the 1931 Nevada Legislature passed two bills. One lowered the residency period for divorce from three months to only six weeks. The other allowed licensed gambling by application to the county sheriff and payment of a fee that would be split by the city, county, and state governments. The action came as no surprise within the state. Both bills had been regularly introduced, and the gambling law was the same one that had been narrowly defeated in 1927. Their passage had been widely anticipated, and many supported the measures. The six-week divorce law, for instance, was heralded as a rational response to recent attempts by Arkansas and Idaho to cut into Nevada's lucrative divorce trade by passing their own three-month laws. The *Ely Daily Times*, edited by Key Pittman's brother Vail, predicted passage of the gambling law and anticipated condemnation by the eastern press. He pointed out, however, that Nevada's "vices" of divorce, horse racing, and gambling were "not seriously regarded by its citizenship" and catered instead to outsiders. As Pittman cynically observed, "after all much of the revenue derived from these sources comes from the critical residents of other states." [15]

Within Nevada's business community, at least that portion of it based on the incipient tourism trade, both the divorce and the gambling laws made sense. Amidst hard times produced by the national depression, which was already affecting Nevada's livestock industry, the measures shored up the tourist-based economy of legalized or tolerated vices that Wingfield and others had been developing in Reno since the 1910s. A shorter residency period would prevent diversion of Nevada's profitable divorce trade to other, more accessible locations. Legalized gambling would allow for policing of existing games and elimination of cheaters, besides giving local and state governments a share of the profits.

Wingfield favored the 1931 legislation as he had done in 1927 and began laying the groundwork fully a year earlier. In June 1930, for instance, he cautioned Walter Bracken about the Clark County Republican convention:

> I think you should advise your delegates not to bring up the gambling proposition, nor the booze racket, as there are many other ways to skin a cat and we don't want to get any groups against us before the election. Those matters can be handled in a different way, if your delegates are inclined to be liberal, and you can elect liberal members of the Legislature.

This strategy obviously worked. The bill was passed by healthy margins in both the Democratic Assembly and the Republican-controlled Senate. As former governor James G. Scrugham editorialized in the *Nevada State Journal*, the people of Nevada approved of "legalized liberality":

> At the present time it appears that a majority of the people desire a trial of open gambling and easy divorce as a means of stimulating business. The opposition to these measures was only nominal and the present state administration were elected largely as avowed advocates of such legislation.

The *Reno Evening Gazette* bemoaned the unsavory reputation that would result from scandalous magazine articles, but acknowledged that passage of the bills "really makes conditions but little different from what they have been in fact for years."[16]

Pleased with the general acceptance of the legislation, Wingfield confided to his bankers at Crocker in March 1931 that he had been "busy with Legislative activities. They got through this morning and we got everything we wanted and killed everything we did not want." Wingfield planned to take off for a round of quarterly bank meetings, but in the light of the new laws he reassured his bankers: "Conditions up here are very much better and I look for a very good season." Wingfield considered passage of these liberal measures Nevada's salvation, and he was not alone in believing so. Reno Mayor E. E. Roberts cheerily proclaimed Nevada "about the only free state left"; and Governor Balzar made plans to publish a book called *Nevada Liberalism*, which would be distributed to every daily newspaper in the United States. As Balzar explained to Wingfield, his book would tout the unique basis of the state's success and "give Nevada some valuable publicity."[17]

Along the same lines, and drawing on the earlier example of the 1910 Johnson-Jeffries prizefight, Reno promoters including Jack Dempsey, Graham, and McKay made plans to host a July 4 heavyweight prizefight between American Max Baer and a Spanish Basque fighter, Paulino Uzcudun. They erected a special stadium on the grounds of the Reno racetrack and predicted confidently that 4,000 people would be attracted to Reno for the occasion. Dempsey's manager told one reporter, "This fight is not merely a fight. It is the big card in the Reno boom. Its object is to put Reno on the map, and get the people with money out here." Presumably they would spend some of that money for lodging, food, and drink, and especially for the newly legalized thrill of gambling. Reno businesses were sprucing up in anticipation of the influx, hoping against hope that the twin attractions could overcome the weight of the economic depression and lure people to Nevada. While George Wingfield owned no gambling clubs himself, Graham and McKay were his tenants in the Golden Hotel. When their Bank Club opened new, luxurious quarters on the ground floor in 1931, they anticipated that "the play should be a little better" than it had been previously, when they were located out of harm's way in the basement. Presumably, their rent was a little higher, as well.[18]

Within Nevada, then, the majority seemed reconciled to the new laws. Both gambling and the divorce trade were touted as part of the state's frontier heritage and they offered in addition the boon of a new source of income for beleaguered local governments. But the legislature's actions created a furor in the rest of the country. As the *Gazette* had gloomily predicted, writers deplored Nevada's status as "a prostitute state," and headlines proclaimed Reno "a mad riot of wine, women, divorce, gambling." Outsiders were horrified especially by Nevadans' cheerful and open admission that the new laws were framed specifically in order to lure tourists to the state. A matter that Nevadans largely cast in terms of potential profit seemed to others a moral travesty, a dangerous subversion of all that was sacred. The national press responded with predictable outrage. Nevada's 1931 legislation piqued the country's interest and titillated a conservative audience that publicly deplored both divorce and gambling.[19]

The resulting surge of media attention rivaled the feverish madness of twenty-five years earlier, at the peak of the Tonopah-Goldfield boom. Writers and reporters from all over the United States came to Nevada to describe its outlaw society. Articles and books about the social experiment proliferated. Most of them prominently featured George Wingfield as "the man to whom most of the credit must go for the building of Reno and for the liberal laws of his State." Once again, Wingfield was the subject of sustained national publicity. This time, however, in marked contrast to the adulation of Nevada's Napoleon during the Goldfield boom, the tone of the articles was not admiring.[20]

The sensationalist *New York Evening Graphic*, published by physical culturalist Bernarr Macfadden, was particularly vitriolic. It began a 20-part series on Reno in July 1931 with the startling declaration: "Nevada is an outlaw state. George Wingfield is its king." For the rest of the month, the *Graphic* series, written by Laura Vitray, explored the steamy panoply of Reno's vices, including the drug trade, prostitution, alcohol, gambling, murder, and graft. The articles knowingly cited Wingfield's origins as a gambler, referred to the lawsuits filed by his common-law wife, and identified him with the criminal empire of Graham and McKay. The Cole-Malley debacle was covered in terms vaguely reminiscent of Pat McCarran's closing statement during the trial, and headlines screamed, " 'King' of Nevada Makes Governor, Judges and Senators Do His Bidding." The *Graphic* series rehearsed the dissatisfaction of some stockholders with Wingfield's handling of the assets of the old Washoe County Bank, which he had incorporated into the United Nevada Bank in 1929. It blamed the scandal of Reno's corruption squarely on Wingfield, whose hotel properties had been made lucrative by "legislation passed against the will of the voters of Nevada, at Wingfield's instigation." Wingfield was blamed as well for the failure of eastern companies to invest in legitimate Nevada mines, because of the scandal associated with the state's social practices. In short, the *Graphic* series repeated many of the charges of the 1928

Sacramento Bee articles, but this time in greater and more lurid detail, and in a national forum.[21]

The shocking 1931 series was reprinted in other papers and attracted attention across the country. Arthur Thomas, a stockbroker in Salt Lake City, and one of Wingfield's associates in the San Rafael venture, wrote angrily to office manager William Zoebel about it:

> I hate these stories. . . . Some dirty, little scurrilous bum probably got a couple of hundred dollars for that story at the most, and for two hundred dollars they would sell the soul of even the Almighty. . . . There ought to be a law that would allow you to go out and shoot these people that say malignant things about you in the press.

Cornelius Vanderbilt, Jr., himself the object of attack in Reno when he published his own relatively mild novel about its divorce colony in 1929, was also concerned about the numerous stories defaming Reno. He wrote confidentially to Wingfield from Los Angeles, to report on some of the sources:

> There are some few people living in Reno at the present time, who are sending out there, from time to time, news and photographs of a derogatory nature. I think this should be stopped. I realize fully that it is none of my business; and that we are powerless to hamper the affairs of the press; but when persons deliberately set out to blacken and ruin a community, then it is high time something were done about it. . . . regardless of all the notoriety which Reno is getting, I love the little town and I hate like the dickens to see it further besmirched. . . . If we had the Vigilantes, they'd take some of these people out and beat the ———— out of them, as should be done now.[22]

Wingfield himself, by now accustomed to such controversy, was resigned. At the end of the *Graphic* series he reported mildly to Hoyt Smith in Chicago, "Everything is going along alright here. While the outside papers are knocking Reno, I would only like to see other towns as good." No doubt he consoled himself that not all the coverage was scurrilous. *Business and Commerce*, a national financial magazine published in New York, attacked the *Graphic* series as "evidently intended for readers of a moronistic tendency" and lauded the gambling legislation as "a fearless step in the right direction." This journal found no dissension in either Reno or the state of Nevada on the issue: "The legalizing of gambling is considered by every intelligent man or woman as a step which should be applauded by all of us who believe in honesty and frankness." A writer for *American Mercury* concluded in 1933 that gambling was fairer now that it was regulated and made fun of its misguided opponents, "the usual group of Methodists, who solemnly predicted that the residents of Reno, suffering a complete moral breakdown, would immediately transfer their homesteads to the roulette dealers." And capitalistic *Fortune* magazine pointed out in 1934 that there were genuine economic benefits to the new arrangement: "Whatever you may think of Reno's morals, the liberality of its rulers toward man's essential appetites has paid its bills." But the shocking story told by the *Graphic* was echoed in milder tones by all the others, who pointed in common to the absolute centrality of George Wingfield to Nevada's new legislation.[23]

Whatever they might think of them, all the national observers agreed that Reno's morals were Wingfield's. As *Fortune* put it, "In Wingfield's flamboyant career is the essence of Nevada's character." Wingfield himself would not have disagreed. He had long been an advocate of personal freedom and had never condemned divorce, drinking, or gambling. While Vitray in the *New York Evening Graphic* was surely wrong in attributing the 1931 legislation solely to Wingfield's influence, the Nevadan was unabashed about his approval of the new laws and expected the state as a whole to profit by them. This was entirely in keeping not only with his frontier morality, but also with his economic faith in diversification. Wingfield owned no gambling clubs himself, but his hotels would profit if the number of visitors increased, either seeking divorce or lured by the games of chance. In that sense, even bad publicity might actually prove favorable. Since the point was to lure outsiders to come and take advantage of Nevada's social tolerance, the national hue and cry might be seen as invaluable, if inadvertent, advertising of Reno's unique atmosphere. As Wingfield reported to his office manager in May 1931, from San Francisco, "I don't know where they are going to put the people this summer as Reno is all you hear around here."[24]

In retrospect, Wingfield proved prescient when he confided to a New York friend immediately after the legislature's adjournment, "I look for quite a revival of business in this community." Legalization of gambling in 1931 spawned an economic boom in Reno. The Baer-Uzcudun fight on July 4 attracted thousands, and a 29-day July race meet took in the unprecedented sum of $586,000. Wingfield himself had "my house packed with people over the Fourth" and expected "of course the town will be filled with people for the whole month." Men and women in elegant evening dress flocked to Graham and McKay's Willows Club, which stood west of Reno on the road toward California until it burned in 1932. In addition to the expanded Bank Club downtown, the partners opened the rustic Cal-Neva at Lake Tahoe, where the state line between Nevada and California ran down the middle of the dance floor and divorce-seekers flirtatiously crossed it in violation of the stipulation that they not leave the state of Nevada while establishing residency. Traditional backroom gambling halls weren't enticing to tourists; but Reno's infamous underworld entrepreneurs set a successful new nightclub style that combined dancing, dining, and drinking with gambling in a luxurious setting, thus catering to wealthy sojourners of both sexes who were starved for entertainment. From an economic standpoint then, the legislation seemed to be a great success. Indeed the tourist-based industry that George Wingfield initially developed and underwrote in Reno still remains the keystone of Nevada's vigorous economy.[25]

But in 1931 the national press focused on Nevada's immorality rather than its economy. By reviving the invidious 1928 allegations of the *Sacramento Bee*, and drawing attention once again to Wingfield's tremendous power and his connections to Reno's underworld figures, the new wave of media attention rendered him even more prominent and ever more controversial. No longer Nevada's Napoleon, its fearless champion, Wingfield was now depicted as its domineering king, an evil man who brooked no opposition and whose will was absolute. "Some [Reno citizens] told me that it would be more than their business lives were worth to have it known that they oppose Mr. Wingfield's policies," reported the *Christian Century*. Gossip linked the banker financially to speakeasies and gambling joints, and to Reno's legal brothel. The existence of the notorious bipartisan political machine was simply assumed, with the lack of substantial Nevada opposition to the 1931 legislation taken as irrefutable evidence. In the "whirlpool of vice" that was Reno, George Wingfield's was depicted, and in some circles accepted, as the ubiquitous and omnipotent guiding hand.[26]

Inured to criticism, and habitually reticent, Wingfield made no public response to the charges. He saw no need to. He was surrounded by eminent men who respected him and his efforts, and he was supremely confident of the rectitude of his activities. Wingfield assumed that most people who were knowledgeable about Nevada's economic and social limitations would agree that the legislated industries of divorce and gambling were its only economic hope, and he disdained the opinions of the ill informed. Soon, however, as the worldwide economic collapse of the 1930s belatedly began to impinge on Nevada, it proved difficult to remain aloof. By 1931, Wingfield was already beginning to feel the pinch of depression, in what proved to be the beginning of a sequence of events that ultimately toppled him from his throne as the reputed king of an outlaw state. In retrospect, it would be clear that he had reached, in the early 1930s, the zenith of his career.

Initially, however, signs of this downturn were murky. Wingfield's economic optimism during this period has already been noted. In October 1931, he was sufficiently confident to contemplate taking over yet another bank, the Nevada First National of Tonopah. He approached Key Pittman, who was one of its stockholders, with a proposal to buy the rival to his own Tonopah Banking Corporation. He explained, reported Pittman, "how [having] one bank in Tonopah with a reduced capital could make money. He also showed me how it was impossible at the present time for two banks to make money." Wingfield planned to merge his oldest banking property, John S. Cook & Co. at Goldfield, into the Tonopah Banking Corporation, because of declining business at the moribund southern Nevada town. Incorporating the other Tonopah bank as well would create an institution that, in Wingfield's opinion, "could make a handsome profit for a number of years to come." He predicted $30,000 annually. Although at least one of the Nevada First National stockholders, Thomas F. Cole, was reluctant to effect the consolidation, it was eventually concluded, and the three banks became one in late July 1932. Wingfield followed his usual procedure with any new bank, determining right away to write off all bad loans against the undivided profits account. As he described it to Senator Pittman, "My idea would be to clean house right there and keep it clean." It was the same course he had followed with the bank in Winnemucca and with others as well. It was the normal procedure of a prudent banker.[27]

The times were not normal, however. By 1932, bad loans were beginning to multiply in all of the Wingfield banks, as the national depression and a series of drought years combined to undermine the always delicate Nevada economy. The trouble began as early as 1929, when the first in a series of dry winters hit the western range, and with it the Nevada cattle and sheep ranchers who were among the principal borrowers of the banks. Winters with less than usual moisture meant that the following season's grass was reduced. This in turn meant that ranchers couldn't successfully feed as many head of stock. The banks traditionally carried ranchers through the year by advancing them operating funds and waiting for the returns when sales were made in spring and fall. But the collapse of national markets following the stock market crash in 1929 meant that prices for lambs, wool, and cattle were declining precipitously, at precisely the same time that ranchers needed money to pay for feed to substitute for the sparse natural grazing and to pay off their bank loans. Both prices and yields declined. Cattle that sold for almost 10 cents per pound in 1928 brought less than 4 cents per pound in 1932, and their average weight declined. The Wingfield banks, especially those in outlying rural areas like Elko and Winnemucca, loaned large sums of money to local ranchers. When the ranch economy suffered, they did too.[28]

As behooves a careful banker whose business depended in large part on ranchers, George Wingfield constantly monitored Nevada range conditions. By November 1929, he was already aware of problems. Wingfield observed the first signs of drought in a letter to Tasker Oddie: "Everything is going along nicely outside of not having had any rains and they have had none in California either and this has made range conditions very bad and the situation in that respect does not look very good." He was right. As early as 1930, there were ominous signs. Deposits in Nevada banks, after peaking at over $52 million in 1928, had fallen to under $47 million. Wingfield's cashiers reported a total of $481,000 in loans labeled "bad and doubtful," many of them made to ranchers. One of Nevada's largest and wealthiest stockmen, John G. Taylor, was in dire straits by 1930, forced to borrow almost half a million dollars to keep his cattle and sheep operations afloat. Unable to provide the needed cash through his banks, George Wingfield turned to his personal bankers at Crocker, agreeing in February 1931 to guarantee Taylor's one-year note.[29]

Meanwhile, he was also borrowing heavily from Crocker on his own account. Throughout 1930 and 1931, he periodically increased his loans at Crocker by $100,000 to $350,000, putting the additional money into certificates of deposit at the Henderson Banking Company in Elko. This bank, where the largest number of livestock loans originated, was chronically short of cash as it tried desperately to keep its ranch customers from bankruptcy. Wingfield's deposits protected the Henderson reserves by providing large amounts of cash that would not be withdrawn until the bank had other cash to replace it. In theory, this would happen once deposits at Henderson rebounded after the fall stock sales, when ranchers repaid their loans and deposited the excess proceeds in the bank. At that point Wingfield could cash in his certificates of deposit and repay his own loans from Crocker. Unfortunately, in the drought years from 1929 to 1935, these deposits continued to plummet, and Wingfield was forced to leave some of his borrowed money on permanent deposit in Elko. When the bank closed in November 1932, he still had $250,000 there.[30]

Henderson in Elko and the First National Bank of Winnemucca were the worst affected by the livestock crisis, but United Nevada Bank also had outstanding livestock loans that had been part of the assets of the failed banks when they were absorbed into the consolidation. In addition, in order to spread the risk of these large, seasonal livestock loans, as well as other large loans, Wingfield had divided some of them and parceled smaller amounts out among the various banks he controlled. There was a certain logic to this system, since the ranchers and companies that were large borrowers almost always operated in more than one area of the state. The practice was not authorized under then current Nevada banking statutes, however, since it effectively consolidated the theoretically independent Wingfield banks into a single operating unit. Still, it was one way of staving off immediate disaster for the banks with large portfolios of ranch loans and buying time for the despairing ranchers.

Another way was to help them pool their resources. George Wingfield was not a man to sit idly by and watch his banks go under. Instead he took action, hiring a ranch expert who had been both a banker and a ranch manager. Robert C. Turrittin had assisted in liquidating the assets of the Washoe County Bank when it was absorbed into United Nevada and had earlier been cashier at the Nixon National. Since 1927, he had been an appraiser, liquidator, and manager of ranch properties. Wingfield gave him responsibility for supervising the ranch operations in all the banks. Beginning in 1930, Turrittin began a systematic survey of ranchers who were indebted to the banks. Carefully noting the number of head of sheep and cattle, land ownership, water rights, buildings, and amount of outstanding loans of each borrower, he painted a bleak picture of the Nevada livestock industry.

Based on his reports, Wingfield decided in 1931 to sponsor two cooperative marketing agreements or pools. Livestock owners, who did not have to be borrowers from Wingfield banks, would assign their animals to the bank's management. Turrittin, in turn, would oversee shipment of all the animals thus collected to feed lots and stockyards in the East, beyond the reach of Nevada's drought. There, presumably, they could be fattened and sold for better prices. Turrittin had authority to ship and sell the animals as he saw fit, with the net proceeds of the pools to be distributed to the participants on a proportional basis and used to pay off their ever-increasing loans.

It was a daring gamble. By the fall of 1931, Nevada agriculture was in shambles, and the only way to protect the investment already made was for the banks to throw good money after bad, by further extending already jeopardized loans in an attempt to outlast the hard times. In September, the newly appointed State Agricultural Relief Committee, of which George Wingfield was chairman, had negotiated emergency reductions in railroad freight rates to accommodate the massive movement of outgoing livestock. Throughout the fall and winter of 1931, Wingfield anxiously followed Turrittin's progress. Over 90,000 lambs were assembled and shipped to Idaho, Colorado, Kansas, and Nebraska for feeding, with occasional sales taking place along the way. Cattle, too, were gathered in a separate undertaking, shipped to feed lots, and then sold at the stockyards in Kansas City and Omaha. Turrittin had estimated that sales of fattened cattle would bring over $382,000; but by mid-September, they had yielded less than $247,000.[31]

Never losing hope, Wingfield continued to monitor the progress of the pools closely, but the news was consistently disappointing. Expenses of the pool arrangement—for transportation, feed, and the salaries of hands to manage the large groups of animals—were high, and returns were low. By January of the new year, 1932, Wingfield was clearly despondent. Far from rebounding, the market for cattle was sinking ever lower. No longer a matter of maximizing profits, it was now a question of just cutting losses: "I don't see any sales coming in whatever and of course the time to sell is when the stuff is ready as the more feed that is put into them after they are finished, the more losses will be sustained." [32]

The pools were an expensive failure, but they were a good-faith effort to assist Nevada stockmen and protect one of the state's bedrock industries. So were the extended loans. George Wingfield the promoter of tourism and gambling was astute enough to recognize that these new leisure-based industries would never support the entire state, and that rural Nevada, in particular, needed the ranchers. As the son of a cattleman, and a person who had first made his living as a cowhand, Wingfield sympathized with the stockman's predicament, pinched between drought and declining markets. He wanted to help, not solely to protect his own banks, but also to save their borrowers.

Against his own better fiscal judgment, he extended loans rather than calling them and sending the borrowers into foreclosure. If Wingfield had foreclosed ruthlessly in 1930, he probably could have saved his banks; but he instead advanced more money. Fussing constantly at his cashiers to reduce outstanding loans to ranchers, he nonetheless authorized increased chattel loans against the questionable security of constantly decreasing herds. He had, as he saw it, no choice. The only other option would be to abandon the ranchers and have the bank take over most of the ranches in rural Nevada. Such a step had its own risks, as he confided to Turrittin in 1932:

> On account of the critical situation we are passing through, I feel that all of the friction and trouble we can avoid for the next six months will be to our advantage, even if it does cost a little more to handle the sheep with some particular person than to bring about a lot of foreclosures. . . . for if a recovery comes, these men in charge of the smaller outfits will put forth greater energy to pay up their indebtedness and it would look better, than if it were in one large concern.

Mindful of the repeated charges of his domination, Wingfield was sensitive to the impression it might create if he were to follow sound business practice and foreclose on all the people who owned him money and couldn't pay. With loans to over 150 ranches that owned seventy percent of Nevada livestock, his banks would then truly have ended up controlling a substantial portion of the state. Increased personal attacks on the banker would have been the predictable result.[33]

And the ranching crisis was merely the beginning of his woes. The nascent gambling industry was suffering along with the rest of the country and hotel receipts in Reno were declining by October 1931. In January 1932, Wingfield's office manager advised a Los Angeles correspondent against expansion into Reno:

> In his [Wingfield's] opinion, present conditions do not justify the construction of a new hotel and casino in Reno. As a matter of fact, we have a plenitude of vacant hotel rooms in the City and many of the gaming places established last year when the law legalized gambling have since gone out of business.

Even Reno Pony Express Days, an elaborate rodeo promotion staged in late June 1932, was not enough to revive the flagging fortunes of the aspiring tourist destination.[34]

Neither Nevada nor its major capitalist ultimately proved immune to economic depression. In 1931, Wingfield signed personal notes to Crocker First National Bank for an unprecedented $850,000. He reluctantly reduced the salaries of even trusted senior employees like Estey Julian in September of that year. The next May, he was making further reductions, laying off some men altogether and cutting wages for Bob Turrittin, John Mueller, and his special banking assistant, Charles P. Weigand. Wingfield wrote to Walter Bracken in Las Vegas that he was now willing to accept less money for his lots there. And, in October 1931, he wrote plaintively to Raymond Benjamin in Washington, hoping that Benjamin could speed up the promised $80,000 government payment for Wingfield's lots along the south bank of the Truckee River, the site for a new federal post office. When he finally got a reduced payment of $78,000 the next January, his relief was palpable.[35]

The money was sorely needed. By 1932, George Wingfield had stopped making personal loans altogether, a long-standing practice that he gave up regretfully. As the depression worsened, more and more of his formerly comfortable friends and acquaintances found themselves in straitened circumstances, swallowed their pride, and turned to Wingfield for help. Unfortunately, the Nevada banker could no longer afford such personal benefaction. As he explained to E. A. Montgomery, whose mining fortune had come from the Bullfrog mines during the same southern Nevada boom that established Wingfield, "I have been using a great deal of money through these strenuous times and have had to refuse all my old friends alike." At the same time he began dunning those to whom he had previously loaned money for payments on their notes, generally without any success. Hard times made collection difficult. Many didn't even bother to answer Wingfield's letters.[36]

Meanwhile, difficulties mounted on other fronts. Sutter Butte Canal Company, in California, had begun an ambitious program of expansion. Now it was running ever-increasing deficits as rice prices fell, and Crocker First National Bank was insisting on refinancing. Wingfield's mining companies, too, were suffering. GCMC sold its Canadian Base Metals property in 1933 for some much-needed cash, and the Boundary Red Mountain Mining Company, another Wingfield gold property located in northern Washington, defaulted on its $220,000 loan from George Wingfield.[37]

In the general press of business, Wingfield had less time and attention than usual for politics, or for the customary details of business management. The banker was struggling now not only for the ranchers, but for his entire empire. The banks were in a critical state, borrowing money from the Federal Reserve Bank in San Francisco and from Crocker. In May 1932, his friend Tasker Oddie wrote sympathetically of his plight:

> I can understand that you have been through hell on earth this year. You have kept the State going under the most terrible conditions it has ever had to face and I hope the people of the State generally will realize what you have accomplished and what you mean to them.

Most were not so solicitous, however. Wingfield's problems were none of their own, and besides it was hard to feel sorry for a man who apparently had so much.[38]

In fact, the year 1932 turned out to be one of the darkest of Wingfield's life. The man described by former governor James G. Scrugham as "apparently imperturbable in any tumult . . . unafraid and calm in times and conditions that sent most men reeling and dizzy" was starting to crack under the mounting strain. The livestock pools were a failure, and borrowers defaulted in record numbers. Beginning in the late summer of 1931, deposits in the Wingfield banks dropped steadily, a total of $9 million over the next fifteen months. In 1932 alone, losses in the twelve banks totaled $3.5 million. Wingfield's personal expenses didn't slacken, with monthly alimony payments of $2,500 due to Maude Murdoch Wingfield, and additional costs associated with the presentation of his daughter at the Court of St. James in England, and his son's education at Stanford. He and Roxy continued to live well at home, dispatching specialty orders to San Francisco for caviar puffs, boneless anchovies, and pâté de foie gras; but all of these expenditures added up.[39]

George Wingfield turned fifty-six years old in August 1932. Instead of celebrating he was fighting for his economic life. Facing insurmountable troubles that no amount of action or acumen could overcome, he had been drinking more heavily than usual and his health had deteriorated. His daughter later credited Roxy Thoma Wingfield with holding her father together and saving him from drinking himself to death because of the stress. Understated as usual, the phrase that Wingfield used in October 1932 about one of his borrowers takes on a special poignancy as a summary of his own situation: "His indebtedness at the present time is causing us considerable worry." [40]

He had every reason to be worried. It was, as one economic historian put it, "an extreme emergency," and Wingfield was right in the middle of it. Accustomed to authority and accomplishment, he suddenly found himself a victim instead, as the proverbial bottom fell out of formerly dependable markets. Yet he was also a man from whom many expected miracles. His prominence as a Nevada political and economic leader made him seem invulnerable to the vicissitudes that were then afflicting so many others. As the economic situation grew ever bleaker in 1932, he struggled to meet his responsibilities and find the solutions that so many people expected of him and that, in truth, he also expected of himself. On January 29, after recounting the number of bank failures in surrounding states, he explained the problem to his friend Oddie:

> By securing relief in these stringent times I am satisfied everything would come out alright through the State as a whole. We are meeting every situation that arises, but, of course, the public don't realize that by hoarding their money they are making the situation worse, in this State as well as all other States . . . and of course, the banks are only making such loans as they have to, which has a bad effect as Depositors withdraw their funds from the banks and make personal loans to their friends.[41]

That very day he had taken the first steps to solve it, dispatching an air mail letter inquiring about the possibility of a loan from the newly created Reconstruction Finance Corporation (RFC) to the state of Nevada. The bill creating the RFC, an emergency relief agency designed to loan federal funds to banks and other financial institutions in order to revitalize private financial markets, had been signed on January 22 by President Hoover. Wingfield was writing to Oddie for details of its operation just five days later, "especially how it will fit in with our situation out here, particularly on ranches, range lands and the livestock industry." The ranchers were clearly uppermost on his mind at the time, but he also took a broader view, implicitly assuming responsibility as well for the general welfare of his state: "I would like this information as soon as possible and will then know about how the wants of our people would fit into this picture after I once get it." In fact, the RFC was not yet authorized to make loans of the sort that Wingfield requested, for direct relief to states; but his inquiry demonstrated the benevolent capitalism that Wingfield had come to regard as his duty. His interest in the potential usefulness of the RFC, as in the Boulder Canyon Project or upstream storage on the Truckee River, seamlessly melded potential economic self-interest with genuine concern for the well-being of his state.[42]

By now, Wingfield's habit of conflating his wishes with Nevada's interests was ingrained. The events of 1932, however, would dramatically and permanently sever the connection. Once the banker learned the parameters of RFC loans, he began to take full advantage of the program. Beginning in February and continuing through October, his banks applied for and received a series of loans totaling over $5 million. Of this amount, slightly over $3 million, beginning in April, went to the flagship institution, the Reno National Bank. The rest was divided among the smaller banks, with the first loan being requested for the First National Bank of Winnemucca, Nixon's old institution and one of the banks most severely affected by the livestock crisis. Temporarily, these loans served their intended purpose, providing enough liquidity to enable the banks to meet their obligations; but they did not solve the problem. The terms of RFC loans, at six months or less, were much too short to give the banks time to solve their problems, and at six percent, their interest rates were high. Because the national economy was still stagnant, depositors' money was flowing out of the banks. Assets pledged in support of loans, meanwhile, were steadily losing value, and foreclosure often didn't recover enough to cover the outstanding balance. Waiting until the economy recovered and assets resumed their value would have been sensible. Unfortunately, with RFC loans that had to be repaid in months rather than years, the Wingfield banks could not afford to wait.

Instead they found themselves involved in a steadily escalating panic. Several 1931 bank failures in nearby states made people nervous, and there were rumors about difficulties in the Wingfield banks as early as February 1932. News of the RFC loans reassured some, but caused other fearful Nevada depositors to withdraw their money from the Wingfield banks. Some people simply needed the cash to meet expenses. As the funds drained out, the banks needed increasing amounts of money to meet the demand. Meanwhile, the RFC insisted that the best assets of the banks be pledged to guarantee the short-term loans that were keeping the Nevada institutions afloat. These assets were conservatively valued by the RFC at only fifty to eighty percent of their market value and were not available during the period of the RFC loan to meet the cash demands on the bank. This meant that desperate banks had to sell other, less marketable assets to meet their cash requirements. Often these assets were sold at a considerable loss on a depressed market, further weakening the banks and doing nothing to stop the hemorrhaging of funds. Ultimately, economic historian James Olson concludes, "the R.F.C. loans themselves sometimes did no more than add new pressures to already over-burdened institutions." Even in the best cases, the loans simply prolonged the agony. Until the livestock industry recovered, and the assets on which loans to ranchers were based assumed something approaching their original values, there was little that could be done to help the Wingfield banks.[43]

As the summer wore on, their circumstances were critical. The Reno National Bank's first loan, for $1,137,000, was approved in early April. Two months later, it was back seeking more, with a third loan request approved later the same month, June 1932. In July, there was a fourth application, first requesting $500,000, then amended and finally approved on July 30 for almost $1,393,000. At that time George Thatcher, bank vice-president Jerry Sheehan, and F. Gloucester Willis, vice-president of the Crocker National Bank, appeared personally before the RFC Board of Directors. The bank had no more collateral to offer, and the men sought a further advance against assets that the RFC already held. The bank building was already pledged to the RFC and Reno National was actually securing its loans with collateral transferred from its sister institution, the Bank of Nevada Savings and Trust Company.

The San Francisco Loan Agency advised the board by telegram: "The situation is critical, and as closing this chain would doubtless tie up entire state, including state government funds, the repercussions in adjacent and other states might be very serious." The RFC board was sympathetic, realizing that "the question to be decided was the preservation of the value of the present collateral through the borrowing institutions continuing in business." Ultimately they decided their initial valuation of assets had been conservative and that the circumstances warranted an additional $400,000 to save the bank from collapse. Two more small applications were approved in August and October. It could not go on indefinitely, however.[44]

The pattern was similar for other Wingfield banks, with a continual series of applications for money requiring ever greater amounts of collateral. The national bank examiner of the San Francisco Federal Reserve District, T. E. Harris, reported that he "not only used my influence but that of my friends" on Wingfield's behalf. Tasker Oddie was pulling every string he knew, seeking to expedite the applications as they poured into Washington. The banks urgently needed new capital; but Wingfield's personal loan from Crocker was up to $850,000, and he had pledged most of his RSC stock to guarantee it. He had no more assets against which to borrow. The RFC itself was not authorized to invest in stock of commercial banks until March 1933, too late to save the Wingfield institutions. Until then, the corporation could only make loans. As RFC chairman Jesse H. Jones recalled in his memoirs, it was a matter of bad timing:

> The chain of Nevada banks dominated by George Wingfield of Reno was broken by the plight of the stockmen. To the Wingfield banks the RFC made several loans; but finally the time came when they had no more available collateral. Under the law requiring us to have full and adequate security, we could render no further help; and we had to watch the banks go to the wall.[45]

And go to the wall they did. In October 1932, the first loans to Reno National, made in April, were coming due. The bank was barely hanging on, the livestock markets hadn't picked up, and depositors were still withdrawing their funds and "hoarding" rather than spending. Disaster loomed once again. By Friday, October 28, Reno National was practically without funds. On Sunday, October 30, Governor Fred Balzar, Wingfield's friend and political ally, flew to Washington, D.C., to make a last-ditch appeal to President Herbert Hoover and the RFC, hoping to secure more money so the bank could open on Tuesday, November 1, following the October 31 Nevada Admission Day holiday. As Balzar testified to the RFC directors, "Our condition out there is most serious." The Wingfield banks needed an additional $2 million to carry them over until spring, and maybe more, since "there is no price on our livestock whatsoever." Balzar explained that the situation was "desperate" because the Wingfield banks held approximately sixty-five percent of all deposits and seventy-five percent of all loans in the state. In addition: "We have practically all our State funds deposited with the Wingfield banks." If they were allowed to fail, the ramifications would be serious and far-reaching. The state deposits were theoretically protected by surety bonds, but these bonds were mostly provided by Wingfield's own Nevada Surety and Bonding Company, and it was presumed to be no stronger than his banks.[46]

When funds were not immediately forthcoming, Balzar instructed lieutenant governor Morley Griswold to declare a banking holiday, until November 15. Although there was no legal basis for any such action, Balzar undertook it, as he told the RFC directors, to protect the other Nevada banks from a run and to buy time for the Wingfield institutions to secure new financing.

Under the provisions of the extralegal holiday, any bank that wished to might stay open for business. One Reno institution, the First National Bank run by Richard Kirman, did so, although local businessmen griped, "Of course the First National is liquid, they are ultra-conservative, but that don't develop the state." All twelve of developer Wingfield's banks took advantage of the moratorium and remained closed, however. None of them was ever to reopen. The depression was making mockery of George Wingfield's proud boast in 1913 that no one in the state had ever lost a dollar in his banks.[47]

At first no one realized the full extent of the crisis. Editor Graham Sanford, in the *Reno Evening Gazette*, proclaimed in a November 1 editorial that there was "No Need for Alarm." Sanford pointed out that it was not the first time that the state had passed through unsettled banking conditions and that the Wingfield banks were planning to reorganize and reopen. Both Reno papers printed Wingfield's reassuring statement, blaming the problems on the collapse of the livestock industry and promising: "I have contributed and will continue to contribute to the limits of my resources to restore the stability of the Wingfield banks." It was a statement similar to the one he had made with his partner, George Nixon, during the 1907 run on John S. Cook & Co. It was reminiscent of his pledge in 1927 that no depositor in the Carson Valley Bank would lose a penny due to the defalcations of its cashier or state officials Cole and Malley. In a curious way, the scenario was so familiar that it was almost reassuring. George Wingfield had faced economic adversity in the past and overcome it. Surely this would be no exception. No one really believed that Nevada's wealthiest man was not equal to the occasion.[48]

There were other encouraging signs as well. Herbert Hoover had promised help, although he said that the decision must come from the RFC. After listening to Balzar, the RFC board dispatched two examiners by plane to study the situation of the Wingfield banks. The men, A. R. LeRoy and John K. McKee, were familiar with regional banking. They had just assisted with the reorganization and reopening of the chain of ten banks that had closed in Idaho in 1931. Newspaper coverage in the days immediately following the closure was generally sanguine, pointing out that the Riverside and United Nevada banks were generally in good shape and giving details of the Idaho reorganization, which was assumed to be the model for any Wingfield plan. After a week, the *Gazette* lauded the state for its calm acceptance of the situation, boasting that "residents of mining and livestock states are accustomed to 'ups and downs.' They accept them as part of their risks. They do so in this instance."[49]

Even *Time* magazine was jaunty, reporting that Nevadans were muddling through, with gambling halls carrying their good customers, divorcees drawing on eastern banks, and stores accepting checks on the closed banks: "The sentiment of the State was that when onetime Gambler Wingfield checked up he would find himself even better than his books and his banking wheels could spin again." Private citizens agreed. The local manager of the Virginia and Truckee Railroad, who had received advance warning of the holiday at 11:30 the night before, was out in the streets the next day taking the pulse of Reno. He reported to the railroad owners in New York that the city's businessmen "have every confidence in Wingfield's ability to re-establish his banks, and are confidently accepting checks on them." [50]

But the prevailing faith was misplaced. As the days stretched into weeks, the Wingfield banks did not bounce back. After an initial survey, the RFC examiners announced that the bank stockholders were entirely wiped out and that depositors stood to lose about $3 million (out of a total of $15 million in deposits). In the meantime public funds totaling over $1.7 million were tied up in frozen accounts. The banking holiday was extended for two weeks while the examiners, in consultation with Wingfield, Thatcher, and Sheehan, devised a proposal for reorganizing the banks, based on the Idaho model. Its basic principle, one on which George Wingfield insisted, was that all depositors and stockholders in Wingfield banks would share equally in any losses. The only other alternative, independent reorganization of each separate bank, would leave some too weakened to reopen in the aftermath of the livestock debacle and others virtually unscathed. Having tried to spread the burden among the banks by splitting the large loans, Wingfield felt it would be unjust now to penalize the smaller or weaker banks, such as Virginia City or Tonopah, on account of those loans. [51]

The plan entailed combining all the assets and liabilities of the twelve banks and creating a single institution, capitalized at $3 million, that would be headquartered in Reno, but have branch operations in the various other locales. There would be a board of directors formulating general policy, with a manager and advisory board in each individual community. To the extent that they shared large loans, the Wingfield banks had already been operating as a chain, but official reorganization would require a change in the state banking law to permit branch banking, which RFC examiner McKee described as "far more flexible than the methods employed by the Wingfield banks." Current depositors in the banks would supply $2 million of the capital for the new bank, to be called the Bank of Nevada, by accepting stock in exchange for some proportion of their deposits. The other $1 million would have to come from different sources. As the United Nevada Bank had done in 1929, the new bank would take over all the good assets of the twelve existing institutions. Bad and doubtful loans would be sequestered in a separate realization company, in which depositors would hold stock representing the amount of doubtful assets in each bank. Since the stockholders' interest would be lost, Wingfield's own equity in the banks—a substantial part of his fortune—would be entirely wiped out.[52]

This plan required the approval of depositors' committees from each bank and also of the RFC Board of Directors. The depositors began meeting on November 18, with George Thatcher, George Wingfield, and the RFC examiners making personal appearances to explain the new plan. Wingfield was particularly impassioned, displaying "the greatest emotion his friends declare he has ever shown in all his spectacular career." He declared repeatedly to the depositors that he would give them the shirt off his back, take any steps necessary to reopen the banks: "I want the depositors protected if it takes my shoes off." The fact that Wingfield was suffering too was emphasized. Newspapers reported that he had no money for household expenses and had been forced to borrow $1,000 from the Bank Club, a fact which he admitted "with tears streaming down his cheeks." A few groups greeted him with cheers. Others, like Sparks, were contentious, demanding that Wingfield give them the property he had transferred to his wife Roxy.[53]

Since the stockholders' interests were to be sacrificed, Wingfield would have no stake in the new bank. He supported the reorganization plan, however, both to assuage his wounded pride as a banker and to avoid the financial embarrassment that receivership would bring. If the banks could be saved and reopened, there was a chance that he might be able to salvage something from his stockholder's equity. If they were closed and liquidated, he would be financially liable, both as a stockholder and as a director, for any losses sustained by the two national banks, at Reno and Winnemucca. Consequently, he was willing to work hard. As he put it, "We have been moving Heaven and Earth to try and get this thing going."[54]

The RFC Board approved the reorganization in principle, after a report by John McKee that "sentiment was most favorable to the plan." The board required, however, that $500,000 in new capital be subscribed by outside corporations. Wingfield was thus busy on several fronts simultaneously. He needed to secure a change in the banking laws from the Nevada legislature, which ordinarily wouldn't meet until January 1933; to solicit the additional capital from California companies that operated in Nevada, such as Standard Oil, Western Pacific Railroad, or Southern Pacific Railroad; and to convince the depositors' committees that the plan was a worthy one. The latter proved to be the most difficult task. In late November and early December, ten depositors' committees agreed to the Wingfield plan, after varying amounts of "rather fiery" discussion. However, two banks, United Nevada and Riverside, proved reluctant to join the reorganization.[55]

Both of these banks were in good financial shape and expected to be able to pay their depositors ninety to ninety-five percent of their accounts. Cashier Roy Frisch at the Riverside Bank had refused to participate in most of the split loans from Reno National, thereby protecting his depositors' money. These depositors were, therefore, naturally reluctant to join in underwriting the losses at other Wingfield banks such as Reno National, which was estimated to be able to pay its depositors only forty-five to sixty percent. In addition, some of the United Nevada depositors were angry at the way they had been treated since the creation of the bank by Wingfield in 1929. Depositors in the old Washoe County Bank had been paid only 75 cents on the dollar in that reorganization and resented the profits that Wingfield had since gained from the new bank. In addition, they objected, as Laura Vitray had pointed out the year before, to the switching of assets between the United Nevada Bank and the realization companies that had been organized to pay stockholders and depositors in the old Washoe County and Scheeline banks. When profits were realized from the sale of some asset classed as "doubtful," it always seemed to go to the new bank (and Wingfield), rather than to the depositors and stockholders. All in all, it was a legacy of sufficient bitterness and mistrust to make the United Nevada depositors decidedly unsympathetic to Wingfield's proposals.[56]

George Wingfield himself was sanguine, confiding to his former office manager, Zoebel, "While there are a few people trying to undermine us, they are in a very small minority, and I have found we have many good friends, who are trying to help the situation and save the State. I hope to see the depositors paid out." But things were not coming together. On November 22, with five days still remaining on the previous order, Governor Balzar extended the banking holiday for another month. By now, only Wingfield's banks and the tiny Battle Mountain State Bank remained closed. Riverside depositors rejected the reorganization and received editorial support from Graham Sanford's *Reno Evening Gazette*, which urged state officials to take a more active role in the bank situation and endorsed separate reorganization efforts for the twelve banks, so that depositors in one didn't subsidize others. As the weeks wore on toward Christmas, the *Gazette* became increasingly critical, blasting Governor Balzar for his failure to act, and condemning George Wingfield for his refusal to turn over his stock in the Riverside Bank to the depositors' committee there, so that they could proceed with plans to reopen independently. The required outside money was also slow to arrive, although Thatcher kept expecting it to come in just a few more days. By early December, Wingfield's assessment was a bit more cautious. He still expected the banks to reopen, but he was painfully aware now of an organized opposition. As he reported to his bankers at Crocker, "The Reno Evening Gazette has been nasty through an imaginary grudge against me, but this has reacted against them and I don't think they will have much more to say. . . . I am satisfied that when the banks reopen, it will bring business back all around."[57]

The *Gazette* was not the only source of nastiness. The collapse of the Wingfield banks brought to the surface all the resentment of George Wingfield that had been brewing for years. He was a figure of mythic proportion in Nevada, where his wealth and power were so vast that he was held responsible for virtually everything that happened. People blamed him for the bank failure just as they credited him with single-handedly procuring the gambling and divorce legislation or supporting the illegal activities of Graham and McKay. Led by the insinuations of McCarran, Waugh, Vitray, and others to expect scandal and corruption, many Nevadans assumed the worst about Wingfield's role in the bank closure. They gossiped among themselves about how he had looted the banks and hidden the funds, had warned friends and employees about the closure so they could get their money out, and had protected his own assets by putting everything in his wife's name. Although Wingfield companies actually had over $41,000 on deposit at the various banks, in addition to $250,000 he had borrowed from Crocker for the certificates of deposit at Henderson Bank in Elko, and personal accounts belonging to Wingfield, his mother, wife, and children, there was a widespread impression that he had not been affected by the bank failure.[58]

People whose money was tied up in the suspended banks were not inclined to be charitable toward the banker whose life underwent no discernible change. When salaries weren't paid and foreclosures resulted, there were anonymous threats against Wingfield and his family. Garbage was dumped on the steps of his house, and his wife's niece and nephew were supervised carefully, lest they become targets for vengeful depositors. Once again, as in the days of the Goldfield strike twenty-five years before, George Wingfield was accompanied by bodyguards, this time John Mueller and Norman Biltz. Reno in 1932 was a tiny town of roughly 19,000, where a prominent man's drinking binges of two or three days at a stretch could hardly have escaped notice; and there was gossip about that, too. Feelings ran high, and resentment was given full voice, not all of it as restrained as the anonymous, ungrammatical poem inscribed "to Mr. George Wingfield":

> YOU'VE GOT YOURS AND
> YOU'VE GOT MINE
> IF YOU'LL KEEP YOURS
> AND GIVE ME MINE
> THEN WELL BOTH
> GET ALONG VERY FINE

In the words of a Santa Barbara, California newspaper editorial, "thousands hate him." [59]

In fact, the toll on Wingfield was substantial. Old friends would no longer speak to him and even his own family caused him anguish. Just four days after the bank failure, he was answering a letter from his daughter, Jean, in which she expressed "disappointment in the management of our income." His reply was icy:

> I am more surprised that a daughter of mine would write me such a letter when I am in distress. When times are so tough, I at least expected a word of sympathy and encouragement. . . . What you have had in the past and what you will have in the future is due to me, because even though you are now nearly twenty-one, you have yet to earn a cent. I have at least taken good care of you up to this date.

His former wife, to whom he owed back alimony payments, was pressing him for money as well; and he was busy liquidating his free assets as fast as possible. On November 27, he sold the sixteen thoroughbreds remaining in his Nevada Stock Farm stable. Even at depressed prices, the star, Hygro, brought $12,000. Horses had always been Wingfield's real love and sacrificing his racing stable was the act of a despondent man. Two weeks earlier he had resigned his membership in the prestigious Bohemian Club, the San Francisco group renowned for its elite membership of national business and political leaders, who gathered for an annual frolic on the grounds of the club's private retreat, Bohemian Grove. A few faithful friends rallied around him during this crisis period, hardly knowing what to say or do, but offering nonetheless, "If I can be of any service, please command me." Others, however, were silent, shunning the man whose predicament now seemed an embarrassment, or, worse yet, pitying him for his fall from the heights of power. One of the latter reported "he thought the blow to your pride was perhaps worse than all else and that he felt sorry for you." [60]

Some popular resentment was expressed politically. Wingfield's bank closed exactly one week before the national election in which Franklin Roosevelt swept to victory over the discredited Republican Hoover. On the state level, Tasker Oddie was up for reelection, running against Wingfield's old nemesis, Democrat Pat McCarran. The preoccupied Republican national committeeman had no time or energy to spare for this 1932 campaign, and Oddie was on his own. The two men plotted no strategy. There was no orchestration of the campaign by Wingfield, and no political gossip about the nuances of party alliances. Perhaps most important, there was no money. One disgusted party worker complained that the "state committee has not had sufficient [funds] to even distribute literature properly." In the aftermath of the spectacular collapse of the banks, and in common with most Republican candidates in that depression year, Tasker Oddie was swept from office by McCarran. Editorial endorsement of Oddie and Congressman Samuel Arentz by the Republican *Reno Evening Gazette*, claiming that, "for the good of the state they should be re-elected," was not enough. Arentz lost to former governor James Scrugham by almost 9,000 votes, although McCarran's margin of victory was less than 1,700 votes out of 41,000 cast. In decided contrast to the phenomenal Republican organization in the 1926 campaign, in 1932 "the whole Republican organization just went to pieces."[61]

The bank failures thus marked the end not only of Wingfield's economic domination of the state, but also, with Oddie's defeat, of a political era in Nevada history. The Wingfield machine, whether effectively bipartisan or not, had always hinged in large measure on access to national political circles. In 1928, with Herbert Hoover's election to the presidency, George Wingfield was at the peak of his power, having gained personal entry even to the White House. Tasker Oddie, meanwhile, remained an important long-term ally and advocate for Nevada's interests at a national level. With the Republican senator's departure, and the Republican president's defeat, Wingfield in 1932 was deprived of both access and advocate. He was not powerless, by any means; but his political reach was now severely limited.[62]

In the next few years, as he fought to preserve his personal finances from entanglement in the bank disaster, the new constraints under which Wingfield operated would become clearer. His influence as a Republican national committeeman was negligible in a Democratic administration. Getting things done in Washington proved to be difficult, if not impossible, and Nevada had new voices. Wingfield was naturally skeptical about the outcome. Democrat McCarran had no misgivings, however. Immediately after the election he eloquently pronounced his victory worth any potential cost. The bank failure was "a blessing of purification" because "the power that controlled the throttle of this state is at an end, and though the people may go back into the throes of impoverishment, they nevertheless will reap the benefit in many ways."[63]

By mid-December, those costs were mounting. Wingfield's twelve banks were still closed, and it was evident that they wouldn't be reopening any time soon. Legal challenges were beginning to mount against them, as the state of Nevada and disgruntled depositors threatened suit for the return of their money. As Wingfield stormed to Estey Julian, "Everything was working very nicely until a few hungry lawyers got their snoots into the pot." Consequently, on December 9, Wingfield reluctantly acceded to the demands that he surrender control of his closed banks. Having officially suspended operations, the nine state banks were turned over to the Nevada state bank examiner, E. J. Seaborn, while the national banks and the savings bank were taken over by Walter J. Tobin (in Reno) and H. A. Streeter (in Winnemucca), representing the U.S. comptroller of the currency. The reorganization plan was not dead, but it was obviously not going to be consummated soon. In the meantime, a custodial receivership would forestall suits and give the proponents of reorganization time to complete all their requisite tasks.[64]

Personally, the receivership was a bitter blow, not at all the consummation that Wingfield had hoped from the bank holiday. For once in his life, the celebrated "Wingfield luck" had failed him. Reviled by the people he had tried to help, and pitied by his friends, George Wingfield in 1932 was no longer fortune's favorite son. Instead, "tired and worn," he was holding himself together by sheer force of will. He went to work every day in the same office and lived in the same house; but after the collapse of his banks Wingfield's life would never resume its old contours. His faith in his own benevolent vision for the state of Nevada, and his confidence in his power to realize it, ultimately betrayed him into bankruptcy.[65]

TEN

"Hitting the Comeback Trail"

THE WINTER OF 1932–1933 was a bleak one, as the national depression belatedly hit Nevada. There was no race meet scheduled that year, and hotel occupancy rates plummeted. Livestock markets remained weak and only the gamblers seemed to have money. Divorce and tourism alone were insufficient to save the state's economy, and no prizefights or highway expositions loomed to pull Reno out of its doldrums. Slowly, the true extent of the calamity became apparent. Wingfield's success in securing his full share of Nevada's state treasury deposits meant that a large amount of public money was tied up when his banks suspended. As a result, salaries at the university and in some school districts couldn't be paid in full. There was talk of a special session to fund the operations of the state government, and the state eventually had to borrow money from the RFC to save itself from bankruptcy. Despite confident pronouncements in newspaper editorials, the Wingfield bank failures weren't just a temporary setback. Business wasn't bouncing back, not even gambling. When Graham and McKay's sumptuous Willows Club burned in June 1932, it wasn't rebuilt.[1]

Superficially, the banker seemed blissfully unaffected by the catastrophe he had helped to create. Although he quit the extensive traveling that had previously characterized his business life, George Wingfield still lived comfortably in his Court Street house, still employed secretaries at his office in the Reno National Bank Building, and still managed his hotel properties and numerous other companies, including GCMC. He still had talented and expensive legal help, in the persons of Thatcher and Woodburn, and a close tie to the Nevada capital, in the person of Fred Balzar. Through the Wingfield Trust Fund he had established for his children, he still controlled considerable property, including important Reno real estate. McCarran's election to the senate had clipped his political wings, but had by no means ended his influence within the state. All in all, the capitalist seemed to the general public to be leading, as he always had, a charmed life.

Things were not as they seemed, however. For the next few years Wingfield's life, though outwardly unchanged, was actually dreadfully harried. Almost until the day he filed for bankruptcy in November 1935, he struggled to salvage the vestiges of his empire against orchestrated political opposition from former allies as well as opponents. In the end he lost the fight. Along the way, he also lost his long-standing pride of ownership in Nevada. The customary "double vision," by which Wingfield identified his own interests with those of his state, and cheerfully worked to further both, vanished entirely during the bank reorganization fight. Vitriolic radio attacks began in January 1933 on KOH radio, and Wingfield experienced the full force of the hatred that had built up against him over the years. Now lacking his former clout as the richest man in the state, he fought back ineffectually. Without the security of a fortune to protect him and deflect the blows of public criticism, and without access to national power in a Democratic administration, Wingfield found himself at a disadvantage. Playing the game was not much fun in these conditions. The stakes were high and he could ill afford to lose.

With the failure of the banks in November 1932, George Wingfield's entire fortune was jeopardized. The bank stock instantly lost all its value, which in turn negated its worth as collateral for Wingfield's huge personal loans from Crocker First National Bank. In self-defense, the bank assumed control of the remaining assets that were pledged, including the Reno Securities Company (RSC) stock and bonds. After 1932, then, both the Riverside and the Hotel Golden were mortgaged to Crocker to guarantee Wingfield's loans, although other company properties, including the Las Vegas lots, were not. Wingfield thus became a salaried manager of his own hotels. By agreement with the San Francisco bank he received $500 monthly to manage the two properties, a reduction from the $2,000 monthly he had been paid by the company in 1932. He was also paid $250 per month for his services in managing GCMC, which continued as well to pay employees like Mueller and Julian, although at reduced salaries.[2]

Meanwhile Wingfield worked feverishly to liquidate assets and reduce expenses elsewhere. His former wife, Maude, remarried in April 1933 in Chicago, and Wingfield settled her claim for back alimony by agreeing to give her all but $5,000 of the proceeds from the sale of their Pacific Avenue home in San Francisco. He and Julian struggled to keep the Sutter Butte Canal Company from bankruptcy, buying back as many of its bonds as they could. The company was unable to meet the interest payment that was due on these bonds on March 1, and Wingfield was trying to stave off a creditors' rebellion and maintain his control over the property. In March he complained to his longtime accountant, George K. Edler, that he had no money to fight an IRS assessment for additional income taxes for 1929 and 1930: "I don't know what to do in this tax matter as I have nothing to pay it with and nothing to spend for expenses to fight it." Under the circumstances, the five-cent GCMC dividend in June, which came from the sale of the Base Metals Mining Company, was most welcome. It only temporarily alleviated the pressure, however. Most of Wingfield's share went to pay down the outstanding balance on his loan from Crocker. Without the banks to bring in dividend income, and with Reno's tourist business in the doldrums, he was hard-pressed to get the money to keep up the interest payments, let alone pay down the principal.[3]

The new circumstances meant a tremendous change in George Wingfield's way of life, one for which he was ill prepared at the advanced age of fifty-seven. No longer did he have the Midas touch that converted everything into gold, yet he was also pitifully unaccustomed to a poor man's economies. Although Wingfield had never lived extravagantly, he was accustomed to a considerable level of comfort. Keeping a car required a driver. Keeping a house required a staff. He was still suppporting his mother and his nieces, and $750 a month did not stretch far. In the waning days of prohibition, good wine was not inexpensive either. It seems safe to conclude that the adjustments were both embarrassing and difficult to a man who always liked things "first-class." In July 1933, on his behalf, GCMC wrote two checks totaling $16,000 to the Bank Club. Either Wingfield had continued to borrow heavily from his friend McKay, from whom he first sought household expense money when the banks closed, or the checks represented sizable gambling losses. In either event, the large checks are extraordinary, recalling the former grand scale of Wingfield's financial dealings amid the generally pinched conditions of 1933. In September, he summarized the situation succinctly to an old friend in New York: "There is practically nothing going on out here."[4]

Of course he meant his remark in a financial way. In fact, in 1933, a great deal was going on for Wingfield, all centered around the high drama of bank reorganization, which continued to be played out on a very public stage. Reorganization and reopening of the banks still hinged on the same three factors: securing outside capital, passage of new state laws to allow branch banking, and agreement of the depositors' committees in the twelve banks. As if this weren't enough, the process was now further complicated by the fact that the banks were controlled by separate entities: the state bank examiner for the state-chartered institutions and the comptroller of the currency for the national banks. This meant that any plan now had to secure approval at two additional levels of authority.

Matters proceeded more smoothly on the first two fronts than on the last. With the assistance of Crocker First National Bank, and the San Francisco Chamber of Commerce, George Thatcher and Wingfield bank associates put together a coalition of California business interests willing to assist in the reorganization efforts. Spearheaded by Victor F. Palmer, treasurer of the Standard Oil Company of California, the group was poised to deposit $500,000 in the reorganized Bank of Nevada, promising not to withdraw the money for a period of three years. This was not precisely the new capital required by the RFC, but it would provide a much-needed financial cushion for the new bank. Palmer, who took an active role in the reorganization campaign throughout 1933, hoped that it would be sufficient to convince the RFC. To that end the group of interested businessmen devised a second, slightly revised plan for bank reorganization, which was approved by the RFC on February 4. Significantly, it did not require participation of every closed bank in order to succeed.[5]

After a full appraisal of the assets of the closed banks, reorganization sponsors announced that, once branch banking legislation was obtained, approximately $2.7 million in liquid assets was available for the new Bank of Nevada. Dubious loans and outright losses in the amount of approximately $9 million would be consigned to twelve separate trust funds for each bank. Any money recovered from these assets would be turned over to the depositors in the respective banks. After depositors were repaid with interest, remaining funds would go to the stockholders. Other assets of the closed banks, classified as good or good-but-slow, would be assigned to a separate mortgage company, which in turn could pledge its assets to the RFC. This mortgage company would purchase assets from the proposed new Bank of Nevada, giving the latter a crucial $1.5 million in cash with which to operate, and in turn use the assets to secure its RFC loans. The mortgage company would maintain the old assets and eventually liquidate them in orderly and presumably profitable fashion. Returns, as with the trust funds, would go to repay depositors and, if anything additional was realized, to mortgage company stockholders. In assuming the assets of the closed banks, the mortgage company would also assume the obligations of the closed banks to the RFC, Crocker, and the Federal Reserve Bank.[6]

The most controversial provision of the new plan was a requirement that depositors invest in the new bank and mortgage company, since all other sources of potential capital had failed to materialize. These investments would be made from funds already on deposit in the closed banks. After outright losses were deducted separately for each bank, depositors would theoretically be entitled to receive their remaining funds. Depending on the bank, these remaining funds ranged from thirty-four percent of the original deposit for Reno National account holders, to ninety-seven percent for Riverside customers. In order for the new bank and mortgage companies to have sufficient capital to operate, however, the depositors in the old banks would have to subscribe some of that money to capital stock. They would be required to accept approximately thirteen percent of their money in the form of stock in the new bank, and twenty-eight percent in mortgage company stock. After these subscriptions, the remaining funds could actually be withdrawn from the closed bank, twenty-five percent immediately, and the remainder at intervals over the next three years. Thus the most fortunate depositors, those at the Riverside Bank, could expect to receive immediately only $144.17 out of a hypothetical $1,000 on deposit in the bank on November 1, 1932. Reno National customers would get only $50.46 of the same $1,000.[7]

Because of this provision for investment in the new bank and mortgage company, the reorganization plan required depositor approval. Before the new bank could be opened, depositors holding at least fifty-one percent of the total funds on deposit at the state banks, and sixty percent (later raised to seventy-five) of the funds in the national banks, had to sign special waivers agreeing to the plan. Approval by both the state bank examiner and the comptroller of the currency was also required. The campaign to secure these waivers began on March 4, 1933. More than fifty clerk-typists donated their services, and a group of Reno businessmen contributed postage money to send more than 30,000 waiver forms. They were mailed on the same day that Franklin Roosevelt was being inaugurated as president and specified that the new bank had to be operational within ninety days. In March 1933, the country was in the midst of an unprecedented national bank holiday, declared by the nation's governors to halt a massive bank run similar to the one that had closed most of Nevada's banks the previous fall. Nevada's had begun on March 2. Thus, while the American financial system apparently crumbled around them, a depositors' committee chaired by Forrest W. Eccles set out to convince battle-scarred Nevadans that reorganization of the former Wingfield banks was in their best interests.[8]

It was not an easy task. The new bank and the mortgage company would be run by a sixteen-member Board of Directors. The California companies that agreed to a deferred deposit would select three of those members and would name the management of both bank and mortgage company during the period of their participation. The depositors' committees of the individual banks would each name one member, and the stockholders of the Wingfield banks would collectively name one member. This arrangement became a sticking point, as opponents charged that the reorganization was, in George Wingfield's words, "a plan sponsored by me and for my benefit." Despite his repeated public denials of the charge, there were many disgruntled depositors who believed it. Wingfield had dominated the state's affairs for so long that no one could really imagine it otherwise. Even though he deliberately remained in the background in the battle over bank reorganization, and was not actively involved in formulating or promoting the new plan, Wingfield was the figure foremost in the public mind. As one constituent informed Key Pittman:

> The group who have dominated our legislature, our courts, and our banking institutions, and who beyond a doubt have violated our banking laws to the detriment or ruin of many of our citizens, and at this writing are forcing their victims to re-organize [*sic*] these banks by bringing pressure upon the bank debtors, are no longer popular, and it is in the minds of the people that they are going to do something about it by any means that they can, not only to them, but to any public official who supports them.[9]

The public resentment was sustained by the charges and countercharges that were traded in the state legislature, which convened in January 1933. As expected the Wingfield banking fiasco was the central topic; and, as Wingfield observed ruefully, "the Assembly especially are the ones making the trouble." On February 4, the same day that the second reorganization plan was approved by the RFC, the Nevada legislature began an investigation of the closed banks, seeking to find out what went wrong the previous year and whether any banking laws had been violated. While a joint committee of the Senate and Assembly took testimony, the rest of the legislature wrangled over a variety of banking bills. One of these, an Assembly bill supported in editorials by Graham Sanford of the *Reno Evening Gazette*, would have provided that the closed banks be reopened only by their depositors, without any provision for the stockholders' equity. Ultimately, with the help of a conservative Senate that included Noble Getchell and other prominent Wingfield supporters, a compromise banking bill was passed on March 28, as the legislative session ended. This bill allowed for reorganization to be initiated by depositors representing at least five percent of the total number of accounts and over fifty percent of the total dollar amount of deposits. It further stipulated that the old stockholders would receive nonvoting stock in any new corporation.

If all depositors and creditors were paid in full with interest, then the stock-holders in the old corporation would receive something for their holdings. The bill also permitted branch banking, as the reorganization plan required.[10]

The banking bill and RFC approval for the second reorganization plan were major victories; but opposition continued to mount. Predictably, it was directed against Wingfield personally. Even though he was not operating the new bank, and would not be an officer, critics of the reorganization feared that he was the true power behind the plan they were offered. Proponents of re-organization were assumed to be Wingfield stooges. A group including Reno attorneys Prince Hawkins, H. R. Cooke, Thomas F. Ryan, and E. F. Luns-ford campaigned against the new reorganization plan. They urged deposi-tors not to sign the waivers, claiming, in Hawkins's words, "This proposed mortgage company would give them [the Wingfield group] the firmest foun-dation ever known for continued political control of the state." The rhetoric of the charge, and of others like it that circulated in 1933, was suggestive. No longer just George Wingfield personally, but members of his "group," busi-ness associates or employees who were loyal to Wingfield and his purposes, were suspect. It was a massive case of guilt by association.[11]

The citizens' committee tried to rebut the perception. In their cover let-ter accompanying the bank waivers, they assured depositors that the former owners of the banks would have no control or management role in the new bank. Wingfield, embroiled in his own financial difficulties by 1933, clearly envisioned no such position for himself. Most of his time and energy was spent in managing RSC and trying to reduce his obligation to Crocker First National Bank. On February 17, "because I feel that in so doing I will ad-vance the reorganization plans, so vital to the depositors and the welfare of our state," even George Thatcher publicly withdrew from the reorganiza-tion efforts. Wingfield was not actively involved in planning strategy for the second reorganization plan and spent neither time nor money in supporting it. Nonetheless, rumors of Wingfield control died hard. In the new Nevada that was emerging painfully out of the depression, George Wingfield was no longer patron saint but devil; and men associated with him were repudiated as well. His friends thought they knew who to blame, recalling "that four years ago that gentleman from Superior California, who runs the Bee, threat-ened to get you if it took years." But Wingfield himself was too beleaguered to debate responsibility. When the newspapers were reporting that bankers' homes had been burned by irate depositors, it was small wonder that the embattled Nevada capitalist felt the need for bodyguards.[12]

Opponents of the reorganization were numerous and well organized. Graham Sanford's *Reno Evening Gazette* began an editorial campaign against the plan that overtly sought to destroy the monolithic power structure George Wingfield had built through his years of political dominance. Someone, assumed by Wingfield's supporters to be Sanford, arranged for regular radio broadcasts of speeches by W. E. Barnard attacking Wingfield's honesty. Blasting "the political trust," Barnard echoed the charges made by the *Sacramento Bee* in 1928, and by the *Evening Graphic* in 1931, that Wingfield had used his power to corrupt the state government for his own profit. He also accused Wingfield of defrauding the bank depositors, thus keeping alive the popular animosity against Wingfield that had surfaced immediately after the November closure. Meanwhile, in a speech to the Reno Chamber of Commerce, H. R. Cooke hinted that opponents might file suit against the plan, on the ground that nonconsenting depositors should not be forced to participate in financing the new institutions. While this was certainly a matter of legal principle, it was also part of an anti-Wingfield backlash. The day after the speech, Cooke went on to delineate the opposition's basic article of faith: "long-continued opposition to Wingfield's domination in financial and political matters." In the battle over bank reorganization, all the resentment of Wingfield's power and wealth that had been building throughout the previous decade arose to haunt him. Even as he reached the nadir of his career, and lost virtually all the authority he had once exercised in the state, his opponents still feared his influence. In the next few months, they took action to curb it once and for all.[13]

The legislative committee issued its report on the banking situation on March 13. After hearing testimony from state government officials, especially bank examiner E. J. Seaborn, and from bank officers including George Wingfield, the six-man committee issued a scathing critique of the state's lax banking system. Fundamentally the committee concluded that "the failure of the Wingfield chain must not be attributed entirely to the depression and the decline in livestock prices, but was due to a great extent to certain managerial policies of the Wingfield chain of banks." They examined each of the closed banks in turn, detailing a host of these dubious policies, including advancing money on faltering livestock operations rather than foreclosing, making loans in excess of legal limits, allowing large loans to be split among the banks, paying dividends before charging off uncertain loans, overvaluing bank buildings, and continuing to operate after cash reserves were impaired. The financial security of Wingfield's Nevada Surety and Bonding Company was also questioned, backed as it was by bonds of the Sutter Butte Canal Company. Since the canal company was experiencing its own financial crisis in 1932, its bonds were virtually worthless; and there had been violations in some of the bonding company's practices. With some exasperation, the committee observed, as was surely true, that "seemingly the Board of Examiners and State Treasurer regarded the solvency of the Nevada Surety and Bonding Company and the Wingfield State banks as depending upon Mr. Wingfield's personal resources."[14]

In one sense the report was a vindication for Wingfield. The committee found no fraud, as Barnard was charging. It concluded that failure of the Reno National, triggered most immediately by a spring 1932 run on the Bank of Nevada Savings and Trust Company, had forced the other banks to close. It did find numerous sloppy or prejudicial practices, however. Reno National borrowed money from the RFC on behalf of the Bank of Nevada Savings and Trust Company, for instance, but used at least part of the proceeds to repay Crocker National Bank. Cashier Roy Frisch, of the Riverside Bank, revealed that Crocker officials "were virtually in charge of all Wingfield banks for a period of 90 days, during the summer of 1932," implying that it was their presence that insured such repayment. In several cases, including Henderson, Tonopah, and United Nevada, excess loans in the various banks had been inherited when Wingfield took them over. But the committee insisted primly that such loans were nevertheless unlawful, and their age or origin "does not appeal to your committee as a valid excuse."[15]

At base, the committee opined, it was a problem not simply of the national depression or bad judgment, but of the failure of state banking officials to enforce the existing laws properly. If they had done so, excess loans would have been reduced, split loans prohibited, and risky loans foreclosed before the losses grew so large. The devastating failure of the Wingfield banks might never have occurred, in other words, if they had been forced by the bank examiner, Seaborn, to follow the letter of the law. Instead the banks were allowed to continue operating "long after the total value of their loans and resources had depreciated to an extent that any reasonable examination on the part of the Bank Examiner and the State Board of Finance would have disclosed that their capital was impaired." The implicit message, nowhere overtly stated in the committee's report, was that George Wingfield's immense power and influence had subverted proper enforcement of the laws of Nevada. They recommended legislation to correct the situation, and the compromise banking bill was the result.[16]

The legislative report was even-handed and relatively moderate in its tone and its conclusions. The *Reno Evening Gazette*, however, editorialized comprehensively against "the political influence of those who composed the Wingfield banking group with the officials of this state, both Democratic and Republican, now and during past years." Within two weeks, on March 26, the battle was joined as Hawkins filed a suit on behalf of United Nevada depositors, seeking appointment of a receiver for closed banks. Meanwhile, Cooke, Hawkins, and Ryan continued their campaign against the waivers. Nevertheless, the reorganization triumphed. In early April, the manager of the Virginia and Truckee Railroad reported to his boss that "the small group in Reno is still preventing the reopening of the Wingfield banks." But supporters waged a tightly organized campaign reminiscent of earlier political battles, with depositors in Winnemucca even threatening to call for a repeal of the 1931 divorce law if the waivers weren't signed. Although separate reorganization was technically an option for each bank, the Winnemucca depositors believed, as was probably the case, that failure of the Riverside and United Nevada banks to participate would "balk the reorganization plan for all banks." By May 9, the supporters of reorganization had prevailed. All the banks but one, the tiny Churchill County Bank in Fallon, had collected sufficient waivers to approve the plan.[17]

Everything seemed to be falling into place. On June 4, under the headline "Nevada Weathers Its Banking Crisis," the *New York Times* confidently announced that the new bank was set to reopen on June 17. Proponents made formal application to the RFC for $2 million on June 13. Just as the reorganization seemed secure, however, a new set of problems arose. On May 22, the judge in the United Nevada case ruled that the court *could* appoint a receiver in place of the state bank examiner, Seaborn. This made it easier for the nonconsenting depositors to force a separate liquidation of the bank. On June 6, the comptroller of the currency responded to an inquiry from Cooke, Hawkins, and Ryan that he would not accept any reorganization plan which forced nonconsenting depositors to accept stock in exchange for part of their deposits in the closed banks. The net effect was to call the new reorganization plans to a screeching halt. By May 23, the citizens' committee was already preparing new waiver cards for all the agreeing depositors, seeking a ninety-day extension of the time to open the new bank, which would otherwise expire on June 17. They got agreement from all but 800 of the original signers, but Cooke, Hawkins, and Ryan had meanwhile filed suit on behalf of nonsigning depositors in all the other banks. To expedite matters, all these suits over reorganization of the state banks were combined into one trial, presided over by Nevada district judge Clark Guild in Carson City.[18]

Reorganization proponents responded to the setback by devising a new plan, which would enable them to buy out the nonconsenting depositors in the two national banks covered by the comptroller's decision. On August 14, George Wingfield was still optimistic, confiding in passing to F. G. Willis at Crocker that "everything seems to be pointing toward the reorganization." However, on October 5, a ruling from Guild included nonconsenting depositors in state banks in the category of those who had to be bought out if the reorganization were to succeed. This required considerably more money. Despite the best efforts of Wingfield and the depositors' committee, including an appeal from Thatcher and Woodburn to Key Pittman to solicit help from A. P. Giannini of Transamerica Corporation, they could not raise the additional $1 million in capital necessary to culminate the plan. Transamerica decided to open a new bank in Reno rather than invest in reviving the old chain, and under the circumstances the RFC was unwilling to advance more money. By November 2, one full year after the Wingfield banks had closed, the Virginia and Truckee Railroad manager was dejected: "The banking situation is back to where it started a year ago, the California interests have refused to step in because of the controversies here." Graham Sanford, in the *Reno Evening Gazette*, was blunter. Quoting Clarence R. Pugh, chairman of the board of the Committee of One Hundred that had supported the reorganization plan, Sanford pronounced the old plan "a corpse." [19]

On November 29, 1933, almost anticlimactically, Judge Guild took the final steps to bury it. Concluding the yearlong bank reorganization drama, he ordered seven of the nine state banks into receivership under Leo F. Schmitt from Iowa (Henderson Banking Company in Elko and Wells State Bank had separate receivers). As he pointed out in making his ruling, Guild had delayed time and time again to allow reorganization supporters to submit acceptable plans, but time had run out. The problem was further complicated by conflicts between state and national bank authorities. The comptroller of the currency would not permit Reno National Bank receiver Walter J. Tobin to make public information about appraisal of assets in that bank, although the national banks were to be incorporated in the proposed new bank. Eventually, acting on behalf of depositors who had gone a full year without access to their money, Guild could wait no longer. Sympathetic to charges of reorganization opponents that Seaborn had been too lenient a receiver and had continued to employ all of Wingfield's old bank employees, Guild appointed the outsider, Schmitt, with instructions to pay a dividend to all depositors within four months. Although the decision was challenged by reorganization attorneys, the Nevada Supreme Court upheld Guild's ruling in February 1934, and Schmitt was formally named receiver for seven of the state banks later that same month.[20]

With Schmitt's receivership and liquidation all hope of reviving George Wingfield's once mighty banking empire vanished. The assets of the banks were liquidated over a period of six years, paying back one hundred five percent to fortunate Riverside Bank depositors, and an average of seventy-five percent to all others, except for Virginia City. The bank buildings were mostly sold to the new First National Bank of Nevada, which had been purchased by Transamerica Corporation in April 1934, after the failure of the reorganization effort eliminated all potential competition. Transamerica even bought Wingfield's headquarters building in Reno, reopening the banking floor on August 1, 1934, in "a blaze of glory" that Wingfield thought testified to their skills as "pretty good show men." It was a melancholy fate for the building he had opened with similar fanfare almost thirty years earlier as the Reno National Bank. Receivership had other melancholy effects, as a number of ranchers and Wingfield friends, including John G. Taylor, were forced into bankruptcy when they could not repay their bank loans. Even the Virginia and Truckee's F. M. Murphy was dubious: "The receiver for the Wingfield banks is hard boiled and doing some great injustices in selling live stock [*sic*] and sheep, in liquidation. . . ." Valuable assets including ranches were sacrificed in order to realize some immediate return for the depositors, and the interests of all the stockholders were permanently wiped out in the process.[21]

The recovery that George Wingfield had bet on did come eventually, but it was too late to save him. As one rural banker's wife remembered: "Had the farmers been allowed to keep their stock only a few months longer the price doubled, and in a year's time it tripled and quadrupled. It was a sorry time." It was also undoubtedly the bitterest period in Wingfield's life. As he told Judge Guild, "Half of the state of Nevada thinks I'm a crook and no good," and it pained him personally to watch good men and loyal employees like his bank vice-president, Jerry Sheehan, lose everything they had in the collapse. In the battle over bank reorganization, politics had proved to be Wingfield's nemesis, against which all his wealth and ambition availed him nothing. In the face of intransigent local opposition, and without additional loans from the RFC and the California corporations, Wingfield and the reorganization proponents just couldn't hold out long enough to wait for the eventual national recovery of the livestock industry. Unable to do what he promised and save the state's banks, he found himself instead fighting desperately for his own financial life.[22]

Not only did the defeat of reorganization mean that Wingfield had lost the entire value of his bank stock; but, as both a director and a stockholder, he also faced additional liability on the losses sustained by the two national banks, in Reno and Winnemucca. On May 2, 1933, receiver Walter J. Tobin, of the Reno National Bank, filed suit against George Wingfield and the other stockholders of that bank, seeking to establish the stockholders' liability for bank losses. For his share in the two national banks, this debt came to more than $500,000 for Wingfield personally. Ironically, the banker had at least twice considered changing the charter of First National Bank of Winnemucca to make it a state bank. In 1926 and again in 1929, he raised the issue, pointing out that membership in the federal reserve system was expensive and that no particular advantage accrued on account of national bank status. In 1929, however, his attorney, William Woodburn, advised against the change, concluding, "It is my judgement that people generally have more confidence in the stability of a national bank than in a state bank. All other factors being equal, a national bank charter is the most desirable." As a consequence, Wingfield did nothing and the change was never made.[23]

In 1933, this decision was one he surely rued. On top of the $850,000 he still owed Crocker, on which interest was accruing, as well as his mounting personal debts, the stockholder's obligation was impossible for him to meet. He spent the next two years attempting to compromise it in some way, beginning with a request through Tobin to the U.S. comptroller of the currency to accept a settlement of approximately $64,000. In support of the offer he submitted a financial statement dated December 31, 1932. It showed assets of $1.08 million and liabilities of $1.33 million, leaving Nevada's formerly wealthiest citizen some $246,000 in the hole. Under the circumstances, the comptroller agreed to the offer, but required that the court also approve it. On August 29, George Wingfield filed a petition in federal court listing his assets and liabilities and pointing out that if he were forced into bankruptcy, the banks might recover considerably less than he was offering them.[24]

Wingfield's supporters noted the pathos of a man once so wealthy now facing bankruptcy solely because of "leniency toward the hard-pressed ranchers." The *San Francisco Argonaut* concluded a laudatory article with a paean to the banker's integrity: "George Wingfield 'played the game' of business, as of life, straight—but with many 'errors' on the side of humanity." Wingfield's political opponents, however, were not so sure. On September 13, they filed a petition objecting to the compromise. They didn't believe the financial statements and charged that Wingfield had deliberately hidden his assets beginning in 1931, once he knew Reno National would be compelled to close. No action was taken on the offer for six months, while the bank reorganization wound down to its dismal conclusion. The hearing was finally conducted in Carson City, on March 1, 1934, by San Francisco federal Judge A. F. St. Sure. After testimony from both Tobin and Wingfield, St. Sure ruled that the offer, then valued at $66,000, was "far from sufficient." Despite Tobin's testimony that "Wingfield is hopelessly insolvent," and Wingfield's own claim that the offer was the best he could do, representing eighty to ninety percent of his free assets, the judge was adamant. Clearly skeptical of Wingfield's 1931 transfer of his home to his wife Roxy and the Crocker Bank transactions, St. Sure implied that the capitalist was hiding his assets. Typically terse, Wingfield described the proceedings graphically to F. G. Willis, at Crocker: "They ducked us in the lake."[25]

By the end of the month, he was back again. This time he offered the receiver all of his free assets, as well as any equity he might have in the assets that were pledged to Crocker as collateral for his loans. Once again Tobin supported the offer, pointing out that there were other secured claims against Wingfield and that forcing him into bankruptcy might risk recovering even less for the depositors. It took St. Sure just two weeks to turn him down again, observing that the offer was "totally inadequate and so small that it is hardly worth noticing." Undoubtedly mindful of the property that Wingfield had protected through the Wingfield Trust Fund, the judge was not inclined to be sympathetic. His rulings reflected the depositors' collective frustration that there should be so little left over for them from the man who had promised to give them everything if they would just let him reopen the banks. The offer was rejected at least in part because it was made contingent on the receiver's waiver of his right to sue Wingfield for recovery against his liability as a director of the national banks. This last liability was much greater than his stockholder's liability, and St. Sure was unwilling to waive the depositors' rights to it.[26]

Consequently, all possibility of compromise faded. Even Tobin's receivership was threatened, as a group of depositors led by W. E. Barnard petitioned J. F. T. O'Connor, comptroller of the currency, for his removal. The Depositors Protective Association of the Closed Wingfield Banks charged that Tobin had taken insufficient steps either to liquidate the bank or to collect from George Wingfield on the debts he owed. The comptroller did not grant their request, but there was continued pressure on the federal receivers to resolve the problem. On May 8, Tobin and Streeter proposed another strategy. If Wingfield would confess his director's liability, and sell all his remaining assets to satisfy the outstanding judgments on his stockholder's liability, they would then consent to have the remaining judgment auctioned off to "someone friendly" for a minimum amount. This would avoid further court proceedings and presumably satisfy the bank depositors that Wingfield had given them all he had.[27]

Wingfield resisted confession of liability and delayed his answer while trying to take steps to protect his other creditors. Finally, in October 1934, the comptroller of the currency ordered the national bank receivers to file suit against George Wingfield to collect against his stockholder's liability for "excessive and improvident loans" in the two national banks. Suits on the director's liability followed shortly. Default judgment in the first of these cases was rendered on the last day of the year, and they continued into 1935. Ultimately, Wingfield's stockholder's liability was $549,000, and his director's liability was $2,244,000, a total of over $2,793,000 he owed to the national bank depositors. Similar attempts to recover against Wingfield on behalf of the state banks were ruled unconstitutional in June 1934, but the national bank liability alone was enough to insure his eventual bankruptcy.[28]

Meanwhile, a startling series of events had focused further public attention on Wingfield's purportedly nefarious connections. In the first days of January 1934, the *Sacramento Bee* once again took up its campaign against the Nevada leader it characterized as a "sagebrush caesar." Beginning on January 2, it published a four-part series by Arthur B. Waugh that garnered the paper a Pulitzer Prize for "meritorious public service." The articles focused on the pending appointments of Frank Norcross to the U.S. Circuit Court of Appeals and Wingfield attorney William Woodburn to Norcross's vacant seat on the U.S. District Court. In characteristically passionate prose, Waugh depicted the disputed appointments, which were later investigated by a U.S. senate subcommittee under McCarran, as deciding "whether the now defunct political machine of Boss George Wingfield—thoroughly disorganized and discredited since the bank crash—shall remain in oblivion or renew its throttle-hold on the State of Nevada." Waugh made unsubstantiated charges against Woodburn and Wingfield, purportedly demonstrating "How Wingfield Ring Fleeced Nevadans with Interlocking Financial Firms." The articles presumed that Woodburn and Wingfield had looted the banks and reiterated many of the charges made by the 1933 legislative committee, concluding that there were "no less than a dozen violations of the law chargeable to officers and directors of the banks, any of which could be classed a felony."[29]

The *Bee* articles drew attention particularly to the 1932 bankruptcy of the Owl Drug Company, over which Norcross presided and which Woodburn had handled on referral from George Wingfield. The gist of the charge was that the Owl Drug bankruptcy was a sham, simply a device to defraud preferred stockholders and void burdensome leases by declaring bankruptcy, but then turning the company back to its original owners. A subsidiary issue involved alleged collusion between Norcross and his former partner, Woodburn, to keep receivership fees for Woodburn's firm and Wingfield's Bank of Nevada Savings and Trust Company. In time these charges, under scrutiny from McCarran's subcommittee, were sufficient to block the Norcross nomination; but their presentation by Waugh was, as he freely admitted, merely a means to attack George Wingfield, "to show how these appointments, in a measure, would assist in rebuilding the now wrecked Wingfield machine."[30]

The *Bee* vendetta brought the level of political debate down to a level of name-calling and innuendo. It was soon eclipsed, however, by the pressure of more immediate events in Reno. Once again, George Wingfield was implicated. On January 31, 1934, William Graham and James C. McKay were indicted on federal charges of mail fraud, in connection with a scheme that duped investors out of money they had purportedly won on horse races out of state. The operation depended on the gullibility of Reno visitors who "found" a deliberately planted purse with money in it. When they returned the purse, they were offered as a reward a tip on a horse race in a distant location such as Texas. When the horses paid off, the recipient would be asked to put up good-faith money, to show that he could have covered the loss. These sums of money, in the form of checks or securities cashed through the Riverside Bank, were consigned to their contacts, while the victims were given a ticket to pick up their "winnings" in Texas. When they got to Texas, of course, there was no money, and the sum they had advanced as a token of good faith was lost. Sometimes the scheme involved investments in the stock market instead of horse races, but always with the same sorry result.[31]

This scheme had initially been run through the Reno National Bank, which became suspicious of so many large sight drafts being cashed in amounts of $30,000 or $40,000. While the Reno National tried to delay payment on these drafts, so that suit was actually threatened in some cases, the business went elsewhere, to the Riverside Bank. At the latter bank, described in the trial as "a place where no questions were asked," cashier Roy Frisch apparently tolerated the "mystery transactions." Graham and McKay were charged as accessories. They did not run the schemes, but they provided the "protection" from Reno police and the banking facilities that perpetrators of the con needed to carry out their frauds. Their charge was fifteen percent of the proceeds.[32]

At first many of the victims were too chagrined to report the swindle, but some complaints were filed and postal authorities began to investigate. They contacted the Riverside cashier, Frisch, who testified to the grand jury about dates, amounts of money, and identities of those who received it. Although he had been under guard due to the nature of his testimony, Roy Frisch was alone on March 22, 1934, when he mysteriously disappeared somewhere between his house on Court Street and a downtown movie theater. His body was never found, but federal agents were pronouncing him dead within weeks, and midwestern gangster Baby Face Nelson, in Reno at the time, was subsequently implicated in his murder. At the time, George Wingfield was as mystified as anyone, assuming that Frisch had decided "to fade out" and wondering what had caused him to do it. As he wrote to his former secretary, William Zoebel, "No one can figure it out and all we can hear is different rumors."[33]

Wingfield was actually more concerned with the recent death of his friend

Governor Balzar, who died in office on March 21. Balzar's death came as both a personal and political blow. Fred Balzar was not a political confidant as Tasker Oddie had been, but he was a reliable Wingfield ally, some said a tool. His death removed one more key link in Wingfield's network, at a time when access to such political influence might be crucial. Wingfield was an honorary pallbearer at the governor's funeral. But public gossip focused on another connection altogether, as F. M. Murphy recounted:

> He [Frisch] was one of the cleanest men I ever knew; when they were transferring securities and funds from all other banks to save the Reno National, he refused to permit them to do it at the Riverside Bank, so it was the only liquid one in the group. It is claimed that Wingfield is tied up with Graham and McKay and the talk in Reno is very nasty, as Frish [*sic*] has been in public life over there for many years, is beloved by all who knew him, naturally suspicion points to those who were most interested in his disappearance.[34]

Murphy obviously numbered George Wingfield among those potentially interested in silencing Frisch. In April 1934, Wingfield was rejoicing in a bank examiner's positive report about the operations of the Reno National Bank in 1932. Obviously pained at public accusations of incompetence, he crowed to his bankers at Crocker: "The next time they speak of improvident loans and directors liability, I want to spring their own report on them." In fact, this was not the only such positive report. An earlier auditor's report was "quite complimentary"; it "refuted all charges made by those who employed him [reorganization opponents]." But the suspicious public, instructed by the *Sacramento Bee*, knew nothing of this report and still suspected the worst. Graham and McKay were arraigned in April in New York. Wingfield was summoned by the grand jury to testify in June. Later, in July, when Wingfield was subpoenaed as a witness in their trial, Las Vegas editor A. E. Cahlan, a prominent opponent of reorganization in the 1933 legislative session, cavalierly described Wingfield as "big boss" to the other two.[35]

Years of close personal relations with McKay made it impossible for Wingfield to distance himself in the public mind from the business dealings of the crime figures. Although McKay testified that he had no business relations with Wingfield, most Nevadans found the claim incredible. Wingfield himself gave no credence to the rumors, attributing them to the same misguided resentment that had turned so many bank depositors against him. He was confined to his home with an acute case of lumbago in July, so he did not attend the trial. It ended with a hung jury, and a retrial was ordered. The second trial, in 1935, ended with another deadlocked jury and the pair remained free until their eventual conviction in 1939, when they were fined $11,000 each and sentenced to nine years in federal prison. Although George Wingfield was not called to testify after the first trial, rumors of his collusion with the crime bosses nonetheless persisted.[36]

Frisch's murder and the indictment of Graham and McKay, on top of McCarran's hearings on Norcross, helped confirm a general impression of Wingfield as the toppled emperor of a corrupt realm. There was no way of combating such a perception, at a time when even the people who had been carried by Wingfield's banks spoke harshly of the banker. In any event, Wingfield didn't try. Steadfast in his reserve, he made no greater attempt to explain himself in 1934 than he had done in 1928, when he was at the height of his power. Although he was highly sensitive to the appearance of unethical behavior, Wingfield never publicly defended himself against such charges. He even turned down an offer from popular writer Ernest Haycox to do a sympathetic article, replying that "he was not interested in becoming the subject of books and stories as much as he could use the money." Privately, Wingfield suffered greatly. In a rare outburst he described his anguish to his old friend Bernard Baruch: "This whole thing is like a nightmare to me, to get wiped out like this through no fault of mine, as even two years ago I *was* very wealthy, and after all the things that I have done for the people here, a very small minority are trying to make a bum of me. And a great deal of it is personal, and politics." Publicly, however, he was stoic as always, pursuing his business and attempting to save what he could for those creditors he considered legitimate.[37]

Foremost among the latter, of course, was Crocker First National Bank. This bank, particularly its vice-president, F. Gloucester Willis, had supported Wingfield loyally through previous crises including the Cole-Malley losses and the collapse of the livestock industry. Now, when they stood to lose the money they had loaned to Wingfield personally, he repaid the favor by working assiduously to protect their interests. Though financially devastated by the bank failures, Wingfield still had resources with which to do this. He controlled GCMC, RSC, and the Sutter Butte Canal Company. After a few disastrous years at the beginning of the decade, each of these made a modest annual profit. The Wingfield Trust Fund, with assets of over $360,000, owned additional real estate and mortgages, and some much-needed cash with which he could make purchases of bonds to protect his remaining business interests. From 1933 until bankruptcy became inevitable late in 1935, Wingfield's sole objective was to manage these various assets so as to preserve them intact from secondary creditors like the bank receivers and repay his enormous debt to Crocker.[38]

Crocker's role instantly became controversial with opponents of reorganization, who naturally resented Wingfield's attempt to protect the interests of the San Francisco bank. Crocker's involvement with the Reno National in the summer of 1932, when they supported the latter bank's emergency request for an additional advance from the RFC, was depicted in a sinister light in newspaper accounts, though Wingfield insisted that he had invited Willis to Reno simply because "I wanted his advice on how to handle things." Wingfield's bank vice-president, Jerry Sheehan, depicted the arrangement in somewhat different light, remembering that "Willis came in and told me that Wingfield had placed the stock in their lap, and it was up to them." The fact that some of the money from that RFC loan was used to repay money that Crocker had earlier advanced to Reno National was also criticized. Men from inside the Wingfield organization, like Sheehan and Frisch, for example, understood the nature of the relationship. As Frisch explained it to the 1933 legislative committee investigating the banks: "My idea is that there was a great deal of friendship between the Crocker organization and Mr. Wingfield and my idea is that they were here to help solve the situation." To cynical bank depositors however, the presence of the San Francisco banker definitely smacked of foul play.[39]

In the next few years, as George Wingfield managed his own properties for the benefit of Crocker, those misgivings grew. The alliance was a close one. Wingfield and Gloucester Willis worked together closely, corresponded at least weekly, and occasionally visited to discuss their mutual business affairs. From the beginning of the management arrangement in 1932, Wingfield kept Willis informed of the details of daily administration, including his progress at reducing expenses and fluctuating occupancy rates at the hotels. The two men consulted about remodeling the Hotel Golden in 1935, about an advertising budget for the hotels, and about whether to raise the rent for the Bank Club when prohibition ended. Wingfield was a good and conscientious manager. When the construction workers went to work on the Hotel Golden in the spring of 1935, he supervised personally, complaining that "this is the slowest and most tedious thing I have ever had anything to do with" and "I make about twenty trips a day over there." He took pride when he materially reduced expenses and increased profits for 1933 compared to 1932.[40]

Similarly, Willis and Wingfield collaborated on financing. When Wingfield finally sold the Las Vegas lots in 1934, for a paltry $15,000 net, the money went not to disgruntled bank depositors, but to pay overdue interest on RSC bonds held by Crocker National Bank and the Wingfield Trust Fund. Both men later worked to secure a 1935 agreement with holders of these bonds to forego interest payments for ten years. At Willis's suggestion,

George Thatcher created a new company, the Nevada Holding Company, to succeed the Bank of Nevada Savings and Trust Company as trustee for Wingfield's trust account for his children. Wingfield's devotion to Crocker's interests in all of these transactions was absolute. He deferred to Willis whenever any decisions had to be made in regard to liquidation of the Henderson Banking Company in Elko, where his $250,000 on deposit was also pledged to Crocker. In May 1934, he reported to Willis an offer to buy the two Reno hotels for $700,000: "Of course, if I were not so involved, I would not consider any such price for the property as I am satisfied in time it will give a good account of itself. My sole object is to see that the bank is paid in full regardless of the condition it leaves me in." His activities during 1934 and 1935 testify to the truth of his remark.[41]

All along, this was an obstacle in Wingfield's attempt to compromise the bank stock cases. In response to demands of the Reno National receiver, Tobin, and reorganization opponents that he turn over all of his free assets, George Wingfield consistently maintained that he could not, because he had other creditors besides the depositors. His primary loyalty was to Crocker. Indeed, in August 1933 he pledged GCMC stock worth over $100,000 to the San Francisco bank specifically to keep it from the bank receivers. Loyalty had long been a virtue in the gamblers' world, and Wingfield's loyalty to his bankers was paramount and unassailable. Crocker had gambled with him on the revival of the Nevada livestock industry, at his instigation. Now that they had both lost, he felt morally obligated to do what he could for Crocker as the innocent party. Toward the bank depositors, by contrast, who reviled him and attacked his honesty, he naturally felt no such sense of obligation.[42]

In return, Crocker managers were magnificently cooperative with their former customer. They treated him as a respected businessman who had been trapped by circumstances, not as a villain. Wingfield was allowed to continue managing his hotel properties, and his advice was followed. In August 1935, after successful negotiation of an extension on repaying its bondholders, RSC bought at auction the 640-acre Spanish Springs Ranch that had formerly belonged to Reno mayor E. E. Roberts. The company paid $3,000 for this property, northeast of Reno, which Roberts had used as a duck preserve. Three days later, they were offered $6,000 for it. Though Wingfield held out for $8,000, he confided to Willis that he thought it might be best to keep it. As it turned out, he would own the property for the remainder of his life. Though the Spanish Springs Ranch was a modest successor to Meadowbrook Ranch or the Nevada Stock Farm, Wingfield gradually built it up into a model hunting preserve, with duck ponds, labrador dogs, and prize-winning quarter horses. In the meantime it provided him with a nearby hunting ground and a comfortable place to entertain guests who shared his passion for the sport.[43]

By that time, too, the partners had legally protected themselves against the threat represented by George Wingfield's looming financial crisis. After the liability judgments were entered against Wingfield, in April and May 1935, the national bank receivers levied attachment on all his remaining free assets and sold them at public auction. Though these included his Churchill County showplace, the Bailey Ranch, a depressed market meant that next to nothing was realized on the sale. Proceeds of the auctions, on April 8 and May 20, 1935, totaled $61,500. With virtually nothing remaining to his name, Wingfield still owed Crocker $850,000, so in March RSC signed a guaranty contract making it responsible for payment of the debt. By this device Wingfield made sure that his greatest remaining asset, the hotel company, would go to Crocker in the event he couldn't repay them. Although he steadily applied hotel profits and dividends from the Henderson Banking Company liquidation to the outstanding balance, it was still over $817,000 on August 30 of that year.[44]

Amidst the consistently dismal financial news, George Wingfield could take some comfort in April 1935 at his official exoneration by a federal grand jury that had been convened to consider the possible criminal liability of the Reno National Bank directors. Acting on a complaint brought by W. E. Barnard, the same man who had attacked Wingfield in radio broadcasts in 1933, U.S. district attorney Edward P. Carville sent the matter to the grand jury despite the fact that there was no criminal liability for overloans. George Thatcher complained about this to Key Pittman and tried to stop the sham process, because "an indictment, regardless of the outcome, carries a stigma which is almost impossible to wipe out." William Woodburn characterized Barnard as "Nevada's foremost and most stinking crook." It went forward anyway, and Wingfield and Jerry Sheehan, among others, appeared to give testimony.[45]

On April 10, George Wingfield delivered a prepared statement where, at last, he told his side of the story. Denying all charges of malfeasance, he told a sorrowful story of being overwhelmed by circumstances:

> I was at all times actuated by a desire to save the banks; a large part of my personal fortune was invested in the so-called Wingfield chain. I was trying to serve the needs of Nevada and particularly one of its basic industries, the livestock and ranching interests. I may have made many mistakes, but they were errors of judgment occasioned probably by my over-confidence in the industries of Nevada. . . . I didn't profit one dollar but on the contrary I have sacrificed my entire personal fortune.

Clearly stung by the charges of fraud, he reiterated again and again that he had acted forthrightly. There were no misleading entries in the books of the banks. His own companies and his family had substantial deposits in the banks, and his personal account at the Henderson Banking Company was five times greater than any other deposit in any of the Wingfield banks. There were no withdrawals from any of these accounts in advance of the bank closure: "Instead of trying to defraud the banks I did everything humanly possible to keep them open." As he concluded movingly, "I have given everything that I have in the world and I do not figure how a man can do any more."[46]

For a man as reserved and private as George Wingfield, it was undoubtedly a humiliating moment; but the grand jury testimony gave him his only opportunity to respond to the rampant suspicion of deceit and corruption, to rebut the charges of bank depositors and the *Sacramento Bee* alike. When the hearings concluded, the grand jury voted not to indict any of the bank officers. Thatcher and Woodburn each had slightly different versions of the vote, but no more than two of the twenty-one men on the jury apparently voted to uphold the charges. As Woodburn jubilantly reported to Pittman, "several of the grand jurors expressed themselves that they have never seen a cleaner or more honest bank failure." The testimony "showed that Wingfield put in his whole fortune." Any triumph that Wingfield may have felt, however, was evanescent. At virtually the same moment, the U.S. marshal's office was conducting the first of two public auctions of his remaining property.[47]

The two national bank receivers had continued to press for settlement of their outstanding judgments, according to the compromise plan they first suggested in May 1934. Wingfield had initially delayed because he was reluctant to let the national bank depositors have assets that he believed, in good conscience, should also be shared with his other creditors. He finally agreed to the plan in January 1935, however, and willingly turned over his property to the U.S. marshal, who sold it on behalf of the two national banks. Unfortunately, in August the comptroller's office refused to allow Tobin and Streeter to auction off the judgments to friendly parties, as originally agreed, because the guaranteed minimum bid of $3,250 was "too small in proportion to the amount of the judgments."[48]

Thatcher and Woodburn increased the offer to $3,500, and even invoked the aid of Senator Key Pittman to try to have the offer accepted. They circulated copies of Wingfield's current financial statements, which showed that he was "$2,700,000.00 worse off than broke with these judgments outstanding." All their efforts came to naught, however, and the judgments remained as current liabilities. As Wingfield fumed to his former Nevada Stock Farm trainer, Preston Burch, "I kept my part of the agreement and they have not kept theirs." The beleaguered capitalist hinted darkly about reasons: "It looks

like there is a lot of spite work coming from some quarter in this whole matter." Unfortunately, under the Democratic New Deal administration, he had
no national connections to call on in his hour of need. In 1935, Wingfield was
helpless in Washington, D.C., as he had not been since Nixon's took office
thirty years before.[49]

By September 1935, George Wingfield was without remaining defenses.
The federal government still sought to collect almost $30,000 for income tax
deficiencies in 1929 and 1930, and all attempts to negotiate a compromise on
the outstanding default judgments were proving fruitless. Wingfield accurately predicted to Burch, "Should the judgments not be put up for sale and
a compromise not made on the income tax claims, I will be forced into bankruptcy." His former office manager, Clarence Burton, by now the president
of City Bank in Washington, D.C., made one last valiant effort on his behalf
and contacted officials in the comptroller's office. He reported back to Wingfield that, although treasury officials were convinced that the bank failure was
honest, they were unwilling to accept the small sum offered to compromise
the debt, "in view of the bitterness prevailing in the State." Burton thought
perhaps the matter could be settled for $50,000 in cash, but Wingfield didn't
want to ask his friends for money that would only be turned over to someone
else. By his lights bankruptcy was the only viable alternative.[50]

The finale came in November, after a carefully orchestrated exchange of
letters with his faithful friends at Crocker. Wingfield described the sequence
of events to his old friend Burton: "As I indicated to them that as long as
I was in such a terrible mess, there was nothing in the future for me and
I could see nothing outside of bankruptcy, they immediately sold me out."
The San Francisco bank made formal demand for payment of his debt on
November 9. Wingfield replied two days later: "I exceedingly regret that it is
impossible to meet your demand. . . . I am helpless in the matter." Crocker,
accordingly, took action and foreclosed. After proper notice, they sold the
collateral they held on the steps of San Francisco City Hall, bidding it in
on their own account since no other bidders appeared. It brought a total of
$403,087, the bulk of it for 200,000 shares of RSC stock. The remaining
sum of over $414,000 became the responsibility of RSC, which signed a new
demand note to Crocker. The bank formally assumed control of the hotel
company and installed George Wingfield as general manager. He earned a
salary of $500 per month, with an additional monthly allowance of $150 for
expenses in entertaining guests and prospective guests at the hotel. Over
7,000 shares of bank stock in the former Wingfield banks were returned to
their chastened owner because "they are considered valueless."[51]

Once these transactions were completed, the way was cleared for the former capitalist to complete the formalities of bankruptcy. After taking steps to establish a small checking account for his wife through RSC, he filed a petition of bankruptcy on November 30, 1935. The erstwhile multimillionaire listed liabilities of $3,098,715 and assets of just over $10,504. As he admitted bitterly to Clarence Burton, his enemies had triumphed:

> I dislike very much to go through this procedure, but it looks like a hopeless proposition to try and go through the situation any further, owing to the fact that there is such a bitter row on here locally by a half dozen people, who were laying for me for a good many years, but who did not dare show their faces until they thought they had me on the run and they are quite correct in the latter assumption.

Burton wrote back to console his former employer, assuring him:

> To compromise was not worth the price you would have had to pay. . . . This is an election year and if any of the Democratic bunch from top to bottom would find some way of taking a kick at you, they would do it and I am inclined to think that they would rather have kept you in the position you have been in so that they could smack at you whenever they felt like it.

Still, when GW walked into the federal court building in November 1935, the mighty had indeed fallen. The reverberations from the final collapse of Wingfield's old and venerable power structure would echo throughout the state of Nevada for years.[52]

The case was heard by U.S. district judge Frank Norcross, the man whose elevation to the appellate court had been halted by the political fallout surrounding George Wingfield. Norcross appointed Arthur F. Lasher as trustee in bankruptcy, and all Wingfield's remaining assets were turned over to him. These included his Packard automobile; several trophies and guns; his watch; a stick pin; and a diamond, platinum, and star sapphire ring. Household furnishings, clothing, and personal memorabilia like framed photographs were exempt. His son later recounted a touching scene, in which his father offered Norcross his watch and ring, saying they were all he had left. According to this version, Norcross refused them with tears in his eyes, saying, "I won't take that away from you, George." In reality, a sale of the personal property was held on February 10, 1936. George Wingfield was in bed with flu at the time, and George Thatcher bought back the trophies and the jewelry on behalf of George Wingfield, Jr. He had a budget of $1,000, but spent only $865.[53]

With very little to do but disperse the paltry profits of the sale, the trustee closed the case in short order. The national bank stockholders' and directors' liability remained almost entirely unpaid, as Tobin had feared would be the case if he sued for recovery. In the end, the bank depositors recovered nothing more than the initial compromise offer that Wingfield had made them in 1933, and that amount came from the sale of the same assets that Wingfield had offered to give them initially. The bankruptcy yielded only an additional $173.83 for the First National Bank of Winnemucca and $539.91 for Reno National Bank. Wingfield was exempted from any further obligation on these debts when he was discharged from bankruptcy on March 17, 1936, in Carson City. At age fifty-nine, he was now ready to begin a new life. His jubilation was palpable in a letter to Bernard Baruch:

> I hope your son felt as happy on his birthday yesterday as I did when I had my hearing in the Federal Court and they discharged me, so that matter is closed. . . . One thing is sure and that is I am going to get out of politics as I am not going to have these birds shooting at me from all directions and I am going to try and get going so I can make both ends meet.

True to his word, he resigned later that year as Republican national committeeman for Nevada, after sixteen years in office: "They have asked me to continue, but I will not do so." [54]

Bankruptcy marked a symbolic death and rebirth for Nevada's most prominent citizen. *Fortune* magazine characterized George Wingfield as "still a personage in Nevada," even though bankrupt; but he was a different sort of personage than he had been before. After the failure of his banks and his agonizing personal ordeal of false accusation and public rejection, Wingfield was a changed man. Although he remained active for another twenty years, his vision was no longer the only one that mattered for the state of Nevada. As the state gradually recovered from the depression, and grew prosperous from the very tourist industries he had helped establish, it also grew larger than the grasp of any single man. The mantle of absolute personal power and authority that Wingfield had enjoyed for so many years had shifted to others. In the booming new society that he had helped to create, he was only one voice among many. After his bankruptcy, and the collapse of the banks, Wingfield truly inhabited a different world. [55]

Wingfield might simply have retired. He became a grandfather in 1936, just one day after the bankruptcy sale of his personal property. Approaching age sixty, and with his fortune gone, Wingfield had suffered a serious blow to his pride as well as his property. Choosing to stop fighting might have been only natural. But Wingfield was never a man to sit back and relax. His restless energy and executive abilities needed an object. He lost his taste for banking in the aftermath of the 1932 collapse, but his thoughts now turned back to mining. Once again he allowed himself to be tantalized by the possibilities. As he wrote to Bernard Baruch in January 1935, "There is very little new in mining out here but some one will run into another good one and I hope to be on the top row when they do." Baruch, of course, had been part of the first good one, GCMC, and had stuck with Wingfield through several others not quite so good, including Buckhorn. In response to that letter, Baruch wrote back a simple, two-sentence reply: "I am sorry you are in such a mixup. When you are ready to get straightened out, I will be glad to help you as I told you before." Baruch's generous offer proved to be critical in Wingfield's astonishing financial recovery, as he built a second, new fortune virtually on the ashes of the first.[56]

Contemporary observers made much of Wingfield's luck, but in the 1930s it was friendship that saved him. George Wingfield had enjoyed throughout his life the esteem of men in high places. In the years following the collapse of his banks, some of those men came to his rescue. His relationship with the Crocker First National Bank, for instance, was not just the natural warmth of a bank for a large and reliable borrower. Their consideration was due in large part to the regard in which Wingfield was held by the president, William H. Crocker. The two men had been acquainted since Nixon first introduced them in the Goldfield days, when Crocker financed the partners' purchase of the Jumbo and Red Top mines. Crocker had never forgotten the favor that Nixon and Wingfield had done him during the Panic of 1907, when their Goldfield bank had supplied more than $1.5 million in cash to stave off a potential run. Consequently, when Wingfield was in trouble, Crocker extended him every courtesy.

The San Francisco bank carried him long after wisdom might have dictated foreclosure, and when foreclosure became necessary, they arranged it to Wingfield's benefit. Not only was he allowed to manage his own properties, but Crocker eventually made it possible for Wingfield to repurchase them, by accepting RSC's guarantee for Wingfield's indebtedness. When William H. Crocker died in September 1937, Wingfield was an honorary pallbearer at his funeral. One of the bank's vice-presidents characterized the relationship between Crocker and Wingfield as "close" and assured Wingfield: "you had his confidence to the fullest extent." As it transpired, events confirmed this analysis.[57]

Crocker had lived just long enough to witness the beginning of George Wingfield's recovery. For more than a year after the foreclosure, RSC was controlled by Crocker First National Bank and the hotels were managed by Wingfield on their behalf. During that time, the company made steady payments on its obligation as guarantor of Wingfield's note. By November 1936, one year after his bankruptcy filing, the balance had been reduced from over $414,000 to $310,000. Wingfield's financial circumstances had improved considerably, and he was once again deemed credit-worthy. Accordingly, on March 19, 1937, Crocker allowed RSC to mortgage the two hotels for $700,000, with the proceeds used to pay off the remainder of Wingfield's original note and buy back the company's outstanding bonds. They also loaned Wingfield $90,000 personally, to enable him to buy back half of the RSC stock held by the bank.[58]

From that point on, the hotel company once again belonged outright to George Wingfield, along with his son and daughter. Characteristically, he went to work immediately to make improvements. By December 1937, he was reporting happily to F. G. Willis that he was tearing out the wooden wainscotting in the Hotel Golden bathrooms and installing modern basins, toilets, and light fixtures. Similar improvements were envisioned for the Riverside in 1938: "At any rate both places will be much more inviting than they have been in the past."[59]

Besides the debt to Crocker, only one additional obligation remained after the bankruptcy, which was the outstanding federal income tax obligation for 1929 and 1930. Bankruptcy did not abrogate this debt, although the trustee had remitted $1,443 on account; and George Wingfield spent much of his postbankruptcy time and energy trying to make an acceptable compromise offer. By 1936, after penalties and interest, the amount he owed had grown to over $28,000. Although he had no money of his own with which to pay it, "If I could get rid of the matter for three or four thousand dollars, I would be willing to attempt to borrow the money to settle it for once and for all." In October 1936, he was hopeful it might be settled for $10,000; but the IRS rejected the offer and filed a lien against Wingfield's personal bank account at Crocker. The money he had there was the remainder of a $100,000 loan he had secured from Bernard Baruch, and IRS intercession was most unwelcome. The only alternative, however, was for Wingfield to follow the advice of his Washington attorney and keep all his funds under Roxy's name and complete his business transactions in the names of others. Even the attorney who gave the advice recognized it was unlikely to be taken: "I know that it will be difficult for you to do this because you have always laid your cards on the table."[60]

Instead, in June 1937, George Wingfield gave up. He withdrew his offer in compromise on the outstanding taxes and borrowed the money to pay the IRS its remaining $20,000. He still believed he didn't owe the money, "and this was more in keeping with a fine on one who they thought could afford to pay." But in 1937 he was beginning to make money again, and he didn't want to have the IRS hovering over him for the rest of his life: "If they did compromise and I should make any real money in the future, they would always have it in for me and say they had been deceived, etc." In 1937, Sutter Butte Canal Company was profitable once again, and GCMC was buying a gold placer property in Alaska. Wingfield still owed money to Crocker on his personal loan, and he owed money to Baruch, but he also had considerable property in his own name. His capital account had been a paltry $17,000 in 1936. By 1937, it was $116,000. As he put it to Baruch in March of 1938: "I . . . am drifting out of debt pretty fast and will certainly not get caught in any more log jams." [61]

In fact, by 1938, George Wingfield was well on his way back to wealth. Crocker's loyalty and support enabled Wingfield to regain control of his beloved Reno hotels, but his second fortune came from elsewhere. The real source of Wingfield's phoenixlike rise from bankruptcy was, fittingly enough, another gold mine, and, once again, friendship was the means of his acquisition. Known as the Getchell Mine, this property was located in rural Nevada, approximately twenty miles northeast of Golconda, where Wingfield had made and lost his first fortune so long before. It was brought to his attention by the man for whom it was named, Noble H. Getchell, although at the time it was known more mundanely as the Chase Prospect.

Like Crocker, Getchell had known Wingfield since Goldfield, though the occasion of their meeting, in the bar brawl, was more colorful. Getchell had gone on to become a Battle Mountain mineowner and banker. He served as Republican state central committee chairman while Wingfield was national committeeman. His Battle Mountain State Bank had also collapsed during the 1932 bank holiday. Getchell was elected to the state senate in 1922 and became president pro temp in 1928. The two men respected each other and were political allies. It was Noble Getchell, in particular, who moderated some of the State Assembly's criticism of Wingfield during the 1933 banking investigation. [62]

It was also Noble Getchell who brought Wingfield the instrument of his redemption, although neither man could have recognized it at the time. Getchell first learned of the strike from a prospector, Emmet Chase, in 1934. He grubstaked Chase and his partners for six months, after which their findings proved promising enough that he began to buy up adjoining railroad land in order to be able to follow through on the vein. In the meantime, Getchell approached George Wingfield in June 1935, as "the only one I will consider on a deal of any kind in this property." Intrigued, Wingfield took his brother-in-law, mining engineer Roy Hardy, along with him to have a look. The two men liked what they saw. Getchell purchased Chase's interest, and, in October 1935, RSC signed an agreement with Noble Getchell for the joint development of the property. The hotel company agreed to pay half of the costs in exchange for 50,000 shares of capital stock. A year later, with the bankruptcy safely behind him, Wingfield purchased the right to receive this stock from RSC for $5,000.[63]

By then the development work at the mine had proven exceptionally promising, and the partners were anticipating full-scale operation, including construction of a mill. This required money that neither of them had, however, so Wingfield went to call on his old friend, Bernard Baruch. The latter's offer of assistance was of long standing. As early as 1933, Baruch had written Wingfield to call on him when the time came:

> After you are all cleaned up and out of debt, I wish you would let me know as I would like to discuss with you then, if I am still in good financial condition, letting you have a small stake to go on with, if you want it. You know, I have great faith in your ability and unswerving belief in your integrity. After all, you are a game guy.

With Getchell's fortuitous acquisition of the Chase Prospect, the time was ripe. George Wingfield went east to New York in October 1936, at Reno Securities expense, to visit with Baruch and explain the situation. He took along assay reports on the ore samples and invited Baruch to invest in the mine, suggesting that he send an independent mining engineer to sample the property. On the strength of these samples, and some Reno real estate that he had redeemed from the Riverside Bank, Wingfield also arranged for a $100,000 personal loan from Baruch.[64]

Upon his return, in November 1936, the partners incorporated their property as the Getchell Mine. There were 1.5 million shares at a par value of $1 each. Wingfield was president and Getchell vice-president. Roy Hardy was their consulting engineer. The officers each took 500,000 shares, and 500,000 remained in the treasury. Wingfield offered his son and daughter each a chance to purchase ten percent of his share of the mine, which they did. Baruch, meanwhile, sent a gold mining expert to investigate the property. Fred Searls, who had been a mining engineer in Goldfield, and who now ran the Newmont Mining Company, was impressed by what he saw. With some urgency, Baruch telegraphed Wingfield late in November 1936: "Sampling almost up to yours. Can you come on. Sooner the better." Once again Wingfield departed for New York, where he found the weather "cold and disagreeable. Would not want any of this country for a steady diet." The

By 1941, when this photograph was taken, George Wingfield was no longer the undisputed "King of Nevada" he had once been. He had, however, recovered control of his hotels and was beginning to be financially comfortable once again. (Courtesy of Nevada Historical Society)

visit was well worth the temporary discomfort, however—he returned with an agreement from Baruch to take the other one-third interest in the mine, in partnership with Newmont, and provide the necessary money to develop it.[65]

The Getchell Mine contained large quantities of low grade oxide ore that proved to be easy and efficient to treat, with the result that the mine was exceptionally profitable. Construction on the mill began immediately. The company poured its first bullion in 1938 and paid its first dividends in September of that year. Monthly payments thereafter amounted to $200,000 over the next three months. From 1939 to 1944, Getchell paid more than $3 million in dividends, with one-third of that going to George Wingfield and his children. Initially traded at only 10 cents per share, stock in the Getchell mine occasionally paid 10 cents per month in dividend. At times, the stock sold for as much as $10 per share. By 1939, Wingfield could boast with justifiable pride to Baruch, "We have a good mine that will last for years to come." Always more ebullient than his partner, Noble Getchell was quoted in *Time*: "We now stand a good chance of making a million or so each."[66]

As news of the strike at Getchell began to spread, Wingfield was once again newsworthy. Writers around the country, captivated by the compelling story of his remarkable recovery from bankruptcy, couldn't resist colorful metaphors. Emphasizing his dramatic past, they added another layer to the growing Wingfield myth. The *San Francisco Chronicle* evoked a cowboy image with its headline: "Wingfield Hitting the Comeback Trail." *Time* preferred a gambling theme, announcing that " 'King George' once more loomed on the Nevada scene with a big stack of blue chips." *Life* characterized him as "No. 1 Reno citizen" and photographed him "symbolically casting his shadow over the State of Nevada." Wingfield's story had come to represent the glittering promise and vaguely sinful overtones of Nevada in general. His saga of rags-to-riches-to-rags-to-riches was repeated as the quintessential western fairy tale. As the main character in the romantic story of his recovery, Wingfield was himself now a facet of the tourist-based economy that he had helped to create and still promoted through his hotels. In his startling comeback, he embodied the allure of Reno as a place for new beginnings, a mecca for the unhappily wed or those aspiring to great good luck. Now no longer Nevada's wealthiest citizen, George Wingfield had become its most symbolically representative.[67]

In the late 1930s, then, Wingfield's recovery was clearly more than just financial. He began to regain reputation and public stature, as well. It was a development that naturally pleased friends like mining engineer William J. Loring, who wrote to congratulate him on the Getchell Mine: "You have always had my fondest hopes for a just return to your former wonderful position." Former *Reno Evening Gazette* publisher Oscar Morgan found the story so inspiring, and potentially salable, that he decided to write a book on Wingfield's life. Even former president Herbert Hoover added his compliments on Wingfield's dignity and persistence. Hoover was a great admirer of self-made men, of whom he was one, and he had reason to extend a special sympathy to those forced to endure unjust public attacks. Like the others, he was pleased to see George Wingfield pull through: "I have long delayed writing you just a short note which has been often in my mind, and that is, to express my admiration for a man of courage and staunchness and my congratulations for the way you have pulled out of a great deal of persecution and injustice."[68]

In the face of sentiment of this sort, George Wingfield may have over-estimated the extent of his rehabilitation with the people of Nevada. In any event, in 1938 he allowed himself to be convinced by University of Nevada president Walter E. Clark that he should run for another term as university regent. Despite his initial reluctance to file for the office, he acceded to Clark's request: "You have been so able a Regent during your years of service that it will be a great loss to the University and to the whole state if you should withdraw. . . . Please file." He did so in May 1938. By then Wingfield's financial circumstances had improved sufficiently that he was once again loaning money to friends and making public gifts. In March 1938, for instance, he donated over $6,000 to the university for necessary improvements to an irrigation ditch which flowed through the campus. In May, he bought a $120 pair of mute swans to be placed on the newly constructed Virginia Lake south of the Reno city limits. He carefully requested, however, that his gifts to the university not be publicized and that no political advertisements be placed in support of his candidacy. As he told Walter Bracken in Las Vegas: "I am very much opposed to sanctioning anything that would be an attempt to bring politics into the University."[69]

Politics evidently intervened nonetheless. Though Wingfield supporters tried to make it clear that he had been asked to run by fellow regents, voters were skeptical. Many in the state remained bitter about the bank collapse, and they saw in George Wingfield's relatively painless recovery further evidence of financial corruption and political collusion. Fearful of his previous power, the people of Nevada were unwilling to give him a new political base. Wingfield was one of three candidates in the primary election on September 6, which he survived; but he was defeated in the general election by Anna H. Wardin. She received almost 9,600 more votes than Wingfield, out of a total of nearly 44,000 cast. To his friends, the defeated candidate expressed relief: "For myself, I am happy to be out of the 'mess' at the University as it is a thankless job and there is a pretty hard crowd to deal with so I am well satisfied with the outcome." Those who knew him, however, felt he had been hurt by his rejection. It was further evidence, if any were needed, of Nevadans' determined repudiation of his vision and proffered leadership for the state. From that time on, George Wingfield would play the game as a private citizen.[70]

On balance, however, there were consolations. The bank reorganization battle had been devastating, but he had survived it. The Getchell Mine, as he put it to Baruch, was "one of the great mines," and its profits were rising steadily. Business in the hotels was brisk, and Wingfield paid off his 1937 personal loan from Crocker in April 1939. He repaid Baruch three months later, with money that he borrowed from Crocker for that purpose, "not that he has ever mentioned it to me or for any reason other than that the banks are the proper loaning agencies." By 1939, Wingfield's credit was improving sufficiently that he didn't have to resort to old friends for financing. As he confided to Baruch in August, "I am getting shaped up in good order." If he was no longer Nevada's king—*Life* magazine notwithstanding—George Wingfield was still a prominent citizen. All in all, it was far cry from the darkest days of November 1932. By the end of the decade, as the *San Francisco Chronicle* announced, "the name Wingfield again means money in Nevada."[71]

ELEVEN

"The Same Old Landmarks Over and Over Again"

I N 1944, due largely to the continued prosperity of the Getchell Mine and Nevada's wartime boom, George Wingfield's long financial nightmare came to a formal end. In August of that year, he wrote to Billy Crocker, the son of his old friend William H. Crocker, now president of the San Francisco bank. Wingfield's prose was businesslike, but his pride was unmistakable:

> Since March 31, 1937, I have dug myself completely out of the foxhole which has been a long row to hoe. I am completely out of debt and so is the Reno Securities Company which owed your bank large sums of money and I likewise was badly involved.
>
> I wish to take this means to thank you and your staff for the many courtesies and favors extended to me and my concerns over the past forty years. Much water has gone over the wheel since then. At any rate, I have dug out regardless of high taxes and other difficulties which I have been forced to face so everything that I now possess is in the clear.

The mixed metaphors bespoke emotion. Badly scarred by his bankruptcy, when debt had sabotaged a lifetime of self-reliant independence, Wingfield was now understandably wary of owing money. His final reemergence from debt was a ceremonious occasion.[1]

Wingfield also wrote of paying the hotel mortgage to a few personal friends, to Baruch, and to his son, George, Jr., then serving as a naval officer in the South Pacific. But the letter to Billy Crocker was the most portentous. It was the Crocker First National Bank, after all, which had made possible George Wingfield's second rise to fortune, by rescuing him from the full consequences of bankruptcy. For the support and friendship thus extended, the Nevada capitalist was profoundly grateful. The bank president wrote a personal reply to his old and honored customer: "You may have had some ups and downs, but around this bank there was never any question about your ability and integrity. You have my heartiest congratulations for the way you have handled your affairs and my sincerest hope for many years to enjoy to the fullest the fruits of your accomplishments." For the 68-year-old Wingfield, this solemn exchange marked the conclusion of a dreadful interval and the beginning of a comfortable old age. During the remaining fifteen years of life, he could once again take pride in his own self-sufficiency and revel in the delicious sensation of being "in the clear."[2]

The costs had been tremendous. Financially, Wingfield had lost an empire and he never recovered his characteristic drive to build a new one. Though he retained his home and some valuable Reno real estate through his wife and his children's trust fund, he was no longer building for the future, no longer financially involved throughout the state. His postbankruptcy ventures, which included a Reno laundry, were modest by comparison to those he had undertaken in his prime. Wingfield after his bankruptcy took Bernard Baruch's financial advice and, as soon as he was able, built up large cash accounts. He invested now in treasury bills rather than innovative fuel processes. No longer a venturesome capitalist, his business was confined to a small number of core properties over which he still retained control, including the centerpiece Reno Securities Company, Getchell Mine, the Sutter Butte Canal Company, and GCMC. While these provided him with wealth, and with scope for his executive abilities, they were all old and established companies that entailed few risks. The second Wingfield fortune was that of an old man.[3]

In addition to financial losses, Wingfield had also suffered personal and political humiliation in the aftermath of the bank collapse. Even in 1940, Reno was still a small town, with just over 21,000 residents. When its most prominent citizen was threatened personally and vilified publicly in the press, there was no salve of anonymity. Although he wrote the attacks off to "politics," Wingfield personally suffered every slight. In his maturity, George Wingfield no longer lashed out physically against his enemies, as he had once drunkenly attacked Boyd Moore, but he nonetheless remembered. In 1940, writing to his former United Nevada Bank partner Herbert Fleischhacker, he recalled how it felt:

> As I have been through some of these things I know what they can do
> to a person when they get the idea they have them on the down-grade,
> and it is a very easy matter for the public to forget the many fine acts of
> charity and good deeds that have been done for them in the past, and

This photograph of a relaxed George Wingfield was taken inside "the cave."
Above his head is a picture of himself and several associates after a successful shoot
at Spanish Springs Ranch. (Courtesy of Nevada Historical Society)

some of those who have benefitted the most are those who can be the most bitter.[4]

In Wingfield's case, the personal opposition that surfaced during the bank reorganization campaign, which far exceeded mere political disagreement, came as a shock. Still faithful to the creed of his prime, Wingfield envisioned himself mildly as a benevolent capitalist who was devoted to the economic betterment of Nevada. Years of power had shielded him from any genuine appreciation of the bitterness that his economic and political domination had engendered. Nevadans were not uniformly grateful for the prosperity that Wingfield saw as his principal legacy to them, and the fact stunned him. His resounding rejection in the mid-1930s permanently destroyed his previous confidence in the congruence of his own interests with those of the state. All the lofty language of empire abruptly ceased. The name Wingfield may once again have meant money, but it no longer meant Nevada.

The bank battle also marked the end to any significant political power for the Nevadan. In dire financial straits, electoral politics were an indulgence he could no longer afford. He took no active part in the 1934 elections, though he observed sarcastically to his bankers at Crocker that "I am becoming the principal candidate on both sides." He was right about that. W. E. Barnard's radio attacks against Wingfield's "bipartisan machine," bolstered by the *Sacramento Bee*'s continued insinuations about Woodburn and Norcross, were given widespread publicity throughout the campaign season. Things got so bad that George Thatcher resigned as Nevada's Democratic national committeeman in March, in order to protect Key Pittman, who was up for reelection. Pittman wrote privately to his old friend Thatcher of his sorrow about these "factional controversies":

> I know that a lawyer can perform professional services without being improperly influenced in any way whatever by the business of personal desires of his client. I know that you and Billy [Woodburn] have always opposed George Wingfield politically. . . . I have for years answered and argued against the assertion of a bipartisan political control in Nevada. No such thing ever existed.[5]

Pittman nonetheless took care to distance himself publicly from charges of bipartisanship. He accepted Thatcher's resignation and maintained in newspaper interviews that Wingfield had always "fought" him. To charges that Wingfield would control him if he were elected, Pittman replied that he had never been connected with the Republican machine: "If I were foolish enough to be connected with that machine, either in the past or at any other time, then I have not got sense enough to represent you in the United States Senate or anywhere else." An astute politician, Pittman realized that the general public would not share his broad-minded view of Nevada's intimate business and political circles.[6]

Republicans, of course, were even more vulnerable than Pittman. Desperate to dissociate themselves from the bank controversy, they fought back by attacking Graham Sanford and the *Reno Evening Gazette.* The *Gazette* was opposing the Republican gubernatorial nominee, acting governor Morley Griswold, and supporting Democrat Richard Kirman, former president of Reno's solvent First National Bank. In a series of political advertisements in the rival *Nevada State Journal,* the party pointed out that Sanford had himself been intimately identified with George Wingfield in the past, and furthermore, that no banker could ever be trusted to be a progressive leader. In particular they harped on the hated Barnard, trying to cast suspicion on him by pointing out that he was not a depositor in any of the Wingfield banks, despite his consistent attacks on the reorganization.[7]

Ingeniously, they tried to turn his bipartisan machine charge against Barnard:

> A certain clique having political ambitions have discovered a bipartisan control, which they claim has been ruling the State of Nevada for many years. Why not analyze this clique who are making these accusations and see if they are not trying to build up a bipartisan machine of their own in the State of Nevada that no one ever dreamed of and, if successful would be controlled by outside interests?

Naming names, they went on to ask, "Why is the Sacramento Bee so interested in Nevada affairs? Why did they purchase Radio Station KOH at Reno? . . . Why do these interests employ W. E. Barnard to peddle their poison? . . . Is this a part of a notorious scheme to sell out the State of Nevada financially and politically?"[8]

It was not enough. The fiscally conservative Kirman soundly beat Griswold in 1934 and inaugurated an era of Democratic dominance in Nevada state politics that lasted until 1950. In this new political world, which the failure of his banks had in part created, George Wingfield was no longer a power broker. He still had influence, and he was still interested in politics, but his resignation in 1936 from the Republican National Committee severed permanently his formal connection to political power. From then on, Wingfield was an observer rather than a player, and a new set of political allegiances came to dominate the state's politics. The Republican party splintered into myriad factions, and the burden of political leadership passed from Wingfield's Republicans to McCarran's Democrats. Some men prominently identified with Wingfield remained active in the Democratic years, including John Mueller and Norman Biltz. Mueller continued as a lobbyist and frequently advised Nevada legislators on issues in which Wingfield was interested. Biltz, a prominent Lake Tahoe land developer who had gotten his start with a loan from Wingfield and accompanied the latter to his bankruptcy hearing, became a supporter and close advisor of Senator McCarran. Neither was exclusively identified as a "Wingfield man," however.

Gradually, the bipartisan label shifted from Wingfield to McCarran. As had always been typical of the small and cozy world of Nevada politics, leaders of both parties continued to know and work with each other. McCarran cultivated a group of talented young men and women, including later director of the mint Eva B. Adams. Their political program consisted primarily, as did McCarran's, and Wingfield's before him, of serving Nevada's interests. Indeed, as the proverb had it, the more things changed, the more they remained the same. Years later, in the 1950 election, a group of young Republicans calling themselves the Young Turks broke with the aging leadership of their party and engineered the election of Republican candidate Charles Russell as governor. To their dismay, they discovered that the Republican Russell was advised by McCarran's confidant, Norman Biltz. As Nevada historian Jerome Edwards has observed, "party affiliation did not mean much in Nevada anyway."[9]

McCarran had a personal touch and a popularity that George Wingfield had always lacked, however. People could vote for (or against) McCarran every six years, and he made frequent trips to Nevada to maintain contact with his constituents. Contrasting favorably with the privacy and reserve of banker Wingfield, the congenial McCarran depicted himself as a man of the people. At least partly as a consequence, his own "bipartisan machine," though perhaps more powerful, was never so controversial as the one attributed to the capitalist.

Wingfield's political power may have evaporated, but his interest in politics did not. He remained a dedicated Republican partisan until the end of his life, adamantly opposed in particular to Franklin Roosevelt's New Deal and all of its "socialist policies." In 1936, in a gesture of defiance, he contributed $100 that he could ill afford to the Republican National Committee, to help fight "the greatest battle in history to save America." Aside from his own animosity toward the Democratic administration that had helped to sink his bank reorganization plan, he also resented the public welfare policy of the New Deal, which "has got people in the humor of not wanting to work." At the outbreak of World War II, he condemned governmental planning efforts to his old friend, stockbroker Alfred Frankenthal: "Any time the people allow a bunch of crackpots to experiment with the laws of supply and demand, as well as with the laws of nature, they will take us back to the horse and buggy days and then some." Predictably, he lamented the growth of bureaucracies as well: "We hope that the new Congress will clean out some of the bureaus as they are getting entirely too thick and some of them do not stop at anything as they consider themselves bosses of the people and not servants of the people and the people are not going to stand for that much longer." He relished the vulgar humor of anti-Roosevelt doggerel circulated by Noble Getchell.[10]

His hatred for the New Deal was an area of agreement with Nevada's Democratic senator, McCarran, who gained national notoriety in 1937 for his opposition to Roosevelt's "court-packing" scheme for the Supreme Court. Despite the history of opposition between the two men, dating back to McCarran's appearance as one of the attorneys for May Baric in Tonopah, they found common ground in their later years. Norman Biltz supported McCarran for reelection in 1938 and later reported the senator's suspicion of his efforts because of McCarran's long-standing distrust of "the boys on the corner," with whom Biltz was closely identified. Yet Biltz also observed that McCarran was more suspicious of Woodburn and Thatcher than he was of Wingfield personally, and it is clear that by the 1940s there was a mutual understanding between the two adversaries. In 1944, Wingfield was working behind the scenes to secure McCarran's reelection, writing to Bernard Baruch that "our friend" would have difficulty only in the primary: "In my opinion, he has done a good job and would continue to do so." A few weeks later, he elaborated: "They are attacking Pat as an Isolationist and they are trying to urge him and it don't [*sic*] look as good for him as it did when I wrote you last. However I think he will win." Indeed, Wingfield's hopes in that year were all with the Democrats. Of congressional aspirant Berkeley Bunker he wrote, "Bunker will no doubt be elected to Congress. He is a democrat and a Mormon and a very good friend of mine."[11]

For George Wingfield, the last phrase was a telling one. Friendship founded on personal respect and loyalty had always assumed central importance in his life, and it had proven crucial in his financial recovery. Friendship had been a key political value throughout his life. Going back as far as George Nixon and including Tasker Oddie, Fred Balzar, George Thatcher, and Key Pittman, the men he supported for political office and relied on for advice had been his friends as well. This made for an intimate politics that many over the years regarded with suspicion, especially when the central figure in the network of friends was as enormously wealthy and powerful as Wingfield.

Yet it seemed almost inevitable in a tiny and backward state such as Nevada, where the pool of potential political leaders was so small.

By the 1940s, in a sensational reversal that no one could possibly have predicted at the time of the 1928 Cole-Malley trial, George Wingfield had added Pat McCarran to that list of friends. The two men consulted on matters of mutual interest, especially wartime mining regulations that affected operations of the Getchell Mine. When the Democratic senator returned to Reno he stayed at the Riverside Hotel. He called on Wingfield in the old familiar office that he had condemned so often as a den of insidious power brokers, on the second story of the bank building. The fact that it was now the First National Bank instead of Wingfield's Reno National, and that it was McCarran who now had the upper hand politically, had clearly changed the complexion of things in the mind of the Democratic senator. Cooperation, once unthinkable for both men, was now expedient. At the time of McCarran's death in 1954, their rapprochement was complete. On the occasion of the senator's birthday in August of that year, Wingfield sent warm greetings: "You are a great American, a great Senator and a good friend; and may you live long and prosper." It was yet another example of the peculiar pliability of partisan politics in Nevada.[12]

In this new political world, however, George Wingfield was no longer a major player. He watched from the sidelines, complaining predictably about high taxes and militant labor unions, but no longer calling the shots. His correspondence narrowed to old friends and associates like Baruch, Julian, and Frankenthal. To them he sent political observations and gossip about his business enterprises, but his operations were no longer so extensive as they had once been. Economically he was once again unencumbered, but the times were changing. As owner of Reno's most prominent hotel, the Riverside, he met numerous celebrities who came to town for a divorce; but he was consulted far less often about new ventures or new policies. Instead, in the years of his old age, Wingfield came full circle and identified himself once again primarily as a mining man.

Temperamentally, mining had probably always suited Wingfield best. The riskiness of the business, from finding and processing the ore to making an advantageous market for the stock, appealed to his gambler's soul. Mining's enormous potential profits had lured him into the game in Tonopah, and the spectacular payoff in Goldfield had made him a lifetime player. As the *Goldfield Tribune* had observed long before, "He was endowed with a speculative spirit and the courage to test his own resources." Although he had lost virtually all of his GCMC stock in the bankruptcy, Wingfield continued his control of the company's board of directors until his death in 1959. Estey Julian was vice-president and general manager of the company, which continued to diversify its activities throughout the 1940s and 1950s. GCMC controlled the Sutter Butte Canal Company and the California Fuel and Utilities Company (which operated a magnesium-based power plant). In 1940, it bought a controlling interest in the Comstock-Keystone mine in Virginia City, and in 1944, in the midst of World War II, it purchased the Dalmo-Victor Company, which made radar antennas for airplanes. In 1947, in connection with Goldfield Deep Mines Company, it resumed development work on its thirty-four claims in Goldfield: "Although most of the claims in the Goldfield area have been pretty well worked over, there is always the chance that something may be uncovered, which was overlooked years ago." [13]

By 1952, Wingfield could boast happily to Baruch: "Goldfield is coming to life again." The company owned a zinc mine in Mexico and the Deep Creek lead mine in Washington State. Goldfield milling operations continued, and GCMC also purchased a majority interest in the American Chrome Company in Montana. In all of this expansion Julian was the central figure, consulting with Wingfield as president, but carrying out all facets of the operations on his own, including frequent trips to Washington, D.C., to consult with government officials. Under the circumstances, it was only natural that Wingfield should contemplate turning over the company to his faithful lieutenant, whom he described as "a very high class and competent engineer." Unfortunately, Julian died unexpectedly in 1955, while examining an ore-bearing region in Ethiopia on behalf of GCMC. His death left Wingfield with no choice but to carry on with the management of his pride and joy, though he complained to Baruch that it "threw a big load on me." Along with everything else, GCMC had to stave off a proxy fight in 1955 and again in 1956, and it had acquired exclusive rights to explore and mine 30,000 square miles in Ethiopia. It was also in the middle of selling its interests in the Sutter Butte Canal Company.[14]

Although he complained of the burden, George Wingfield continued to serve as president of GCMC until his death. His sentimental attachment to the company was considerable, and he saw no viable successor. Julian's consulting engineer, Willis A. Swan, became the new general manager. Together Swan and Wingfield renewed the company's original Wyoming charter for another fifty years when it expired in 1956. Wingfield continued to sign by hand all GCMC stock certificates sent in for transfer, because he wanted to know who was buying and selling the stock. He fought back still another unfriendly takeover attempt against the company in 1959, the year of his death.[15]

In the end, GCMC was to prove Wingfield's most lasting affiliation. Although he no longer profited substantially from the company's success, he remained committed to its integrity and achievement. He would no doubt 'have taken some satisfaction from the fact that his famous Nevada gold-rush creation actually outlived him. In deference to its president, the company maintained a Reno office until his death. Then, from San Francisco in 1960, it purchased the Getchell Mine from the estates of George Wingfield and Noble Getchell. In 1966, as the Goldfield Company, it finally cut its symbolic ties to its birthplace and sold all its remaining property in Goldfield, Nevada. Over all the previous years, however, it had been the single consistent business interest in Wingfield's life.[16]

GCMC was Wingfield's first love, and he remained faithful through the trials of fifty-three years, long after profit had ceased to be a motive. Bernard Baruch acknowledged the seductiveness of mining fully forty years after their first investment together in GCMC, when he wrote to Wingfield about a proposed law regulating the flotation of mining securities: "As you and I know, they are not gilt-edged investments. Thank Heavens! If they had been, you and I would never have done anything with them." George Wingfield had done a great deal indeed with GCMC, from the initial organizational stages, through the boom years in Goldfield and subsequent diversification and management by skilled subordinates. It was a testimonial to his devotion that this company, which had initially been his creation, remained affiliated with him long after he lost his ownership interest and survived to become his final economic legacy.[17]

Wingfield's attachment to the Getchell Mine was more recent, but no less intense. By 1945, the Getchell was famed as "the second greatest gold mine in America," largely because of the demand for strategic minerals created by World War II. It seemed to be one more incidence of "Wingfield Luck." As soon as war broke out in Europe in 1939, Wingfield conferred with Bernard Baruch and with Newmont Mining Company president, Fred Searls, about building a new mill to process the tungsten ore they already knew was located on their property. Wingfield confidently predicted that, "should the tungsten plant be built and the prices stay at their present level, we could get our money back from profits within one year." The combination of tungsten and arsenic, both found on the Getchell property and both strategic wartime minerals, meant that the mine could avoid complying with the government orders closing down gold mines. Tungsten alone wasn't profitable enough to support the high costs of wartime operation, but arsenic couldn't be produced without also producing gold—and the combination was enormously lucrative. Even after taxes that Wingfield considered to be little short of confiscatory, the company continued to pay dividends.[18]

Wartime labor problems were serious. Workers were hard to find, demanded high pay, and sometimes didn't return to the mine after getting drunk on payday. But the company attempted to combat the problem by providing comfortable housing and work facilities at the site. It also lobbied for a Mexican guest-worker policy similar to the *bracero* program developed for agricultural employers. In 1945, the accumulated difficulties finally stopped active operations; but the mine reopened again after the war. In 1947, with new sulfide gold ore proving to be refractory, Newmont Mining Company sold its Getchell shares on the open market, and by 1949 the company had 1300 public stockholders, including Joseph P. Kennedy. The original owners maintained their interests, however, with George Wingfield remaining as president. In 1950 the company experimented with new milling processes for the sulfide ore. The company repeated its World War II experience during the Korean War, closing its gold plant in 1951 and producing tungsten instead.[19]

Though Getchell's gold production never reached previous levels, the mine continued to be moderately profitable. By 1956, its twenty-year anniversary, the company had produced over $38 million in dividends for its stockholders. Less spectacular than GCMC's nearly $30 million in thirteen years, this was still a respectable record. For George Wingfield it was the financial basis of a prosperous old age, as well as being the emblem of his recovery from the dark days of the bank collapse. His personal share of the dividends amounted to over $10 million, and his estate realized an additional profit of over $500,000 from the sale of his stock to GCMC in 1960.[20]

Getchell Mine always meant more than profits to George Wingfield, however. In contrast to GCMC, which he merely supervised, Wingfield participated actively in the operation of Getchell Mine. As president of the company he visited the mine frequently for inspections and communicated with the managers daily by teletype from his office in Reno. Always anxious to know what was going on, Wingfield remained interested and engaged by company affairs, planning improvements to the physical plant and strategies for new treatment methods. He clearly relished the chance for active connection with the mining industry that Getchell afforded him at the end of his long business career, when other entrepreneurial activities had lost their appeal. As he wrote to Bernard Baruch in 1956, at age seventy-nine, "the mining is all I care to do."[21]

By that time, in the final years of his life, mining was all that Wingfield did do in a business way. But he continued as president of RSC until 1955 and oversaw in those years another phase in the expansion and improvement of the Golden and Riverside, as Reno entered a wartime hotel boom that solidified its status as a tourist town. Wingfield was preparing for the boom even before it developed. As soon as he recovered the hotels in 1937, he began a series of improvements and planned for expansion. He also instituted a number of promotional measures, including elaborate brochures for distribution in other hotels and a hotel hostess at the Riverside. The latter greeted sojourning divorce-seekers, treated them to drinks, and arranged social occasions and outings for the amusement of hotel guests. In 1940, he was sounding out his bankers at Crocker about the possibility of building a $250,000 addition to the Riverside, which he confidently predicted "should discourage any competition for years to come." [22]

Eventually the decision was made to postpone the Riverside addition "in these troubled times," but minor improvements such as new elevators for the Golden continued to be made, and the company's financial reports didn't suffer. Indeed, in time even Wingfield's bankers noted his monthly ritual of apologizing as president because the company was making so little money, when it seemed to them that Reno Securities was "going along in excellent shape." With the outbreak of war and the sudden and unexpected eruption of hotel business, things got even better. Despite Wingfield's constant complaints about the difficulties of keeping reliable employees during World War II, the hotels didn't suffer. They were regularly packed, and the money just seemed to roll in. Reno Securities increased its monthly mortgage payments to Crocker from $5,000 to $10,000, and the note was paid in full on August 12, 1944. Wingfield was once again the principal owner of his two hotel properties, valued respectively at $535,000 for the Golden and $692,000 for the Riverside.[23]

The proprietor did not entirely approve of his customers, despite the profits they brought him. In 1944, he complained to John Mueller, then an army major in the Pacific: "There are entirely too many people travelling who have no business to be and they are setting a very poor example. While it is very good at the hotels, I would prefer that they stayed home." Reno was now attracting more visitors who came only to gamble, men and women of newfound leisure and unaccustomed money, who sought frenzied distraction from wartime austerity. Wingfield's scorn for them was absolute, and he vented it to Mueller. In the old Reno, December had been a slow month, especially the week between Christmas and New Year's Day. In the new Reno, of December 1944, none of the old rules applied. Even on December 29:

> The town is well filled with people yet and a certain element of them
> are spending every dollar they can get hold of and will be right back
> where they started when the war is over. I have never come in contact
> with such people before as we have had around here in the last year or

so. I don't know where they come from and I never knew that so many morons existed before.[24]

Those morons, however, were the means of his emergence from debt. More importantly, their leisure-time habits were also the powerful stimulus for a new, postwar Reno economy that would be based on the national merchandising of gambling as a popular entertainment. After World War II, gambling gradually gained respectability to become a mainstream recreation that appealed to men and women alike. Times were changing, and the reluctant Wingfield was forced to change with them to remain competitive. Eventually, he allowed gambling even in his sacrosanct Riverside Hotel.

In October 1946, RSC sold the aging Golden Hotel for $1.5 million, to a group of investors including John Mueller and Norman Biltz. A substantial portion of the proceeds was devoted to a $600,000 expansion of the Riverside. As Wingfield explained to Baruch, who was perpetually curious about the Nevadan's finances, the profits were better off in a building than being eaten up by inflation. And besides, he needed improved facilities in an up-to-date building to attract the new Reno tourists: "We are almost forced to put an extension on the Riverside Hotel . . . and to make it the 'headquarters' for Nevada. There is a tremendous shortage of rooms here." In 1949, he was at it again, this time to the tune of $850,000, including an enlarged kitchen and large dining room suitable for entertainment. When the construction was completed, in 1950, there was "a grand blow-out," complete with popular performer Jimmy Durante. Wingfield's commitment to the property was absolute. When a devastating flood swept through at Thanksgiving, he put emergency crews to work immediately and the Riverside was reopened before Christmas.[25]

The building program of these years accomplished what Wingfield wanted. It made the Riverside a major property and RSC reliably profitable. It also made George Wingfield proud. By 1952, the former cowboy could look around him and see almost everywhere the results of his years of effort to promote Reno as a tourist destination. The town's growth owed much to his own efforts in building bridges over the Truckee River, in financing buildings and businesses, and in constantly improving his own hotels. His sense of ownership in what had resulted was palpable in a letter to Bernard Baruch, inviting him to visit and see how "things have changed materially around this village, especially at the Riverside, as you will see by the enclosed folder. We have quite an institution there now and I imagine that, should you arrive, I would have a lot of trouble in keeping you from bucking the tiger. At any rate, it is a beautiful place." [26]

Part of the reason for this success was Wingfield's personal oversight. For many years Wingfield stopped at the Riverside on his walk to work each day and checked in with its manager. He monitored minor details like the location of the taxi stand and the appearance of retail stores in the lobby. Until he was in his late seventies, he closely supervised the various hotel managers, and he remained associated with his beautiful institution until 1955. In that year Wingfield and his children sold RSC to the men who had leased the Riverside casino since 1949, eastern underworld figures Lou and Mert Wertheimer. The price was over $4 million, but even the sale didn't sever Wingfield's sense of responsibility to the property. One of his attorneys for the sale, Virgil Wedge, remembered Wingfield patting his shoulder holster and threatening the notorious Wertheimer brothers that, if they didn't abide by the terms of the contract in exact detail, they would see him coming up the street and they would know why. The Riverside Hotel was Wingfield's monument in the Reno landscape, and he was fiercely protective of virtually every aspect of it. Throughout his lifetime, it retained that status as Reno's preeminent hotel.[27]

By virtue of Wingfield's supremacy in the hotel business, however, he also managed to discourage serious competition for the Riverside. Successful casino operators like the Smith family at Harolds Club, and William F. Harrah at Harrah's, had taken over where Graham and McKay left off and pioneered a popular new middle-class style of gambling; but they were slow to build hotels to accompany their casinos. Increasing numbers of people were being attracted to Reno, by skiing promotions at nearby Lake Tahoe as well as by gambling, but there were few first-class lodgings to serve their needs. When the Mapes family completed the 12-story Mapes Hotel across the Truckee River from the Riverside, in 1947, it was the first substantial rival for Reno's growing tourist trade. Only in 1953 did Wingfield finally sell his own prime hotel site, adjacent to the Reno post office, to Norman Biltz and John Mueller. In such an environment, with little competition, the Riverside continued almost inevitably to grow and prosper, and George Wingfield with it.[28]

Indeed, prominent Reno advertising man Thomas Wilson claimed that Wingfield actively suppressed any potential contender. M. A. Diskin, for instance, was attorney for the Smith family and also a close friend of Wingfield. Wilson, who also worked for the Smiths, maintains that "the Wingfield organization found it necessary to manipulate and direct some of the power of Harolds Club," in order to protect the Riverside Hotel, and that this was accomplished through Diskin. Wilson reported that Wingfield was able to forestall the development of competing resort hotels by urging friendly local casinos to purchase all the suitable sites and not build on them, or by convincing local families not to sell their land except for inflated prices. When Wingfield withdrew from the hotel business in 1955, he had the satisfaction of recognizing that he had fostered an important industry, with the exquisite timing to get out of it just as serious competition loomed. He and his children made a tidy profit in the process, and George Wingfield retired at the age of seventy-nine from the company he had run for forty years.[29]

The decade from 1940 to 1950 was one of explosive growth for Reno and for the state of Nevada. The city's population increased over fifty percent, to more than 32,000, while the state reached 160,000, from 110,000 in 1940, a growth rate almost as spectacular. This postwar boom transformed both state and city almost beyond recognition to men of Wingfield's generation. Accustomed to the state's pitifully small scale and to the boom-and-bust cycles of their youth—which were typified by the fate of Goldfield after the ore ran out—they were unprepared for the consistent expansion that would characterize Nevada's population and economy thereafter. As Las Vegas began the steady growth spurt which led to its emergence as Nevada's major city, Reno was three times the size of the village that Wingfield had come to in 1908. The prosperity he had helped to initiate had exceeded his capacity to envision it, and the future was no longer his to plan.

Politics changed, too, as so many newcomers to the state found different causes and followed new leaders. With few exceptions the old Tonopah-Goldfield crowd was no longer in office or in power. A new generation was running the banks, tourism was growing explosively, and gambling was gradually being integrated into the state's economy. As historian Mary Ellen Glass has pointed out, the 1950s were years of major change in the state, marking "Nevada's entry into the modern era." It was indeed a different world, one which George Wingfield no longer controlled or even fully appreciated. As he withdrew from active business involvement, Wingfield found that he no longer knew virtually everyone in Reno. In his last years, he was still a prominent figure, but no longer the dominant player. As everyone recognized, it was now a new game, and it was being played by a new generation of men.[30]

Wingfield thus inhabited in the 1940s and 1950s a far narrower universe than he had commanded at his peak in the 1920s. He remained a spirited observer of the local scene, for instance, but was scarcely touched by the cataclysmic events preceding and during World War II. In 1939 and 1940, he worked assiduously on behalf of the Finnish Relief Fund as the Nevada state chair; but his efforts were clearly a personal response to the request from Herbert Hoover, who was the national chair, rather than a matter of deep principle. In July 1941, he remarked blandly to a friend in New York, "I think eventually the Dictators will hang themselves," but the war scarcely intruded into his correspondence except as an obstacle to his plans or as a source of anxiety about his son and John Mueller, both of whom served in the Pacific. Instead his letters centered on his mines and his hotels and the difficulties of operating them under adverse circumstances. Increasingly, his was a vision not of the future, or even of the welfare of the state, but of the past.[31]

This was surely the tone of the group of Wingfield cronies who met for lunch each day at the Grand Cafe on Second Street. This miscellaneous assemblage included prominent cattle rancher William H. Moffat, John Mueller, Noble Getchell, Roy Hardy, First National Bank president William Hopper, attorney Virgil Wedge, and banker Jordan Crouch, among others. They met each day to gossip and listen to stories from Moffat, Getchell, and Wingfield, who were older than the others and regaled the group with tales of Reno's past. The stories were legendary, and the comradeship was important, but the mood was unfailingly retrospective. Wingfield had given up smoking at age seventy-three and continued to be a teetotaler, but he loved to eat, and he relished the lunchtime salon. These sessions were paramount among the pleasures remaining to him as he retired from business and watched friends and associates die.[32]

Inevitably, old age was marked by its share of such deaths. Wingfield's mother died in 1940, at the age of ninety-one; and his friend and banker F. Gloucester Willis of Crocker died at age fifty-four in 1942. Wingfield could not attend Willis's funeral, but officials at the bank made sure to write and describe the service as one that would have pleased the banker: "no ostentation—simplicity itself." It was an even bigger blow when George Thatcher died in 1946, and the pace quickened in subsequent years. McCarran died of a heart attack in 1954, and Estey Julian met a similar fate the next year. Maude Murdoch Wingfield also died in 1955, predeceasing her much older former husband. Even William Woodburn died before his longtime client, in 1957. As the circle of his associates shrank, George Wingfield sought consolation with his remaining close friends, including the group at the Grand Cafe. With them he was generous and relaxed, a wonderfully amusing companion whose stories of the early days were delightful. But he was no longer a force for change in either the state or the city.[33]

Friendship was one of Wingfield's chief satisfactions in his final years, as it had been during his prime. In his old age he shared the pleasures of his Spanish Springs Ranch with friends who hunted or fished and made gifts to others of the pedigreed labrador dogs he raised there. After his financial recovery, much of his effort went into making this ranch property a hunting preserve. It was Wingfield's customary weekend retreat and he probably would have lived there all the time if his wife had agreed. He hunted grouse and ducks whenever he could and planned the ranch with his pastime in mind: "I don't attempt to call the ducks as I don't speak their language very well. I catch them on the fly or put out wooden decoys and when they come by, let them have it, and I have had very good shooting so far." Frequent visitors like John Mueller had their own blinds. When RSC was sold in 1955, Wingfield kept the ranch. He continued to hunt there until the end of his life and remained by all accounts an excellent shot.[34]

Beginning in 1941, Wingfield also bred and raised quarter horses at Spanish Springs Ranch, along with his son. In the mid-1950s, they had about fifty head and had embarked on an ambitious sales program. Family members always maintained that horses were George Wingfield's true love, and although the Spanish Springs operation never approached the scale of his beloved Nevada Stock Farm, it was renowned in its day. Horses introduced Wingfield to a new group of associates with similar interests, including surrounding ranchers and department store magnate Wilbur May, whose Double Diamond Ranch south of Reno also raised quarter horses. Horses also caused him serious injury in July 1947, when a herd that was being unloaded became frightened, jumped a fence, and knocked a 16-foot gate down on top of the onlooking owner. The accident fractured his right knee and left ankle, leaving him with two casts and damaged ligaments in his left knee. He was almost seventy-one years old, and the injuries were slow to heal. They left him with arthritis in both knees and ankles. More cautious thereafter, Wingfield nonetheless continued to supervise the animals, and the herd remained intact until his death. Like his mining companies, the ranch and horses were something he was reluctant to relinquish.[35]

Meanwhile, as the years passed, contemporaries died, and bitter memories of the bank collapse faded, Wingfield gradually emerged from the sinister shadow of rumor and innuendo that surrounded him in the 1930s to undergo the final transformation of his long lifetime in Nevada. By the 1950s, as the new Nevada was being born in the aftermath of World War II, George Wingfield emerged somewhat unexpectedly as an icon of Nevada's rapidly fading pioneer past. Bereft of power and no longer a political or economic menace, he had become a community treasure. Wingfield was characterized fulsomely by Lucius Beebe in *Holiday* magazine as "Nevada's best-loved citizen," "an authentic giant out of the heroic Nevada past." More understated, a who's who guide referred to him blandly as a "pioneer mining executive."[36]

In 1956, on his eightieth birthday, the old wounds were symbolically healed. Wingfield was feted at an elaborate dinner organized by his wife and children at the Riverside Hotel. Engraved invitations summoned guests to cocktails at the house on Court Street and then to a seven-course meal, accompanied by four wines, at the hotel. A chartered airplane brought boyhood associates from Lakeview. Both Baruch and Herbert Hoover, among many others, sent congratulatory telegrams. No hint of the former controversy intruded, and the *Nevada State Journal* characterized the celebrant neutrally, as a man "extremely active in the business and political affairs of Nevada and the West Coast."[37]

The next year, in 1957, the rhetoric of public approbation grew even stronger, as both George Wingfield and Noble Getchell were awarded honorary degrees by the University of Nevada. Wingfield's citation as a doctor of mining economics was effusive in the customary style of such documents, extolling his accomplishments as an "organizer of dynamic ability," an "executive with vision and abiding faith in the future of Nevada," and, most significantly, as a "self-made man whose life stands as a symbol of American ambition and enterprise." In the celebratory context, no hint of past controversy was allowed to surface. Two years later, shortly before his death, there was a proposal to name a new engineering mines building (subsequently Scrugham Engineering) after him; but it was opposed because there was no evidence that he intended to leave anything to the university. Still, considering the defamation of Wingfield only twenty years earlier, the award of an honorary degree was surprising, and the unremittingly laudatory language of the citation was little short of miraculous. Improbably, George Wingfield had lived long enough to witness his own revival.[38]

He had never depended on public approval to maintain his self-esteem, however, and the shift in public image seems to have had little personal effect. The self-contained Wingfield spent his final years surrounded by friends and family, having recovered both his dignity and his wealth in the community with which he had long identified himself. He had six granddaughters and his son worked with him daily in the same office, leaving the room when important visitors came to call. Wingfield took pride in the growing prosperity of his state and his city, and he blamed himself for nothing. In his last years, he continued to loan money to friends, including the perpetually needy Tasker Oddie and considerably more reliable James McKay. He donated money in substantial amounts to worthy causes like the Nevada State Museum, but never again approached the sums he had given with such abandon in 1928. It was a moderate but entirely consistent old age after such a flamboyant career.[39]

When it came, Wingfield's death, too, was gentle. His 1947 accident marked the beginning of accelerating health problems including a prostate operation in 1949 and frequent stomach trouble. He spent increasing

George and Roxy Thoma Wingfield on his seventy-fifth birthday,
August 16, 1951. (Courtesy of Nevada Historical Society)

amounts of time in San Francisco visiting doctors for diagnosis and treatment. Although the cause of the intestinal difficulties remained obscure, it was apparently cancer. In 1957, he was in San Francisco for an operation to remove a throat tumor believed to be malignant, but, in 1958, another one appeared. This time it was treated with radiation therapy rather than being removed. Still vigorous and generally healthy, Wingfield proclaimed at age eighty-two: "I feel good." But he was reminded of his advancing age by the various aches and pains attendant on it. He walked to work, but his pace was slower and the trips were less regular. Still, he remained active until the last weeks of his life. In September 1959, at the age of eighty-three, he embarked on a trip back to Oregon, to visit his sister, Mary, six years his senior. Three months later, in December 1959, he had a stroke. After thirteen days in a coma, he died in a Reno hospital on Christmas night. There was a certain poignancy in the fact that the last words of Nevada's most powerful twentieth-century citizen were about horses.[40]

In death, as in life, George Wingfield was a very public citizen. On the day he died, the Reno morning paper had featured a front-page photograph of children caroling in the park that he had given to the city. On subsequent days, newspapers throughout the state and the nation assessed the meaning of his life. His passing was noted by the *New York Times* and the *San Francisco Examiner*. The latter reported the death under the headline "Fabulous Nevada Figure Dies," describing Wingfield as "a gambling cowpoke" and "Nevada's most powerful out-of-office political leader." The *Las Vegas Sun* labeled him "one of Nevada's most colorful developers and early mining figures," a "Nevada tycoon," a theme that was repeated by the *San Francisco Chronicle*. His obituaries left no doubt of his central importance to the history of Nevada. The *Reno Evening Gazette*, edited now by Graham Sanford's son John, depicted Wingfield's death as more significant than one man's mortality. It marked the end of an era which had begun in the boom towns of Tonopah and Goldfield: "Probably no Nevadan in the 95 years in which the state has been a member of the commonwealth has been so prominent for so long a period of time."[41]

Though twenty-five years had elapsed since the bank controversy, Sanford had not forgotten Wingfield's former might. He editorialized in the same issue against the bipartisan machine, with its "power of life and death over business and individuals. Any criticism of the Wingfield machine's methods and operations, any rebellions against its rule, were quickly and mercilessly put down. Only a few strong individuals dared to stand up against it at the height of its power." But he went on to concede the truth that all the obituaries granted: that Wingfield's life had genuine significance:

For the first half of this century Nevada and George Wingfield were synonymous. His friends and associates admired him intensely, his critics and enemies hated him with equal fervor. But all respected his power and his ability, and all agree that he had a profound effect on the history of the state.

That effect, according to the *Las Vegas Sun* editorial, was because "George made his money in Nevada and did not emigrate to California or to some eastern metropolis . . . he stayed with the state that made him one of its biggest men."[42]

It was a constant theme of the obituaries. The lengthy one in the Nevada Mining Association *Newsletter* was more personal than most, noting that Wingfield was "a firm believer in private enterprise," a man "loyal to his friends and tolerant toward those who thought they were his enemies due to misinformation, misunderstandings, or failure to look beneath the surface." The writer, possibly Wingfield's brother-in-law Roy Hardy, even included a gratuitous anti–New Deal barb: "His idea of WPA was to Work, Persevere, and Aspire." The memorial concluded on a note remarkably similar to the more antagonistic *Gazette*, however: "He left an indelible mark upon the history of his State and it does not seem probable that anyone will ever wield the influence that he did in mining, banking, business, and politics in the State of Nevada."[43]

George Wingfield left an estate valued at over $3 million and a will dated July 1958. George Wingfield, Jr., was his executor. The Spanish Springs Ranch, minus the quarter horses, was left to Roxy, along with one-half of the community property. The remaining assets, after generous bequests to his granddaughters, his nieces, and five employees, were to be divided by his son and daughter. His intangible legacy to the state, however, is far more difficult to trace, and its shape is still a matter of controversy. After Wingfield's death scores of letters poured in to his son. They praised the dead man as loyal, honest, understanding, thoughtful, "moved by the best with which man is endowed," in the words of Bernard Baruch. Yet he was also a man with numerous enemies, as Virginia City's *Territorial Enterprise*, then edited by Lucius Beebe, observed in its obituary: "A man of true character and importance gains stature by his enemies. If Mr. Wingfield had them in abundance, more power to him. He was a product of times when men played rough." Long after his death, Wingfield continued to be regarded in this divided fashion, as he had been during his life. Some revered him, while others reviled him. All agreed on the magnitude of his power, but not on its consequences.[44]

To the contemporary observer, almost thirty-five years after Wingfield's demise, the continuing debate is perhaps the most surprising aspect of his career. Even death has not put an end to the speculation about his character, or the suspicion about his illicit activities. Instead of fading away, the myth of George Wingfield continues to grow in Nevada, threatening with its black-or-white depiction of the past to overwhelm the subtle realities of Nevada's chiaroscuro history. In truth, George Wingfield was neither devil nor saint. He was a man of rough origins, considerable intelligence, deep friendships, and remarkable fortune. As a master of many situations, his early successes taught him to have great faith in himself and in his assessments of the men around him. His money brought him power, which he exercised as he saw fit, in order to develop a small and economically backward state. He pursued Republican political programs and economic diversification with religious fervor.

The very fact that he was located in a place like Nevada made the phenomenon of George Wingfield possible in the first place. A similar fortune and political program could never have had such an extraordinary effect in a more populous state like California. Nevada's isolation intensified Wingfield's potency due to the absence of any significant counterbalancing individuals or institutions. At the height of his career, in the 1920s and early 1930s, George Wingfield *was* Nevada and he knew it. No one else was big enough and cared enough to dominate the state in similar fashion.

Inevitably, so much power and self-confidence, combined with a moralistic distrust of his socially liberal views, made enemies for Wingfield. Economic realism dictated deference toward a major capitalist willing to remain in an impoverished state, however, and his critics were circumspect. Wingfield cavalierly ascribed the malignant gossip that did circulate to obstructionists, "reformers" who short-sightedly sought to block the economic progress and stability that he offered the state. He assumed that those who disagreed with him simply didn't understand his progressive vision for the future. He never recognized that resentment of his high-handed initiatives for the state ran deeper than mere "politics."

It was only after the Cole-Malley settlement, when the disparity between Wingfield's notions of fairness and those of the rest of the state were fully revealed, that attacks became overt. At first they came primarily from outside the state. Only when Wingfield finally weakened, when his fortune and his vision proved insufficient to support the burden of an entire state during the Great Depression, did they become widespread within Nevada. By then a considerable store of bitterness had been laid up, and the situation was further complicated by political animosities outside the state. The result was not just economic catastrophe, but also the end of an empire. With Wingfield's staggering fall from grace into the mundane life of a wealthy private citizen came a forfeiture of his previous leadership. Yet he nonetheless had reason to be proud of what he had accomplished. His checkered reputation notwithstanding, George Wingfield had in fact set the course for the economic and social development of his state in the twentieth century.

He had been involved in virtually every significant Nevada economic initiative of the early twentieth century, including mining, ranching, reclamation farming, banking, and hospitality. He had practically created the state's tourist industry, through his encouragement of road building and maintenance, his support for special events to attract visitors, and his building of luxury hotels to house them. Furthermore, by promoting toleration of illegal alcohol, and by lobbying for horse racing, for legalized gambling, and for lenient divorce legislation, he helped make and sustain consumer demand for the tourist services that profited him and many others. Modern Nevada's phenomenally successful gambling-based economy, though it has been refined by many people over the years, is founded on the initial vision of George Wingfield, who understood that mining and agriculture alone would not be enough to sustain his adopted desert state. Ultimately, Wingfield and Nevada were a good match. The modern society that he did so much to shape still bears the stamp of his personality and beliefs—socially liberal, fiscally conservative, and determinedly self-reliant. All in all, it was a remarkable achievement for a cowboy-gambler from Arkansas.

NOTES

Chapter One: Owner and Operator of the State of Nevada

1. The description of southeastern Oregon is from native-son William Kittredge, in *Owning It All* (St. Paul, Minn.: Graywolf Press, 1987), p. 21.

2. George Wingfield was almost universally labeled Nevada's king: e.g., "Passion in the Desert," *Fortune* 9 (April 1934): 107; *San Francisco Chronicle*, September 16, 1933, p. 3. A confused undertaker in Nebraska once sent him a telegram addressed to the governor of Nevada, seeking advice on what to do with a corpse (H. O. Wildy to George Winfield [*sic*], December 29, 1930, George Wingfield Papers, Nevada Historical Society, Reno, Nevada). Henceforth citations to the Wingfield Papers are identified only by correspondent and date.

3. During his lifetime, there were several requests to do biographies of George Wingfield (henceforth GW in notes). With the exception of his old friend, former *Reno Evening Gazette* editor Oscar Morgan, GW turned them all down. One such request, by western novelist and screenwriter Ernest Haycox, is documented in a letter from Forrest E. Cooper to Guy Rocha, December 4, 1979 (photocopy in author's possession). Haycox was hopeful that GW would give permission for preparation of a biography because the latter's financial circumstances were dismal in 1934. However, "he reported that George gave him a cordial reception but that he was not interested in becoming the subject of books and stories as much as he could use the money." This reticence was consistent throughout his life. GW's disinterest in offers to make movies based on his life was reported by his niece, Alice Hardy Paulsen, in an interview, November 22, 1988, Reno, Nevada. See also William E. Zoebel (GW's secretary) to W. A. Mundell, July 27, 1929: "Since Mr. Wingfield is reluctant about any glorification emanating from his office, I am unable to supply even a brief history of his rise, this, notwithstanding that volumes could be written without exhausting the subject."

4. Sally Springmeyer Zanjani, *The Unspiked Rail: Memoir of a Nevada Rebel* (Reno: University of Nevada Press, 1981), pp. 102–103; "Wingfield Again Averts Bank Crisis in Nevada," *San Francisco Bulletin*, July 31, 1929, p. 2.

5. GW, quoted in *Goldfield Tribune*, August 9, 1914; Laura Vitray, "Nevada Is Outlaw State Controlled by One Man; Reno Whirlpool of Vice," *New York Evening Graphic*, July 1, 1931, p. 3.

6. Vitray, "Nevada," p. 3.

7. Ralph D. Paine, *The Greater America* (New York: Outing Publishing Co., 1907), p. 294.

8. Andrew Ginocchio, "The Ascent of Reno Iron Works" (Oral History Program, University of Nevada, Reno, 1987), p. 18.

9. Max Miller, *Reno* (New York: Dodd, Mead, 1941), pp. 103–104.

10. Many of these legends about GW were recounted orally to the author in the course of doing research for this biography, most frequently by older Nevada residents. I am indebted to Warren Anderson of Cedarville, Utah, for passing along additional facets of the GW oral tradition.

The story about the Goldfield strike has been told in many versions. See, for example, Joseph F. McDonald, "The Life of a Newsboy in Nevada" (Oral History Program, University of Nevada, Reno, 1970), p. 24. Contemporary newspaper accounts of the strike never mention any such highly charged encounters. This particular version comes from an unpublished outline for a biography of GW prepared by one-time *Reno Evening Gazette* editor Oscar Morgan. The original typescript is in the possession of Morgan's descendant, Audrey Thoreson, in Fremont, California. The quotation comes from pp. 4–5 of the outline. A fleshed-out version was published in "The Knave" column of the *Oakland Tribune*, August 8, 1948. Baruch's variant account, also slightly breathless with the excitement of the times, can be found in John Hersey, "The Old Man," *New Yorker* 23 (January 3, 1948): 28.

11. For the controversy over GW's market manipulations, see chapter 4. "Nevada's Napoleon" is explained by the *Goldfield Tribune*, April 27, 1909. For GW's importance relative to the governor, see *San Francisco Argonaut*, September 29, 1933. Quotation is from "Passion in the Desert," p. 107; John Sanford, "Printer's Ink in My Blood" (Oral History Program, University of Nevada, Reno, 1971), p. 47.

12. *Sacramento Bee*, October 19, 1928 ("octopus"), January 5, 1934. It is perhaps worth noting that the *Bee* was a Democratic paper.

13. Both the Vitray articles in the *New York Evening Graphic* and the 1934 *Fortune* article cited earlier assume that GW, who did not disapprove of either drinking or gambling, was a partner of notorious Reno underworld figures James McKay and William Graham. In *Unspiked Rail*, Zanjani charges that Wingfield thwarted prohibition enforcement in Reno in the 1920s (pp. 260–326). *Fortune* (April 1934): 124; Miller, *Reno*, p. 248.

14. For background on the Wingfield family I am indebted to Nancy E. Welch, who generously shared her research on the origins of the Wingfield family in Arizona. This branch was founded by brothers of Thomas Y. Wingfield and thus consisted of cousins of George Wingfield. A 1936 affidavit of Martha M. Spradling Wingfield, in the GW Papers, gives the date of her marriage as February 2, 1868. A 1906 obituary of GW's father, Thomas, in the Wingfield clippings file at the Nevada Historical Society in Reno gives the year as 1867. GW's mother's WCTU membership and church attendance were recalled by Alice Hardy Paulsen in an interview on November 22, 1988.

15. In Morgan, "Biography of George Wingfield," p. 14.

Chapter Two: Roots

1. This account of GW depends heavily on the unpublished biography by Reno newspaperman Oscar Morgan cited earlier. This untitled manuscript, ca. 1940, was the only biography to be completed during GW's lifetime with his active assistance and contains details found nowhere else in the historical record. To the extent that

these can be verified, they seem accurate and are evidently based on interviews with GW himself. Morgan began the book in 1938 and wrote a few sample chapters and an outline for the projected book-length manuscript, which he submitted as a prospectus to publishers. In 1941, he informed GW that no publishers were interested in the book (Oscar Morgan to GW, May 31, 1941). The other standard source for GW's early years is Barbara C. Thornton, "George Wingfield in Nevada from 1896 to 1932" (M.A. thesis, University of Nevada, Reno, 1967). Information on family background was also supplemented by George Wingfield, Jr., in an interview on August 19, 1983.

2. For the cattle industry in southeastern Oregon, see J. Orrin Oliphant, *On the Cattle Ranges of the Oregon Country* (Seattle: University of Washington Press, 1968), and Peter K. Simpson, *The Community of Cattlemen: A Social History of the Cattle Industry in Southeastern Oregon, 1869–1912* (Moscow: University of Idaho Press, 1987).

3. Interview with Virgil Wedge, November 3, 1989 ("rough talker"); Thornton, "George Wingfield," p. 2; *Tonopah Miner*, August 19, 1905.

4. Morgan, "Biography," p. 15.

5. The description of Wingfield as "incorrigible" is reported in Thornton, "George Wingfield," p. 2, and confirmed in John R. Leach to Mrs. Hugh Brown, October 30, 1968 (photocopy in author's possession). The latter adds the anecdote that Wingfield "was escorted to the city limits [of Lakeview] and told not to come back." Forrest E. Cooper to Guy Rocha, December 4, 1979 (photocopy in author's possession), notes Wingfield's aspirations to be a professional gambler.

6. Thornton, "George Wingfield," p. 6. For the lynching, see Phillip I. Earl, "Lynch Law Prevailed in Reno 80 Years Ago," *Nevada State Journal* (henceforth *NSJ*) November 3, 1971. Family legend places GW at the scene, but has somewhat obscured the details. See Bill Phillips, "Controversial Wingfield Built a Nevada Empire," *NSJ*, August 15, 1976; interview with George Wingfield, Jr., August 19, 1983. Thornton speculates that GW was thirteen or fourteen at the time of the jockey episode.

7. For the cattle industry generally, see James A. Young and B. Abbott Sparks, *Cattle in the Cold Desert* (Logan: Utah State University Press, 1985). Wingfield's experiences were recounted by him in an interview by L. S. [Les Shaw] published in the *Lakeview Examiner*, undated but after September 28, 1952. The interview can be located in the newspaper clippings scrapbooks at Schminck Memorial Museum, Lakeview, Oregon.

8. In addition to the Shaw interview, details of the drive can be found in George Wingfield's obituary in the *Battle Mountain Scout*, December 31, 1959.

9. For the nickname, see *Goldfield Tribune* (henceforth *GT*), April 26, 1909; also Morgan, "Biography," p. 24. For activities during the Winnemucca years, see GW to Mrs. Avery D. Stitser, January 23, 1941; Morgan, "Biography," pp. 13–21, *passim;* GW obituary, *Battle Mountain Scout*, December 31, 1959.

10. Cooper to Rocha, December 4, 1979.

11. Pansilee Larson, North Central Nevada Historical Society, to author, August 31, 1988.

12. Morgan, "Biography," p. 20.

13. Carl B. Glasscock, *Gold in Them Hills* (1932; reprint Las Vegas: Nevada Publications, 1988), pp. 40–41.

14. The figure on GW's net worth at this time comes from Morgan, "Biography,"

p. 20. Independent verification is impossible, but Morgan's source was undoubtedly GW himself. Information on mining at Golconda can be found in Stanley W. Paher, *Nevada Ghost Towns and Mining Camps* (Las Vegas: Nevada Publications, 1970), p. 154, and *Winnemucca Silver State*, September 22, 1898.

15. *Golconda News*, February 18, 1899.

16. Elliot J. Gorn, *The Manly Art: Bare-Knuckle Prize Fighting in America* (Ithaca: Cornell University Press, 1986), p. 133.

17. Details of the property purchases are contained in the Humboldt County Assessment Rolls for 1899 and 1901 and the Deed Record Book for 1899. For representative newspaper coverage, see *Golconda News*, August 3, 1899, and *Winnemucca Silver State*, June 10, 1899.

18. *Golconda News*, August 3, 1899.

19. *Winnemucca Silver State*, June 22, July 5, 1899; *Golconda News* April 7, June 23, 1900.

20. Typescript autobiography, GW Papers [1915]. The text is similar to, but not identical with, a published version that appeared in John P. Young, *Journalism in California and Pacific Exposition Biographies* (San Francisco: Chronicle Publishing Co., 1915), p. 338. Internal evidence suggests that the manuscript version was drafted or at least substantially prepared by Wingfield himself.

21. Roy A. Hardy, "Reminiscence and a Short Autobiography" (Oral History Program, University of Nevada, Reno, 1965), p. 5.

22. GW to H. H. Atkinson, September 19, 1929. For more on Taylor, see chapter 9.

23. The best summary of Nixon's career can be found in W. B. Lardner and M. J. Brock, *History of Placer and Nevada Counties* (Los Angeles: Historic Record Co., 1924), pp. 1011–1012.

24. Oscar Morgan, in "The Knave," *Oakland Tribune*, August 22, 1948 ("twinkling"); Bessie Beatty, *Who's Who in Nevada: Brief Sketches of Men Who Are Making History in the Sagebrush State* (Los Angeles: Home Printing Co., 1907), p. 29 ("genial"); *GT*, June 4, 1912.

25. Quoted in Morgan, "Biography," p. 178. The other four were financier and federal bureaucrat Bernard M. Baruch, San Francisco banker William H. Crocker, and mining engineers J. Wellington Finch and John H. Mackenzie.

26. *Tonopah Miner*, August 10, 1905 (source of quotations); Laura Vitray, "Nevada's 'King' Started Rise to Top with Poker Cards and $300 in Cash," *New York Evening Graphic*, July 9, 1931. See also Barton Wood Currie, "Pluck and Luck in the Desert," *Harper's Weekly* 52 (April 4, 1908). Biographer Thornton, who interviewed family members for her thesis, repeats the story of Nixon loaning Wingfield the money to travel to Tonopah.

27. Typescript autobiography, GW Papers [1915].

28. Morgan, "Biography," pp. 21–22; *Winnemucca Silver State*, articles in 1900–1901.

29. I am indebted to my research assistant, Anita Watson, for this observation, based on a comprehensive survey of the Winnemucca and Golconda newspapers for the relevant years.

30. See chapter 4 for details of the May Wingfield allegations. Findings in the suit of Wingfield *v.* Wingfield are in the Patrick A. McCarran Papers, Nevada Historical Society, Reno. May's claim about Alaska was *not* part of the suit. It was made at the time of GW's marriage, in the *San Francisco Examiner*, August 1, 1908, p. 9. There May claimed, "He ought to give me at least $50,000 considering I helped him to get his start in Alaska and helped him to make money when we first went to Nevada." This article also features a photograph of GW and May Baric together.

31. Reprinted in the *Goldfield News*, January 1, 1926, this article was singled out by George Wingfield, Jr., as being more accurate than most about his father's life.

Chapter Three: "Young Men Who Are Willing to Rough It"

1. Chapter title and quotation from *Winnemucca Silver State*, January 29, 1901. The best general source for Tonopah history is Russell Elliott, *Nevada's Twentieth-Century Mining Boom* (1966; reprint, Reno: University of Nevada Press, 1987). See also Jay A. Carpenter, Russell Richard Elliott, and Byrd Fanita Wall Sawyer, *The History of Fifty Years of Mining at Tonopah, 1900–1950* (Reno: Nevada Bureau of Mines, 1953); Lucile Rae Berg, "A History of the Tonopah Area and Adjacent Region of Central Nevada, 1827–1941" (M.A. thesis, University of Nevada, 1942); and Byrd Fanita Wall Sawyer, "The Gold and Silver Rushes of Nevada, 1900–1910" (M.A. thesis, University of California, 1931).

2. The two dates are from GW manuscript autobiography [undated], GW Papers, and T[om] W. Kendall to GW, October 27, 1938. The care with which GW distinguished between them suggests that it is not simply a typographical error of substituting April for May. The account of the Reno interval can be found in Morgan, "Biography," pp. 23–25.

3. GW to T. W. Kendall, October 31, 1938.

4. *Winnemucca Silver State*, May 26, 1901; Carpenter et al., *History*, p. 11; Morgan, "Biography," pp. 51–52; Sawyer, "Rushes," pp. 32–33.

5. Oscar Morgan, in "The Knave," *Oakland Tribune*, August 22, 1948; 1906 Wingfield biography reprinted in *Goldfield News*, January 1, 1926.

6. For Kendall, see James G. Scrugham, ed., *Nevada, A Narrative History of the Conquest of a Frontier Land* (Chicago: American Historical Society, 1935), vol. 3, pp. 149–150. Quotations from Tasker L. Oddie to "Mother," January 14, 1901, Tasker L. Oddie Papers, NHS; Glasscock, *Gold*, p. 41.

7. Compare Glasscock, *Gold*, pp. 41–42; Morgan, "Biography," pp. 45–48; and Glenn Chesney Quiett, *Pay Dirt: A Panorama of American Gold-Rushes* (New York: Appleton-Century, 1936), p. 437. These accounts differ in several details, including the amount of money that Wingfield actually won the night that the gambling concession was organized. Jack Hennessy is credited by Morgan and by Sawyer with being Wingfield's partner in the Tonopah Club.

8. Curie, "Pluck and Luck in the Desert," p. 28; Morgan, in "The Knave," *Oakland Tribune*, August 22, 1948; Sawyer, "Rushes," p. 44; George Graham Rice, *My Adventures with Your Money* (1913; reprint New York: Bookfinger, 1974), p. 154.

9. Nye County Assessment Records, 1901–1904; [P. La Montagne], *Nevada— The New Gold State* (San Francisco: D. G. Doubleday, 1905); Carpenter et al., *History*, pp. 13–14. Kendall continued to be assessed individually for the Tonopah Club until 1915, when GW appeared as the owner of record. He sold it the next year. Sometime before that, however, Wingfield had loaned money to Kendall with the Tonopah Club, among other buildings, as security. In 1913, Kendall owed $8,000 and Wingfield was threatening to take over the buildings and collect rents on them (J. O. Walther to GW, November 30, 1912; C. F. Burton to T. W. Kendall, May 15, 1913). See also GW correspondence with H. H. Bacon, his Tonopah agent, 1915–1916.

10. For the epidemic, see Guy Louis Rocha, "Regulating Public Health in Nevada: The Pioneering Efforts of Dr. Simeon Lemuel Lee," *Nevada Historical Society Quarterly* 29 (Fall 1986): 201–209; Scrugham, *Nevada*, vol. 1, p. 401. In a letter to his mother dated January 13, 1902, Tasker Oddie reports that most of those who died were drunkards living in tents (Oddie Papers). See also Sawyer, "Rushes," p. 32; *Tonopah Bonanza*, January 18, 1902, September 6, 1902; Carpenter et al., *History*, pp. 13–14.

11. Florence Burge and Noble H. Getchell, "From Grease Paint to Gold: The Life of Noble Hamilton Getchell" (unpublished manuscript, Florence Burge Papers, Special Collections Department, University of Nevada, Reno, March 1958), pp. 46–47. William Woodburn, Jr., recounted another version of the Getchell-Wingfield meeting, which he had from both Noble Getchell and GW, in an interview on October 4, 1985, Reno, Nevada. According to the Woodburn version, some "big bully" had encountered GW in an alley, where Wingfield hit him on the head with the butt end of his gun. Getchell came running out of a saloon nearby to ask if Wingfield needed any help and then introduced himself.

12. *Fortune* magazine put the matter succinctly in 1934: "Everybody who ever was anybody in Nevada came from Tonopah" ("Passion in the Desert," p. 100). See Jerome E. Edwards, *Pat McCarran: Political Boss of Nevada* (Reno: University of Nevada Press, 1982), p. 7, for an account of the extended network of cronies that developed in Tonopah and later came to dominate Nevada's political structures. Information on May Baric comes from her unsuccessful divorce suit, Wingfield *v.* Wingfield, filed March 2, 1906, for which see the decision, dated August 13, 1906, in the Patrick A. McCarran Papers at NHS. *Tonopah Miner*, November 28, 1903.

13. Morgan, in "The Knave," *Oakland Tribune*, August 22, 1948; *Tonopah Bonanza*, September 27, 1902, *Winnemucca Silver State*, October 16, 1902. For Wingfield's account of the partnership, see manuscript drafts of his biography [ca. 1912] in the GW Papers, and Young, *Journalism in California*, p. 338.

14. GW autobiographical sketch [ca. 1915], GW Papers. For the pattern of the early Nixon and Wingfield business dealings, see the George S. Nixon Papers, NHS (e.g., GSN to GW, December 24, 30, 31, 1902, November 2 and 7, 1903). See also *Tonopah Miner*, August 19, 1905, a particularly detailed account of the early years of the partnership.

15. *Tonopah Miner*, January 9, 1903; GSN to Dr. H. B. McDonald, May 4, 1903, GSN Papers; Morgan, "Biography," p. 48.

16. *Tonopah Miner*, August 19, 1905. This account is particularly valuable because

it describes the operations of Nixon and Wingfield *before* their famous formation of the GCMC, which colored all subsequent accounts.

17. *Tonopah Bonanza*, May 31, 1902; for the Boston-Tonopah transactions, see the Nixon Papers, NHS.

18. GSN to J. F. McCambridge, November 2, 1903, GSN Papers.

19. GSN and GW to J. F. McCambridge, November 7, 1903, GSN Papers. See, e.g., *Tonopah Miner*, May 25, 1907: "The fact is, that the Senator believes in doing those things which will be of real benefit to the people of the State generally, and his operations have been conducted from an honest desire to promote and advance the great mining industry of this State." For profits from mines, not stocks, see *San Francisco Call*, May 26, July 14, 1907, and Morgan, "Biography," p. 175: "Senator Nixon and I are trying to make mines and not markets."

20. Glasscock, *Gold*, p. 60; GSN to [Clarence] Van [Duzer], December 28, 1902; GSN to GW, July 11, 1904, GSN Papers; Esmeralda County Miscellaneous Records, Book B, Power of Attorney, p. 310.

21. *Tonopah Miner*, August 19, 1905; Rodman W. Paul, *The Far West and the Great Plains in Transition, 1859–1900* (New York: Harper and Row, 1988), p. 254.

22. GSN to GW, July 11, 1904, GSN Papers. Harry Ramsey was another former cowhand and gambler who was an early arrival in Tonopah, where he invested in mining claims and leases. Described by Glasscock as a "fighter with a reputation" (*Gold*, p. 60), he invested with GSN (but not GW) in several exceptionally rich mines in Goldfield and ultimately owned a one-half interest in the Combination mine.

23. George Wingfield, Jr; reported his father's nervous habit, interview, August 19, 1983. Morgan, "Biography," pp. 47–48; Thornton, "George Wingfield," p. 9; *Tonopah Miner*, August 19, 1905.

24. GW to Elizabeth McLaughlin, October 17, 1958 (in the possession of the Wingfield family); *GT*, January 27, 1911; Glasscock, *Gold*, p. 87. Throughout his life, GW repeatedly claimed proudly that he was the first man to put money into the ground at Goldfield.

25. This account of Goldfield's founding is drawn from Sawyer, "Rushes," p. 39; Quiett, *Pay Dirt*, p. 437; Glasscock, *Gold*, pp. 87, 101; and Helen Downer Croft, *The Downers, the Rockies—and Desert Gold* (Caldwell, Idaho: Caxton Printers, 1961), p. 97. For a detailed history of the discovery and growth of Goldfield, see Sally Zanjani, *Goldfield: The Last Gold Rush on the Western Frontier* (Athens: Swallow Press/Ohio University Press, forthcoming).

26. *Tonopah Miner*, June 13, October 31, 1903. See Esmeralda County Mining Records and Deeds for examples of the transactions involving the two partners and the various investment groups with which they were involved. Nixon began his purchase of the Mohawk property in January 1904, when he obtained a one-quarter interest in the four claims, as well as a similar interest in Goldfield townsite, for $5,000 (Morgan, "Biography," pp. 100–105; *Tonopah Miner*, August 19, 1905; *Tonopah Bonanza*, May 30, 1903; Glasscock, *Gold*, pp. 101ff.). See chapter 4 for Wingfield's involvement with the Mohawk.

27. Croft, *Downers*, p. 113; Glasscock, *Gold*, p. 113; Quiett, *Pay Dirt*, p. 438; Morgan, "Biography," pp. 104, 118. The story of their investment in the Florence claims

appears in Van Dyck and Watson [Goldfield mine promoters and attorneys] to Frank Ehrgood, January 8, 1908, Goldfield, Nevada Mining Company Records, Bancroft Library, Berkeley, California. According to this account—which was authoritative since Van Dyck and Watson were involved with Lockhart in several properties, including the Florence—when Lockhart first came to Goldfield he was "enviegled [*sic*] into the purchase of a 60% interest in the Florence group of claims, which 60% interest was paid for by him and Mr. A. D. Parker, of Denver, Colorado. The remaining 40% was in the hands of George Wingfield, George Nixon, J. P. Hennessy and John McKane. For some time, the property was not incorporated and when it was incorporated [1905] each partner took stock to the amount of his interest." *Tonopah Miner*, August 19, 1905.

28. *San Francisco Call*, September 3, 1904. These companies included the Columbia Mountain and Sandstorm Mining companies, on the ground that Wingfield had purchased from Stimler and Marsh; the Conqueror Mining Company, on Wingfield's independently owned Tonopah Club claim; the Goldfield Kendall and Nevada Boy Goldfield Mining companies, on the ground the two partners were jointly interested in with Tom Kendall, Harry Ramsey, and five other men; and the Mohawk, Booth, and Blue Bull mining companies, on the ground that Nixon was individually interested in with other partners. See Esmeralda County Assessment Records, Deeds, and *GT*, September 27, 1908.

Chapter Four: Nevada's Napoleon

1. Evidence of Wingfield's lack of social standing is largely implicit. He does *not* figure in the newspaper social columns reporting the activities of Tonopah's elite. He is never referred to in Mrs. Hugh Brown's *Lady in Boomtown: Miners and Manners on the Nevada Frontier* (Palo Alto: American West Publishing Company, 1968), an account of life in Tonopah by one of the city's prominent society matrons, even though Wingfield was one of her husband's clients and business associates. See also Minnie P. Blair, "Days Remembered of Folsom and Placerville, California; Banking and Farming in Goldfield, Tonopah, and Fallon, Nevada" (1968), and Amy Gulling, "An Interview with Amy Gulling" (1966), both in the Oral History Program, University of Nevada, Reno, for impressions of Wingfield's unsuitability for polite society.

2. Aileen Cleveland Higgins, *A Little Princess of Tonopah* (Philadelphia: Penn Publishing Co., 1909), pp. 102–103. I am indebted to Jerome Edwards for bringing this novel to my attention.

3. The fullest reference to GW as Nevada's Napoleon is in the *GT*, April 27, 1909; but see also *Tonopah Sun*, May 25, 1905. Rice, *My Adventures with Your Money*, p. 154.

4. Morgan, "Biography," p. 113.

5. Thornton, "George Wingfield," p. 16. For a discussion of the bipartisan machine, see C. Elizabeth Raymond, "George Wingfield's Political Machine: A Study in Historical Reputation," *Nevada Historical Society Quarterly* 32 (Summer 1989): 95–110. See also chapter 8.

6. *Tonopah Sun*, April 4, 1905. For May's ministrations, see her suit, Wingfield *v.* Wingfield, in the McCarran Papers, NHS.

7. *Goldfield Review,* June 22, 1905; *Tonopah Bonanza,* February 4, 1905; *Tonopah Sun,* April 14, 1905; GSN to Frank C. Miller, August 7, 1905, GSN Papers, NHS; Croft, *The Downers,* p. 120.

8. *Tonopah Sun,* May 13, 26, June 2, 1905; GSN to Miller, August 7, 1905, GSN Papers.

9. Sewell Thomas, *Silhouettes of Charles S. Thomas* (Caldwell, Idaho: Caxton Printers, Ltd., 1959), pp. 83–84.

10. *Tonopah Sun,* August 4, 1905.

11. *Tonopah Sun,* October 28, 1905. The Montgomery Hotel was named after Mrs. E. A. Montgomery, whose husband discovered the richest mine in the Bullfrog district, the Montgomery-Shoshone, in October 1904. Mrs. Montgomery came from San Francisco for the occasion, on October 21, 1905.

12. "George Wingfield," *Goldfield News,* January 1, 1926; *Tonopah Miner,* August 19, 1905; Morgan, "Biography," pp. 118–119.

13. *Tonopah Sun,* September 23, October 11, 1905, January 17, 1906. Population statistics for Columbia come from *Nevada-California Gazetteer and Business Directory* (San Francisco: Suits-Shuman Co., 1905). Wingfield continued to own real estate in Columbia until 1910, according to the Esmeralda County Assessor's Records.

14. Sawyer, "Rushes," pp. 44–50; *GT,* January 7, 1907 (Beach quotation); Charles S. Thomas, "Autobiography," typescript copy, Charles S. Thomas Papers, Colorado Historical Society, Denver, p. 127. For more detail on Goldfield history, see Sally Springmeyer Zanjani, "To Die in Goldfield: Mortality in the Last Boomtown on the Mining Frontier," *Western Historical Quarterly* 21 (February 1990): 47–69, and her forthcoming history, *Goldfield: The Last Gold Rush on the Western Frontier.*

15. Albert S. Watson to E. C. Brown, October 16, 1905, Goldfield Mining Company Correspondence and Papers, Bancroft Library, Berkeley, California; Reginald Meaker, *Nevada Desert Sheepman* ([Sparks]: Western Printing and Publishing, 1981), p. 65; Emmett L. Arnold, *Gold Camp Drifter, 1906–1910* (Reno: University of Nevada Press, 1973), pp. 83–84; Anne Ellis, *The Life of an Ordinary Woman* (Boston: Houghton Mifflin, 1929), pp. 247–252. The population estimates are for the greater Goldfield area, from Charles W. Riehl, "Goldfield, Nevada," *The Banker's Magazine* 74 (May 1907): 789. All such estimates are notoriously unreliable. Russell R. Elliott, in his *History of Nevada* (Lincoln: University of Nebraska Press, 1973), p. 396, conservatively estimates Goldfield's peak population at 15,000 in the years 1907–1908. For sanitary conditions in Goldfield, which were generally good, see Simeon L. Lee to John Sparks, governor of Nevada, February 14, 1905, reprinted in Guy Louis Rocha, "Regulating Public Health in Nevada: The Pioneering Efforts of Dr. Simeon Lemuel Lee," *Nevada Historical Society Quarterly* 29 (Fall 1986): 207–209.

16. Sawyer, "Rushes," p. 50; Elliott, *Nevada's Twentieth-Century Mining Boom,* pp. 78–90; Rice, *My Adventures,* p. 151; Chester Lyman to his mother, July 3, 1907, Goldfield Consolidated Mines Company file, Central Nevada Historical Society, Tonopah. See Ellis, *Life of an Ordinary Woman,* p. 250, for evidence of stock ownership at very modest economic levels in Goldfield society.

17. For details of the Hayes-Monnette lease, see Sally Springmeyer Zanjani, "George Wingfield: The Goldfield Years," *Nevada Historical Society Quarterly* 32 (Summer 1989): 111–113. Morgan, "Biography," pp. 124–128, has an atmospheric account of the partners' decision to leave Goldfield just before the big discovery was made. See also *Tonopah Miner*, June 16, 1906. See *GT*, May 26, 1910, and Morgan, "Biography," pp. 155–157, for the increase in Mohawk stock prices; *San Francisco Call*, May 26, 1907, February 20, 1910, for details of Wingfield's purchases. The "mining king" characterization is from *Tonopah Bonanza*, June 30, 1906.

18. Morgan, "Biography," pp. 107, 162–164; *Goldfield Review*, August 30, 1906; *GT*, October 22, 1906, June 27, 1908.

19. For the Gans-Nelson fight's publicity value, see Elliott, *Twentieth-Century Mining Boom*, pp. 83–84; *GT*, October 29, 1906; Croft, *The Downers*, pp. 156–157; Sawyer, "Rushes," p. 68. Letting ordinary people benefit from a phenomenal rise in stock prices is the basis for the heroism of the Wingfield character, Ned Osborne, in *A Little Princess of Tonopah*.

20. Morgan, "Biography," p. 128.

21. Ibid., p. 172; *GT*, November 5, 1906.

22. This suit was case number 18857 in Nevada's Third District Court. A photocopy of the Findings of Fact and Conclusions of Law rendered by Judge Peter Breen on August 13, 1906, is in the McCarran Papers, NHS. For the *lis pendens*, see Nye County Miscellaneous Records, Book I, 41, and Esmeralda County Miscellaneous Records, Book A, 142. Both documents are dated March 21, 1906.

23. Nye County Miscellaneous Records, Book J, 15. See the Findings of Fact and Conclusions of Law in the McCarran Papers for the language of the complaint. May Baric had at least one daughter, Olivette, who was a teenager at the time of GW's marriage in 1908 and was not his child.

24. For acknowledgments of May's relationship to Wingfield, see Blair, "Days Remembered of Folsom," p. 42; *San Francisco Call*, January 3, 1907. The *San Francisco Examiner* of August 1, 1908, has a photograph of George Wingfield and May Baric together. For the earthquake, see *Tonopah Sun*, April 25, 1906.

25. Nye County Miscellaneous Records, Book I, 299; Nye County Deeds, Book 4, 253. The documents were actually recorded on April 21, 1906; see *San Francisco Call*, December 29, 1907.

26. *San Francisco Call*, December 29, 1906 (emphasis added).

27. *San Francisco Call*, January 3, 1907.

28. This account depends heavily on Morgan, "Biography," pp. 161–168, and Glasscock, *Gold*, pp. 242–245. The quotation is from Samuel Freedman, in *Goldfield, Its Gold, Its Founders, Its Romance* (Goldfield, Nev.: Samuel Freedman, 1907), p. 19.

29. *Tonopah Miner*, November 10, 1906; *NSJ* July 6, 1936. See also Charles F. Spilman, "The Story of the Consolidated," in clippings scrapbook at the Central Nevada Historical Society, Tonopah, but probably from the *Goldfield Chronicle*, August 24, 1907. This same version is contained in Freedman, in *Goldfield*, pp. 19–20.

30. Morgan, "Biography," pp. 162, 167–168; GW to David Ryder, October 23, 1958, in the possession of the Wingfield family; Bernard M. Baruch, *Baruch: My Own Story* (New York: Henry Holt, 1957), p. 249.

31. For customary capitalization, see Sawyer, "Rushes," p. 50. For criticisms, see Charles S. Thomas, manuscript autobiography, Colorado Historical Society, Denver, p. 128; Van Dyck and Watson to Henry S. Van de Carr, New York Consolidated Stock Exchange, January 14, 1908, Goldfield Mining Companies Correspondence and Records, Bancroft Library. See also citations in Zanjani, "George Wingfield: The Goldfield Years." *GT*, July 30, 1908. For a defense of the capitalization, see *Goldfield News*, June 8, 1907, October 30, 1909; Frederick S. Harris letter, *Mining and Scientific Press* 94 (January 5, 1907): 16. Wingfield's comments are in *Tonopah Bonanza*, November 16, 1906. *GT*, July 30, 1908. GCMC capitalization was *not* the largest of the mining companies identified as the best dividend payers for the year 1909 (*GT*, November 19, 1909).

32. *GT*, May 30, July 23, 1907. In 1907, after the merger had been completed, GW was still buying stock in the constituent companies, including Mohawk, Jumbo, and Goldfield Mining; see correspondence with Kenneth Donnellan Co., January 15, 16, 1907; G. M. Lee to GW, March 3, 1907.

33. Watson and Van Dyck to D. H. Louderback, April 10, 1906, Goldfield Mining Companies Correspondence and Papers, Bancroft Library, Berkeley, California; Morgan, "Biography," p. 174; *Tonopah Miner*, November 10, 1906; *Goldfield News*, November 10, 1906.

34. Rickard's opinion is so reported in the *Goldfield Chronicle*, February 8, 1908, although he actually described GCMC as "the most productive gold mine in the world in 1907."

35. For the Botsford option, see *Goldfield Chronicle*, January 18, 1908; Freedman, in *Goldfield*, pp. 19–21, Sawyer, "Rushes," pp. 69–70; "Statement of Charles E. Knox," enclosed June 28, 1910, Box 62, GCMC, GW Papers. For GW's father, see *GT*, November 15, 1906.

36. Spilman, "Story of the Consolidated"; Thomas autobiography, p. 130; Morgan, "Biography," p. 178; Bernard Baruch to George Wingfield, Jr., December 26, 1959 (in the possession of the Wingfield family); Jordan A. Schwarz, *The Speculator: Bernard M. Baruch in Washington, 1917–1965* (Chapel Hill: University of North Carolina Press, 1981), p. 15.

37. Thomas autobiography, p. 130; Hersey, "The Old Man," p. 28; Carter Field, *Bernard Baruch: Park Bench Statesman* (New York: McGraw-Hill, 1944), pp. 59–61; Baruch, *My Own Story*, p. 250.

38. C. S. Thomas to W. H. Bryant, January 24, 1907, Central Nevada Historical Society, Tonopah; Baruch, *My Own Story*, p. 251; Freedman, p. 21.

39. *GT*, November 9, 1906, September 23, 1907; *Tonopah Sun*, November 12, 1906. The negative editorial opinion of Nixon and Wingfield's merger comes from the *Sun*, and the more positive estimation from the 1906 *Tribune* article. *NSJ*, July 6, 1936; Glasscock, *Gold*, p. 307; *Goldfield News*, March 18, 1913, January 1, 1926. GCMC dividend payments were noted in the Goldfield newspapers and summarized in the annual reports of the company, which were also given newspaper coverage. Eventually GCMC paid some additional dividends, bringing the total payment to over $30 million. These were from sources other than the Goldfield property, however. The industrial ranking is from Alfred D. Chandler, Jr., *The Visible Hand: The Manage-*

rial Revolution in American Business (Cambridge: Belknap Press of Harvard University Press, 1977), appendix A, p. 503.

40. "George Wingfield," in *Press Reference Library* (Los Angeles: Los Angeles Examiner, 1915), p. 365; *San Francisco Call*, February 20, 1910; "Story of the Goldfield Consolidated Mines Company," *The Woman Citizen*, Nevada Edition (November 1912): 34–35; Morgan, "Biography," p. 180.

Chapter Five: "Compromise Be Damned"

1. Chapter title from GW, quoted in *Tonopah Sun*, March 30, 1907. Morgan, "Biography," p. 180: this estimate of Wingfield's fortune, although the most common, is almost certainly inflated. A promotional annual edition of the *Goldfield Tribune*, which could also be expected to adopt a sanguine view, put his worth at $15 million in 1907 (*Goldfield Tribune Annual Review*, March 25, 1907). In 1934, *Fortune* magazine put the amount at $6 million; "Passion in the Desert," 9 (April 1934); *San Francisco Journal of Commerce*, reprinted in *Goldfield Review*, August 30, 1906. When George Nixon died in 1912, after the dissolution of Nixon and Wingfield, his estate was "over $5 million" (*GT*, June 19, 1912). For the car, see *GT*, July 28, 1907.

2. Wingfield's refreshing lack of pomp was cited admiringly in most published accounts and confirmed by personal interviews. See, for example, Alfred H. Dutton, *Notable Nevadans in Caricature* (Los Angeles: Out West Corporation, 1915), p. 40: "With all his vast accumulation of wealth—the wealthiest in Nevada—he still remains just plain George Wingfield." Reporter George Arnold observed in 1929, "He loves life and the good things in it, but eschews display and ostentation": "George Wingfield, Nevada's Foremost Citizen," *Coast Investor and Industrial Review* 7 (April 1929): 26, 57–60. George Wingfield never admitted to his children that he had actually owned a saloon or been a gambler, although he saved a photograph of himself in a bartender's apron.

3. *NSJ*, August 15, 1976, and interview with George Wingfield, Jr.; T. A. Rickard, *Retrospect, An Autobiography* (New York: McGraw-Hill, 1937), p. 78. The writer of a 1910 mug book observed approvingly, "With his sudden acquisition of vast wealth, Wingfield has been able to do what few other men could under similar circumstances—hold his coolness of judgment and clearness of brain and buckle down to the great work which his possessions have entailed upon him" (*Notable Nevadans: Snapshots of Sagebrushers Who Are Doing Things* [Reno: n.p., 1910], p. 29).

4. *Goldfield Review*, March 15, 1906. See Elliott, *Twentieth-Century Boom*, pp. 78–92, for an account of the mining craze that swept the country, and for a summary of stock promoters' abuses. For examples of expanding Nixon and Wingfield mining activities, see *Tonopah Miner*, May 25, 1907; *Goldfield Chronicle*, December 23, 1908. A comprehensive list of their properties appears in the *Goldfield Tribune Annual Review*, March 25, 1907. For Fairview, see Hugh A. Shamberger, *The Story of Fairview, Churchill County, Nevada* (Carson City: Nevada Historical Press, 1973).

5. Rickard, *Retrospect*, p. 77. An interesting variation of stock manipulation charges circulated during the labor disputes of 1907. At that time it was alleged that

the IWW leaders prolonged the strike in collusion with stockbrokers in order to profit from the fall in stock prices. Others made similar claims about the owners: Laura A. White, "History of the Labor Struggles in Goldfield, Nevada" (M.A. thesis, University of Nebraska, 1912), p. 81.

6. *Tonopah Miner*, November 30, 1907. In 1913, Rice published a richly detailed autobiography, *My Adventures with Your Money*, which provides exceptionally perceptive descriptions of the Goldfield boom, and of Nixon and Wingfield personally, but generally refrains from self-criticism. The most balanced account of his Nevada activities is Elliott, *Twentieth-Century Boom*, pp. 90–98, but see also Morgan, "Biography," pp. 140–143, 179–180, and *passim*. Morgan explains Rice's animosity toward Nixon and Wingfield on the grounds that they had rebuffed his offer to make a deal, in "The Knave" column, *Oakland Tribune*, August 1, 1948. Rice was not the only critic of Nixon and Wingfield, but he was certainly the most vocal. Aside from "Diamondfield" Jack Davis, little other direct personal criticism of the partners survives.

7. Morgan, "Biography," p. 141; *Tonopah Bonanza*, November 10, 1907.

8. *Tonopah Sun*, November 9, 1907; Morgan, "Biography," pp. 141–143.

9. Rice, *Adventures*, p. 149.

10. For the pattern of accusations and denials, see *Tonopah Sun*, November 15, 1907, January 15 (source of the headline), June 12, 1908; *Goldfield News*, June 29, July 27, 1907, February 1, December 12, 1908; *San Francisco Call*, July 30, October 13, 1907. Nixon's statement is from the *San Francisco Call*, May 26, 1907, p. 47. In June 1908, George Wingfield took a delicious revenge against Rice by purchasing the controlling interest in Goldfield's Combination Fraction Mining Company. While this property was of interest to GCMC because it lay between the Mohawk and Florence ground, it was also an attractive target because Rice needed it to cover his short position in the stock. In collusion with Fraction owner Al Myers, who sold him the stock, Wingfield caused Rice, who had effectively been betting that the price of the stock would go down, to take a substantial financial loss. This deal is detailed in the *San Francisco Call*, June 27, 1908, and *GT*, June 23, 1908. Wingfield and Nixon achieved control in September (*Goldfield News*, September 26, 1908).

11. *Goldfield News*, October 30, 1909. The *News* was specifically rebutting Rice's charges that its mining reporting was not credible because the paper was a publicity arm of GCMC (Watson and Van Dyck to J. Oliver Williams, 2 July 1907, Goldfield, Nevada Mining Companies, Correspondence and Papers, Bancroft Library). Rice astutely exploited the animosity between himself and GCMC for all its considerable publicity value. Jack Davis reported in 1911: "Rice told a friend of mine the other day that the editor of his magazine told him that they received thousands of subscriptions through the advertising given the story by the Goldfield News and if it was not for the Goldfield News lambasting Rice he would have quit talking about you and the Senator in his articles after the first attack. The general impression here in the East is that where there is so much smoke there must be some fire, and that the Goldfield News would not have roasted him half as hard as it did if Rice had not stepped on your corns." Davis, revealingly, appealed to Wingfield's manhood in advising him to stop the public feud with Rice: "People are beginning to think down here that you are a hard loser and that of the two Rice is gamer because he has stood all the punishment

the Goldfield News gave him and cried for more, while from the moment his articles began to mention your name the Goldfield News went into hysterics" (Jack Davis to GW, July 15, 1911).

12. For conservative GCMC policies, see *Goldfield Chronicle*, September 23, and 24, 1907; *GT*, July 30, 1908. *GT*, June 6, 1908; December 17, 1909 (source of Baruch quotation); *Goldfield News*, November 21, 1908. For a New York brokerage prediction that GCMC would reach $15 per share, see *GT*, December 17, 1908. During these years GCMC prices occasionally sank below $5 per share, especially during the height of the labor disputes. It seldom sold above par. The owners of the Combination took their stock in the merger company on the basis of $7.50 per share, while Baruch's option valued it at $7.75.

13. *GT*, October 20, 1911; *San Francisco Call*, February 7, 1908; *GT*, April 19, 1909. For Rice's wildcatting, see *GT*, April 14, 1911, which describes how he profited by circulating rumors that inflated the price of Jumbo Extension stock (then involved in a controversy with GCMC) and sold quantities of the stock to his customers. When the outcome of the controversy was less profitable to Jumbo Extension than Rice had predicted, the stock immediately fell in price, leaving the buyers to absorb a loss. For a defense of Wingfield and Nixon from charges of stock jobbing, see the *Goldfield Tribune Annual Review*, March 25, 1907, p. 2.

14. Estimates of the influence of the displaced Colorado miners varied from twenty to fifty percent of the new union. Useful accounts of Goldfield's labor conflict include Vernon H. Jensen, *Heritage of Conflict: Labor Relations in the Nonferrous Metals Industry up to 1930* (Ithaca: Cornell University Press, 1950); Guy Louis Rocha, "Radical Labor Struggles in the Tonopah-Goldfield Mining District, 1901–1922," *Nevada Historical Society Quarterly* 20 (Spring 1977): 3–45; Guy Louis Rocha and Sally Zanjani, *Ignoble Conspiracy* (Reno: University of Nevada Press, 1986); and White, "Labor Struggles." See also Elliott, *Twentieth-Century Boom*, pp. 103–144. The following synopsis of Goldfield labor difficulties is based largely on these works. The IWW preamble is from White, pp. 15–16.

15. Typescript autobiography, Charles Thomas Papers, pp. 127–128; GW to Laura A. White, June 30, 1911.

16. Lindley C. Branson to GW, December 1, 1912. Throughout his letter, Branson reiterates the charge that the fight was Wingfield's and not his: "I could have settled that affair in twenty ways, but you asked me to go on with it and insisted that you would see that I did not lose anything by so doing. The result was that I went on with the fight purely, simply and solely because it was your wish. . . ." Branson had borrowed $1,145 from GW in 1904: GW to L. C. Branson, May 19, 1910. *Tonopah Sun*, September 10, 1906. Anti-union newspapers were not the only sources of admiration for Wingfield's courage. See Joseph F. McDonald, "The Life of a Newsboy in Nevada" (Oral History Program, University of Nevada, Reno, 1970), p. 24; T. A. Rickard, "Wingfield, Lockhart and Parker," *Mining and Scientific Press*, March 16, 1908, reprinted in Martin C. Duffy, comp., *Goldfield's Glorious Past* (privately published, n.d.).

17. For the leasers' tolerance of high grading, see T. A. Rickard, "Rich Ore and Its Moral Effects," in Duffy, *Goldfield's Glorious Past*, and Sawyer, "Rushes," pp. 82–

83. The latter points out that leasers were often friends of the men they employed as miners and didn't object to their employees sharing in their good fortune: "High-grading was the accepted local custom and employees and employers alike thought it humorous that visitors to the camp were outraged at this common practice of stealing ore." Arnold, in *Gold Camp Drifter*, pp. 51–52, describes miners concealing ore in their mouths with chewing gum, under their armpits, and in their rectums in rubber receptacles. For payments in order to obtain preferred shifts, see Sawyer, "Rushes," and GW to J. H. Fulmer, October 20, 1920.

18. Information on the Northern, which reportedly fell into receivership after the practice of highgrading was quelled, can be found in a letter, probably from attorneys Campbell, Metson, and Brown to an attorney in Galveston, Texas, November 7, 1908, in the possession of Allen Metscher, Tonopah, Nevada. Assayer Mel Downer is quoted in Glasscock, *Gold*, p. 118.

19. For the Reno seizure, see *Tonopah Sun*, December 14, 1906.

20. Albert S. Watson to W. L. Morrison, December 31, 1906, Goldfield Mining Company Records, Bancroft Library.

21. *Tonopah Sun*, December 31, 1906; Watson to Morrison, December 31, 1906.

22. "Arrival of Wingfield Expected to Settle Strike," *Tonopah Sun*, January 5, 1907.

23. White, "Labor Struggles," p. 37.

24. Rocha and Zanjani, *Ignoble Conspiracy*, provides an exhaustive account of this event and its judicial aftermath, although I differ with them in my estimate of Wingfield's culpability. They tend to make GW the scapegoat for everything that went on in Goldfield during the labor disputes. I see him, rather, as one among many disgruntled mineowners and operators, each of whom had a stake in the outcome. See, however, F[red] J. Siebert to Tasker L. Oddie, July 7, 1911, Tasker L. Oddie Papers, Huntington Library, San Marino, California: "We [Siebert and GW] both agree that it would be best to let Smith go on parole, as he has been sufficiently punished and was only a poor boob in the thing in the start. So far as Preston is concerned, however, we sincerely hope that he will stay there until he rots." Preston and Smith were posthumously pardoned in 1987, largely as a result of evidence presented by Rocha and Zanjani (White, "Labor Struggles," pp. 57–58).

25. J. W. Finch to Cripple Creek District Mine Owners and Operators' Association, March 22, 1907, in the possession of Allen Metscher, Tonopah, Nevada. The purported notices to leave are reported in *San Francisco Call*, March 13, 1907. The Cook incident and threats to kill are from *Reno Evening Gazette* (henceforth *REG*), March 13, 1907. Farrington's opinion was issued in the suit that GCMC brought in December 1907 to dissolve the WFM. It was quoted in *GT*, March 11, 1908.

26. As White points out, "Labor Struggles," p. 74, note 6, the IWW and WFM had split at the national level in September 1906, and the WFM refused by 1907 to recognize the IWW as a legitimate labor organization.

27. "Bill in Equity," March 1907, in the possession of Jon Aurich, Jr., Woodland Hills, California. The document offers interesting proof of the direct influence of the Cripple Creek incidents on Goldfield's labor troubles. Frequent citations of the cost or violence of events in Colorado are offered as establishing a pattern and thus

justifying the injunction being sought. I am grateful to Mr. Aurich for sharing his collection of GCMC material with me.

28. Intimates of GW perceived the labor agreement as a personal victory for him. Attorney Hugh H. Brown, for instance, congratulated Wingfield in a letter seeking a retainer for his law firm: "All Tonopah was greatly elated over the settlement of the strike. I know what a great burden has been lifted off your mind. I hope that your course may be plain sailing for at least two years to come so far as labor troubles are concerned": *GT*, April 22, 1907; Arthur Winslow to J. W. Finch, April 29, 1907; J. W. Finch to Tonopah and Goldfield Railroad, May 26, 1907; GW to W. H. Bryant, July 8, 1907, all in the possession of Allen Metscher, Tonopah, Nevada.

29. Quoted in White, "Labor Struggles," p. 112.

30. *Goldfield News*, August 31, 1907. Evidently even the change rooms were not a foolproof solution to the problem of highgrading. In an interview on June 16, 1989, Marshall Giusti reported that years later, when his family eventually tore down the GCMC change rooms, they found enough gold nuggets that had fallen through the floorboards to fill a "large coffee can."

31. GW to Laura A. White, June 30, 1911; "Report of Special Commission on Labor Troubles at Goldfield, Nevada," 60th Congress, 1st Session, House Documents, vol. 105 (Washington, D.C.: Government Printing Office, 1908), p. 21; *Goldfield News*, August 24, 1907.

32. *GT*, December 16, 1913; *San Francisco Call*, October 28, 1907, p. 1; Sawyer, "Rushes," pp. 78–80.

33. *Goldfield Chronicle*, October 15, 1907; *San Francisco Call*, October 15, 1907, p. 5; Sawyer, "Rushes," pp. 79–80.

34. Sawyer, "Rushes," pp. 77–78. For the "smelter trust," see *GT*, October 22, 1907. T. A. Rickard, "Squandering of Gold," July 11, 1908, *Mining and Scientific Press*, reprinted in Duffy, *Goldfield's Glorious Past*, p. 50.

35. *Tonopah Sun*, October 24, 1907; *San Francisco Call*, October 28, 1907, p. 1; *GT*, December 16, 1913, November 3, 1910. There was an alternate, less benevolent view of Nixon and Wingfield's role in saving the Goldfield banks, as reported to Key Pittman by his brother William: "He also spoke of Nixon going down in his own pocket and putting up $1,500,000.00 to protect his banks and save the poor depositors from losing. Now in reality Geo. Wingfield told me that the amount put up by him [Nixon] at Goldfield was something like $450,000.00. . . . His action was not due to any big heart or generosity on his part, purely a business proposition" (William B. Pittman to Key Pittman [henceforth KP], October 28, 1910, KP Papers). Although these two versions don't, in fact, contradict each other, the animus of each is decidedly partisan.

36. GW to David Ryder, October 23, 1958, in the possession of the Wingfield family; *Goldfield News*, November 2, 1907. The Northern was owned by Ole Elliott and Tex Rickard, among others. The Casey Hotel was operated by J. Casey McDannell, who later named one of his children after GW.

37. White, "Labor Struggles," pp. 130–132; *Goldfield News*, November 2, 1907.

38. The smelter meeting was also held on December 4, however, and Wingfield

did attend, as reported in the Reno newspapers. See *Goldfield Chronicle*, December 5, 1907. Telegram, John Sparks to Theodore Roosevelt, December 3–4, 1907, quoted in "Report of Special Commission," p. 3.

39. Mine operator Malcolm MacDonald of Tonopah telegraphed his friend, Congressman George Bartlett, with some surprise on December 5, 1907: "What is all this I see in United Press dispatch about governor's request to president[?] We have no trouble here nor can I learn of any in Goldfield" (George Bartlett Papers, Special Collections Department, University of Nevada, Reno). *Goldfield Chronicle*, December 9, 1907. J. H. Mackenzie to George Bartlett, September 30, 1908, in the Bartlett Papers encloses a copy of minutes of MOA meetings of November 18 and 23, 1907, to show that wages were in fact lowered before arrival of the troops, although cards announcing the fact weren't printed up until later (J. H. Mackenzie to "Dear Friend," December 11, 1907, in the possession of Allen Metscher, Tonopah, Nevada). See *Tonopah Miner*, January 13, 1908, for GW's recruiting trip to Utah.

Finch's resignation, which was announced on November 23, 1907, was not publicly explained, although relations with the company were purportedly cordial. Given his central role in previous labor negotiations, his resignation at this particular time, when the company was in the midst of another union confrontation, is curious. At roughly the same time, the Goldfield MOA was being reorganized to exclude businessmen and represent only mine operators. This may have been done to make it easier for the mineowners to obtain the two-thirds vote necessary for them to declare a lockout or it may possibly have had something to do with Finch's departure (*Goldfield Chronicle*, December 16, 1907).

40. *Goldfield Chronicle*, January 7, 1908. For a summary of the December suit, which charged that the union had "instituted a reign of terror in the district so that citizens have been deprived of their personal rights," see *Goldfield Chronicle*, December 27, 1907.

41. For Sage, see Rocha and Zanjani, *Ignoble Conspiracy*, pp. 15–16; *GT*, September 5, 1911. For Thiel detectives, see GW to Manager, Thiel Detective Agency, August 30, 1914. The "shit-ass list" is given in [C. F. Burton] to Billy [William H. Webber], Nevada Hills Mining Company, November 13, 1910. Quotation from personnel records of C. B. Comsford, Mohawk miner discharged on December 27, 1914, in the possession of Jon Aurich, Jr., Woodland Hills, California. William Covert to *Goldfield News*, April 26, 1910, in *Goldfield News*, April 30, 1910; GW to Laura A. White, June 30, 1911 (emphasis added).

42. GW to Maurice J. Sullivan, acting governor, March 31, 1915, Governor's Papers, Nevada Division of Archives and Records, Carson City, Nevada. Sullivan responded by forwarding the sticker to the head of the State Police and asking him to investigate (GW to Key Pittman, January 7, 1920). In 1912, one of the items kept in GW's office safe was a list of members of the Goldfield miners' union.

43. *GT*, January 25, 1908; *Goldfield Review*, September 5, 1908; *Goldfield Chronicle*, December 24, 1908; *Tonopah Sun*, November 17, 1908. See Hugh A. Shamberger, *Goldfield: Early History, Development, Water Supply* (Carson City: Nevada Historical Press, 1982), for details of the Goldfield Hotel financing and operation.

Nixon and Wingfield invested in the Bonanza Hotel company along with Al Myers, J. F. Douglass, G. W. Hayes and M. J. Monnette of the famous lease, and the partners of the latter, John W. Smith and Harry Benedict.

44. For details of the Baruch settlement, see *New York Times*, September 21, 1907; *Tonopah Sun*, September 24, 1907; *Tonopah Miner*, November 2, 1907. Mackenzie's assessment is in *GT*, May 5, 1908.

45. *GT*, May 22, July 14 and 25, November 19, December 27, 1908; *Tonopah Sun*, April 3, 1909.

46. The wedding was undoubtedly rushed because of threats from May Baric (e.g., *GT*, December 11, 1908). I am grateful to Melinda Price, San Rafael, California, for providing information on her grandmother, Maude Murdoch Wingfield. Harry H. Atkinson, in his oral history, observed that the wedding brought GW social standing he didn't previously have "Tonopah and Reno: Memoirs of a Nevada Attorney" (Oral History Program, University of Nevada, Reno, 1970), p. 77.

47. Blair, "Days Remembered of Folsom," pp. 42–43. Wingfield's marriage was reported in the *San Francisco Call*, July 31, 1908, p. 4. The Baric imbroglio appears in *San Francisco Examiner*, August 1, 1908, p. 9; *San Francisco Call*, August 2, 1908, p. 6; and finally, belatedly, *GT*, August 4, 1908. The Goldfield celebration was reported in *GT*, August 1, 1908.

48. *San Francisco Examiner*, August 1, 1908, p. 9 ("cur"); *San Francisco Call*, August 2, 1908 (Olivette).

49. *GT*, August 5 and 25, 1908; *San Francisco Call*, August 27, 1908, p. 4.

50. A fire was reported in their Reno home on October 22 (*GT*, October 23, 1908). For a different view of Wingfield's departure from Goldfield, depicting a broken town "so successfully subdued that Wingfield could safely leave its affairs in the hands of his lieutenants," see Zanjani, "Wingfield: The Goldfield Years," pp. 111–125. Goldfield's population at its peak in 1907–1908 was conservatively placed at 15,000. By 1910, in the wake of the strike and declining production, it was approximately 4,800. Sustained by the county seat, which was moved there in 1907, its 1990 population was under 500. For Wingfield's return visits, see the register of the Goldfield Hotel for the year 1909, Central Nevada Historical Society, Tonopah, Nevada.

51. GW to Chester L. Lyman, March 20, 1909, Central Nevada Historical Society, Tonopah; *REG*, December 16, 1912.

Chapter Six: "I Have Took Over Everything"

1. Chapter title from GW to George K. Edler, March 31, 1909. Chandler, *Visible Hand*; Dutton, *Nevadans in Caricature*, p. 40.

2. On GW operating through lieutenants, see editorial, "Vindication of Goldfield Consolidated," *GT*, November 19, 1909; *GT*, July 10, 1910. GW to Tasker L. Oddie, July 1, 1912; Arnold, "George Wingfield," p. 59; *GT*, July 31, 1908. This same pattern of operation was also attributed to George Nixon. See *GT*, September 16, 1908, for GSN's "heart-to-heart talks with his constructive lieutenants."

3. Burton had Nevada connections through his uncle, Charles J. Kappler, the same man who shared with George Wingfield the August 1905 ordeal of walking forty miles back to Tonopah after their car broke down in the desert. Burton was an early arrival in Goldfield, where he was a teller at the John S. Cook & Co. bank. In Reno he married Lucille Golden, the daughter of jeweler, banker, and hotel proprietor Frank Golden, the man who had prompted Wingfield's initial venture into Tonopah in 1901. Information on Burton comes from *GT*, May 13, 1920; Newsletter, Nevada State Board of Accountancy, spring 1988; interview with Elizabeth Burton, Reno, Nevada, March 7, 1989. Clarence Burton, in turn, acknowledged Wingfield's significant influence on his career: "If I make good I think it will be a pleasure to yourself also because your influence upon my business career has been so profound that my success will reflect credit upon yourself as well. I want you to know that I appreciate your many kind acts toward myself and I shall never be able to feel entirely weaned away from the outfit" (Clarence F. Burton to GW, July 19, 1920).

4. For Julian, see extensive correspondence files in the GW Papers; *GT*, September 8, 1911; *San Francisco Chronicle*, August 10, 1955; Shamberger, *Story of Fairview*. During their long association Estey A. Julian also came to be a close friend of GW. Clarence Burton always addressed his employer as "Mr. Wingfield" and in turn was referred to as "Burton." Julian, by contrast, referred to Wingfield respectfully, but warmly, as "Chief" and was known in turn as "Julie." A lifelong associate and beneficiary of Wingfield's patronage, Julian died in his employ, in Ethiopia, where he had gone to investigate chromium mining prospects for GCMC.

5. Young, *Journalism in California*, p. 338; *Tonopah Miner*, August 19, 1905; *San Francisco Call*, February 23, 1913; GW to Tasker L. Oddie, July 1, 1912. For a sense of the range of Wingfield's investments, see C. Elizabeth Raymond, *A Guide to the George Wingfield Papers* (Reno: Nevada Historical Society, 1988).

6. Young, *Journalism in California*, p. 338; F. J. Siebert to Tasker Oddie, March 17, 1915, TLO Papers, NHS. Edward Chase Kirkland, in *Dream and Thought in the Business Community, 1869–1900* (1956, reprint Chicago: Elephant Books, 1990), notes that most late-nineteenth-century businessmen sincerely believed that material progress must precede other forms of progress.

7. James D. Finch to KP, November 25, 1913, KP Papers.

8. In Goldfield, when the popular Roman Catholic priest Father Dermody needed money for his church, GW gave him literal *carte blanche*. Though his Methodist forebears would no doubt have scowled, GW offered Dermody a checkbook on his account, with the privilege of using as much money as was needed (*Tonopah Miner*, August 19, 1905; Croft, *The Downers*, p. 136). For other examples, see *GT*, April 17, 1908; General Executive Committee, Fourth of July Celebration, 1912, Central Nevada Historical Society, Tonopah. For representative personal loans, see GW to Ruby Van Patten, January 24, 1928, and H. Lavenroth to GW, December 24, 1928. This pattern also extended to significant individuals such as Tasker L. Oddie (see chapter 8). For gifts to the Elks, see Blair, "Days Remembered of Folsom," p. 33; *GT*, May 25, 1907, February 12, 1910, April 13, 1912; Forest E. Cooper to Guy Rocha, December 4, 1979. GW's personal financial statements confirm the ongoing pattern of small but numerous donations to both public and religious charities. See

monthly summaries of personal expenses, Series II, Personal Financial Records, GW Papers.

9. *Goldfield News*, February 27, 1909; *Tonopah Sun*, Mining Edition, March 20, 1909, April 19, 1909. The federal suit is discussed in *San Francisco Call*, February 5, 1909, p. 1 (source of quotation), April 27, 1909, p. 4. May Baric is referred to in the first article as Mrs. Charles Barrick, and the amount of damages has increased to $750,000 in the second article. The duration she cites for their common-law marriage would put its beginning a few months earlier than the December 1902 date she claimed in the Tonopah suit.

10. The text of Baric's agreement with Wingfield, dated January 7, 1911, is in the GW Papers.

11. Clare Hofer Hewes, "The Hofer Family of Carson City" (Oral History Program, University of Nevada, Reno, 1966), p. 8. For female disapproval of George Wingfield, see Silas E. Ross, "Recollections of Life at Glendale, Nevada, Work at the University of Nevada, and Western Funeral Practice" (Oral History Program, University of Nevada, Reno, 1970), p. 280.

12. *Goldfield News*, April 3, 1909; *GT*, April 9 and 11, 1909; *REG*, December 15, 1909; *Tonopah Bonanza*, May 22, 1909; *Tonopah Sun*, April 29, 1909.

13. GW to George Bartlett, March 12, 1909, George Bartlett Papers, Special Collections Department, University of Nevada, Reno; GW to George K. Edler, February 27, 1909; *Goldfield News*, April 3, 1909. Wingfield was at pains to deny the Frick rumor: "I never saw the man; never wrote or received a letter from him, and wouldn't know him if I saw him" (*GT*, April 11, 1909). For political speculation about Nixon's reasons for selling, see *San Francisco Call*, March 30, 1909, p. 9; *Tonopah Miner*, November 5, 1910; *Goldfield News*, April 17, 1909. The timing of Wingfield's trip tantalizingly suggests that the Baric suit may have had some influence on Nixon's decision to extricate himself from their partnership, although, true to form, the matter was not publicized in Nevada newspapers.

14. *Tonopah Sun*, April 29, 1909; GW to George K. Edler, March 31, 1909.

15. *Tonopah Sun*, Mining Edition, May 1, 1909; *GT*, April 9, 1909; Sawyer, "Rushes," p. 136; Malcolm Macdonald to George Bartlett, April 17, 1909, George Bartlett Papers; *Goldfield News*, January 1, 1910. Sam C. Dunham to KP, August 4, 1910, KP Papers, notes that Rice is "after Nixon's scalp."

16. The undated *Telegram* article is found in a scrapbook of clippings in the GW Papers.

17. The profit figure for Nixon and Wingfield is from *Tonopah Sun*, April 29, 1909. *Tonopah Sun*, Mining Edition, May 1, 1909.

18. *Goldfield News*, May 8, 1909; *GT*, January 27, 1911, March 6, 1912.

19. For the bullion tax controversy, see *Goldfield News*, November 29 and 30, 1909; *GT*, April 29, 1910.

20. For highgrading, see *GT*, February 5, August 7, 1910; February 5, August 8, 1911. The *Wall Street Journal* article is reported in *GT*, March 18, 1910. For NYSE listing, see *GT*, June 23, 1910; *Goldfield News*, June 26, July 2, 1910.

Some refused to believe that Nixon and Wingfield had actually severed their association in GCMC. In anticipation of the 1910 senatorial race between George Nixon and Key Pittman, one of Pittman's advisors suggested, "I think I would call attention to the fact that Nixon and Wingfield have been successfully bearing the property of all other companies in Goldfield . . . for the purpose of embarrassing the companies that own these properties and prevent them from borrowing money, that they may at their leisure gobble them up. . . . They are not activated by any public spirit whatever, but the basest selfishness. Their ruthless policy has absolutely ruined the business men of Goldfield" (Sam C. Dunham to KP, August 9, 1910, KP Papers).

21. For information on the Buckhorn and Nevada Hills deals, see GW correspondence with J. Horace Harding, 1911–1917, GW Papers; GW to Bernard M. Baruch, April 23, September 8, 1910, GW Papers; Shamberger, *Story of Fairview*. The quotation about Nevada Hills is from *GT*, July 6, 1910. Buckhorn and Nevada Hills both ceased operations later in the decade, due to the combined effects of wartime shortages of material, difficulty in securing water, and lack of sufficient good ore. The Buckhorn Mines Company was formally dissolved in October 1919 (GW to Miss M. A. Boyle, December 1, 1920).

22. Wingfield purchased stock in the Lander County company personally, over a period of years, eventually dissolving the company and selling its assets in 1917. The Pyramid operation, which controlled over 150,000 acres of public range in addition to the land it owned, was initially controlled through the Nixon National Bank, in Reno. In 1918, it was sold to a Wingfield holding company, the Reno Securities Company. For Lander County Livestock Company, see *Goldfield News*, May 7, 1910, and GW to Maurice Phipps, November 12, 1916. For the Pyramid Land and Stock Company, see details of purchase in 1918 Reno Securities Company files, GW Papers. The Goldfield Hotel was owned by the Bonanza Hotel Company: see *GT*, December 31, 1910, and correspondence files by that title in the GW Papers. The company was organized in 1909 to take over the Casey Hotel and the Goldfield Realty Company, which owned the Goldfield Hotel.

23. *Goldfield News*, December 25, 1909; *NSJ*, September 27, October 3, 1913; *GT*, November 3, 1913. See also affidavit of Clarence F. Burton, January 10, 1917; Scrugham, *Nevada*, vol. 2, p. 14; John Townley, *Turn This Water into Gold* (Reno: Nevada Historical Society, 1977).

24. *GT*, June 12, 1914; *Las Vegas Age*, November 8, 1913 ("Success"); Sam Wingfield to GW, October 8, 1917; GW to J. W. Hamm, March 20, 1922; *GT*, October 28, 1913 ("blossom"). The State Agricultural Society became the State Board of Agriculture in 1920, and Wingfield remained a member until 1940.

25. State officials were particularly concerned about the perceptions outside the state if the beet sugar industry should fail. See C. A. Norcross, Nevada Bureau of Industry, Agriculture, and Irrigation, to Tasker L. Oddie, November 19, 1913, Oddie Papers, Huntington Library. For Wingfield's involvement, see *GT*, November 27, 1915; Leonard J. Arrington, *Beet Sugar in the West: A History of the Utah-Idaho Sugar Company, 1891–1966* (Seattle: University of Washington Press, 1966).

26. *Humboldt Star*, March 27, 1911; Hardy, "Reminiscence," p. 7; Charles E. Chambliss, *Rice Growing in California* (Washington, D.C.: U.S. Department of Agriculture, Farmers' Bulletin 1141, 1920); John A. Ford, "Raising Rice—A Modern Wonder Tale," *Illustrated World* 34 (September 1920): 112–114. For detail on the

Sutter Butte Canal Company, see GW correspondence with William Johnson, Estey A. Julian, and re Sutter Butte Canal Company, GW Papers.

27. For Meadowbrook Ranch, see Tim I. Purdy, "Wingfield's Meadowbrook Ranch," *Lassen County Times*, March 21, 1979; correspondence re Meadowbrook Ranch, 1911–1923, GW Papers. I am indebted to Purdy for sharing his research on the Pacific Coast Bear Club, formed by E. C. Brown and several prominent Nevadans in 1906. Wingfield's shooting skill is widely documented (e.g., *NSJ*, January 24, 1912; *GT*, March 25, 1913). See also GW to George K. Edler, September 14, 1908. About a trip to Walley Hot Springs in Carson Valley, Wingfield writes, "Am going to kill a bunch of ducks up there. . . ." Virgil Wedge, in an interview on November 3, 1989, noted that Wingfield retained his ability as a duck hunter into his old age. In an article about their subsequent divorce, June 4, 1927, p. 4, the *San Francisco Chronicle* claimed that the first signs of friction between George and Maude Wingfield occurred over her lavish spending on Meadowbrook.

28. GW to George Bartlett, May 19, 1910, Bartlett Papers, UNR; *GT*, September 10, 1910, October 25, 1911; *Lassen Mail*, March 29, 1912.

29. Correspondence files relating to the various Wingfield companies give the best picture of the growing complexity of the "Wingfield organization," although the personal correspondence files, which contain notes between GW and Burton, are also revealing. Many of the letters which went out from Wingfield's office were in fact written by Clarence Burton or by a succession of supervising engineers, including Frederick J. Siebert (brother-in-law of Tasker Oddie) and later the stalwart Estey A. Julian. In general, Wingfield initiated new ventures and set policy for ongoing ones, but left the details of daily administration to his office managers.

30. *REG*, August 27, 1910, reports GW's homecoming, as well as the rumors purportedly circulated by Rice. For GW's influence as a public figure, see Scrapbooks in the GW Papers, or his correspondence with TLO during the latter's term as governor, TLO Papers, Huntington Library. References to GW in the California newspapers are particularly numerous during the 1910s.

31. *REG*, August 27, 1910.

32. GW to TLO, February 18, 1911, TLO Papers, Huntington Library. GW was not the only one to feel this way—see Congressman E. E. Roberts to GW, September 14, 1914: "You have been the only man in the history of the State who has spent his money there in the development of the State's natural resources. . . . I believe that when a man invests his money in the state and tries to develop it on a large scale, he should be encouraged in his endeavors. . . ."

33. See, for instance, *GT*, May 17, 1912, where GW complains of the Churchill County's tax levy against Nevada Hills ("The Nevada Hills Mining company is a corporation which is controlled by people who are residents and business people of this state; people who have always spent in the state the money that they made there"); GW to TLO, April 30, 1911, seeking road improvements from Fallon to Fairview; GW to TLO, August 28, 1912, offering to pay TLO's expenses if he would go south and "boost Massey and Roberts." Both of the latter are in the TLO Papers at the Huntington Library. For Wingfield's suffrage interview, see *San Francisco Chronicle*, March 16, 1914.

34. Wingfield's justification is contained in the *San Francisco Chronicle* interview, March 16, 1914; *Manhattan Post*, March 21, 1914; *Carson City Appeal*, March 24, 1914; Anne Bail Howard, *The Long Campaign: A Biography of Anne Martin* (Reno: University of Nevada Press, 1985), pp. 74–98. See Minnie Bronson to GW, March 26, 1914; GW to Minnie Bronson, April 24, 1914; GW to C[larence] A. Sage, August 31, 1914. GW assured Bronson that "I really think that we have the suffragettes very badly beaten."

35. *REG*, December 16, 1912, p. 7; GW to Bernard M. Baruch, August 27, 1910.

36. GW to Hon. George S. Nixon, March 12, 1912: "There is no denying the fact of Roosevelt's strength among the people of Nevada. His picturesque personality appeals especially to the people of a State like this. . . . Except for the policy, which Pinchot put up to Roosevelt, he would have carried this and other western states almost unanimously. . . . I am satisfied that with careful manipulation that we can carry this State for Mr. Taft." GW to George Bartlett, May 18, 1910, Bartlett Papers.

37. The Fallon "Get-together" speech was reported in the *Carson City News*, March 14, 1914. See also *Lakeview Examiner*, January 15, 1914, where Wingfield condemns "office chasing and political jockeying" by candidates who talk about running the state on business principles but borrow money and go into debt to run for office: "They know just how to run the State or the nation, but they never did run anything else except to run it into the ground." I would not contend that GW was a progressive in the classical mode represented by Nevada's Senator Francis Newlands (see William L. Rowley, "Francis G. Newlands and the Promises of American Life," *Nevada Historical Society Quarterly* 32 [Fall 1989]: 169–180). However, he shared certain elements of the progressive faith, especially in the desirability and efficacy of administrative reform. As the state's chief taxpayer, Wingfield sought efficiency in government operations, not just penny-pinching. In 1911, for example, he discussed the advisability of state automobiles for the prison warden and the Publicity Commission, noting that it would provoke a backlash: "I am afraid it is going to raise a big howl for the farmer is in favor of the horse and is prejudiced against the automobile because he don't know." Wingfield, however, did know and approved (GW to TLO, May 4, 1911, TLO Papers, Huntington Library). On the other hand he also disapproved of many progressive reform measures designed to protect weak members of society and was consistently suspicious of the motives of would-be reformers. In 1919, in a rare moment of political philosophizing, he described his reservations to Nevada Republican senator Charles B. Henderson in classic conservative language: "We must at some point put a stop to this tendency toward complete paternalism in the government. It is a big stepping stone toward Socialism and I do not believe that any considerable portion of the people of the United States are ready to accept that doctrine" (GW to Hon. C. B. Henderson, July 23, 1919).

38. For the funeral, see *GT*, June 11, 1912. Years later, after Nixon's estate was dissipated and his widow and family had fallen on hard times, GW privately endowed the Nixon mausoleum in the Masonic section of Mountain View Cemetery in Reno, so that it would be properly cared for (Ross, "Recollections of Life at Glendale, Nevada," p. 579). The text of Oddie's appointment of GW, dated June 12, 1912,

from which the quotation is taken, is in the Oddie Papers, Huntington Library. For editorial reaction, see *Carson City News,* June 12, 1912; *GT,* June 17 (compilation of editorial opinion from throughout the state), June 24, 1912; *NSJ,* June 13, 1912. The vast majority of the papers quoted favored the appointment—e.g., the *Salt Lake City Tribune:* "Mr. Wingfield has shown himself to be a man of vast capacity, of strong organizing force, and of rare administrative ability. That he will be a good and useful senator for his state . . . there can be no doubt." However, the *Wells Herald* is quoted in the *GT* compilation as disapproving: "The appointment is meeting with much adverse criticism all over the state. It does seem that some person could have been found for the exalted position who has more to recommend him than the mere possession of money." The *Elko Weekly Independent,* June 21, 1912, bemoaned the appointment of a man "well known as one of the proprietors of Tonopah's notorious boom-day resort, the 'Tonopah Club,' and lately of some affluence by reason of lucky investment in mining stocks. . . ." Wingfield's response asking for time to consider, GW to TLO, June 13, 1912, is in the GW Papers.

39. GW to H. C. Frick, June 14, 1912; H. C. Frick to GW, June 19, 1912. The petition is undated, but its receipt was acknowledged on June 29, 1912. J. D. Finch to KP, June 10, 1912, KP Papers. The story about going fishing is from Morgan, "George Wingfield Outline," p. 5; GW to H. C. Frick, June 27, 1912.

40. GW to TLO, July 1, 1912; Arthur Dunn, "The Cowboy Who Refused a Toga," *Sunset* 29 (October 1912): 446–447; Robert Lawrence, "George Wingfield," *Town Talk* 9 (November 1912), n.p.

41. *GT,* July 1, 1912. The *New York Mining Age* clipping, undated, is in a scrapbook in the GW Papers. Dunn, "Cowboy," p. 446; "George Wingfield," in *Notables of the Southwest* (Los Angeles: Press Reference Library, 1912), p. 367. The GW scrapbooks contain a cross-section of the publicity that ensued after the senate appointment.

42. Key Pittman to A. B. Gray, January 8, 1912, KP Papers. Pittman also added, "While George is not equipped to hold a position as U. S. Senator, there is no doubt that he has considerable executive ability, and would at least make a firm Governor." Pittman was a Democrat who had run unsuccessfully against Nixon in 1910 and was elected to the U.S. Senate in 1912, when he defeated the Reno judge William Massey, who was appointed in Wingfield's place to succeed Nixon. Despite these credentials, however, he was a business associate from the Goldfield years, and his assessment of Wingfield was a judicious one. In later years, Pittman and Wingfield would be political allies in the interests of the state, and investment partners (see chapter 8). For Wingfield's dislike of publicity, see Thornton, "George Wingfield," p. 18, and *NSJ,* August 16, 1976. Thornton confirms his discomfort in the East, but see in addition GW's plaintive note to his office manager, Clarence Burton, December 7, 1912, from New York: "I think a man would go nutty in two weeks around this place."

43. Wingfield's refusal of the senate seat is directly attributed to his fear of revelations about May Baric by his associate and later U.S. district attorney Harry Hunt Atkinson, "Tonopah and Reno," p. 77. TLO to GW, July 24, 1912. The second quotation is from the State Police Report, as related by Oddie in the letter.

44. *Washington, D.C. Pathfinder,* July 20, 1912; "From Faro-Table to Senate," *Literary Digest* 45 (July 6, 1912): 33–36.

45. Jack Davis to T. L. Oddie, October 26, 1913, TLO Papers, NHS. Davis was also infuriated that Wingfield had failed to look after May Baric's daughter Olivette, who had become another man's mistress at age seventeen—"an honorable man will take care even of his mistress, but May was George's wife through the common law of Nevada, and he was the little girl's natural guardian"—and that Wingfield had failed to pay him all of the money that Davis felt he was owed for witness costs "and other things in the trial of Smith and Preston." I am grateful to Guy Rocha for bringing this important and candid letter to my attention. In an earlier letter to Key Pittman, Davis described GW as "a two faced cheap tin horn" (Jack Davis to KP, December 18, 1912, KP Papers).

46. Jean Wingfield Filmer died on April 13, 1986, in Palm Desert, California. Wingfield first rented the Court Street residence in 1909, from Charles F. Snyder, manager of the Western Ore Purchasing Company in Reno, for $250 per month. His wife Maude gave birth to stillborn twin boys in 1910, and the move was probably related to her pregnancy. Wingfield eventually purchased the house from Snyder later in the decade. Although he and his wife redecorated extensively, the home was relatively modest by contemporary standards and paled by comparison to the magnificent Nixon Mansion, completed in 1908. For the banks, see *GT*, January 2, 1910, October 21, 1912; *San Francisco Call*, August 17, 1912; *New York Curb*, May 10, 1913. Nixon and Wingfield purchased the property at Virginia and Second streets in 1908, at a cost of approximately $100,000 (*Goldfield Chronicle*, September 3, 1908).

47. *NSJ*, October 12, 1914, p. 6; November 20, 1914, p. 4; *GT*, May 24, 1914. The banking interview, reprinted from *REG*, appeared in *GT*, January 18, 1914: "I believe that the law as a whole is a good one and that bankers should do everything possible to aid in working it out so as to bring the greatest advantages to themselves and to the nation." GW was also lobbying Nevada's Senator Francis Newlands on banking matters: see GW to Newlands, January 31, 1914. For GW's motives in purchasing the banks, see GW to Mrs. George S. Nixon, August 12, 1914: "When I went into them I went in with the idea of helping you out of a serious situation and I think I have done so" (GW to Mrs. George S. Nixon, September 1, 1914).

48. *GT*, February 26, 1915. For Tonopah Banking Corporation, see *GT*, January 21, 1918, and Blair, "Days Remembered of Folsom," p. 47.

49. The authoritative mining journal, San Francisco's *Mining and Scientific Press*, praised GCMC's candor about the difficulty of properly estimating ore reserves in 1912 (*GT*, February 8, 1912). The New York Stock Exchange controversy is reported in the market publication, *New York Curb*, May 10, June 7, June 21, 1913; but see also *GT*, June 9, 1913. Burch's comments are reported and commended in *GT*, January 14, 1914. For GCMC generally, see Spilman, "Drama and Romance in Story of Goldfield Mines," *NSJ*, July 6, 1936.

50. *GT*, August 17, 1915, March 10, 1916 (source of quotation). For the Goldfield Consolidated Mines Exploration Company (GCME), see correspondence files under that title beginning in 1917, as well as correspondence with E. A. Julian in the GW Papers. Julian continued to supervise the San Francisco office until his death. GCME was officially reabsorbed into GCMC in 1936.

51. The 1917 GCMC report was quoted in *GT*, March 29, 1918. GW to Clarence A. Sage, October 18, 1918. The decline of Goldfield was further symbolized by

the reduction in the capital stock of John S. Cook & Co., from $250,000 to $150,000, late in 1917 (*GT*, January 12, 1918). GCMC's successor in Goldfield was the Goldfield Development Company, headed by H. G. McMahon, which purchased some GCMC properties and leased others beginning on February 1, 1919 (*GT*, January 31, 1919).

52. Clarence F. Burton to Mrs. GW, September 29, 1913. The *San Francisco Examiner* headline, dated from internal evidence, was kindly shared with me by Jean Wingfield's daughter Melinda Price. For the hand-rolled cigarettes, see *NSJ*, August 16, 1976, and interview with George Wingfield, August 19, 1983, Reno, Nevada. For Wingfield's personal attention to his correspondence, see Robert Lawrence, "George Wingfield," *Town Talk* 9 (November 1912); *NSJ*, March 23, 1914, p. 5. The *Tribune* was quoted in *GT*, June 2, 1913; *San Francisco Chronicle*, May 17, 1929.

53. *REG*, May 5, 1914, p. 8; *NSJ*, May 8, 1914, p. 8. George Wingfield, Jr., was born May 4, 1914, and died November 11, 1987, in Reno, Nevada. *San Francisco Examiner*, May 18, 1916, p. 1; *NSJ*, July 24, 1917, p. 8; *San Francisco Examiner*, July 24, 1917, p. 5; *NSJ*, September 25, 1917, p. 8. Details of the property agreement are disclosed in the records of the hearing, case #12,702 in Second Judicial District Court, contained in the George Bartlett Papers.

54. *San Francisco Chronicle*, May 10, 1918, p. 1; *San Francisco Examiner*, May 18, 1918, p. 11. The damage to Maude Wingfield's nose was presumably another instance of GW resorting to violence when provoked, as Baric had charged. GW to W. H. Metson, June 14, 1918; *San Francisco Examiner*, October 9, 1918, p. 6; *San Francisco Chronicle*, October 9, 1918, p. 8; *NSJ*, November 8, 1918, p. 6.

55. *REG*, March 23, 1914, p. 5; *NSJ*, February 5, 1914, p. 8. The justification for horse racing comes from *San Francisco Chronicle*, November 18, 1919, p. 10; but see also *GT*, April 2, 1917, where GW is quoted: "In our appeal for favorable legislation to restore the racing game in various sections of the country we have pointed out the necessity to encourage the breeding industry, so that a high standard of horse would be raised for the cavalry."

56. For community opposition to horse racing, see Anne H. Martin to [Anna Howard] Shaw, May 17, 1915, Nevada Equal Franchise Society Papers, NHS, Reno. Martin attributed Wingfield's support of racetrack gambling to Wingfield's desire "to postpone the day when *women* should exercise their influence." GW to Hoyt, Gibbons & French, August 31, 1914; *NSJ*, August 15, 1915, p. 6; *GT*, March 13, 1916; GW to A. Frankenthal, March 28, 1919. One of the English horses they purchased was the famous stallion Honeywood, which was considered one of the best horses in the country in 1916 and was sold in 1919 for $12,000. Throughout his life GW bred cattle, horses, dogs, and even hogs. For these activities, in addition to the Churchill Creamery stock importation, see Nevada Stock Farm records and records of the Spanish Springs Ranch belonging to the Reno Securities Company, GW Papers.

57. *NSJ*, May 15, 1915, p. 1. Anne Martin suggested that, in order to secure this bill, Wingfield traded votes that also secured passage of the reduced residency period for divorce; Martin to Shaw, May 17, 1915. For a discussion of Wingfield's political maneuvering on these issues, see chapter 8. For the Nevada Derby, see *NSJ*, August 1, 1915, p. 8. For the State Racing Commission, see correspondence files with that title in the GW Papers.

58. Al Paulsen provided information about GW's perusal of his breeding library in an interview on November 22, 1988, Reno, Nevada. Burch's remark was made to Wingfield's son, George Wingfield, Jr. (George Wingfield, Jr., to Peter L. Bandurraga, February 18, 1983 [in the possession of the author]). Details of the defense offer are in *GT*, April 2, 1917. For Wingfield's racing venues, see *Denver Post*, June 20, 1915; *GT*, July 21, 1915; *San Francisco Chronicle*, January 12, 1916, p. 49; GW to KP, December 1, 1917; *San Francisco Chronicle*, October 22, 1920, p. 14; and records of the Nevada Stock Farm in the GW Papers. For famous NSF horses, see GW to J. C. McKay, May 15, 1923; Tasker L. Oddie to GW, May 12, 1924; *Nevada the Silver State* (Carson City: Western States Historical Publishers, 1970), p. 846; and Wingfield, Jr., to Bandurraga. According to Tommy Thompson in "Saddle Chatter," GW's NSF never ranked below seventh among money-winning thoroughbred stables in the nation (undated newspaper clipping in the author's possession, dated from internal evidence ca. 1953). For GW's betting on horse races, see correspondence with Al Frankenthal and Hoyt Smith, who placed bets on his behalf, respectively, in New York and Chicago.

59. Records for RSC in the GW Papers include correspondence files related to RSC affairs and records of the company from 1915 to 1955. Initially Wingfield, Burton, and rancher H. G. Humphrey (owner of the Union Land and Cattle Company) were co-owners of RSC. The three men subscribed a total of $15,000 in cash to purchase the Hotel Golden, which they took over from the Golden family at a total cost of $291,000. The initial down payment was made up of $8,500 from Humphrey, $4,000 from Burton, and only $2,500 from GW. By 1919, Wingfield had bought out his partners and acquired full control of the company. In addition to the hotel, GW took over a number of other properties from the estate of Frank Golden, who died in 1911, including Reno real estate along the south bank of the Truckee River.

60. My observation about Wingfield's strong economic interest in what would later be characterized as tourism is far from original. For a view of his involvement as somewhat more perfidious than I consider it in subsequent chapters, see William L. Rowley, "Reno and the Desert of Buried Hopes," in *East of Eden, West of Zion*, ed. Wilbur S. Shepperson (Reno: University of Nevada Press), pp. 117–133; and Walter Van Tilburg Clark, "Reno, the City State," in *Rocky Mountain Cities*, ed. Ray B. West, Jr. (New York: W. W. Norton, 1949), pp. 29–53.

Chapter Seven: "Probably the Wealthiest Man in Nevada"

1. The chapter title comes from a 1932 radio broadcast, "The Story of Gold, Chapter No. 51," by Ray B. Harris of Goldfield, the text of which is in the GW Papers. This chapter is concerned primarily with Wingfield's economic activities. GW's acquisition and exercise of political power are discussed subsequently in chapter 8.

2. *San Francisco Call*, December 6, 1912, p. 1. George B. Thatcher, later GW's attorney, was appointed to succeed Baker.

3. For the threatening letters, see *GT*, July 9, 1915, and *NSJ*, July 14, 1915, p. 1.

4. The Boyd Moore fight, in which GW knocked Moore out and broke his nose in two places, is reported with glee to KP, by an unsigned correspondent, November 4, 1915, KP Papers ("Awful sorry to have our enemies fighting among themselves"). The description of GW's swearing comes from an interview with Robert Drake (October 6, 1989). CFB to GW, September 9, 1915.

5. Arthur Thomas to Lou Gordon, June 24, 1927. Confirmation of Thomas's appraisal of Wingfield is offered by Harold S. Gorman, a former Reno National Bank employee, in "Recollections of a Nevada Banker and Civil Leader" (Oral History Program, University of Nevada, Reno, 1973): "He always made a comment that if there was going to be any drinking or gambling done, he'd take care of that and the rest of us would leave it alone" (p. 20). For examples of Wingfield temporarily quitting drinking, see GW to TLO, December 28, 1926; Pearl to George Bartlett, July 8, 1930, Bartlett Papers. The Woodburn-Thatcher incident was recounted by William Woodburn, Jr., October 4, 1985, in an interview at Reno, Nevada. Information on GW's ultimate success in quitting comes from interviews with GW, Jr., March 24, 1984, and Al and Alice Hardy Paulsen, November 22, 1988, both in Reno, Nevada.

6. Frank P. Murphy to Ogden Mills, enclosed in Murphy to A. A. Hartmann, March 17, 1930, Virginia and Truckee Railroad Collection, Special Collections Department, University of Nevada, Reno (henceforth V&T Collection). Wingfield's health is documented in passing comments to correspondents and employees throughout his life. Spurred by May Baric's allegations in her lawsuit, and apparently substantiated by Wingfield's frequent hospitalizations at the Adler Sanitarium in San Francisco, rumors were rampant that he had syphilis. Although there is no evidence in the GW Papers to support this assertion, venereal disease would not be inconsistent with the rough life that Wingfield led as a young man. The first effective method to control syphilis was discovered in Germany in 1909 and used by American physicians beginning in 1910, according to Allan M. Brandt, *No Magic Bullet: A Social History of Venereal Disease in the United States since 1880*, revised edition (New York: Oxford University Press, 1987), p. 40.

7. For "Betsy," see Norman Biltz, "Memoirs of 'The Duke of Nevada': Developments of Lake Tahoe, California and Nevada; Reminiscences of Nevada Political and Financial Life" (Oral History Program, University of Nevada, Reno, 1969), p. 56. The gun's make was provided by Virgil Wedge in an interview conducted on November 3, 1989, in Reno, Nevada. According to Wedge, GW was not unusual in this regard. Most lawyers in Tonopah and Goldfield in that era customarily carried sidearms. GW's suits were custom-tailored to accommodate his pistol, according to William Woodburn, Jr. References to the Bohemian Club and its annual frolic, known as "The Jinks," are scattered throughout the GW Papers.

8. For the Tonopah Divide Mining Company, see correspondence between H. C. Brougher and GW. See also *Salt Lake City Tribune*, August 30, 1912; *GT*, October 14, 1916, January 23, April 1, 1918; *NSJ*, March 29, 1918, p. 5; *San Francisco Examiner*, May 29, 1919, p. 8; March 28, 1919, p. 7; GW to Alfred Frankenthal, March 28, 1919. For the banking situation, see Blair, "Days Remembered of Folsom," pp. 47–48.

9. For the strike, see Blair, "Days Remembered of Folsom," p. 56; Scrugham,

Nevada, vol. 1, pp. 518–525; GW to S. C. Mitchell, August 18, 1919: "At any rate we don't intend to give them an inch. Will close down everything first and stay closed until such time as conditions change"; also telegram, GW to Mitchell, August 19, 1919: "Close all our properties and keep them closed until further orders"; both of the latter in the possession of Alan Metscher, Tonopah, Nevada. GW believed the strike was caused by the IWW; GW to Alfred Frankenthal, August 20, 1919. The Simon Lead incident is reported by the *San Francisco Examiner*, May 29, 1918, p. 8. Accounts such as this helped create the pervasive media image of "Wingfield Luck." See also *San Francisco Examiner*, March 28, 1919, p. 7.

10. For the Goldfield Deep Mines Company, see *GT*, January 31, 1919. For the continuing saga of the Goldfield Hotel, see records of the Bonanza Hotel Company and correspondence with V. L. Ricketts (editor of the *Goldfield Tribune*) in GW Papers; *GT*, March 10, 11, and 29, 1920; Esmeralda County Deeds, Book 3, 41.

11. For the Dolly Varden mine, see *NSJ*, December 30, 1922, p. 6; *GT*, January 8, 1923. For Base Metals, see *NSJ*, February 5, 1929, p. 2; GW to Alfred Frankenthal, January 10 and 18, 1929; GW to Bernard M. Baruch, January 30, 1929. GCMC received 1,300,000 shares in the new company and sold 280,000 of those on the open market. It invested in the California oil fields in 1929. The assessment of GCMC's finances at the decade's end is contained in GW to Bernard M. Baruch, September 20, 1929.

12. For Trent Process Corporation, see correspondence and records in the GW Papers and the KP Papers. GW purchased capital stock in the undertaking then known as the Power Plant Corporation on August 9, 1919. GW to KP, November 12, 1919; KP to GW, November 4, December 21, 1921, KP Papers.

13. CFB to GW, August 9, 1920; GW to Stanislaus C. Mitchell (henceforth SCM), April 6, 1922. For GW representation by others, see GW to SCM, December 17, 1922.

14. For developments in 1923, see CFB to GW, February 26, June 25, 1923. Pittman's statement about protecting Wingfield is found in KP to GW, January 10, 1926, KP Papers. For details of the company's new fuel, see EAJ to GW, December 30, 1926; J. W. Hutchinson to EAJ, January 30, 1928; GW to Guy Standifer, August 15, 1929.

15. Information on SCM comes from *GT*, May 13, 1920; SCM to H. C. Brougher, May 17, 1920; GW to William E. Zoebel (henceforth WEZ), December 26, 1925; as well as from his personal correspondence with GW.

16. For Wingfield's running battle with the Internal Revenue Service, see tax returns and correspondence in regard to taxes in the GW Papers. For one example of an ongoing argument, as to whether Wingfield's activities qualified him as a stockbroker, so that any losses on stock sales were not deductible from his income, see CFB to E. C. Yellowsley, October 16, 1918.

17. For Zoebel, see *Who's Who in Nevada: Biographical Dictionary of Men and Women Who Are Building a State* (Reno: Who's Who in Nevada Publishing Co., 1931), vol. 1, p. 63, and extensive personal correspondence with GW. Mitchell and Zoebel both ran the Corporation Securities Company, created in 1920 to try and realize something from the apparently worthless investments made by the defalcating cashier

of the Tonopah Banking Corporation. When Wingfield became a stockholder of the Tonopah bank, he took over all the questionable security and consigned it to his new secretaries with instructions to recover from it whatever they could.

18. For GW's economic caution, see GW to CFB, July 5, 1920. For his purchase of the Humphrey interests, see GW to Wellington Gregg, June 15, 1921. The Churchill County Creamery sale is covered in Townley, *Turn This Water into Gold*. For the banks, see *NSJ*, August 6, 1921 (Churchill County); August 11, 1921 (Virginia City); CFB to GW, February 8, 1921 (Bank of Sparks); *NSJ*, December 15, 1919, p. 8, and records of the Hotel Humboldt Company (First National Bank of Winnemucca).

19. For Knowles and Sheehan, see *GT*, November 24, 1923.

20. GW's active supervision of his banks is evident after reading any of the bank correspondence files in the GW Papers. A representative example is the Churchill County Bank, whose cashier, Ernie W. Blair, was a longtime Wingfield bank employee and exceptionally responsive to Wingfield's desire to be consulted about all decisions.

21. GW to Wellington Gregg, vice-president, Crocker National Bank, June 15, 1921; Gregg to GW, June 21, 1921.

22. *San Francisco Examiner*, November 28, 1921, p. 11; James Garland to SCM, November 9 and 26 (source of quotation), December 6, 1921; GW to W. E. Johnson, December 20, 1921; GW to William H. Metson, July 14, 1922. For the resignation, see GW to Metson, June 23, 1922. The issue of this resignation and varying interpretations of its cause are considered in chapter 8. GW to SCM, December 25, 1922: "Am still in bed and don't know how long it will be before I can get out. I have terific [*sic*] pains in the back of my neck and over my right eye. especially of a morning. am getting very tired of it. [all punctuation *sic*]"

23. WEZ to GW, October 17, November 12, 1924; *NSJ*, November 13, 1924, p. 8.

24. WEZ to GW, February 9, 1925. The Center Street bridge campaign is covered in more detail in chapter 8. For the bond election, see *REG*, December 31, 1925, p. 8. GW billed the county $24,000 for the portion of the lots north of the courthouse that they agreed to purchase, unsigned memo [WEZ to GW], December 3, 1925. For a malevolent view of these sales, with GW "forcing" the county to pay him money for the lawn adjacent to the county courthouse, see Laura Vitray, "Choice of Lethal Gas or Life Is Reno's Way of Guarding Blood Gold," *New York Evening Graphic*, July 13, 1931, p. 4. GW announced the decision to build the Riverside Hotel after consulting his bankers at Crocker: GW to J. B. McCargar, vice-president, Crocker First National Bank, May 26, 1926. The figure on the Riverside's value comes from GW to TLO, March 8, 1927.

25. GW's continued interest in mining is obvious in the pattern of his private investments and the activities of GCMC, especially its exploration subsidiary. For his lobbying for federal reclamation dollars, see GW's extensive correspondence regarding the proposed Spanish Springs project: e.g., GW to Emmet D. Boyle, January 28, 1924; GW to TLO, January 28, April 11, 1924, March 3, 1926; SCM to John F. Richardson, February 5, 1924; True Vencill to GW, January 3, 1925. Wingfield believed that Spanish Springs, along with a proposed private project he was involved

in on the Humboldt River at Red House, would be a great blessing to Nevada: "[the Humboldt Project] is going to help out that section of the country immensely and with the Spanish Springs Project going through I think Nevada will be able to hold her own irrespective of other developments" (GW to TLO, April 11, 1924).

Walter Van Tilburg Clark made insightful observations about the development of an incipient tourist industry in post–World War I Nevada in "Reno, the City State." The same article also contains an atmospheric depiction of the Reno underworld in the 1920s, which was confirmed by Robert A. Drake, a Reno resident at the time, in an interview on October 6, 1989, Reno, Nevada. For a view of GW's involvement in tourism as more malevolent, see Rowley, "Reno and the Desert of Buried Hopes." GW was by no means the only Nevadan interested in promoting tourism. Governor James G. Scrugham, for instance, began an active campaign to induce people to visit Nevada in connection with the pageants celebrating the 2,000-year-old pueblo ruins at Lost City, Nevada, in 1925 and 1926. See Thomas Woodnutt Miller, "Memoirs of Thomas Woodnutt Miller, A Public Spirited Citizen of Delaware and Nevada" (Oral History Program, University of Nevada, Reno, 1966) p. 196; Marie Harrington, *On the Trail of Forgotten People* (Reno: Great Basin Press, 1985), pp. 160–173.

26. The phrase, with its overtone of disapproval, comes from "Passion in the Desert," p. 128. The development of Nevada's divorce industry is traced in Anita Watson, "Tarnished Silver: Popular Image and Business Reality of Divorce in Nevada, 1900–1939" (M.A. thesis, University of Nevada, Reno, 1989).

27. GW's speech is quoted in *Carson City News*, February 17, 1914.

28. *GT*, August 9, 1914.

29. J. D. Finch to KP, February 17, 1915, KP Papers.

30. See chapter 6 for the details of Wingfield's stand on horse racing. Anne Martin suggested that, in order to secure his horse racing bill in 1915, GW traded votes that also secured passage of the reduced residency period for divorce, Martin to [Anna Howard] Shaw, May 17, 1915, Nevada Equal Franchise Society Papers, NHS. For Nevada racing profits, see records and correspondence of the Nevada State Racing Commission, of which GW was a founding member. The biggest single year was 1923, when the total take from two Reno race meets was $1,771,843 and the state's share $23,624. The comment on people coming to town for the races is from GW to Hoyt P. Smith, July 10, 1929.

31. GW to J. H. Miller, September 7, 1916.

32. Unsigned note, WEZ to GW, January 31, 1925. For the 1927 bill, see Watson, "Tarnished Silver," pp. 49–51. Wingfield's attendance at the legislature was noted by WEZ to Alfred Frankenthal, March 17, 1927. The comment on haste is from *NSJ*, March 19, 1927; Frank P. Murphy to Ogden Mills, March 30, 1927, V&T Collection.

33. On Nevada road building, see Scrugham, *Nevada*, vol. 1, pp. 452–453, 498–502, 525–526, 545–547; Elliott, *History of Nevada*, pp. 264–265.

34. On the Mt. Rose matter, GW issued a memo clearly stating his strategy:

The Mt. Rose project must be recognized by the Nevada State Administration and also by the Federal Bureau as a new and independent project so that work can be started, even if it can not be provided for or completed at once. It is up to

Governor Balzar to do everything possible to get this started so far as the State is concerned. Senator Oddie will handle the Federal end of it in Washington, which appears to be a difficult proposition under the present system of securing an extra appropriation after the regular appropriations bills are passed.

This memo was included in correspondence to both TLO and governor-elect Fred B. Balzar. See GW to TLO, December 11 and 28, 1926. Fred B. Balzar to GW, January 6, 1927, in response to Wingfield's lobbying, states that "the state administration will do all in its power to further this road"; Governor's Papers, Nevada Division of Archives and Records, Carson City, Nevada. Oddie had a long history of interest in good roads, dating back to his days as governor. In 1928, he secured passage of the Oddie-Colton Public Domain Highway Act and the Oddie-Colton Forest Highway Act, which greatly increased the amount of federal highway funds available to Nevada. Both bills were vetoed by Coolidge but were signed in 1930 by Hoover.

35. GW to J. B. McCargar, July 29, 1926; unsigned memo, WEZ to GW, January 9, 1925; WEZ to TLO, January 28, 1928; Arthur Thomas to GW, January 31, 1928. GW's interest in building up Reno involved him in various undertakings. For example, in 1928 he had RSC invest in five proprietary memberships in the city's new golf club, and in July 1929 he invested in 500 shares of stock in the new Nevada Airlines.

36. GW to TLO, February 21, 1927. For some of the flavor of the debate about Reno's new economy, see George Wharton James, "What's the Matter with Nevada?" *Outwest* 7 (April 1914): 173–182.

37. Information on Dodge Brothers and Dudley is found in correspondence files in the GW Papers. For Nevada Surety and Bonding Company, see the company records series, GW Papers. In fact GW's company functioned mainly as an agency, writing bonds for other, larger bonding companies outside the state.

38. For GW's activities at Elko, see *Elko Independent*, February 23, 1919. For Quartz Mountain, see GW to James Garland, April 17, 1926. Garland wrote enthusiastically to GW in May that he had the San Francisco exchange "all 'pepped up' and the boys are all 'raring' to go. . . . There is a much improved feeling here in regard to mining stocks and inasmuch as all the other markets are dull and quiet, we can put over another mining deal. The time is ripe and if you have some luck, in having the San Rafael ore body go down in depth, we can successfully 'shoot' things and get away with it" (May 21, 1926). For the fate of the mining operations, see the records of the San Rafael Development Company and San Rafael Consolidated Mines Company, GW Papers.

39. GW's loans from Crocker are documented in annual notes from the audit department in the correspondence files, which also document his relationship to William H. Crocker.

40. GW to William H. Crocker, July 15, 1929.

41. For details of GW finances, see his financial records in the GW Papers, as well as records of the Wingfield Trust Fund. The 1925 income figure comes from an unsigned memo, WEZ to GW, November 27, 1925. Each year the Wingfield office paid corporation license tax for all the companies it was responsible for. The 1927 list

is dated June 23. GW's estimate of his fortune comes from grand jury testimony he delivered on April 10, 1935.

42. Information on GW's habits and his wife's establishments comes from interviews with GW, Jr., August 19 and 26, 1983, March 24, 1984, Reno, Nevada. The San Francisco home was located at 2324 Pacific Avenue. After one of his inspection tours of the hotels, GW issued testy instructions: "The elevator girls should not read books and magazines on duty. I have seen them doing this several times and it looks like the management could see these things without me having to call their attention to it" (GW to WEZ, June 20, 1928).

43. GW's generosity is amply documented in his correspondence files. For his generosity to his mother, see [Martha M. Wingfield] to GW, November 6, 1926, asking if he would mind if she donated a recent gift of stock to the church: "It was very much of a supprise [*sic*] to me, and very lovely in you. and I thank you." Walter Hawkins's story was recounted to me by his son, Jim Hawkins, in a telephone interview, July 19, 1991. Specific gifts were reported to the author in interviews with Eva Adams (labrador dog), Virgil Wedge (hunting rifle), and William Woodburn, Jr. (automobile).

44. For GW loans, see, e.g., TLO to GW, March 1, 1921, asking to borrow $1,500 to cover medical expenses; J. P. Hennessy to GW, January 10, 1925, seeking money to cover defalcations by an employee involved in "the very thing that you warned against, namely bootlegging." The caution about too much charity is from GW to J. P. Hennessy, May 18, 1925.

45. For Belle Isle, see *GT*, December 5, 1914; Reno City Council Resolution #326, January 27, 1920, in the GW Papers; *NSJ*, January 17, 1920, August 19, 1976. The fact that Martha Spradling Wingfield never tasted alcohol was relayed by her grandson, George Wingfield, Jr., in an interview on March 24, 1984, Reno, Nevada. According to GW, Jr., his grandmother refused even a taste offered to her on her ninetieth birthday. For the 1928 restoration, see *NSJ*, March 27, 1928; Walter E. Clark, president, University of Nevada, to GW, April 2, 1928.

46. *NSJ*, May 17, June 6 and 7, October 2 and 9, 1928. For Wingfield's disinterest in getting credit for his gifts, see Gorman, "Recollections of a Nevada Banker," p. 48.

47. *NSJ*, July 12, 1927; Thornton, "George Wingfield," p. 48. For Wingfield's career as a regent, see correspondence files 1927–1938. In 1928, he donated the cost of a retaining wall along the irrigation ditch that ran through the campus, at an estimated cost of $3,700 to $4,500 (Walter E. Clark to GW, April 2, 1928). Wingfield was defeated for reelection in 1938.

48. GW to J. F. Shuman, May 16, 1927; GW to Hoyt P. Smith, January 14, 1927. The comment about "old hens," apropos of opposition to the Riverside Bank from other Reno bankers, is from GW to TLO, March 8, 1927. In an interview on December 28, 1988, former Riverside Bank assistant cashier Joe Fuetsch recounted the fact that the Riverside Bank was established partly to keep the business of long-term hotel residents away from the rival First National Bank, which otherwise would have been the bank closest to the new hotel. Reno's population rose fifty percent between 1920 and 1930, from 12,000 to 18,000.

49. GW to TLO, March 8, 1927. See also petitions and copies of letters accompanying unsigned memo, WEZ to GW, March 13, 1927. Wingfield's interest in this bill is presumably the principal reason that GW was attending the 1927 legislative sessions. For slot machine profits see unsigned memo, WEZ to GW, December 31, 1925. The Golden slot machines netted $8,003, for instance, in 1923, and $11,102 in 1924, although only $1,614 in 1925, due to constant harassment by "the reformers," for which see unsigned memos, WEZ to GW, March 24, July 18, October 16, November 27. In the last Zoebel expostulates: "My information now is that the University bunch is responsible for the closing of the games. They appointed a committee of 5 to visit all of these places, and one of them tipped it off to Kirkley who passed the word around before they made their rounds, with the result that everyplace [*sic*] was closed when they came. They are wondering how the word got out. Everything is still closed tighter than a drum and you couldn't even make a bet here on the ponies yesterday."

50. Laura Vitray, "Reno's Divorce Machine Cuts the Splice on One Couple Each 5 Minutes," *New York Evening Graphic*, July 8, 1931, p. 4. For Reno gambling in the period before legalization, see Raymond I. Sawyer, *Reno, Where the Gamblers Go!* (Reno: Sawston Publishing Co., 1976); [C. F. Burton] to Hon. W. C. Adamson, May 25, 1916; GW to C. F. Burton, January 25, 1917; Basil Woon, *Incredible Land: A Jaunty Baedecker to Hollywood and the Great Southwest* (New York: Liveright Publishing, 1933), p. 229.

51. Unsigned memo SCM to GW, November 27, 1923; *Elko Independent*, July 7, 1928; Frank Murphy to Ogden Mills, March 1, 1927, V&T Collection.

52. For GW support of antiprohibition groups, see John J. Donnelley to GW, June 25, 1917; unsigned letter [possibly CFB] to Frank Golden, Jr., May 19, 1919. Wingfield's 1924 statement comes from GW to Clemens Horst, August 8, 1924. The political controversy over prohibition, involving U.S. district attorney George Springmeyer, as well as John Donnelley, is covered in chapter 8.

53. For the McKay raid, see *GT*, December 17, 1923; *Carson City Appeal*, March 17, 1924. GW's memo to CFB about taking over the Golden's whiskey is worth quoting at length: "There is a little #6 whiskey at the hotel. have this put in a large jug and kept for me. Whiskey has took another raise and I hear all Bonded whiskey is to be took over by the Gov't. raise the price on Scotch and Cocktails to 25 [cents] as there is nothing in it for less [all punctuation *sic*]" (GW to CFB, April 25, 1918). Nevada's prohibition initiative passed by a margin of 4,000 votes out of more than 22,000 cast. The measure took effect in December 1918. For the raid on GW's house, see Atkinson, "Tonopah and Reno," p. 70; GW to TLO, March 21, 1930. GW was not alone in his opposition to prohibition. Nevada voters passed two antiprohibition initiative measures in 1926.

54. GW to TLO, December 18, 1923; GW to J. P. Hennessy, January 10, 1925; SCM to GW, December 30, 1922; unsigned memo, WEZ to GW, August 24, 1925.

55. Unsigned memo, WEZ to GW, January 20, 1926. For an evocative depiction of Reno during this period, including the world of the racetrack and the nightclub, see Walter Van Tilburg Clark's novel, *City of Trembling Leaves* (New York: Random House, 1945), esp. pp. 70–85, 339–358.

56. For GW's toe, see F. G. Willis to GW, July 25, 1927. For the divorce, see suit #24222, Washoe County Clerk's Office, Reno, Nevada; *San Francisco Chronicle*, June 4, 1927, p. 1; *NSJ*, August 22, 1927, p. 6.

57. Wingfield's attendance during his wife's illness is chronicled in the *NSJ*, March 20, 1928, p. 8; but see also George B. Thatcher to Theodore Roche, December 19, 1928. Details of the property settlement were sealed by the court, but are contained in an agreement dated May 16, 1929, in the possession of the Wingfield family. The lump-sum payments were to cover more than $33,000 in outstanding bills. Maude Murdoch Wingfield later remarried, becoming Mrs. Paul Hamlin. She predeceased her first husband, dying in 1952.

58. GW to J. B. McCargar, January 6, 1928. The 1928 bank earnings figures are found in GW to W. W. Jones, February 25, 1929; GW to TLO, January 16, 1929. For the banker's comment on the hotels, see J. B. McCargar to GW, March 6, 1928. For the Henderson Banking Company building, see *NSJ*, April 10, 1928, p. 2. The quotation is from GW to W. W. Jones, February 25, 1929.

59. For the 1927 sugar beet attempts, see Arrington, *Beet Sugar in the West*, p. 187; *Lassen Advocate*, October 29, 1926; Blair, "Days Remembered of Folsom," p. 75.

60. GW to Walter R. Bracken, January 9, 1928 [1929], December 14, 1928; *NSJ*, December 30, 1928, p. 1; unsigned memo, WEZ to GW, January 10, 1929. The Boulder Canyon Project Act was signed by President Coolidge on December 21, 1928.

61. GW to Walter R. Bracken, March 28, 1929. GW's comment about his Las Vegas plans is from GW to Bracken, January 9, 1928 [1929]. The fulsome praise for Wingfield's genius is from Leigh Hunt to Walter Bracken, June 10, 1930, and relates to the potential founding of a new national bank, rather than to the hotel. It was typical of the sentiment of some Las Vegas development interests, however, including Bracken himself.

62. GW to Bracken, June 10, 1929.

63. GW to W. G. Willis, July 5, 1929; GW to W. W. Jones, July 6, 1929; *San Francisco Bulletin*, July 31, 1929, p. 2.

64. GW to W. W. Jones, July 6, 1929; GW to W. G. Willis, July 15, 1929; GW to E. S. Jernegan, August 8, 1929; Herbert Fleishhacker to GW, August 8, 1929.

65. *NSJ*, July 16, 1929, p. 1; GW to Crocker First National Bank Note Department, August 10, 1929; Crocker First National Bank Note Department to GW, August 13, 1929; GW to W. W. Jones, August 14, 1929.

66. GW to TLO, July 25, 1929; *San Francisco Bulletin*, July 31, 1929, p. 2.

Chapter Eight: Playing the Game

1. Amy Gulling, former Republican national committeewoman, "Interview," p. 79; Woon, *Incredible Land*, pp. 227–228.

2. Gulling, "Interview," p. 81.

3. The close-knit nature of Nevada politics was observed both by contemporaries (e.g., "Passion in the Desert") and by historians of the period (e.g., Jerome E. Edwards, "Wingfield and Nevada Politics—Some Observations," *Nevada Historical*

Society Quarterly 32 [Summer 1989]: 126–139). For Wingfield's personal loans, which have been previously mentioned, see the list headed "Notes Charged Off," in his files for 1918. In a list of sixty-four names, several bear the notation from CFB, "You instructed me not to bother him."

4. GW to KP, May 13, 1917, KP Papers; *GT*, August 9, 1914.

5. *GT*, July 23, 1914; GW to A. C. White, July 27, 1914. For more detail on Wingfield's political positions on the three issues of divorce residency, horse racing, and woman suffrage in 1914–1915, see chapter 7. E. E. Roberts to GW, July 17, 1914. GW's appeal to the state's business interests is from a speech to a cattleman's banquet in Reno, quoted in *Carson City News*, February 17, 1914.

6. GW advocated applying business principles to government even in January, when he was not running for office and emphatically denied having any political ambitions. See *Lakeview* (Oregon) *Examiner*, January 15, 1914. The Fallon meeting is reported in the *Carson City News*, March 14, 1914. For GW's political philosophy, see *GT*, August 9, 1914. GW to E. E. Roberts, August 6, 1914.

7. *NSJ*, August 16, 1914, p. 6; *REG*, August 15, 1914, p. 1. For Wingfield buying the banking properties of the Nixon estate, see *NSJ*, October 12, November 20, 1914. CFB to GW, December 28, 1914.

8. See handwritten note, GW to WEZ, January 29, 1925; GW to True Vencill, January 27, 1927.

9. GW to J. H. Miller, September 7, 1916.

10. For the sample ballots, see GW to A. H. Westfall, November 2, 1916. Handwritten note, GW to CFB, February 17, 1917.

11. For Mueller, see Scrugham, *Nevada*, vol. 2, pp. 205–206; *REG*, August 1, 1963. For the recruitment, see John V. Mueller to George Bartlett: "Not long ago I was in Thatcher's office with Mr. Wingfield and he asked me to go to work for him. He did not make any proposition at the time but told me to see him later" (April 15, 1926, Bartlett Papers). The father-son relationship was noted by Eva Adams in an interview, November 7, 1987, in Reno, Nevada. Admiration for Mueller's talent was widespread, shared in interviews by Marshall Giusti (June 16, 1989), Peter Echeverria, who as a legislator was lobbied by Mueller (March 30, 1988), and John Sanford (March 19, 1988). His *REG* obituary in 1963 noted that Mueller was registered as a Republican, but exercised considerable influence in both parties in the legislature.

12. For Mueller's association with Getchell, see *NSJ*, December 6, 1939. Cahlan's description is from *Las Vegas Sun*, September 26, 1967.

13. "If Harry Atkinson [being considered for U.S. district attorney for Nevada] were living here, he would be the logical man for he has more sense than most of them and can always be depended on to play the game" (GW to TLO, February 10, 1926). GW to TLO, March 3, 1926.

14. GW to C. J. Travers, November 5, 1926.

15. GW to TLO, December 28, 1926.

16. For contrasting partisan accounts of the Reno meeting where Wingfield was selected, see *GT* and *Carson City Appeal*, both April 26, 1920. The former extolled the choice of Wingfield as neutral, while the latter suggested more coercion: "All through Saturday's session the steam roller was in evidence. It was worked with a considerable

degree of finesse and left no jagged wounds, but it cut deep. Consequently, the healing process will be slow." Wingfield was the unanimous choice only after the withdrawal of Sam Platt. The quote about service comes from *GT*, April 14, 1920. Wingfield's "principals" were described in an undated draft of his biography for the National Committee, in the 1920 political file, GW Papers. The 1920 Republican convention trade is detailed by Miller, "Memoirs," p. 77.

17. *GT*, June 15, November 1, 1920. For GW's role in supervising the 1920 campaign, see GW to TLO, October 18, 1920, TLO Papers, NHS: "You will see some good results from the places I have visited. I will go to Fallon and Virginia City before election. I shall go to S.F. tomorrow for a further conference. I will assure you that every thing is being done that can be done."

18. For GW financial involvement with Oddie, see, e.g., TLO to GW, March 1, 1921; Carroll Henderson to SCM, January 6, 1922; GW to TLO, April 16, 1924. By 1930, Oddie's total indebtedness to Wingfield, which dated back to 1917, exceeded $25,000; see Memorandum, T. L. Oddie Note, November 17, 1932, GW Papers. Correspondence in the GW Papers on matters of political patronage is substantial beginning in 1921, and virtually nonexistent, except for the occasional request for recommendations, before then.

19. GW to TLO, August 11, 1912, TLO Papers, Huntington Library. For "conservation blight," see *Owens Valley Herald* (Bishop, California), March 22, 1912. Wingfield's animus against Roosevelt is explained in *NSJ*, May 12, 1912. Oddie's biographer sees him as Wingfield's stooge: "Throughout the decade, Tasker Oddie played the role that the machine and his own personality assigned him: a dutiful lieutenant" (Loren Chan, *Sagebrush Statesman: Tasker L. Oddie* [Reno: University of Nevada Press, 1973], p. 170). Though Wingfield's power and influence in Nevada were considerable, the tone of the extensive correspondence between the two men in the GW Papers suggest an instinctive political congruency more than a political boss giving orders.

20. TLO to GW, March 15, 1927; GW to TLO, March 19, 1927.

21. GW to W. V. Hodges, September 30, 1926. One admiring party worker observed that Wingfield was probably the only man who could afford to be the national committeeman because of the necessity of attending national conventions and meetings; Merialdo, "Memoirs," pp. 74–75.

22. For the bands at political rallies being paid by GW, see Lester J. Hilp, "Reminiscences of a White Pine County Native, Reno Pharmacy Owner, and Civil Leader" (Oral History Program, University of Nevada, Reno, 1968), p. 11; GW to J. Grant Crumley, June 23, 1922. A rare note of appreciation was sounded by San Francisco banker William H. Crocker, who was also a national committeeman: "I know that the Republican Party owes to you solely the victory which you secured on election day. I am thankful that you kept your membership in the National Committee, and I hope that you will continue to take an interest in this line of work. We can hold the radicals down if men like you will continue to interest yourselves in the political welfare of our country" (William H. Crocker to GW, November 6, 1924).

23. For GW's successive elections to the post of national committeeman, see TLO to GW, May 12, 1924; *NSJ*, April 25, 1928, p. 8.

24. GW to TLO, February 4, 1924, March 24, 1926.

25. Frank Murphy to Ogden Mills, August 30, 1926, V&T Collection. Wingfield's political practices were pragmatic. In the 1924 presidential campaign he and other Nevada Republicans encouraged circulation of a petition to nominate Robert LaFollette on a third-party Progressive ticket. They reasoned that a LaFollette candidacy would draw away from the Democratic candidate, John W. Davis, votes that President Calvin Coolidge couldn't get under any circumstances. See GW to William M. Butler, July 22, 1924.

26. Regarding the Spanish Springs Project, the economic reasons are contained in GW to TLO, December 4, 1924, and the political rationale in GW to C. B. Slemp, February 25, 1924. The remark about meritorious legislation comes from the former of the two letters.

27. Blair, "Days Remembered of Folsom," p. 43.

28. For the bipartisan machine, see my article "GW's Political Machine," which covers the range of prevailing views on the matter. See also Edwards, "Wingfield and Nevada." Oral histories of Wingfield contemporaries almost all discuss the machine. John Sanford, "Printer's Ink in My Blood," pp. 45–46. Graham Sanford was a sometime Wingfield opponent and aspirant to Republican party office. During the financial chaos that followed the collapse of Wingfield's banks in 1932, Sanford and the *Gazette* were active in defeating Wingfield's plans for reorganizing and reopening the banks.

29. For information on Thatcher and Woodburn, see Scrugham, *Nevada*, vol. 2, pp. 9–11, 204–205; unsigned memo [GW] to Jerry Sheehan, November 5, 1924; Atkinson, "Tonopah and Reno"; *NSJ*, October 16, 1946, January 24, 1957.

30. Handwritten memo, GW to SCM, January 5, 1923. The chronology of the Thatcher and Woodburn firm, including Woodburn's comment, was recounted in some detail by the two principals in the course of testimony before a federal investigator in 1934. See U.S. Congress, Senate, Subcommittee of the Committee on the Judiciary, *Hearings*, 73rd Cong., 2nd sess, 1934, pp. 5–6. Both Thatcher and Woodburn died before GW, the former in 1946 and the latter in 1957.

31. For Thatcher and Woodburn's political influence, see Woodburn's obituary, *NSJ*, January 24, 1957. The opinion that Thatcher was especially close to GW, who was generally a loner, was advanced by John Sanford in an interview on March 19, 1988, Reno, Nevada. It is confirmed by evidence in the GW Papers, where most of the correspondence and references to Wingfield's attorneys are specifically to Thatcher. Elliott, *History of Nevada*, p. 270.

32. Telegram, GW to John T. Adams, Republican National Committee Chair, June 6, 1922; *NSJ*, June 11, 1922, p. 6; GW to J. Grant Crumley, June 23, 1922.

33. *San Francisco Examiner*, June 11, 1922, p. 14; TLO to GW, June 12, 1922; GW to William H. Metson, June 23, 1922; GW to TLO, June 24, 1922.

34. For Pittman's membership in the Pacific Coast Bear Club, see KP to E. C. Brown, December 28, 1909, KP Papers. Woodburn's claim of responsibility for GW's resignation is in William Woodburn to KP, July 3, 1922, KP Papers. The text of the petition, undated, is in the GW Papers, 1922 political file. Clarence Oddie confirmed GW's support for Pittman, reporting to his brother that "his [GW's] real reason for resigning is due to his ill health and to the further fact that he is reluctant to conduct

the campaign this Fall against Key Pittman" (Clarence M. Oddie to TLO, June 19, 1922, TLO Papers, NHS).

35. William Woodburn to KP, October 16, 1922, KP Papers; GW to John T. Adams, September 25, 1922; GW to KP, November 15, 1922; GW to John T. Adams, November 14, 1922.

36. "G.W. [*sic*] . . . is dead against Scrugham and is going to make a determined effort to elect Johnnie Miller [for governor]. It is likely that before it is over that on account of us fellows standing with Scrugham that he may get in and support the whole Republican ticket, but he won't have much luck in view of the fact that a great many of his associates have already committed themselves to vote for you" (William Woodburn to KP, August 29, 1922, KP Papers). Pittman's claim comes from a letter to his brother Vail, May 21, 1926, KP Papers: "[Wingfield] embarrassed me very much in the presence of the assembled crowd by stating that he voted for me last election and intended to vote for me again. This is the first time he ever made such a statement, and he probably would not have made it then if he had been entirely calm." For Republican organization, see William Woodburn to KP, August 21, 1921, KP Papers: "There is no question but what they are going to organize; in fact, they are organizing right now" (KP to GW, November 3, 1922, KP Papers).

37. The comment about Oddie's election is from KP to Vail Pittman, May 21, 1926, KP Papers. I am grateful to Bob Nylen of the Nevada State Museum for bringing this important letter to my attention. In 1921, Pittman requested from Wingfield letters to certain key Republican senators in support of an amendment that Pittman had offered. The amendment had to do with reducing taxation on shares of stock worth less than $100, a matter in which both KP and GW had an obvious financial interest (KP to GW, November 4, 1921, KP Papers).

38. Anne Martin, "Nevada: Beautiful Desert of Buried Hopes," *Nation* 115 (July 26, 1922): 89–92. The 1923 city election is discussed at length by Rowley in "Reno and the Desert of Buried Hopes" and *Reno: Hub of the Washoe Country* (Ontario: Windsor Publications, 1984).

39. GW to J. C. McKay, May 15, 1923.

40. GW to TLO, April 20, 1923. In fact, Roberts did challenge Oddie for the Republican senatorial nomination in 1926. Roberts was also supported by Democratic party leaders Thatcher and Woodburn, GW's attorneys. The latter claimed that "we were actively supporting Roberts as a liberal before Wingfield took any part" (William Woodburn to KP, May 18, 1928, KP Papers).

41. Clark, "Reno, the City State," p. 43. Walter Van Tilburg Clark, who wrote the description, was the son of University of Nevada president Walter Clark, who congratulated GW for his generosity during the 1928 flood. For Graham and McKay, who are figures of legend in Reno history, see their obituaries, *REG*, June 21, 1963 (McKay), and November 6, 1965 (Graham). Oral histories are also revealing, including H. H. Atkinson; John F. Cahlan, "Reminiscences of a Reno and Las Vegas, Nevada, Newspaperman, University Regent, and Public-Spirited Citizen" (1970); William Fisk Harrah, "My Recollections of the Hotel-Casino Industry and as an Auto Collecting Enthusiast" (1980); McDonald, "Life of a Newsboy"; Peter C. Petersen, "Reminiscences of My Work in Nevada Labor, Politics, Post Office, and Gaming

Control" (1970), all Oral History Program, University of Nevada, Reno. Harrah, for instance, obviously knew both Graham and McKay well, though he knew GW only to say hello to him. The description of the two men is Harrah's, confirmed by McDonald and Petersen. Details of the fraud scheme can be found in Gorman, "Recollections." Graham's remark is from McDonald, p. 104.

42. Petersen, "Reminiscences," p. 61. Evidence of Wingfield's lifelong friendship 'with McKay is scattered throughout the GW Papers. In 1957, for example, McKay was repaying a loan of over $5,000 from Wingfield (see GW Revolving Fund Ledger, 1953–1960). Although at least one oral history account associates Wingfield with both Graham and McKay (Cahlan, "Reminiscences," p. 41), it was only the latter with whom he corresponded. And when George Cole and Ed Malley arrived at Wingfield's home in 1927, it was only McKay, and not Graham, who was visiting the bedridden Wingfield. See GW testimony reported in *NSJ*, September 13, 1927, p. 2. Some of the political costs of GW's association with McKay were evident in the 1928 election campaign, covered below.

43. For rumors about the Reno Social Club, see Sanford, "Printer's Ink," pp. 55–56. For the Riverside Securities Company, see GW to James G. Scrugham, January 10, 1929. For the bank loan, see GW to J. Sheehan, July 1, 1926. For other disavowals of business connections with Graham and McKay, see WEZ to Jay L. Wickham, May 9, 1928; WEZ to Palace Dry Goods House, January 15, 1929; SCM to GW, November 26 and 27, 1923. See also *REG*, November 27, 1923, p. 6.

Evidence for Wingfield's lack of involvement is largely circumstantial. GW took an exceptionally active role in overseeing the management of every business venture he was involved in; but there is absolutely *no* evidence in the GW Papers of his interest in either the Reno Social Club or the Riverside Securities Company. It would have been uncharacteristic of him to have a financial stake without active participation, and he certainly did not need the money that such illicit ventures would presumably have brought him. After his move to Reno and respectability, mindful of the notoriety that his colorful past had already occasioned, Wingfield carefully kept his distance from such questionable activities. Even when gambling was legal, he had no stake in Graham and McKay's Bank Club, which leased its quarters in the Hotel Golden on a month-to-month basis.

44. One of GW's bank employees, Joseph Fuetsch, reported in an interview in 1989 that he thought GW "tolerated" Graham and McKay rather than approving of them. GW was certainly not alone in his support for legalizing alcohol and gambling. In 1925, the Nevada legislature passed a resolution calling for a constitutional convention to amend the eighteenth amendment, and Democratic governor James G. Scrugham acknowledged the difficulty of enforcing laws against "practices recently made illegal, such as public gambling and the liquor traffic." See Scrugham, *Nevada*, vol. 1, pp. 549–551.

45. GW to TLO, January 27, 1927.

46. GW to TLO, March 8, 1928.

47. GW to TLO, January 5, July 26, 1922. Wingfield was responsible for Donnelley's appointment as well (telegram, GW to TLO, June 22, 1921; GW to TLO, July 9, 1921). For another version of the Springmeyer affair, which differs consider-

ably in tone although not in substance from mine, see Zanjani, *Unspiked Rail*, pp. 250–325.

48. The remark about Donnelley's scalp is from GW to TLO, May 18, 1923. The comparison of Reno to Washington, D.C., is from GW to TLO, December 18, 1923, and of Nevada to other states from GW to TLO, May 30, 1923. Springmeyer's quip is quoted in TLO to GW, December 12, 1923.

49. Both quotations are from GW to TLO, December 18, 1923. The proposed resignation, which never came, was discussed in TLO to GW, January 12, 1924; GW to John T. Adams, January 21, 1924; and GW to TLO, January 21, 1924. For the Veteran's Bureau offer to Springmeyer, see Miller, "Memoirs," pp. 219–220; George Springmeyer to TLO, January 18, 1924 (copy in GW Papers).

50. For Springmeyer's promises to "be good," see GW to TLO, February 29, 1924. Springmeyer's threats against the Republican leadership are discussed in GW to TLO, February 10 (source of quotation), April 13, 1926. The comparison of Springmeyer and Atkinson is from GW to TLO, March 24, 1926. For Atkinson's appointment, see GW to TLO, March 6, 1926, TLO to GW, April 3, 1926; GW to TLO, April 13, 1926.

51. For the bond election, see *REG*, December 31, 1925, p. 8. Zoebel's efforts on behalf of the bridge were reported to GW throughout 1925 in unsigned memos in the GW Papers. The quotation is from WEZ to GW, June 4, 1925.

52. Unsigned memos, WEZ to GW, June 17 (source of quotation), June 15 (sporting element), November 28 (apathy), December 1, 1925 (campaign).

53. See unsigned memos, WEZ to GW, November 30, December 4, 9, and 11, 1925; William Woodburn to GW, December 17, 1925. The newspaper difficulty is traced in William Woodburn to GW, December 19, 1925. Roberts's analysis of the opposition and Barbash's ambition are reported in unsigned memo, WEZ to GW, December 20, 1925. GW to WEZ, December 20, 1925; WEZ to GW, December 21, 1925. Wingfield's letter is dated December 19, 1925, in draft.

54. Unsigned memo, WEZ to GW, December 26, 1925; GW to James G. Scrugham, January 2, 1926, Governor's Papers, Nevada Division of Archives and Records, Carson City.

55. Unsigned memo, WEZ to GW, October 27, 1926: "Roberts has had abundant funds provided by the gambling interests of Reno [pointedly *not* including GW], but am reliably informed that they are very tired of their bargain and their present contributions are being given under protest" (Frank E. Murphy to Ogden Mills, August 30, 1926, V&T Collection). For Roberts, see also Murphy to Mills, October 27, 1926, V&T Collection.

56. For Fleishhacker's financial backing, see unsigned memo, WEZ to GW, October 19, 1926; Frank Murphy to Ogden Mills, September 24, 1926, V&T Collection. For GW contributions, see Murphy to Mills, September 24, October 27, 1926, V&T Collection. The latter is also the source of the quotations about Pittman's role in the 1926 campaign.

57. *REG*, June 2, 1926. For Scrugham's campaign, see Frank Murphy to Ogden Mills, October 13, 1926, V&T Collection. Murphy surmised that Scrugham jeopardized his own campaign by using his state political organization to back Baker in the

senatorial race. The admiring account of the 1926 state campaign is from Merialdo, "Memoirs," p. 75.

58. Frank Murphy to Ogden Mills, October 13, 1926, V&T Collection, is the source of the information on Wingfield's turn around the circle. Congratulatory letters include GW to Noble Getchell, November 5, 1926, Noble Getchell Papers, Special Collections Department, University of Nevada, Reno; GW to C.J. Travers, November 5, 1926.

59. The Cole-Malley scandal is covered succinctly in Edwards, *McCarran*, pp. 33–42. GW gave a detailed account of his actions at the time during the August 1927 trial of Cole and Malley (*REG*, September 1, 1927, p. 1; September 3, 1927, p. 1).

60. Statement made by H. C. Clapp to GW, May 10, 1927, GW Papers.

61. George Thatcher was a good friend of Democrats Cole and Malley, a fact which GW knew. When the matter first developed, GW gave Thatcher the option of withdrawing from the case, but after conferring with Woodburn, Thatcher advised GW that "they saw no reason why they should not continue as their first duty was to their client." Apparently GW thought it better to retain them than to risk their withdrawal, "which would leave them completely beyond control." These conversations and conclusions were reported in Edward Bergner to GW, June 17, 1927 (in the possession of the Wingfield family). William H. Crocker to GW, May 4, 1927. GW to William H. Crocker, May 3, 1927, contains the details of the collateral Wingfield gave to secure the Crocker loan.

62. GW to William H. Crocker, May 3, 1927. In fact there was disagreement about liability for the shortage. Thatcher and Woodburn assumed that the bank would have to stand the entire loss, while Shuman and the Crocker attorneys advised GW that he should offer to pay only one-third of the total amount. They reasoned that the bank should be liable only for the amount of Clapp's shortages (approximately $67,000) and GW's obligation on the officials' bonds ($75,000). Documents on the legal strategy are in the possession of the Wingfield family, including Memorandum, Thatcher & Woodburn to GW, June 8, 1927; and J. F. Shuman to GW, August 15, 1927.

63. "Statement of Geo. Wingfield, President of the Carson Valley Bank," May 7, 1927. For the timing of the release of the statement, see telegram, GW to bank cashiers, May 7, 1927; GW to TLO, May 10, 1927. According to records in the possession of the Wingfield family, GW had the Carson Valley Bank keep careful track of withdrawals following the announcement. For the first two days these averaged approximately $27,000 daily, but by May 10 they had fallen to less than half that level. See also Frank E. Murphy to Ogden Mills, May 11, 1927, V&T Collection: "while there were some few withdrawals they were comparatively light. . . ."

64. GW to William H. Crocker, May 5, 1927. The private investigator's records and reports are in the possession of the Wingfield family, including J. F. Shuman to GW, May 18, 1927; Edward Bergner to GW, May 18, 1927; Bergner to GW, June 17, 1927. One thing GW probably *wasn't* prepared for was an anonymous letter mailed on May 11, 1927, at Reno, which attacked Thatcher and Woodburn: "You have one attorney that is a rank Catholic and who has made some remarks already. Wont [sic] you please put a protestant attorney with them; *Don't trust them.*"

65. GW to Hoyt P. Smith, May 25, 1927. For GW's liability on Malley's bond, see GW to Frank Shuman, June 17, 1927. The Cole-Malley trial began on August 15, 1927, and was covered by both Reno newspapers. For the conviction, see *NSJ*, September 11, 1927; *REG*, September 12, 1927. McCarran was also the attorney for the Nevada Signal Hill Oil Company, where much of the money Cole and Malley embezzled had gone.

66. McCarran was not the only one to voice suspicion of GW. Los Angeles attorney Gilbert F. Boreman sent a confidential letter to attorney general Diskin speculating that the Cole-Malley money was invested in GW's Quartz Mountain mining companies. Boreman further charged that GW had known of the shortage for some time and was scheming to shift the liability to the state. See Boreman to Diskin, May 14, 1927, Attorney General's Papers, Nevada Division of Archives and Records, Carson City. I am grateful to Chris Driggs for bringing this letter to my attention. McCarran's plea is quoted in *NSJ*, September 11, 1927 (summation), and *REG*, September 12, 1927 ("They know what I want"). McCarran conveniently glossed over the fact that GW would be liable as Malley's bondsman if the two men were convicted of criminal wrongdoing.

67. GW to J. F. Shuman, September 7 and 12, 1927; telegram, William H. Crocker to GW, September 12, 1927. All three men involved in the Cole-Malley scandal were released from prison in 1931 by the Nevada Board of Pardons.

68. GW to Fred B. Balzar, November 26, 1927. This public letter was carefully planned, and Frank Shuman in San Francisco, among others, was asked to comment on a draft version, GW to J. F. Shuman, November 21, 1927.

69. See "Memorandum," "Comments on Special Session," November 30, 1927; GW to J. B. McCargar, December 1, 1927. The Singer Sewing Machine representative's opinion (all punctuation *sic*) was reported in Paul M. Hursh to GW, December 3, 1927; *Carson City News*, December 6, 1927, attached to J. H. White to GW, December 6, 1927.

70. John G. Kirchen to Fred Balzar, December 7, 1927, copy in GW Papers. A complete list of the business interests represented by such letters is in *REG*, January 21, 1928, p. 1.

71. *REG*, January 23 and 31, 1928, p. 1; *NSJ*, February 4, 1928, p. 1. Thatcher and Woodburn had long advised the special session, arguing that "the legislature will take a very kindly view of your position, particularly in view of the fact that you have acted so handsomely in this matter up to this point. Neither of us believe that it will be the disposition of the legislative committee to treat you unfairly, no matter what your obligations might be under the strict letter of the law" (memorandum, Thatcher & Woodburn to GW, June 8, 1927, in the possession of the Wingfield family).

72. The text of GW's letter, from which the quote is drawn, is reprinted in *REG*, January 21, 1928. Sanford's editorial is from *REG*, January 25, 1928. At least one prominent opponent of the Cole-Malley compromise settlement, M. C. Hamlin of Mineral County, had also vigorously opposed the 1927 gambling bill that Wingfield was associated with (*REG*, January 24, 1928).

73. For comment on the Board of Examiners, see Nevada State Legislature, "Report of the Joint Committee on Investigation of Closed Banks," March 13, 1933: "it

was largely due to a similar laxness on the part of a prior board of examiners in exercising the functions assigned to it by statute that the Cole-Malley defalcation remained so long undiscovered . . . if any lesson were to be learned from the prior instance, it was the one of guarding against the loose administration of public affairs by public officers, boards and commissions" (p. 22).

74. GW to S. S. Arentz, November 21, 1927; Margaret Bartlett to "Big Boss," June 13, 1928.

75. GW to TLO, February 13, 1928. Frank Murphy to Ogden Mills, July 7, 1928, V&T Collection.

76. GW to the People of Nevada, August 20, 1928. For GW's lobbying efforts see, e.g., GW to Walter J. Cox, September 22, 1928; GW to M. L. Requa, October 6, 1928; GW to Dick Vanetta [*sic*], September 24, 1928. The Hoover rumor is reported in GW to A. H. Lawry, September 24, 1928, Central Nevada Historical Society, Tonopah, Nevada. GW's self-characterization is from GW to S. S. Arentz, November 21, 1927. For a general assessment of GW's campaign activities by a nonparticipant, see Frank Murphy to Ogden Mills, September 8, 1928, V&T Collection: "Wingfield is very much interested and naturally ambitious to win out"; September 28, 1928: "George Wingfield is very much in earnest in his work to put over the entire republican ticket."

77. GW to Hubert Work, September 18, 1928. *Las Vegas Review*, July 11, 1928; *Humboldt Star*, July 10, 1928. Statement "Given to the Gazette," July 17, 1928, GW Papers.

78. For the 1928 editorial campaign, see GW to Hubert Work, October 6, 1928; Archie Trewick to Editor, *Elko Free Press*, October 8, 1928. Blake's editorial is quoted in the latter. Arthur B. Waugh, "Bootleggers and Bone Drys Form Unholy Alliance for Hoover in Sagebrush State," *Sacramento Bee*, October 18, 1928, p. 1; Waugh, "Wingfield Uses Strangle Hold on Nevada to Secure Votes for Herbert Hoover," *Sacramento Bee*, October 19, 1928, p. 1.

79. *Sacramento Bee*, October 19, 1928; GW to Hubert Work, October 6, 1928. Murphy to Ogden Mills, October 28, 1928, V&T Collection. For Nevada reprints, see, e.g., *Nevada State Herald* (Wells), October 26, 1928.

80. Frank Murphy to Ogden Mills, October 28, 1928, V&T Collection; Waugh, October 18, 1928. Even within Republican circles, the involvement of Graham and McKay was controversial. See Jake Wainwright to GW, October 23, 1928: "The main thing as concerns this important campaign before us is that the Republican party must bear the stigma of the support of McKay and Graham and they are not delivering the vote which they are credited with. . . . All these boot leggers hoars [*sic*] and pimps know is force. I suggest the club to insure the vote where it should belong to a Republican administration that has tolerated this element."

81. GW to Hayden Henderson, October 6, 1928. This direct request for political involvement by bank employees below the level of cashier was unusual and indicates the extremity of Wingfield's irritation. Joseph Fuetsch, for example, who was assistant cashier of the Riverside Bank, reported during an interview on December 28, 1988, that GW never exerted any political pressure on him, either directly or indirectly.

82. William Woodburn to KP, May 18, 1928, KP Papers.

83. J. J. McNeary to GW, October 11, 1928.

84. GW to the People of Nevada, October 25, 1928. See GW to M. L. Requa, October 15, 1928: "Pittman eventually answered my letter [of August 20] through a circular, or attempted to, but I shall trim his sails up as he does not quote facts by any means, which I can prove through the Congressional Record, so I will have to go after him on this."

85. Frank Murphy to Ogden Mills, December 10, 1928, V&T Collection.

Chapter Nine: *"Thousands Hate Him"*

1. Chapter title from editorial, *Santa Barbara Daily News*, February 14, 1933. Worried eastern correspondents included Alfred Frankenthal of New York and Hoyt P. Smith of Chicago; see Frankenthal to GW, October 3, 1929. For the political impetus of the stock market crash, see GW to Frankenthal, November 9, 1929. Wingfield's rhetoric is from GW to Smith, January 27, 1930.

2. For GW economic activities, see GW to Bernard M. Baruch, March 18, 1930; GW to A. Frankenthal, March 29, 1930; unsigned memo [WEZ to GW], January 16, 1930; GW to W. W. Jones, February 26, 1930. WEZ to Charles P. Weigand, March 1, 1930.

3. GW to Walter Bracken, June 6 and 28, 1930; GW to TLO, January 7, 1930. For GW's loan transactions with Crocker First National Bank (henceforth CFNB), see CFNB to GW, July 25, 1930, January 14, July 3, 1931. GW to Raymond Benjamin, September 4, 1931.

4. GW to TLO, February 26, 1930; GW to Walter R. Bracken, January 22, 1930.

5. GW to Hoyt P. Smith, April 29, 1932; GW to Walter R. Bracken, January 22, 1930.

6. See GW to TLO, January 7 and 20, February 26, 1930.

7. GW to TLO, January 20, 1930; GW to Fred Balzar, May 9, 1931, Governors' Papers, Nevada Division of Archives and Records, Carson City.

8. Roxy Thoma had at one time dated Bertram Nixon, the son of Wingfield's partner George S. Nixon.

9. I am indebted for accounts of the courtship and marriage to Alice Hardy Paulsen and Royce Hardy, Roxy Thoma Wingfield's niece and nephew. See also *San Francisco Chronicle*, July 27, 1930, p. 1, and GW personal financial records for 1930 in the GW Papers.

10. Impressions of the Thoma-Wingfield marriage were shared in interviews by Jordan Crouch, Peter Echeverria, Royce Hardy, Al and Alice Hardy Paulsen, and Virgil Wedge. Joe Fuetsch reported that he and his bride were given the massive dining room set formerly owned by Maude Wingfield.

11. For the Taylor episode, see M. L. Requa to GW, September 2, 1929; GW to Requa, September 4, 1929; GW to TLO, July 1, 1930; TLO to GW, July 17, 1930. For the state Republican convention, see GW to Requa, June 24, 1930. GW to F. B. Balzar, March 18, 1931.

12. GW to TLO, February 4, 1929. For the arrangements on the *Journal*, see GW

to E. W. Campbell, January 19, 1929 (source of quotation); GW to W. W. Chapin, May 18, 1929. GW to TLO, June 4, 1930.

13. *Elko Independent*, July 17, 1928; Woon, *Incredible Land*, p. 228; Glasscock, *Gold*, p. 291.

14. Impressions of political insiders include Charles H. Russell, "Reminiscences of a Nevada Congressman, Governor, and Legislator" (1967), p. 179; Milton B. Badt, "An Interview with Milton Badt" (1965), p. 77; Biltz, "Memoirs," p. 130; all from the Oral History Program, University of Nevada, Reno. See also Gorman, "Recollections," pp. 29–30.

15. *Ely Daily Times*, March 7, 1931, p. 4. I am grateful to Eric Moody of the Nevada Historical Society for calling the Pittman editorial to my attention.

16. GW to Walter R. Bracken, June 13, 1930; *NSJ*, March 19, 1931; *REG*, March 19, 1931. The vote in favor of the gambling bill was 24-11 in the Assembly and 13-3 in the Senate. The divorce bill had even less opposition, no opposing votes in the Assembly and only 1 in the Senate.

17. GW to W. W. Jones, March 21, 1931; *REG*, March 21, 1931; F. B. Balzar to GW, September 3, 1931.

18. Information on the fight comes from Laura Vitray, "Dempsey Divorce and Fight Merely Reno Sucker Baits," *New York Evening Graphic*, July 18, 1931, p. 4. "Of course, I have personally nothing to do with any of the gambling rackets or anything in that line": GW to Judson Douglass, March 30, 1931. For the Bank Club relocation, see GW to Hoyt Smith, March 30, 1931. According to Raymond Sawyer, the basement operation had consisted of card games only, while the ground floor Bank Club boasted an elaborate bar, oil paintings, faro layouts, and a roulette wheel (*Reno*, p. 23).

19. Paul Hutchinson, "Nevada—A Prostitute State," *Christian Century* 48 (November 25, 1931): 1488–1490; Laura Vitray, "Reno Is Big Gold Mining Camp; Vice Sieve Nets Suckers' Coin," *New York Evening Graphic*, July 3, 1931. Even outraged critics of the wide-open laws conceded that the majority of Nevadans favored them. Paul Hutchinson, for example, observed: "There is a strong *minority* in the state which is opposed to the open gambling and prostitution, and would like to see the divorce laws drastically changed"; but admitted that the majority favored them (p. 1489, emphasis added). For condemnation of Nevadans' profit motives, see both Hutchinson and Vitray. The former sadly concluded in "Can Reno Be Cured?" that only a failure to profit could put an end to the divorce and gambling businesses.

20. The quote about GW is from Woon, *Incredible Land*, p. 227.

21. The *New York Evening Graphic* series ran from July 1 through 24, 1931. It was also reprinted in other papers, including the *Philadelphia Ledger*.

22. Arthur Thomas to WEZ, July 28, 1931; Cornelius Vanderbilt, Jr., to GW, December 22, 1931.

23. GW to Hoyt P. Smith, August 5, 1931. *Business and Commerce*, August 15, 1931, p. 7. Anthony M. Turano, "Nevada's Trial of Licensed Gambling," *American Mercury* 28 (February 1933): 192; "Passion in the Desert," p. 106.

24. "Passion in the Desert," p. 106; GW to WEZ, May 22, 1931.

25. GW to Alfred Frankenthal, March 21, 1931; GW to Hoyt P. Smith, June 17,

1931. The postlegalization boom is well documented in the GW Papers and was confirmed by John Sanford (son of *Reno Evening Gazette* editor Graham Sanford) in an interview, March 19, 1988, Reno, Nevada. For the race meet, see Nevada Racing Commission to Governor Balzar, June 30, 1932.

Nevada gambling continued to evolve over the years. Beginning in the late 1930s, it was refined and extended to a mass market of middle-class Americans by the Smith family at Harold's Club and by Bill Harrah in a succession of clubs. These gambling pioneers filled the void between the backroom games and the Graham and McKay nightclubs and attracted a whole new audience to Reno. Las Vegas club owners in the 1950s further expanded the market by offering big-name entertainment and creating a series of destination resorts. Despite these changes in style, however, a recent popular history of Nevada gives credit to GW for his pivotal role in shaping the modern state: "Wingfield's influence, combined with others, produced Nevada's famed legalized gambling, the constitutional prohibition against the imposition of a state inheritance tax, and other progressive laws which changed Nevada from a largely agriculturally oriented state to one which attracted many of the country's wealthy to make Nevada their legal residence, and which led to the development of the tourist industry as seen today" (*Nevada the Silver State*, p. 846).

26. The term "king" was used by both Vitray and *Fortune*. "Whirlpool of vice" is the former's term. The description of cowed Reno citizens comes from Paul Hutchinson, in "Reno—A Wide-Open Town," *Christian Century* 48 (December 2, 1931): 1520.

27. KP to Mrs. John G. Kirchen, October 23, 1931; GW to KP, February 11, 1932, both KP Papers. For Cole's reluctance, see the latter, as well as KP to B.M. Aikins, April 13, 1932, KP Papers. GW's profit prediction comes from GW to KP, May 5, 1932, KP Papers, which is also the source of the final quotation.

28. For the varying fortunes of the Nevada livestock industry, see Clel Georgetta, *Golden Fleece in Nevada* (Reno: Venture Publishing Company, 1972), pp. 403–425; Young and Sparks, *Cattle in the Cold Desert*; and U.S. Congress, Senate, *Report on the Western Range*, 74th Congress, 2nd Session, 1936, S. Doc. 199: 119–133, 193–211. Cattle prices and yields come from C. A. Brennen, *The Main Reasons Why Range Cattle Ranchers Succeed or Fail* (Reno: University of Nevada, Agricultural Experiment Station Bulletin #133, September 1933), p. 7.

29. GW to TLO, November 6, 1929. GW's bank administrators, including J. O. Walther and C. P. Weigand, were busy compiling comparative statistics and recommending changes in banking legislation throughout this period. For the itemized list of loans, see typewritten memoranda from individual banks dated February 12, 1930, and handwritten cover sheet dated February 10, 1930, in the banking correspondence file, GW Papers. For the Taylor loan, see "Memorandum to Crocker First National Bank," February 16, 1931. For Taylor, see Sessions Wheeler, *The Nevada Desert* (Caldwell, Idaho: Caxton Printers, 1971), pp. 121–148.

30. GW's own loans and the certificates of deposit at Henderson Banking Company are extensively documented in the CFNB correspondence files, but see GW to F. G. Willis, July 25, September 17, October 17, 1930, October 17, 1931. The amount on deposit was verified in a 1933 audit, see George K. Edler to CFNB, March 6, 1933.

31. R. C. Turrittin's activities and reports are documented in correspondence files under his name for 1930 and 1931 in the GW Papers. See also GW to F. G. Willis, November 16, 1931. For the freight reductions, see J. F. Shaughnessy to GW and Cecil Creel, September 24, 1931.

32. GW to R. C. Turrittin, January 29, 1932.

33. GW to R. C. Turrittin, October 26, 1932. This letter was written less than one week before the closure of the Wingfield banks. GW's growing desperation and desire to reduce the livestock loans is evident in correspondence with his bank cashiers: see especially records of the First National Bank of Winnemucca and Henderson National Bank. Observers of the scene agreed that Wingfield might have saved his banks if he had acted harshly at the beginning of the decade (see Georgetta, *Golden Fleece*, p. 404). Cecil W. Creel, in his *History of Nevada Agriculture*, points out that Nevada agricultural returns in 1932 were only $7.5 million, representing a loss of almost $12 million from the 1929 figures (Carson City: State Printing Office, 1964, p. 21). Statistics on the Wingfield banks' livestock loans are from Susan Kennedy, *Banking Crisis of 1933* (Lexington: University of Kentucky Press, 1973), p. 62.

34. WEZ to W. H. Marshall, January 11, 1932. For Pony Express days, see Sam Garrett to GW, April 10, July 19, October 20, 1932.

35. The 1931 loans are documented in CFNB to GW, August 30, 1935. Of that total, less than $100,000 had been repaid by the date of the letter. For the salary reductions, see EAJ to GW, September 1, 1931; GW to C. P. Weigand, May 6, 1932. GW to Walter R. Bracken, August 21, 1931; GW to Raymond Benjamin, October 29, 1931; GW to TLO, January 2, 1932.

36. GW to E. A. Montgomery, January 11, 1932. For a representative exchange on the old notes, see WEZ to P. M. McLeroy, June 17, 1932; P. M. McLeroy to WEZ, June 24, 1932.

37. The Sutter Butte Canal Company was one of EAJ's principal responsibilities, and details concerning its finances can be found in his correspondence files, as well as those bearing the company names. The problem is described in EAJ to GW, February 5, 1932. For the Boundary Red Mountain Mining Company, see GW to W. J. Tobin and H. A. Streeter, Receivers, June 17, 1933.

38. TLO to GW, May 3, 1932. The Wingfield banks had borrowed almost $590,000 from the Federal Reserve Bank and slightly over $215,000 directly from CFNB.

39. Scrugham, *Nevada*, vol. 2, p. 14. The banking crisis is summarized in James S. Olson, "Rehearsal for Disaster: Hoover, the R. F. C., and the Banking Crisis in Nevada, 1932–1933," *Western Historical Quarterly* 6 (April 1975): 149–161, from which the statistics on loan defaults are drawn. GW himself gave the statistic on falling deposits as part of the U.S. District Court hearings on his proposed bank reorganization. See Attorney General's Records, George Wingfield Stockholder's and Director's Liability, 1932, Nevada Division of Archives and Records, Carson City. For the gourmet shopping list, see GW to Goldberg, Bowen Co., August 20, 1932.

40. Jean Wingfield Filmer's assessment of Roxy Wingfield's role was recounted by Alice Hardy Paulsen. The quotation is from GW to R. C. Turrittin, October 26, 1932.

41. Olson, "Rehearsal for Disaster," p. 152; GW to TLO, January 29, 1932.

42. For the Reconstruction Finance Corporation, see James S. Olson, *Herbert*

Hoover and the Reconstruction Finance Corporation, 1931–1933 (Ames: Iowa State University Press, 1977), on which this account heavily relies. GW to TLO, January 27, 1932.

43. The rumors are reported by F. M. Murphy to A. A. Hartmann, February 19, 1932, V&T Collection. Murphy's opinion was that the RFC loans should stabilize the situation, but he reported with surprise that the Reno National Bank was calling the V&T loan. Detailed records of the individual transactions can be found in the *Index to the Minutes*, Reconstruction Finance Corporation Records, National Archives, Washington, D.C. For a summary of the RFC dealings with Wingfield's banks, see Olson, "Rehearsal for Disaster" (quotation from p. 155), and *Herbert Hoover*, pp. 94–95.

44. Telegram, Governor Calkins to Talley, July 26, 1932, in RFC Records, vol. 6, pp. 1014, 1179. The transfers from Bank of Nevada to Reno National were controversial for several reasons, including the fact that no consideration was given. The items were simply carried on the Bank of Nevada books as "available assets," while actually being pledged by Reno National to the RFC. After the collapse, the receiver of the state bank sued to set aside the assignment by Reno National to the RFC. See RFC *Minutes*, vol. 26, p. 5809, RFC Records, where the Bank of Nevada receiver also charged that the RFC knew about the transfers when the loans were made.

45. T. E. Harris to GW, July 5, 1932. For TLO's efforts, see TLO to GW, June 2, 1932: "I immediately took the matter up with General Dawes [president of the RFC] and asked him especially to watch out for the applications when they came in from you and to arrange to have them expedited and the red tape cut" (Jesse H. Jones with Edward Angly, *Fifty Billion Dollars: My Thirteen Years with the Reconstruction Finance Corporation (1932–1945)* [New York: Macmillan, 1951], pp. 42–43).

46. Information on the precarious condition of the Reno National comes from a conversation with GW reported by F. M. Murphy to A. A. Hartmann in New York, November 1, 1932, V&T Collection. Balzar's testimony is recorded in "Proceedings before the Board of Directors of the Reconstruction Finance Corporation, at a Meeting Held on November 1, 1932, at 11:00 A.M." in the RFC Records.

47. The comments of Reno businessmen were reported by F. M. Murphy to A. A. Hartmann, the New York businessmen representing the owners of the Virginia and Truckee Railroad, in a letter dated November 1, 1932, V&T Collection.

48. *REG*, November 1, 1932, p. 4.

49. For LeRoy and McKee, see Balzar's RFC testimony, pp. 2–3; *REG*, November 3, 1932, p. 1. Coverage of the crisis occupied the front pages of both *REG* and *NSJ* daily after the bank closing of November 1. The *REG* editorial is from November 10, 1932, p. 4.

50. "Glory Hole," *Time* 20 (November 14, 1932): 48; F. M. Murphy to A. A. Hartmann, November 1, 1932, V&T Collection.

51. *New York Times*, December 11, 1932.

52. Harold S. Gorman, who was an auditor at Reno National Bank at the time of its closing, explains in his oral history the differences between chain banking, which the Wingfield banks were practicing, and branch banking. In branch banking one corporation controls the entire operation, and the capital of the main bank supports any loan. In chain banking, by contrast, each little bank may take a piece of a large loan,

but must rely on its own capital to absorb any losses. See "Recollections," p. 38. For details of the reorganization plan, see *REG*, November 19 and 28, 1932, p. 1; *Las Vegas Review-Journal*, November 21, 1932, p. 1 (source of McKee's statement); George B. Thatcher, memorandum, November 9, 1932, in KP Papers.

53. Information about the depositors' meetings, including the request for property conveyed to Roxy, was shared by Les Gray, who attended the Bank of Sparks meeting as a youth, in an interview on September 19, 1989. Both GW's passion and his tears were reported by the *Las Vegas Review-Journal*, November 21, 1932. GW was quoted as offering his shoes in *REG*, November 21, 1932, p. 1, the same article that recounted his borrowing money from Graham and McKay. For a slightly different version, see *Las Vegas Review-Journal*, November 21, 1932, p. 1. In an interview, Robert Drake, who at the time owned a taxi business that kept its money in Reno National, reported a similar promise when he asked GW privately about when he could expect to get his company's money: "Kid, if they'll leave me alone, you'll get your money back." Cheers were reported by the *Las Vegas Review-Journal*, November 29, 1932.

54. GW to WEZ, November 29, 1932.

55. *Minutes*, vol. 10, p. 1339, RFC Records. The description of the depositors' meetings is from F. M. Murphy to A. A. Hartmann, December 3, 1932, V&T Collection.

56. Information about Frisch's banking practices was provided in an interview by Joe Fuetsch, assistant cashier at the Riverside Bank. For confirmation, see F. M. Murphy to A. A. Hartmann, March 20, 1934, V&T Collection. Estimated percentage returns to depositors are from *REG*, November 19, 1932, p. 1. Gorman describes the bitterness of United Nevada Bank depositors, but concludes that the 75 cents GW paid to the Washoe County Bank depositors was in fact generous. See "Recollections," pp. 40–46, for his account of the reorganization.

57. GW to WEZ, November 29, 1932; *REG*, November 22, 23, 24, and 30, December 10, 1932; GW to F. G. Willis, December 2, 1932.

58. Judge Clark J. Guild, who later presided over the state bank reorganization cases, recalled tremendous animosity toward GW. Although Guild did not blame Wingfield for the bank failure, he noted that many others did. See Clark J. Guild, "Memoirs of Careers with Nevada Bench and Bar, Lyon County Offices, and the Nevada State Museum" (Oral History Project, University of Nevada, Reno 1971), p. 139; Russell, "Reminiscences," p. 180. In an interview, attorney Peter Echeverria recalled that many people in Reno seemed to want to blame GW for the entire depression. For losses of GW companies in the banks, see GW to E. J. Seaborn, November 18, 1932. His personal losses are obvious in GW's personal financial records for 1932. His Reno National Bank account had over $2,900 in it when the banks closed, a $3,000 deposit having recently been made. GW opened a personal checking account at Crocker on November 9.

59. Information about the personal attacks on GW comes from interviews with family members Royce Hardy, Al and Alice Hardy Paulsen, and George Wingfield, Jr. Biltz reported in his oral history walking to and from work each day with Wingfield and Mueller, though he tactfully did not mention the drinking binges mentioned by

family members (Biltz, "Duke of Nevada," p. 56). The poem is preserved in the 1933 banking reorganization file in the GW Papers (all spelling and punctuation *sic*). *Santa Barbara Daily News*, February 14, 1933.

60. Roxy Thoma Wingfield later reported that the failure of old friends to speak to him after the bank collapse was her husband's greatest disappointment (*NSJ*, August 16, 1976). GW to Jean Wingfield, November 5, 1932; *NSJ*, November 27, 1932, p. 7; Wally Gelatt to GW, December 16, 1932; Arthur Thomas to GW, December 17, 1932.

61. GW's disregard of politics is obvious in his correspondence with TLO during 1932. It is confirmed by Virginia and Truckee Railroad manager F. M. Murphy, who reported to his employer in New York about the meager Republican campaign finances (F. M. Murphy to A. A. Hartmann, November 1, 1932, V&T Collection). *REG* 2 (source of quotation), November 5, 1932, p. 4; Joseph F. McDonald, "Life of a Newsboy," p. 172.

62. In Tasker Oddie, GW lost not only a political ally, but also a close political friend. When the banks closed, GW returned to TLO his personal note for just over $25,000, representing money which Oddie had borrowed over the years, beginning in 1917 and running through 1926. The banker had never carried it on his books and didn't want Oddie (or himself) to be embarrassed by its disclosure. He sent the note, along with the stock he held as collateral against it, in a letter to Oddie's sister, Sarah, in San Francisco. The latter replied to this action with great feeling: "Once more I should like to express my very sincere appreciation, and to assure you that we do not consider this matter closed by your very generous act of confidence." In fact the note was never repaid, and GW subsequently advanced Oddie additional sums of money as part of this "loan." See GW to TLO, November 17, 1932; Memorandum: T. L. Oddie Note, October 17, 1932; Sarah Oddie to GW, November 21, 1932.

63. Patrick A. McCarran to sister Margaret P. McCarran, February 12, 1933, quoted in Edwards, *McCarran*, p. 51. Shortly after taking office, McCarran wrote formally to GW, indicating his willingness to be "of service" to the Nevada capitalist. He did not offer, however, the kind of political gossip or access that Oddie had provided, and communication between the two men was decidedly formal in nature (Patrick A. McCarran to GW, March 10, 1933).

64. *REG*, December 10, 1932, p. 1; Olson, "Rehearsal," p. 157; GW to EAJ, December 10, 1932.

65. The description of GW is from Arthur Thomas to GW, December 17, 1932.

Chapter Ten: "Hitting the Comeback Trail"

1. "Wingfield Hitting the Comeback Trail," *San Francisco Chronicle*, August 29, 1937, p. 10. Interviews with those who experienced the bank collapse, including especially Robert Drake, Peter Echeverria, and Alice Hardy Paulsen, reflect the prevailing sense of gloom and uncertainty at the time. For the salaries, see Alice Terry, "Recollections of a Pioneer: Childhood in Northern Nevada, Work at the Univer-

sity of Nevada, Observations of the University Administration 1922–1964, WICHE, and Reno Civic Affairs" (Oral History Program, University of Nevada, Reno, 1976), p. 124.

2. For GW's salary from RSC, see Malvina Rice to F. G. Willis, March 26, 1934. For GCMC salary, see Malvina Rice to George B. Thatcher, July 3, 1935. Julian's salary was reduced once again (to $750 monthly) in March 1933. In 1932, due to tuberculosis, possibly aggravated by the stress of financial conditions, WEZ left GW's office for treatment in a San Francisco sanitarium. Initially thought to be near death, he survived in a weakened condition and moved to Arizona. GW continued to correspond with him and to subsidize his medical expenses. Zoebel was replaced by a woman, Malvina Rice (henceforth MR), who served GW capably throughout the 1930s, but functioned primarily as an executive secretary. She was never a political confidante or office manager on the model of either CFB or WEZ.

3. Maude married Chicago capitalist Paul Delano Hamlin on April 26, 1933. Details of the financial settlement with her are in MR to George K. Edler, April 25, 1933. For Sutter Butte Canal Company (SBCC) finances, see GW to E. J. Seaborn, April 4, 1933; EAJ to GW, April 5, 1933; Open Letter to Holders of SBCC Bonds, June 12, 1933; G. S. Burk to GW, September 11, 1933. For the income tax dilemma, see GW to G. K. Edler, March 10, 1933. GW's correspondence with various officials of Crocker, particularly Vice-President F. Gloucester Willis, exhaustively documents his finances from 1932 through 1935. For the GCMC dividend and its use, see GW to B. M. Baruch, October 2, 1933; GW to F. G. Willis, August 31, 1933.

4. GW's preference for quality was recounted in a 1989 interview with Robert Drake. The two checks, for $10,000 on July 18 to the Bank Club and for $6,000 on July 19 to R. P. Kindle (Bank Club manager), are regularly made out and countersigned by MR. They are in the GCMC Records, Series IV, GW Papers; GW to A. Frankenthal, September 22, 1933.

5. *REG*, January 11, February 4, 1933. Telegram, KP to Thatcher & Woodburn, February 4, 1933, KP Papers. Ultimately, three Wingfield banks elected to reorganize separately: Churchill County Bank, Henderson Banking Company, and Wells State Bank.

6. See *REG*, January 5, 1933, p. 8; George B. Thatcher, memorandum, November 9, 1932, KP Papers.

7. *REG*, February 22, 1933.

8. *REG*, February 28, 1933. The reorganization committee initially sought only sixty percent participation from national bank depositors, but the federal legislation which permitted national banks to participate in such reorganizations, which was passed on March 9, 1933, provided that seventy-five percent of all depositors must agree to the plan. See William Woodburn to KP, August 4, 1933, KP Papers. The donated clerical help is reported in *NSJ*, February 28, 1933. Nevada's banking holiday is covered in Georgetta, *Golden Fleece*, pp. 407–410.

9. For GW's denials, see GW to Victor F. Palmer and Forrest W. Eccles, April 17, 1933: "My interest in the success of the reorganization is absolutely impersonal and I advocate it for the benefit of the state and as in the best interests of the deposi-

tors." Clearly there were two sides to this issue. On February 14, for instance, editor Thomas M. Storke of the *Santa Barbara Daily News* described the same plan that opponents claimed would maintain GW's power in quite a different light: "The plan adopted to save Wingfield's banks from disaster removes him from authority and strips him of the power which has made it possible for him to control cities, corporations, and politics." Storke didn't unduly lament this fact, but did label it as the end of a twenty-five–year era in Nevada, though "it is yet too early to write the word finis to the colorful career of a man who, right or wrong, is far from whipped." See also *NSJ*, April 21, 1933; *REG*, March 5, 1933; J. M. Heizer to Senator Pittman, May 16, 1933, KP Papers.

10. For RFC approval, see Minutes, RFC Records, vol. 13, pp. 254–256. GW to F. G. Willis, March 21, 1933; Georgetta, *Golden Fleece*, pp. 406–407; *REG*, February 25, 27, and 28, 1933; Assembly Bill 268, Chap. 190, Nevada Statutes, 36th Session, 1933, pp. 293–332. For Noble Getchell's political career and persuasions, see Burge and Getchell, "From Grease Paint to Gold" (Florence Burge Papers, Special Collections Department, University of Nevada, Reno, 1958).

11. *REG*, February 4 and 24 (source of Hawkins quotation), 1933. Hawkins and Cooke, along with C. H. Knox and J. La Rue Robinson, signed a letter urging depositors not to sign the waivers that was published in *REG*, March 6, 1933. In the letter they claimed that "the Wingfield organization, or those connected with or supporting its plans and purposes, desire you to sign it [waiver]."

12. *REG*, February 4, 17 (source of Thatcher quotation), and 24, 1933. Thatcher and Woodburn, both of whom worked extensively and without pay on the various bank reorganization plans, were themselves directors and stockholders in several of the banks and thus had an independent interest in securing reorganization. W. R. McRea to GW, March 9, 1933. The destruction of a banker's home in Dayton, Ohio, by a depositor, who said, "Now you know how it feels," was reported in *REG*, March 10, 1934.

13. Graham Sanford had wanted to be Republican national committeeman in 1927 and had opposed the Cole-Malley settlement in 1928, though the two men had never broken publicly. See GW to TLO, April 11, 1927, January 25, 1928. Representative Sanford editorials opposing reorganization include February 13, March 14 and 23, April 25, July 4, 1933. In his oral history, Graham Sanford's son John claimed that *REG* and its employees suffered retaliation for their stance against the bank reorganization, including withdrawal of advertising, as well as threats against mortgages on their homes and against the political jobs of relatives. He attributes these to the "Wingfield machine": see Sanford, "Printer's Ink," pp. 259–260. Barnard's phrase is quoted by Venice J. Daniels in *NSJ*, February 27, 1933. Daniels criticized Hawkins and urged instead: "Let the backyard fight between Mr. Hawkins and his confederates and Mr. Wingfield and the so-called political trust be counted out and the normal minded people get to opening the banks." On the other hand, F. M. Murphy, a generally respectful observer of GW, considered that "most that is said [by Barnard] is true" (F. M. Murphy to A. A. Hartmann, January 14, 1933, V&T Collection). Georgetta, *Golden Fleece*, pp. 412–413; *REG*, February 28, 1933.

14. *Report of the Joint Committee on Investigation of Closed State Banks* (Carson City: State Printing Office, 1933), pp. 19, 14.

15. *Committee on Closed Banks*, pp. 4, 8, 12. Details of F. G. Willis's activities on behalf of Crocker are in *REG*, February 18, 1933.

16. *Committee on Closed Banks*, p. 11. There was clearly a difference between GW's philosophy of bank management and that espoused by the legislative committee or practiced by Richard Kirman of the First National Bank of Reno. In 1914, shortly after the outbreak of World War I, GW described his cautious philosophy about "cleaning things up" in the Nixon banks: "While everything is not just as I would like to see it, it has got to be corrected gradually without starting something that could not be stopped" (GW to Mrs. George S. Nixon, September 1, 1914). As the legislative report correctly observed, this reluctance to intervene and take forceful action to cut his losses, regardless of the consequences, underlay the 1932 failure.

17. F. M. Murphy to A. A. Hartmann, April 5 ("small group") and 28 (Winnemucca divorce repeal), 1933, V&T Collection; *REG*, April 13, May 9, 1933.

18. *REG*, May 22 and 23, June 6 and 13, July 5, 1933; Ryan, Cooke, and Hawkins to Comptroller of the Currency, May 13, 1933 (copy in KP Papers).

19. See Georgetta, *Golden Fleece*, pp. 414–421, for a summary of the reorganization struggle in 1933; GW to F. G. Willis, August 14, 1933; *REG*, October 11 and 31, 1933; William Woodburn to KP, October 18, 1933, KP Papers; F. M. Murphy to A. A. Hartmann, November 2, 1933, V&T Collection; *REG*, November 2, 1933. Woodburn's letter to KP contains a somewhat different slant on the Transamerica matter than was reported by Murphy and the *REG*. According to Woodburn, Transamerica was smarting from a recent controversy in Oregon, where they had been charged "with being an octopus." They wanted to avoid a similar situation in Nevada and "are perfectly willing to enter the Nevada field if they 'will be invited' so as to escape the charges which were made against them in Oregon. They want to be placed in the position of being requested to come in to save the situation." In any event, letters of protest received from Nevada convinced Transamerica that the situation was too volatile for comfort.

20. *REG*, November 29, 1933; Guild, "Memoirs," pp. 151–153, 120; *REG*, September 11 and 14, 1933, February 9, 1934.

21. Joe Midmore, *First National Bank of Nevada* (Sparks: Western Printing and Publishing, 1975); GW to F. G. Willis, August 1, 1934; Guild, "Memoirs," p. 123; F. M. Murphy to A. A. Hartmann, April 28, 1934, V&T Collection. For payout rates on the state banks, see *NSJ*, December 29, 1940. The unfortunate Virginia City depositors received only 43 cents on the dollar.

22. Blair, "Days Remembered of Folsom," p. 77; Guild, "Memoirs," p. 134. Banking experts and other informed observers seem to agree that the reorganization plan would have been better for the state than enforced liquidation. See Gorman, "Recollections," pp. 29–30; Guild, "Memoirs," p. 148; Larry Schweikart, "A New Perspective on George Wingfield and Nevada Banking, 1920–1933" (1990; manuscript in author's possession). As Georgetta points out, "In just a few months after the receivers were appointed the price of sheep and wool came back up to a point

where if the Wingfield banks had never closed, or had been allowed to reopen, they would have been completely solvent" (*Golden Fleece*, p. 421).

23. *REG*, May 2, 1933. Just over half of the outstanding Reno National Bank stock belonged to GW, 3,521 of 7,000 shares (*REG*, November 28, 1932). GW to J. B. McCargar, March 23, 1926; memorandum, William Woodburn to GW, June 27, 1929.

24. Statement of GW Assets and Liabilities, December 31, 1932. It is worth noting that this list of assets did not include the TLO note that was returned to the senator in the weeks immediately following the bank failures. W. J. Tobin to GW, August 15, 1933; *REG*, August 29, 1933.

25. "A Friend of Nevada," *San Francisco Argonaut*, September 29, 1933. The objecting petition is found in Attorney General's Records regarding George Wingfield Stockholder's and Director's Liability, Box 051, Nevada Division of Archives and Records, Carson City. *REG*, March 1 and 2, 1934; GW to F. G. Willis, March 1, 1934. William Woodburn, Jr., in an interview in Reno, Nevada, October 4, 1985, recalled being told by his father that GW had a lucrative offer from a local musician who wanted to buy his house at the time of the bank failure and that GW had decided to accept it. He came back to the office the next day to cancel the deal, saying that he had forgotten he had put the house in Roxy's name and that she absolutely refused to sell.

26. *REG*, March 29, April 13, 1934; *NSJ*, March 30, 1934; *San Francisco Chronicle*, March 30, 1934, p. 8; *Las Vegas Review-Journal*, April 13, 1934 (source of quotation). Tobin's defense of Wingfield's offer is found in Attorney General's Records, Box 51, Nevada Division of Archives and Records, Carson City.

27. For the charges against Tobin, see *REG*, May 7, 8, 1934. Graham Sanford supported the complaint, pointing out, among other things, that Tobin had allowed GW to pledge some of his assets to Crocker after the failure of his banks. GW to F. G. Willis, May 8, 1934.

28. Details of the receivers' judgments against GW are found in Bankruptcy Case #571, U.S. District Court Records, District of Nevada, National Archives and Records Administration, San Bruno, California. *REG*, June 16, 1934; GW to F. G. Willis, October 10, 1934.

29. *Sacramento Bee*, January 2 (source of quotations), 3, 4 (source of headline), and 5, 1934. The paper won the Pulitzer Prize in 1935 for "the most disinterested and meritorious service of any newspaper during the past year": see *Sacramento Bee*, May 7, 1935.

30. The Owl Drug case, which did not involve GW except peripherally, was covered at length in the hearings on Norcross's nomination, U.S. Congress, Senate Committee on the Judiciary, *Hearings on the Nomination of Frank H. Norcross*, 73rd Cong., 2nd session, 1934. *Sacramento Bee*, January 5, 1934.

31. *REG*, January 31, July 6, 1934. This account of the Graham and McKay scam comes from Gorman, "Recollections," pp. 46–48. He supplied further details in an interview in Reno, Nevada, October 25, 1985.

32. For the three separate Graham and McKay trials, see *NSJ*, February 2, 1934,

September 12, 14, and 17, 1935; *REG*, June 13, 25, and 26, 1934, September 10 and 20, 1937; *Tonopah Daily Times*, June 5, July 18, 1939. Frisch was not indicted, but was named as co-conspirator.

33. *REG*, March 23, 24, and 26, April 18, 1934, January 16, February 4, April 3, July 11 and 13, 1935. Additional background was supplied by Joe Fuetsch in an interview in Reno, Nevada, December 28, 1988. Fuetsch was assistant cashier of the Riverside Bank under Frisch and was called to testify against Graham and McKay after Frisch's death. GW to R. C. Turrittin, March 24, 1934; GW to WEZ, March 24, 1934.

34. F. M. Murphy to A. A. Hartmann, March 30, 1934, V&T Collection. Murphy was hoping to sell lots at Lake Tahoe to Graham, McKay, and Frisch, and reported the entire incident in the guise of a disappointed salesman.

35. GW to F. G. Willis, April 19, January 10, 1934; *REG*, April 2, 1934; *NSJ*, June 24, 1934; *Las Vegas Review-Journal*, July 6, 1934; *REG*, July 14, 18, and 27, 1934.

36. For GW's illness, see MR to Alfred Frankenthal, July 5, 1934; GW to Frankenthal, July 12, 1934; GW to John G. Jackson, July 20, 1934; *REG*, March 29, September 9 and 18, 1935. Graham and McKay's trials are recounted in Sawyer, *Reno*, p. 24.

37. For bank customers reviling Wingfield, see Clarence J. Thornton, "C. J. Thornton, Entrepreneur: Agriculture, Business, Politics" (Oral History Program, University of Nevada, Reno, 1983), p. 137. GW's sensitivity to accusations of un-ethical behavior was reported by Virgil Wedge in an interview in Reno, Nevada, November 3, 1989. His response to Ernest Haycox, then on retainer for the popular magazine *Saturday Evening Post* and later a Hollywood scriptwriter, is in Cooper to Rocha, December 14, 1979. GW to BMB, November 5, 1933, Bernard M. Baruch Papers, Princeton University (henceforth BMB Papers).

38. For the circumstances of the Wingfield Trust Fund, see George K. Edler to GW, December 28, 1934; GW to F. G. Willis, January 15, 1935. The trust fund lost over $56,000 because of the bank failure and $112,000 of the remaining assets were of doubtful value. For GW's use of the trust fund to support his business interests, see GW to F. G. Willis, August 17, 1935.

39. *REG*, February 18 (source of Sheehan, Frisch quotations) and 20 (source of Wingfield quotation), 1933.

40. GW to F. G. Willis, January 3, March 24, 1934, April 11, June 19 (source of quotation), 1935.

41. RSC to CFNB, March 16, 1935; MR to F. G. Willis, April 1, 1935; F. G. Willis to GW, March 20, 1933; GW to Willis, August 20, 1934. For Henderson Banking Company affairs, see GW to Willis, September 1, 1934. GW to Willis, May 14, 1934 (source of quotation).

42. This accusation was part of a depositors' suit seeking removal of Walter J. Tobin as the Reno National Bank receiver, on the grounds that he had "failed to liq-uidate the bank expeditiously" (*REG*, May 7, 1934). For GW's position, see GW to Willis, January 11, 1934.

43. GW to F. G. Willis, August 20 and 23, 1935. The Spanish Springs Ranch is covered in greater detail in chapter 11.

44. For the marshal's sale of Wingfield assets, see memorandum of "Items included in U.S. Marshall's sale," May 20, 1935, GW Papers. The arrangements between RSC and CFNB are detailed in Guaranty, RSC to CFNB, March 19, 1935 (in the possession of the Wingfield family); RSC to CFNB, April 24, 1935; CFNB to GW, August 30, 1935.

45. George B. Thatcher to KP, April 2 (source of quotation) and 13, 1935, KP Papers. William Woodburn to KP, April 13, 1935, KP Papers.

46. See GW Statement to Grand Jury, April 20, 1935.

47. William Woodburn to KP, April 13, 1935, KP Papers.

48. GW to F. G. Willis, May 8, 1934; George B. Thatcher to N. J. Barry, February 7, 1935, copy in GW Papers. For GW's reluctance, see H. A. Streeter to George B. Thatcher, July 14, 1934; W. J. Tobin to George B. Thatcher, July 14, 1934, August 7, 1935. The dates of GW's agreement with the receivers were January 25 and 28, 1935, according to GW to CFB, November 29, 1935. George B. Thatcher to W. J. Tobin, August 7, 1935; copies in GW Papers.

49. For the efforts of Thatcher and Woodburn, including the quotation, see George B. Thatcher to KP, August 12, 1935, KP Papers. GW to Preston M. Burch, September 10, 1935.

50. GW to Preston M. Burch, July 10, 1935. On the income tax liability, GW was offering $200 in compromise and seeking Burch's help to do what he could to assist the matter. It is a measure of GW's loss of power that he had no contacts more powerful than his former trainer in Franklin Roosevelt's Washington—previously, he could have summoned senators and congressmen to his aid. Clarence F. Burton to GW, November 25, 29, 1935.

51. GW to CFB, December 3, 1935. CFNB to GW, November 9, 1935; GW to CFNB, November 11, 1935; CFNB to RSC, November 19 and 25, 1935; F. G. Willis to GW, November 25, 1935 (source of bank quotation). The information on Crocker's bidding on his property comes from GW to Raymond Benjamin, December 3, 1935. The 200,000 shares of RSC were GW's entire holding of the stock. For GW's salary, see F. G. Willis to RSC, December 17, 1935.

52. For the bankruptcy, see GW to Willis, November 23, 1935; Petition of Bankruptcy, November 30, 1935, GW Papers; *REG*, November 30, 1935; Bankruptcy Case #571, U.S. District Court Records, National Archives, San Bruno, California. GW to CFB, November 29, 1935; CFB to GW, December 2, 1935.

53. For GW's health, see MR to F. G. Willis, February 21, 1936. GW, Jr.'s story about Norcross was also repeated by Georgetta, *Golden Fleece*, p. 422, and *NSJ*, August 15, 1976. The sale is recorded in the bankruptcy records, and Thatcher's role is recounted in Memorandum, MR to GW, February 10, 1936.

54. GW to BMB, March 18, 1936; GW to Raymond Benjamin, May 15, 1936. The resignation was made public on May 20.

55. "Passion in the Desert," p. 106.

56. GW's daughter, Jean, had married Chauncey McKeever in Chicago in April 1934 (*NSJ*, April 12, 1934, February 11, 1936). CFB, who had spent his professional life as a banker after leaving GW's employ, recalled the latter's change of heart: "I also remember you saying you would never want anything to do with banking again after

going through the former drought which just about ruined the live stock business at the time" (CFB to GW, July 17, 1959, in the possession of the Wingfield family). GW to BMB, January 9, 1935, BMB Papers; BMB to GW, January 12, 1935.

57. Crocker's gratitude to Wingfield was widely known. See Biltz, "Duke of Nevada," p. 55; Gorman, "Recollections," p. 46. It was recalled by Dan Murphy to GW, August 15, 1944. The 1907 transaction was recounted by GW to David Ryder, October 23, 1958 (in the possession of the Wingfield family). Telegram, William W. Crocker to GW, September 27, 1937.

58. GW to CFNB, March 26, 1937; GW to F. G. Willis, March 30, 1937; F. G. Willis to RSC, March 31, 1937; CFNB to RSC, March 31, 1937.

59. *NSJ*, September 2, 1937; GW to F. G. Willis, December 16, 1937.

60. J. F. Shuman to GW, October 24, 1936; Raymond Benjamin to GW, June 19, 1936; GW to Raymond Benjamin, May 21, 1936 (source of quotation); GW to BMB, October 26, 1936; C. F. Rothenberg, December 17, 1936. Details of the Baruch loan are given below.

61. GW to BMB, June 3, 1937; Sutter Butte Canal Company, Profit and Loss Statement, December 31, 1937. For GCMC, see GW to Alfred Frankenthal, August 7, 1937. Information on GW's capital account is found in his ledger, 1936–1957 (in the possession of the Wingfield family). GW to BMB, March 11, 1938.

62. For background on Getchell, see Burge and Getchell, "From Grease Paint to Gold."

63. Noble H. Getchell to GW, June 10, 1935; GW to Noble H. Getchell, June 12, 1935, Noble H. Getchell Papers, Special Collections Department, University of Nevada, Reno. GW to F. G. Willis, July 13, 1936; RSC to GW, October 27, 1936; MR to F. G. Willis, November 3, 1936; GW to F. G. Willis, November 5, 1936.

64. BMB to GW, November 13, 1933; F. G. Willis to RSC, September 21, 1936; GW to MR, October 9, 1936; GW to BMB, October 28, November 10, 1936. GW eventually forwarded 400,000 shares of Getchell Mine to serve as collateral for this loan.

65. GW to F. G. Willis, November 5, 1936; GW to GW, Jr., Jean Wingfield McKeever, September 21, 1936; telegram, BMB to GW, November 26, 1936. According to GW, Jr., in an interview in Reno, Nevada, March 24, 1984, GW had given Fred Searls his first mining job in Goldfield following his graduation from the University of California as a mining engineer. For a general history of the Getchell Mine, see Cheryl A. Fox, "George Wingfield's Comeback: The Getchell Mine, 1936–1945," *Nevada Historical Society Quarterly* 32 (Summer 1989): 140–158; and Robert H. Ramsey, *Men and Mines of Newmont: A Fifty-Year History* (New York: Farrar, Strauss and Giroux, 1973), pp. 82–83.

66. Ramsey, *Men and Mines*, pp. 82–83; Fox, "Comeback," p. 146. For dividends, see also GW to BMB, September 26, October 1, 1938. Information on stock prices was provided by GW, Jr., in an interview in Reno, Nevada, March 24, 1984. GW to BMB, September 2, 1939. *Time*, September 13, 1937, p. 51.

67. *San Francisco Chronicle*, August 29, 1937, p. 10; " 'King George,' " *Time*, September 13, 1937, p. 51; "The Mechanics of a Reno Divorce Are Simple and Swift," *Life*, June 21, 1937, p. 38.

68. W. J. Loring to GW, October 28, 1938; Oscar Morgan to GW, May 12, 1938; Herbert Hoover to GW, July 20, 1938. For Hoover's veneration of the self-made man, see Roderick Nash, *The Nervous Generation: American Thought, 1917–1930* (Chicago: Elephant Paperbacks, 1970, 1990 reprint), pp. 132–133.

69. Walter E. Clark to GW, February 19, 1938. For GW's renewed charity activities, see A. D. Myers to GW, May 10, 1939; Walter E. Clark to GW, March 21, 1938; E. H. Beemer to GW, May 21, 1938. GW to Walter Bracken, October 26, 1938. Despite his objection to political advertisements, an independent group of businessmen had already placed such an ad in the *Las Vegas Review Journal*, August 31, 1938. It listed his donations to the university, detailed his service, and pointed out that he had no part in formulating the advertisement.

70. GW won the primary by a 1,600-vote margin over Frank Davison, in an election in which almost 33,000 votes were cast. *NSJ*, October 20, 1938. GW to H. J. Amigo, November 11, 1938; interview with Peter Echeverria, March 30, 1988, Reno, Nevada.

71. GW to BMB, August 28, 1939, BMB Papers (source of both GW quotations); memorandum, April 17, 1939, personal file, GW Papers; GW to BMB, July 12, 1939; GW to F. G. Willis, July 10, 1939; *San Francisco Chronicle*, August 29, 1937, p. 10.

Chapter Eleven: "The Same Old Landmarks Over and Over Again"

1. Chapter title from GW to Bert Clark, January 6, 1941. Congratulating Clark on the publication of his book *One Hundred Thousand Miles by Automobile through the West*, Wingfield wrote: "While I have travelled several hundred thousand miles in automobiles, I have never enjoyed seeing the things that you have as my travels were over the desert and it was a case of seeing the same old land marks over and over again"; GW to W. W. Crocker, August 12, 1944.

2. Will Crocker to GW, August 24, 1944.

3. "I buy short time Treasury notes and tax free bonds and try and keep a good supply of cash on hand" (GW to BMB, January 13, 1956, BMB Papers).

4. GW to Herbert Fleischhacker, August 17, 1940.

5. For GW's lack of participation, see GW to George F. Getz, September 28, 1934; Frank M. Murphy to A. A. Hartmann, October 12, 1934, V&T Collection: "Since the campaign of 1898, I have been actively connected with the political situation in Nevada, but in all that time have never seen such a jumble in both parties. . . . George [Wingfield] has personally not been taking the active part he usually does. . . ." GW to F. B. Willis, August 30, 1934; KP to George B. Thatcher, March 19, 1934, KP Papers.

6. *Las Vegas Review-Journal*, August 17, 1934.

7. For examples, see *NSJ*, October 13, 16, and 20, 1934. I am indebted to Phil Earl of the Nevada Historical Society for calling these advertisements to my attention.

8. The attack on Barnard, dated August 6, 1934, is in the GW Papers, 1934 political correspondence file.

9. This account of the McCarran years is drawn from oral histories of the period, including Biltz, "Duke of Nevada," pp. 162–166; McDonald, "Life of a

Newsboy," pp. 104–120; Thornton, "C. J. Thornton," pp. 232–235; Thomas Cave Wilson, "Reminiscences of a Nevada Advertising Man, 1930–1980, or Half a Century of Very Hot Air, or I Wouldn't Believe It If I Hadn't Been There" (Oral History Program, University of Nevada, Reno, 1982), pp. 410–411; and interviews with Les Gray, September 19 and 28, 1989, and Virgil Wedge, November 3, 1989. Edwards, *Pat McCarran*, p. 182.

10. GW to C. B. Goodspeed, October 23, 1936; GW to Alfred Frankenthal, June 1, 1935, February 25, December 22, 1942. Examples of Getchell's anti-Roosevelt material can be found in the GW Papers, in political and personal correspondence files for the 1930s and 1940s. GW also approved of the One Sound State campaign launched by a coalition of Nevada business leaders in the late 1930s. This public-relations effort sought to attract wealthy people to take up residence in Nevada by promoting its fiscal conservatism and low taxes.

11. Biltz, "Duke of Nevada," pp. 163–164. The phrase is McCarran's. The rapprochement was reported in interviews by Eva Adams and Virgil Wedge. GW to BMB, April 23, 1943; GW to BMB, August 9 ("in my opinion"), August 28 ("Isolationist"), November 1 (Bunker), 1944, BMB Papers.

12. GW to Patrick A. McCarran, August 4, 1954 (in the possession of the Wingfield family). This view of the respectful friendship between the two men was confirmed by Eva Adams in an interview in Reno, Nevada, November 17, 1987.

13. *GT*, July 31, 1908. GW retained 182 shares of GCMC out of over 1 million he had once owned. See GW Statement of Assets and Liabilities as of March 14, 1940, in Crocker First National Bank correspondence file, GW Papers. For activities of GCMC, see GW to Alfred Frankenthal, January 21, February 23, 1943 (re California Fuel and Utilities, National Metals Company), November 24 and 28, 1944 (re Dalmo-Victor), March 10, 1947 (re Goldfield Deep Mines Company); GW to BMB, July 23, 1940 (Comstock-Keystone); GW to J. F. Sullivan, April 25, 1949 (Goldfield Deep Mines); George M. Spradling to W. J. Schlegel, February 20, 1950 (re Goldfield Deep Mines, source of quotation). GCMC controlled Sutter Butte Canal Company by virtue of having loaned it money.

14. GW to BMB, May 19, 1952, BMB Papers. Details of 1950s operations are found in an enclosure on GCMC letterhead following GW to BMB, October 18, 1955, BMB Papers. Examples of EAJ's range of responsibility for GCMC can be seen in his correspondence files in the GW Papers for 1947 and 1948. For GW's intention to turn GCMC over to EAJ, see GW to BMB, April 25 (source of quotation), June 4, 1955, BMB Papers. The "big load" remark comes from GW to BMB, October 28, 1955, BMB Papers. For the proxy challenge, see GW to BMB, April 12, 1955, BMB Papers; and the GCMC records for those years.

15. GW to BMB, February 13, 1956, November 10, 1958, BMB Papers. GW's resistance to a signing machine for GCMC stock was described by George Wingfield, Jr., in an interview in Reno, Nevada, March 24, 1984. The April 1959 proxy battle is mentioned in *REG*, December 26, 1959.

16. Willis A. Swan to GW, Jr., and William K. Woodburn, August 4, 1960; Esmeralda County Records, Deed Book U, pp. 155–157.

17. BMB to GW, June 29, 1948.

18. The phrase about the Getchell Mine is from A. E. Cahlan, "From Where I

Sit," *Las Vegas Review-Journal*, April 9, 1945; BMB to GW, September 26, 1939; GW to BMB, September 30, 1939 (source of quotation). Fox, "Getchell Mine," remains the best source for these years. For details of wartime operations, see GW to BMB, October 3, November 21, December 18, 1942, June 18, 1943. "The Getchell Mine is not affected by the closing order for gold mines as they produce arsenic and tungsten and have a serial number. However, they take everything for taxes so it really doesn't make much difference whether they are closed or not" (GW to Alfred Frankenthal, November 19, 1942).

19. On the labor situation, see GW to Alfred Frankenthal, November 21, 1942; GW to John V. Mueller, September 29, 1943; GW to BMB, October 6, 1943, BMB Papers. For Newmont's sale, see Ramsey, *Men and Mines*, 83; BMB to GW, February 7, 1947, BMB Papers. For the stockholders, see GW to Fred Searls, February 15, 1949. Information on Kennedy came from George Wingfield, Jr., in an interview in Reno, Nevada, August 19, 1983. GW to J. F. Sullivan, CFNB, October 9, 1950. Getchell's Korean War experience is found in GW to Patrick A. McCarran, January 3, 1951.

20. The figure on dividends is from Burge and Getchell, "From Grease Paint to Gold," p. 155. The sale of GW's Getchell stock was reported in *Nevada Mining Association News Letter* 90 (September 15, 1960), p. 1. He held 350,600 shares and the price per share was $1.50; GCMC to Estate of GW and Estate of Noble H. Getchell, August 4, 1960.

21. GW's involvement in the management of Getchell Mine is documented in company records and confirmed in an interview with Royce Hardy in Reno, Nevada, June 12, 1989. GW to BMB, January 13, 1956, BMB Papers.

22. For the Riverside hostess, see memorandum, T. L. Willcox to GW, November 30, 1937. GW to F. G. Willis, February 16, 1940.

23. F. G. Willis to GW, April 25, 1940, July 17, 1941. For wartime business in the hotels, see GW to John V. Mueller, September 29, 1943, April 4, 1944; GW to J. F. Sullivan, CFNB, March 29, 1944. Records of the Reno Securities Company payments on the 1937 note to Crocker First National Bank are found in a memorandum in the GW Papers, Reno Securities Company records, labeled Loan No. 17215. The figures on values of the hotel come from insurance valuations, GW to Crocker First National Bank, June 26, 1942.

24. GW to John V. Mueller, April 4, December 29, 1944.

25. GW to Dan Murphy, CFNB, October 12, 1946; GW to BMB, October 21, 1946; GW to Dan Murphy, December 27, 1946; GW to BMB, January 22, 1946 (source of quotation); GW to J. F. Sullivan, CFNB, May 13, 1949, July 12, 1950; GW to Charles Baad, August 17, 1950; GW to Arthur Buel, December 6, 1950. For the Golden sale, see Sawyer, *Reno*, p. 61. The Golden Hotel burned in 1963.

26. GW to BMB, May 19, 1952, BMB Papers.

27. GW's personal involvement at the Riverside is clear from his correspondence and was confirmed in interviews with Eva Adams, Robert Drake, Virgil Wedge, and George Wingfield, Jr. For the sale, see Sawyer, *Reno*, pp. 61–62.

28. The property was sold for $53,750 and later became the site of the Holiday Hotel.

29. Wilson, "Reminiscences," pp. 494, 534. Wilson actually blames "GW's

people" for Reno's failure to develop into a high-class resort, arguing that they aimed at low-income groups and cheapened the market due to their reluctance to pay the expenses of maintaining first-rate hotels. This view is belied by GW's emphasis in his correspondence on the luxury and elegance of the Riverside, although his tastes may have been less highly refined than Wilson's. In 1992, both the Riverside and Mapes hotels remained closed, ironically derelict examples of Wilson's observations about Reno's sleazy, rundown character.

30. Mary Ellen Glass, *Nevada's Turbulent '50s: Decade of Political and Economic Change* (Reno: University of Nevada Press, 1981), p. 6.

31. GW's work for the Finnish Relief Fund can be traced in correspondence files by that title for 1939 and 1940 in the GW Papers. See especially telegram, Herbert Hoover to GW, December 16, 1939. GW to Alfred Frankenthal, July 3, 1941.

32. The Grand Cafe lunches were remembered fondly by several participants, including Jordan Crouch and Virgil Wedge. Wedge recalled trying to write down GW's stories after hearing them, but finding that they lost their dramatic impact in the transcription. The list of participants was largely supplied by George Wingfield, Jr., who also furnished information about his father giving up smoking in an interview in Reno, Nevada, March 24, 1984. GW's healthy appetite was remembered by William Woodburn, Jr., in an interview in Reno, Nevada, October 4, 1985.

33. George J. Kern, CFNB, to GW, November 19, 1942.

34. For the labrador dogs, see Dean Witter to GW, March 16, 1940; GW to Lee Baldock, September 27, 1951. GW to BMB, August 9, 1944, BMB Papers; F. G. Willis to GW, November 25, 1941. The hospitality at Spanish Springs Ranch was recalled in interviews by Eva Adams and Peter Echeverria. The latter remarked in particular on GW's skill with a shotgun. The quotation is from GW to Frank M. Newbert, December 31, 1940. GW reported going duck and pheasant hunting to BMB, November 10, 1958, BMB Papers.

35. For the quarter horses, see Tommy Thompson, "Saddle Chatter," *NSJ*, October 2, 1955, and the Spanish Springs Ranch files in the RSC records, GW Papers. The accident and its aftermath are recounted in GW, Jr., to BMB, July 31, August 11, 1947; GW to BMB, December 27, 1947.

36. Lucius Beebe, "Reno," *Holiday* 24 (November 1958), pp. 91, 170; Clifford C. Walton, comp., *Nevada Today* (Portland, Ore.: Capitol Publishing Co., 1949), p. 422.

37. *NSJ*, August 19, 1956. *REG*, significantly, did not cover the eightieth birthday celebration.

38. Citation entitled "George Wingfield," Archives, University of Nevada, Reno. He was nominated for the degree by Dean Vernon Scheid of the MacKay School of Mines (*REG*, January 4, 1957). The proposal to name the building after Wingfield was made by Newton Crumley of Elko (University of Nevada Board of Regents Minutes, November 21, 1959). It was never officially turned down, but the building was named for Scrugham in 1962. Frederick M. Anderson gives the reasons for the regents' decision in his oral history, "Frederick M. Anderson, M.D.: Surgeon, Regent and Dabbler in Politics" (Oral History Program, University of Nevada, Reno, 1985).

39. George Wingfield, Jr., recalled being told to leave the office whenever Senator McCarran arrived, for instance. For the loans to Oddie, see GW to F. G. Willis,

May 18, 1941; GW to George J. Kern, CFNB, June 23, 1942; George J. Kern to GW, September 30, 1943. GW loaned McKay $20,000 in 1957, which was repaid within three months. See GW Ledger, 1936–1957 (in the possession of the Wingfield family). For donations, see Clark J. Guild to GW, January 22, 1940.

40. GW to Arthur Buel, December 6, 1950; GW to NHG, September 21, 1957; GW to BMB, March 20, April 26, June 10, August 6, 1958 (source of quotation), September 7, 1959, BMB Papers. *NSJ*, December 25, 1959, p. 24. In an interview in Reno, August 25, 1983, George Wingfield, Jr., reported that though his father was comatose during the last days of his life, he could occasionally be heard mumbling about the thoroughbreds he had raced.

41. *NSJ*, December 25, 1959; *New York Times*, December 27, 1959; *San Francisco Examiner*, December 27, 1959; *Las Vegas Sun*, December 27, 1959; *San Francisco Chronicle*, December 27, 1959; *REG*, December 26, 1959.

42. "George Wingfield," *REG*, December 26, 1959; *Las Vegas Sun*, December 27, 1959 (ellipsis in original).

43. Nevada Mining Association *Newsletter*, January 15, 1960, pp. 9–10.

44. *Last Will and Testament of George Wingfield*, July 9, 1958; BMB to George Wingfield, Jr., December 26, 1959; *Territorial Enterprise*, January 1, 1960, p. 11.

BIBLIOGRAPHY

Interviews

Eva Adams, November 17, 1987, Reno, Nevada.
Elizabeth A. Burton, March 3, 1989, Reno, Nevada.
Jordan Crouch, October 3, 1983, Reno, Nevada.
Robert A. Drake, October 6, 1989, Reno, Nevada.
Peter Echeverria, March 30, 1988, Reno, Nevada.
Joseph Fuetsch, December 28, 1988, Reno, Nevada.
Marshall Giusti, June 16, 1989, Reno, Nevada.
Harold Gorman, October 25, 1985, Reno, Nevada.
Les Gray, September 19, 28, 1989, Reno, Nevada.
Royce Hardy, June 12, 1989, Reno, Nevada.
Al and Alice Hardy Paulsen, November 22, 1988, and March 9, 1989, Reno, Nevada.
John Sanford, March 19, 1988, Reno, Nevada.
Virgil Wedge, November 3, 1989, Reno, Nevada.
George Wingfield, Jr., August 19 and 25, 1983, March 24, 1984, Reno, Nevada.
William Woodburn, Jr., October 4, 1985, Reno, Nevada.

Manuscript Sources

Bartlett, George. Papers. Special Collections Department, University of Nevada, Reno.
Baruch, Bernard. Papers. Princeton University, Princeton, New Jersey.
Burge, Florence, and Noble H. Getchell. "From Grease Paint to Gold: The Life of Noble Hamilton Getchell." Unpublished manuscript, Florence Burge Papers, Special Collections Department, University of Nevada, Reno, 1958.
Esmeralda County Records. Esmeralda County Courthouse, Goldfield, Nevada.
Getchell, Noble. Papers. Special Collections Department, University of Nevada, Reno.
Goldfield Consolidated Mines Company. By-Laws. 1907. Special Collections Department, University of Nevada, Reno.
Humboldt County Records. Humboldt County Courthouse, Winnemucca, Nevada.
Lake County Records. Lake County Courthouse, Lakeview, Oregon.
Miscellaneous Goldfield Mining Company Records. Bancroft Library, University of California, Berkeley, California.
Morgan, Oscar. "Biography of George Wingfield." Unpublished manuscript in the possession of Audrey Thoreson, Fremont, California [1940].

Nevada Attorney Generals' Records. Nevada State Archives, Carson City, Nevada.

Nevada Governors' Papers. Nevada State Archives, Carson City, Nevada.

Nixon, George S. Papers. Nevada Historical Society, Reno, Nevada.

Nye County Records. Nye County Courthouse, Tonopah, Nevada.

Oddie, Tasker L. Papers. Huntington Library, San Marino, California.

Oddie, Tasker L. Papers. Nevada Historical Society, Reno, Nevada.

Pittman, Key. Papers. Library of Congress Manuscript Division, Washington, D.C.

Reconstruction Finance Corporation Records. Manuscript Division, National Archives, Washington, D.C.

Sawyer, Byrd Fanita Wall. "The Gold and Silver Rushes of Nevada, 1900–1910." M.A. thesis, University of California, 1931.

Thomas, Charles S. Papers. Colorado Historical Society, Denver, Colorado.

Thornton, Barbara C. "George Wingfield in Nevada from 1896 to 1932." M.A. thesis, University of Nevada, Reno, 1967.

U.S. District Court Records. George Wingfield Bankruptcy. National Archives, San Bruno, California.

Virginia & Truckee Railroad Collection. Special Collections Department, University of Nevada, Reno.

Welch, Nancy. "The Wingfield Family in Arizona: An Overview." 1989.

White, Laura A. "History of the Labor Struggles in Goldfield, Nevada." M.A. thesis, University of Nebraska, 1912.

Wingfield, George. Papers. Nevada Historical Society, Reno, Nevada.

Newspapers

Carson City Appeal, Carson City, Nevada.

Golconda News, Golconda, Nevada.

Goldfield Daily Sun, Goldfield, Nevada.

Goldfield News, Goldfield, Nevada.

Goldfield Review, Goldfield, Nevada.

Goldfield Tribune, Goldfield, Nevada.

Mining and Scientific Press, San Francisco, California.

Nevada State Journal, Reno, Nevada.

New York Graphic, New York, New York.

Oakland Tribune, Oakland, California.

Reno Evening Gazette, Reno, Nevada.

Sacramento Bee, Sacramento, California.

San Francisco Call, San Francisco, California.

San Francisco Chronicle, San Francisco, California.

San Francisco Examiner, San Francisco, California.

Tonopah Bonanza, Tonopah, Nevada.

Tonopah Daily Sun, Tonopah, Nevada.

Tonopah Miner, Tonopah, Nevada.

Winnemucca Silver State, Winnemucca, Nevada.

Oral Histories

All oral histories are part of the Oral History Program, University of Nevada, Reno.

Anderson, Frederick M. "Frederick M. Anderson, M.D.: Surgeon, Regent and Dabbler in Politics." 1985.

Atkinson, Harry Hunt. "Tonopah and Reno: Memories of a Nevada Attorney." 1970.

Badt, Milton B. "An Interview with Milton Badt." 1965.

Biltz, Norman. "Memoirs of 'The Duke of Nevada': Developments of Lake Tahoe, California and Nevada; Reminiscences of Nevada Political and Financial Life." 1969.

Blair, Minnie P. "Days Remembered of Folsom and Placerville, California; Banking and Farming in Goldfield, Tonopah, and Fallon, Nevada." 1968.

Cahill, Robbins E. "Recollections of Work in State Politics, Government, Taxation, Gaming Control, Clark County Administration, and the Nevada Resort Association." 1977.

Cahlan, John F. "Fifty Years in Journalism and Community Development." 1987.

———. "Reminiscences of a Reno and Las Vegas, Nevada, Newspaperman, University Regent, and Public-Spirited Citizen." 1970.

Ferris, Lehman A. "Life of a Busy Man: Recollections of My Work as an Architect, Building Inspector, and Civil Leader." 1971.

Foster, Verne. "Verne Foster and the Nevada Mining Association." 1988.

Gallagher, Charles D. "Memoir and Autobiography." 1965.

Ginocchio, Andrew. "The Ascent of Reno Iron Works." 1987.

Gorman, Harold S. "Recollections of a Nevada Banker and Civic Leader." 1973.

Guild, Clark J. "Memoirs of Careers with Nevada Bench and Bar, Lyon County Offices, and the Nevada State Museum." 1971.

Gulling, Amy. "An Interview with Amy Gulling." 1966.

Hardy, Roy A. "Reminiscence and a Short Autobiography." 1965.

Harrah, William Fisk. "My Recollections of the Hotel-Casino Industry and as an Auto Collecting Enthusiast." 1980.

Hewes, Clare Hofer. "The Hofer Family of Carson City." 1966.

Hilp, Lester J. "Reminiscences of a White Pine County Native, Reno Pharmacy Owner, and Civic Leader." 1968.

Kofoed, Leslie S. "Kofoed's Meanderings in Lovelock Business, Nevada Government, the U.S. Marshal's Office, and the Gaming Industry." 1972.

McDonald, Joseph F. "The Life of a Newsboy in Nevada." 1970.

Merialdo, Peter B. "Memoirs of a Son of Italian Immigrants, Recorder and Auditor of Eureka County, Nevada State Controller, and Republican Party Worker." 1968.

Miller, Thomas Woodnutt. "Memoirs of Thomas Woodnutt Miller, A Public Spirited Citizen of Delaware and Nevada." 1966.

Petersen, Peter C. "Reminiscences of My Work in Nevada Labor, Politics, Post Office, and Gaming Control." 1970.

Petricciani, Silvio. "The Evolution of Gaming in Nevada: The Twenties to the Eighties." 1982.

Ross, Silas E. "Recollections of Life at Glendale, Nevada, Work at the University of Nevada, and Western Funeral Practice." 1970.

Russell, Charles H. "Reminiscences of a Nevada Congressman, Governor, and Legislator." 1967.

Sanford, John. "Printer's Ink in My Blood." 1971.

Terry, Alice. "Recollections of a Pioneer: Childhood in Northern Nevada, Work at the University of Nevada, Observations of the University Administration 1922–1964, WICHE, and Reno Civic Affairs." 1976.

Thornton, Clarence J. "C. J. Thornton, Entrepreneur: Agriculture, Business, Politics." 1983.

Wilson, Thomas Cave. "Reminiscences of a Nevada Advertising Man, 1930–1980, or Half a Century of Very Hot Air, or I Wouldn't Believe It If I Hadn't Been There." 1982.

Secondary Sources

Arnold, Emmett L. *Gold Camp Drifter, 1906–1910.* Reno: University of Nevada Press, 1973.

Arnold, George. "George Wingfield, Nevada's Foremost Citizen." *Coast Investor and Industrial Review* 7 (April 1929): 26, 57–60.

Atherton, Lewis. "The Mining Promoter in the Trans-Mississippi West." *Western Historical Quarterly* 1 (January 1970): 35–50.

Baruch, Bernard M. *Baruch: My Own Story.* New York: Henry Holt, 1957.

Beatty, Bessie. *Who's Who in Nevada: Brief Sketches of Men Who Are Making History in the Sagebrush State.* Los Angeles: Home Printing Company, 1907.

Beebe, Lucius. "Reno." *Holiday* 24 (November 1958): 90–92, 166–173.

Brennen, C. A. *The Main Reasons Why Range Cattle Ranchers Succeed or Fail.* Agricultural Experiment Station Bulletin 133. Reno: University of Nevada, 1933.

———. *The Public Range and the Livestock Industry of Nevada.* Agricultural Experiment Station Bulletin 139. Reno: University of Nevada, 1935.

Brown, Mrs. Hugh. *Lady in Boomtown: Miners and Manners on the Nevada Frontier.* Palo Alto: American West Publishing Company, 1968.

Carpenter, Jay A., Russell Richard Elliott, and Byrd Fanita Wall Sawyer. *The History of Fifty Years of Mining at Tonopah, 1900–1950.* University of Nevada Bulletin 47 (January 1953), Geology and Mining Series No. 51.

Chan, Loren. *Sagebrush Statesman: Tasker L. Oddie.* Reno: University of Nevada Press, 1973.

Chandler, Alfred D., Jr. *The Visible Hand: The Managerial Revolution in American Business.* Cambridge: Belknap Press of Harvard University Press, 1977.

Chandler, Alfred D., Jr., and Herman Daems, eds. *Managerial Hierarchies: Comparative Perspectives on the Rise of the Modern Industrial Enterprise.* Cambridge: Harvard University Press, 1980.

Clark, Walter Van Tilburg. "Reno, the City State." In *Rocky Mountain Cities*, edited by Ray B. West, Jr. New York: W. W. Norton, 1949.

Coit, Margaret L. *Mr. Baruch.* Boston: Houghton Mifflin, 1957.

Creel, Cecil W. *History of Nevada Agriculture.* Carson City: State Printing Office, 1964.

Croft, Helen Downer. *The Downers, the Rockies—and Desert Gold*. Caldwell, Idaho: Caxton Printers, 1961.

Currie, Barton Wood. "Pluck and Luck in the Desert." *Harper's Weekly* 52 (April 4, 1908): 28–29.

Davis, Sam P. "Nevada's Safeguard for Mine-buyers." *Harper's Weekly* 52 (April 4, 1908): 16–17.

DeArment, Robert K. *Knights of the Green Cloth: The Saga of the Frontier Gamblers*. Norman: University of Oklahoma Press, 1982.

Duffy, Martin C., comp. *Goldfield's Glorious Past*. Privately published, n.d.

Dunn, Arthur. "Cowboy Who Refused a Toga." *Sunset* 29 (October 1912): 446–447.

Dutton, Alfred H. *Notable Nevadans in Caricature*. Los Angeles: Out West Corporation, 1915.

Edwards, Jerome E. *Pat McCarran: Political Boss of Nevada*. Reno: University of Nevada Press, 1982.

———. "Wingfield and Nevada—Some Observations." *Nevada Historical Society Quarterly* 32 (Summer 1989): 126–139.

Elliott, Russell R. *History of Nevada*. Lincoln: University of Nebraska Press, 1973.

———. *Nevada's Twentieth-Century Mining Boom*. Reno: University of Nevada Press, 1966.

Ellis, Anne. *The Life of an Ordinary Woman*. Boston: Houghton Mifflin, 1929.

Field, Carter. *Bernard Baruch: Park Bench Statesman*. New York: McGraw-Hill, 1944.

Fox, Cheryl A. "George Wingfield's Comeback: The Getchell Mine, 1936–1945." *Nevada Historical Society Quarterly* 32 (Summer 1989): 140–158.

"From Faro-Table to Senate." *Literary Digest* 45 (July 6, 1912): 33–36.

Georgetta, Clel. *Golden Fleece in Nevada*. Reno: Venture Publishing Company, 1972.

Glad, Betty. *Key Pittman: The Tragedy of a Senate Insider*. New York: Columbia University Press, 1986.

Glass, Mary Ellen. *Nevada's Turbulent '50s: Decade of Political and Economic Change*. Nevada Studies in History and Political Science No. 15. Reno: University of Nevada Press, 1981.

Glasscock, Carl Burgess. *Gold in Them Hills*. Indianapolis: Bobbs Merrill, 1932.

Goldfield, Its Gold, Its Founders, Its Romance. Goldfield, Nev.: Samuel Freedman, 1907.

Grover, David H. *Diamondfield Jack: A Study in Frontier Justice*. Reno: University of Nevada Press, 1968.

Hersey, John. "The Old Man." *New Yorker* 23 (January 3, 1948): 28–37.

Higgins, Aileen Cleveland. *A Little Princess of Tonopah*. Philadelphia: Penn Publishing Company, 1909.

Howard, Anne Bail. *The Long Campaign: A Biography of Anne Martin*. Reno: University of Nevada Press, 1985.

Hutchinson, Paul. "Can Reno Be Cured?" *Christian Century* 48 (December 16, 1931): 1592–1594.

———. "Nevada—A Prostitute State." Ibid. (November 25, 1931): 1488–1490.

———. "Reno—A Wide-Open Town." Ibid. (December 2, 1931): 1519–1520.

———. "Reno's Divorce Mill." Ibid. (December 9, 1931): 1557–1559.

An Illustrated History of Central Oregon. Spokane: Western Historical Publishing Company, 1905.

Jensen, Vernon H. *Heritage of Conflict: Labor Relations in the Nonferrous Metals Industry up to 1930*. Ithaca: Cornell University Press, 1950.

Jones, Jesse H., with Edward Angly. *Fifty Billion Dollars: My Thirteen Years with the Reconstruction Finance Corporation (1932–1945)*. New York: Macmillan, 1951.

Kennedy, Susan. *Banking Crisis of 1933*. Lexington: University of Kentucky Press, 1973.

[La Montagne, P.] *Nevada—the New Gold State*. San Francisco: D. G. Doubleday, 1905.

Martin, Anne. "Nevada: Beautiful Desert of Buried Hopes." *Nation* 115 (July 26, 1922): 89–92.

Meaker, Reginald. *Nevada Desert Sheepman*. [Sparks]: Western Printing and Publishing, 1981.

Midmore, Joe. *First National Bank of Nevada*. Sparks: Western Printing and Publishing, 1975.

Miller, Max. *Reno*. New York: Dodd, Mead, 1941.

Notable Nevadans: Snapshots of Sagebrushers Who Are Doing Things. Reno: n.p., 1910.

Oliphant, J. Orrin. *On the Cattle Ranges of the Oregon Country*. Seattle: University of Washington Press, 1968.

Olson, James Stuart. *Herbert Hoover and the Reconstruction Finance Corporation, 1931–1933*. Ames: Iowa State University Press, 1977.

Ostrander, Gilman. *Nevada: The Great Rotten Borough, 1859–1964*. New York: Alfred A. Knopf, 1966.

Paher, Stanley W. *Nevada Ghost Towns and Mining Camps*. Las Vegas: Nevada Publications, 1970.

Paine, Ralph D. *The Greater America*. New York: Outing Publishing Company, 1907.

"Passion in the Desert." *Fortune* 9 (April 1934): 100–107, 124–132.

Paul, Rodman W. *The Far West and the Great Plains in Transition, 1859–1900*. New York: Harper and Row, 1988.

Peterson, Richard H. *The Bonanza Kings: The Social Origins and Business Behavior of Western Mining Entrepreneurs, 1870–1900*. Lincoln: University of Nebraska Press, 1977.

Quiett, Glenn Chesney. *Pay Dirt: A Panorama of American Gold-Rushes*. New York: Appleton-Century, 1936.

Ramsey, Robert H. *Men and Mines of Newmont: A Fifty-Year History*. New York: Farrar, Strauss and Giroux, 1973.

Raymond, C. Elizabeth. "George Wingfield's Political Machine: A Study in Historical Reputation." *Nevada Historical Society Quarterly* 32 (Summer 1989): 95–110.

Rice, George Graham. *My Adventures with Your Money*. 1913; reprint New York: Bookfinger, 1974.

Riehl, Charles W. "Goldfield, Nevada." *Banker's Magazine* 74 (May 1907): 788–799.

Rocha, Guy Louis. "Radical Labor Struggles in the Tonopah-Goldfield Mining District, 1901–1922." *Nevada Historical Society Quarterly* 20 (Spring 1977): 3–45.

Rocha, Guy Louis, and Sally Zanjani. *Ignoble Conspiracy*. Reno: University of Nevada Press, 1986.

Rowley, William L. "Francis G. Newlands and the Promises of American Life." *Nevada Historical Society Quarterly* 32 (Fall 1989): 169–180.

———. *Reno: Hub of the Washoe Country*. Ontario: Windsor Publications, 1984.

———. "Reno and the Desert of Buried Hopes." In *East of Eden, West of Zion*, edited by Wilbur S. Shepperson. Reno: University of Nevada Press, 1989.

Sawyer, Raymond I. *Reno, Where the Gamblers Go!* Reno: Sawston Publishing Company, 1976.

Schwarz, Jordan A. *The Speculator: Bernard M. Baruch in Washington, 1917–1965*. Chapel Hill: University of North Carolina Press, 1981.

Scrugham, James G., ed. *Nevada, A Narrative of the Conquest of a Frontier Land*. Chicago: American Historical Society, 1935.

Sears, Marian V. *Mining Stock Exchanges, 1860–1930: An Historical Survey*. Missoula: University of Montana Press, 1973.

Shamberger, Hugh A. *Goldfield: Early History, Development, Water Supply*. Carson City: Nevada Historical Press, 1982.

———. *The Story of Fairview, Churchill County, Nevada*. Carson City: Nevada Historical Press, 1973.

———. *The Story of Rochester, Pershing County, Nevada*. Carson City: Nevada Historical Press, 1973.

———. *The Story of Weepah*. Carson City: Nevada Historical Press, 1975.

Simpson, Peter K. *The Community of Cattlemen: A Social History of the Cattle Industry in Southeastern Oregon, 1869–1912*. Moscow: University of Idaho Press, 1987.

Thomas, Sewell. *Silhouettes of Charles S. Thomas*. Caldwell, Idaho: Caxton Printers, Ltd., 1959.

Townley, John. *Turn This Water into Gold*. Reno: Nevada Historical Society, 1977.

Travers, James W. *Tonopah, Past, Present and Future*. N.p., 1902.

Turano, Anthony M. "Nevada's Trial of Licensed Gambling." *American Mercury* 28 (February 1933): 190–192.

U.S. Congress. House. *Papers Relative to Labour Troubles at Goldfield, Nev*. 60th Congress, 1st Session, 1908. H. Doc. 105.

U.S. Congress. Senate. *Report on the Western Range*. 74th Congress, 2nd Session, 1936. S. Doc. 199.

Warns, Melvin O. *The Nevada "Sixteen" National Banks and Their Mining Camps*. Washington, D.C.: Society of Paper Money Collectors, 1974.

Who's Who on the Pacific Coast. Chicago: A. N. Marquis Company, 1949.

Woon, Basil. *Incredible Land: A Jaunty Baedecker to Hollywood and the Great Southwest*. New York: Liveright Publishing, 1933.

Young, James A., and B. Abbott Sparks. *Cattle in the Cold Desert*. Logan: Utah State University Press, 1985.

Zanjani, Sally Springmeyer. "George Wingfield: The Goldfield Years." *Nevada Historical Society Quarterly* 32 (Summer 1989): 111–125.

———. "Power to Rule or Ruin: Goldfield's Long Shadow over Nevada Politics." *Nevada Historical Society Quarterly* 34 (Summer 1991): 321–339.

———. "To Die in Goldfield: Morality in the Last Boomtown on the Mining Frontier." *Western Historical Quarterly* 21 (February 1990): 47–69.

―――. *The Unspiked Rail: Memoir of a Nevada Rebel.* Reno: University of Nevada Press, 1981.

Zanjani, Sally Springmeyer, and Guy Louis Rocha. "A Heart for Any Fate: Vincent St. John in Goldfield." *Nevada Historical Society Quarterly* 27 (Summer 1984): 75–91.

INDEX

Atkinson, Harry H., 171

Baer-Uzcudun prizefight (1931), 195, 198
Balzar, Fred, 154, 174, 179–80, 192, 195,
    209–10, 234
Bank Club (Reno, NV), 195, 212, 236
Bank holiday (1932, 1933), 209–11, 213, 222
Bank of Nevada Savings & Trust Co., 108,
    208, 226, 232
Bank of Sparks, 124
Bank reorganization, 220–28
Baric, May, 21, 29–30, 49–51, 82, 84, 91–92,
    299n.45
Barnard, W. E., 225, 231, 238, 255
Bartlett, George S., 98, 128, 159
Baruch, Bernard, 53, 56–57, 64, 81, 95, 235,
    242–43, 246, 260
Biltz, Norman, 214, 256, 257, 263
Bipartisan machine, 6, 41, 153–54, 159–63,
    185–86, 192–93, 254–56, 310n.11
Bonanza Hotel Co., 81, 120
Boston-Tonopah Mining Co., 28, 32–33
Botsford, Charles H., 55
Boulder Canyon Project, 189–90
Bracken, Walter R., 143, 188–89, 190, 194,
    204
Branson, Lindley C., 66–67
Buckhorn mine, 95
Bunker, Berkeley, 257
Burton, Clarence F., 88, 98, 114, 116, 122,
    123, 150, 240–41

Carey, Jack, 26
Carson Valley Bank, 108, 175–77, 179, 181
Carstairs, J. H., 48
CFB. See Burton, Clarence F.
CFNB. See Crocker First National Bank
Chandler, Charles S., 162–63
Churchill County Bank, 124, 227
Churchill Creamery Co., 96
Clapp, H. C., 175–77
Cole-Malley scandal, 175–81
Columbia, NV, 39, 45

Cooke, H. R., 224, 225, 226
Crocker First National Bank, 53, 76, 133–34,
    176, 189, 201, 204–5, 208, 221, 224, 226,
    235, 240, 251–52
Crocker, William H., 53, 56, 133–43, 176,
    178, 243, 251

Davis, "Diamondfield" Jack, 67, 71, 108
Depression in Nevada, 218. See also Panic of
    1907
Diskin, M. A., 177, 180, 264
Divorce laws, 127–28, 130–31, 193–95, 199
Donnelley, John P., 168, 170

EAJ. See Julian, Estey A.

Finch, John Wellington, 52, 58, 66, 69, 71,
    72, 291n.39
First National Bank of Winnemucca, 18, 108,
    124, 201, 207, 229–30, 242
Fleishhacker, Herbert, 174, 252
Florence-Goldfield Mining Co., 37, 281n.27
Frick, Henry C., 48, 95, 105
Frisch, Roy, 165, 213, 226, 233–35, 236

Gambling laws, 113, 128, 130, 193–95, 199
Gans-Nelson prizefight (1906), 48
GCMC. See Goldfield Consolidated Mines
    Co.
Getchell Mine, 245–46, 248–49, 260–61
Getchell, Noble G., 29, 152, 223, 245–46,
    266
Golconda, NV, 13–16
Golden, Frank, 23, 26, 42
Goldfield Consolidated Mines Co., 39, 58,
    60, 68–69, 76, 82, 109–10, 120, 220, 258–
    60; dividends, 64–65, 74, 77, 81, 91, 220;
    finances, 55–57, 81, 120, 205; formation,
    52–57; stock prices, 53, 64–65, 188; and
    unions, 72–73, 74, 79
Goldfield Hotel. See Bonanza Hotel Co.
Goldfield Mohawk Mining Co., 36, 47–49,
    51–52, 68, 74

347